THE ENGLISH RENAISSANCE STAGE

Terence, *Andria* (Strasbourg, 1496)

The English Renaissance Stage

Geometry, Poetics, and the Practical Spatial Arts 1580–1630

HENRY S. TURNER

OXFORD
UNIVERSITY PRESS

OXFORD

UNIVERSITY PRESS

Great Clarendon Street, Oxford OX2 6DP

Oxford University Press is a department of the University of Oxford.
It furthers the University's objective of excellence in research, scholarship,
and education by publishing worldwide in

Oxford New York

Auckland Cape Town Dar es Salaam Hong Kong Karachi
Kuala Lumpur Madrid Melbourne Mexico City Nairobi
New Delhi Shanghai Taipei Toronto

With offices in

Argentina Austria Brazil Chile Czech Republic France Greece
Guatemala Hungary Italy Japan Poland Portugal Singapore
South Korea Switzerland Thailand Turkey Ukraine Vietnam

Oxford is a registered trade mark of Oxford University Press
in the UK and in certain other countries

Published in the United States
by Oxford University Press Inc., New York

© Henry S. Turner 2006

The moral rights of the author have been asserted
Database right Oxford University Press (maker)

First published 2006

British Library Cataloguing in Publication Data

Data available

Library of Congress Cataloging in Publication Data

Data available

Typeset by Newgen Imaging Systems (P) Ltd., Chennai, India
Printed in Great Britain
on acid-free paper by
Biddles Ltd, King's Lynn, Norfolk

ISBN 978–0–19–928738–3

3 5 7 9 10 8 6 4 2

To Harriet S. Turner and Sarah C. Turner

Acknowledgements

Parts of several chapters have appeared first in a different form as 'Plotting Early Modernity' in Henry S. Turner (ed.), *The Culture of Capital: Property, Cities, and Knowledge in Early Modern England* (New York: Routledge, 2002), 85–127, and I am grateful to Routledge for granting permission to reprint that material here. An early version of Chapter 5 appeared as '*King Lear* Without: The Heath' in *Renaissance Drama*, NS 28 (1997), 161–93, and I thank Northwestern University Press for granting permission to reproduce portions of it here. At the generous request of the late David Woodward, parts of the Introduction were originally written for 'Literature and Mapping in England, 1520–1688' in Woodward (ed.), *The History of Cartography*, iii: *Cartography in the European Renaissance* (Chicago: University of Chicago Press, forthcoming 2007), and the Press has graciously allowed that material to appear here, despite the fact that it has not yet appeared in print.

Figures 1.1–1.3, 2.1, 2.2, 4.2–4.6, 6.1, 6.2, and 6.6–6.9 are reproduced by courtesy of the Department of Special Collections, General Library System, University of Wisconsin–Madison; the figure on page ii and Figures 4.1, 4.7, 4.8, and 7.1 are reproduced by permission of the Folger Shakespeare Library; Figure 5.1 is reproduced by kind permission of the Governors of Dulwich College; Figures 6.3 and 6.4 are reproduced by permission of the Clothworkers' Company; Figure 6.5 is reproduced by kind permission of Christ's Hospital, Guildhall Library MS 12805; Figure 8.1 is reproduced from M. 10. 32, p. 22, by permission of the Syndics of Cambridge University Library; Figure 8.2 is reproduced by permission of Library Services, University of London.

I have silently modernized u, v, i, j, long s, and scribal contractions.

Preface

Although this book pertains specifically to England during the late sixteenth and early seventeenth centuries, its exposition introduces several larger topics and theoretical problems that it will be useful to describe briefly here so as to clarify the arguments that follow and to indicate their relevance to scholars working in different historical periods, cultural contexts, disciplines, or media. In its broadest orientation, the book offers case studies of the changing relationship between practice and theory, as these two categories developed during the Renaissance in response to specific problems concerning epistemology in two primary domains of intellectual and social activity: poetics and early scientific thought. Taken as a whole, the book presents one stage in the historical formation of the disciplines that we today identify as 'literature' and 'science' by examining the pre-modern intellectual categories and networks of social relations out of which both emerged. Its purpose is to examine the development of English drama as a distinct domain of professional activity characterized by a recognizably modern vocabulary, set of theoretical principles, system of values, and authorizing figures, including the 'critic' as well as the 'author'. But it argues that these developments cannot be adequately explained without also considering how poets and playwrights employed habits of thought that were flourishing in contemporary technological fields: modes of inductive and probabilistic argument, an interest in mathematics as a distinctive system for producing knowledge about the natural and social world, the use of diagrams to solve technical problems and to communicate knowledge to others. Although the book deals most directly with the history of the theatre and of performance, it touches also on the history of print as a distinctive technology of communication, and it raises broader questions that pertain to the history of pedagogy, of literacy and numeracy, and of interpretative practices that involve graphic as well as linguistic modes of representation.

Most specifically, the book focuses on the term 'plot', its cognate terms during the sixteenth and early seventeenth centuries, and the different ideas of structure and form that these terms implied. It concentrates on theatrical performance because the theatre provides a particularly clear example of how the social formations in which the term 'plot' was embedded and the techniques of practical thinking associated with the term informed the early-modern literary domain, or the domain of imaginative and 'invented' writing. But this influence is also visible in the work of other writers on poetics more generally, such as Philip Sidney and George Puttenham; despite that fact that they were not professional playwrights, I have devoted particular attention to Sidney's and Puttenham's treatises because they provide crucial evidence for the way in which habits of thought derived from practical mathematics informed Renaissance ideas about mimesis and semiosis in the drama, a form that was itself coming to be understood to be a distinct mode of 'poesy'. The book then examines several plays, across a variety of genres and types of playing spaces, to demonstrate how contemporary modes of practical thinking influenced aspects of English dramatic form. It should perhaps go without saying that I am not proposing geometry and the practical spatial arts as the *only* influences on the development of English dramatic form during the Renaissance period but am introducing them as *significant* influences, and ones, surprisingly, that have been largely overlooked.

Methodologically, the book follows recent work by scholars in the history and sociology of science who have revised the 'history of ideas' as it has traditionally been practised in favour of a historical account of 'epistemology' that emphasizes the social and institutional production of knowledge, as well as the representational modes through which knowledge is legitimized and transmitted. The book reiterates the principle that the 'history of ideas' must in fact be understood as the history of the relationship between institutions, social structures, and, most importantly, the *forms* in which ideas are shaped and expressed: it is the last category that deserves greater scrutiny from intellectual historians and the one that invites the particular resources of literary and cultural critics. The book also argues that the history of ideas is best examined through the changing meanings of specific words and the movement of words among different domains of intellectual and social activity. This method will be familiar to students of Raymond Williams's *Keywords* or of Foucault's *Archeology of Knowledge*; among early-modern scholars, it bears some resemblance to the work of intellectual historians such as J. G. A. Pocock and Quentin Skinner, although I have drawn upon a broader range of evidence than much intellectual history has tended to examine, from textbooks, essays, letters, and plays to practical manuals of mathematics, maps, and other visual documents.

This range of evidence raises two main types of theoretical problems, which may be characterized as semiological, on the one hand, and institutional, on the other: they are problems that lie at the heart of what has come to be called cultural studies, as practised in any historical period or discipline. The first includes all 'internal' problems of representation in its different modes and conventions: the intricate problem of how meaning occurs. A central concern of the book is thus with the semiotic aspects of knowledge production and on the different conventions that characterized diagrams, maps, words, objects, and human actions, especially in a theatrical context. The second encompasses the many 'external' relationships among actual institutions, such as the university, the court, the workshop, or the theatre, and institutionalized social relationships, such as patronage, employment, or modes of professional collaboration, in which texts and other artefacts were produced. These institutions and institutionalized relationships provided the fundamental categories through which texts were understood: habits of thinking and working; logical, grammatical, and conceptual categories that are implied in the semiological dimension of any text but which remain distinct from it as its intellectual horizon.

As I argue at more length in the Introduction that follows below, what we conventionally regard as the 'form' of any text results from a dialectical movement between the semiological and the institutional aspects of its existence, or what Fredric Jameson has described as 'the jumping of a spark between two poles' (1971: 4): 'form' is the mode through which ideas are made thinkable and distinct, according to precise and often highly self-conscious interpretative protocols that are themselves the product of the different social and institutional contexts through which texts, in their formalized state, begin to circulate. To argue in this way is, first, to reassert the indispensability of a category of 'form' to any mode of criticism that seeks to provide a complex account of the relationship between acts of cultural expression and the social life from which they emerge, and thus especially to historicist criticism: it is 'form' that makes the dialectical relationships between representation, institution, value, and power available to analytic thought. But it is to argue further that the category of 'form' also offers a privileged tool for a genealogical study of the modern disciplines: for if 'disciplines' are institutionalized ways of knowing that employ distinctive intellectual categories and techniques of research and argument, it is in the forms these disciplines produce, analyse, and value that their history may be traced—a history not of always already reified disciplines but of disciplines emerging through their specular relation to their formalized objects.

Finally, a word about the structure of the book. The Introduction lays out its primary arguments, theoretical methods, and organization. Although the remainder of the book has been divided into two sections—the first devoted to key ideas, terms, institutional contexts, and points of contact, the second to the way in which practical thinking informed notions of dramatic form—many of the chapters may be read as complementary pairs. Readers interested in the history of mathematics and early scientific thought in the context of English humanism, for instance, will find Chapters 2 and 3 most relevant; those interested in the history of urbanization and semiotics will wish to turn to Chapters 4 and 6; those interested in Shakespeare will want to read Chapters 5 and 6; those interested in the work of Dekker, Chapters 4 and 6; those interested in Jonson, Chapters 7 and 8. At the same time, later chapters often elaborate on ideas first introduced in earlier ones, and my largest arguments—as well as the philological investigation of the term 'plot' that serves as their primary organizing thread—are developed over the course of the entire book. Chronologically, the book progresses from the 1570s and 1580s (Chapters 2 and 3) to the first decade of the seventeenth century (Chapters 4, 5, 6, and 7) and then into the second decade of the seventeenth century, concluding in approximately 1630 (Chapter 8). These dates are meant to indicate the general historical span of the evidence that forms the core of the book's arguments, from Sidney's *Defence of Poesie*, composed in approximately 1579–1582 and Elizabeth's proclamation prohibiting new urban building, issued in 1580, to Jonson's encounter with neo-Aristotelian literary theory in 1629.

It is a pleasure to have the opportunity to thank publicly the many people who supported me as I wrote this book. I owe a great debt, first and foremost, to Jean

Howard, who supervised the project as a dissertation and who has continued to provide counsel at every subsequent stage: in her clarity, candour, professionalism, and her humour she is a model to all her students. Martha Howell welcomed me into her courses and indeed her entire discipline with unusual generosity, encouragement, and rigour; David Kastan's charm was surpassed only by the acuity of his insights. Coursework and conversations with Howard Bloch, Caroline Bynum, Anthony Grafton, and Anne Prescott had a transformative effect on my thinking and made this book possible in ways that they may not realize. At Oxford University Press I have Andrew McNeillie to thank for his warm support for the project and Tom Perridge, Val Shelley, and Laurien Berkeley for their expert assistance in preparing it for publication; all remaining errors are my own. The readers for the Press offered many helpful and sometimes sceptical suggestions, for which they have my thanks. At the University of Wisconsin–Madison, Sara Friedemann Uckelman, Xochitl Gilkeson, Hillary Higgins, Sara Phillips, Cody Reis, and Martisha Turk provided superb research support; Jason Cohen passed on the perfect Bacon epigraph; the library students at the School of Library and Information Studies at UW–Madison and the staff in UW–Madison's Memorial Library's Special Collections have shown unfailing good humour when faced with my many requests. Generous funding for the project was provided by the Whiting Foundation, the National Endowment for the Humanities, and the University of Wisconsin Vilas Foundation.

Early versions of several chapters were presented at Harvard University, the University of Michigan, the University of Nebraska–Lincoln, the UW–Madison History of Science Colloquium, the UW–Madison Rhetoric Colloquium, and the UW–Madison Renaissance Colloquium; to the Medieval and Renaissance Drama Society at Kalamazoo and to the Shakespeare at Kalamazoo Society; and at the annual meetings of the Shakespeare Association of America, the Renaissance Society of America, the Modern Language Association, and the Group for Early Modern Cultural Studies. I would like to thank my hosts and the audiences on all those occasions for their helpful comments.

Many friends have ensured that the long process of writing a book remained happy and satisfying; many colleagues have offered professional support and words of advice. On both counts, I owe particular thanks to Gina Bloom, James J. Bono, Amanda Claybaugh, Lisa Cooper, Mary Thomas Crane, Guillermina De Ferrari, Lee Edelman, Erika Gaffney, Marjorie Garber, William Germano, Jonathan Goldberg, Maria Grahn-Farley, Sara Guyer, Nick Havholm, Marlene Villalobos Hennessey, Barbara Johnson, Louise Keely, Carole Levin, Jacques Lezra, Joseph Litvak, Mun-Hou Lo, Jon McKenzie, Madhavi Menon, Josh Miller, Monica Miller, Scott Newstok, John Niles, Lena Cowen Orlin, Mario Ortiz-Robles, Margaret Pappano, Martin Puchner, Sherry Reames, Bryan Reynolds, Donald Rowe, Arielle Saiber, Scott Straus, Nancy Taggart, Gary Taylor, Ayanna Thompson, Catherine Toal, Richard Walker, Daniel Walkowitz, Judith Walkowitz, Carl Wennerlind, and Chloe Wheatley. Several friends made particular efforts and gave generously of their time to offer comments on extensive sections of the book, making it that much stronger for their expertise and care. For this I would like to express my warm appreciation to Heather Dubrow, Theresa Kelley, Aaron Kitch, Richard Knowles, Michael LeMahieu, Caroline Levine, David Loewenstein, Eric Rothstein, Matthew Stratton, John Tiedemann, Steven Walton, Andrew Weiner, William West, and Susanne Wofford. It is difficult for me to express my appreciation for three extraordinary friends: Jonathan Gil Harris, for his mindfulness, his intellectual company, and his generosity, in this project and in others; Jan Koettner, for his uncompromising gifts of self; and Douglas Pfeiffer, for his deep intellectualism, his integrity, and his intoxicating humour. Sarah Turner, my sister, and Harriet S. Turner, my mother, have provided the kind of support that exceeds acknowledgement; my dedication of this book to them is a small token of my love and gratitude. It has been my greatest good fortune to have Rebecca Walkowitz as a life partner: there is no day in which I am not filled with admiration for her many talents, with delight at her wit and insight, and with deep love for her sympathy, care, and companionship.

'In the case of most books, once we have read a few lines and looked at a few of the diagrams, the entire message is perfectly obvious. The rest is added only to fill up the paper.'

(Rene Descartes)

Contents

List of Illustrations

1

Introduction

. . . I will now attempt to make a general and faithful perambulation of
learning, with an inquiry what parts there of lie fresh and waste, and not
improved and converted by the industry of man; to the end that such a plot
made and recorded to memory may both minister light to any public
designation, and also serve to excite voluntary endeavours.

(Francis Bacon, *The Advancement of Learning*)

'DRAMA' AND THE PLATFORM STAGE

This book began as an attempt to re-evaluate the development of English public
drama during the late sixteenth and early seventeenth centuries and to do so by
drawing on some twenty-five years of scholarship by new historicist and cultural
materialist critics, historians of the theatre, and students of print culture, all of
whom had emphasized how English drama had been determined by its social, economic, and political conditions. As the project developed, it became increasingly
clear that some of the most innovative recent scholarship had come to overlook
important intellectual traditions that also informed English drama during the
period; earlier scholarship that did address these traditions either simplified or dis-
torted them, resulting in accounts of Continental or classical influences on
English drama, for instance, that were either out of date or narrowly defined in
scope. Certainly much ground-breaking work has examined the intellectual
content of early-modern plays; indeed, the discursive turn typical of new historicism has had the happy effect of widening the purview of the critic, who now finds
in the language of the drama a rich and eclectic palimpsest of contemporary ideologies and belief. But a discursive history of dramatic *form* rather than of dramatic content—a detailed analysis of the habits of thought that made theatrical
representation possible in the first place to early-modern playwrights, and one
undertaken in light of the many theoretical and methodological developments of
the last thirty years—has not received the same degree of critical attention.

At the same time, a growing interest among historically minded critics in the
history of the book and in drama as a *printed* form has meant, somewhat paradoxically, that much of the most imaginative and consequential recent scholarship has

tended to avoid a sustained engagement with the performative aspects of the drama and the formal presuppositions that made the theatre such a complex and popular mode of representation. Since the pioneering work of Harley Granville-Barker, Bernard Beckerman, J. L. Styan, Robert Weimann, David Bevington, and Alan Dessen, among others, critics have come to recognize the fundamental importance of staging when considering the interpretative possibilities of early-modern plays. In several important ways, too, attention to the performative nature of early-modern drama became a hallmark of the Foucauldian and Marxist-derived critiques of new historicism, particularly in the early work of Stephen Greenblatt and Louis Montrose. But because new historicism sought to define a dialectical methodology that could embed the drama in early-modern culture more broadly, it tended to emphasize the unique *institutional* realities of the public theatres; critical interest in the formal techniques of performance tended to become restricted to an analysis of the actor and his 'playing', such that one element among many different theatrical codes came to assume a paradigmatic status that could be extended into analyses of the performative nature of royal power or the inherent theatricality of everyday social life. As a consequence, a more complete analysis of drama in performance tended to become subordinated to a formal analysis of power, on the one hand, or to an analysis of social contradictions mediated through symbolic form, on the other, and in this way the drama came to be regarded either as the source of those aspects in early-modern culture that new historicism found most compelling or as the consequence of the broader social transformations that such criticism sought to explain. In the process, fundamental questions concerning the semiotic conventions of theatrical representation, for instance, or the definition and function of basic representational units such as the scene, slipped out of the dialectical equation.

This book takes as its point of departure the deceptively obvious premiss that the English drama of the late sixteenth and early seventeenth centuries must be considered above all as a highly spatialized mode of representation performed in the public theatres and not simply as an artefact of print. Indeed, in strict terms it will be necessary to distinguish a critical and theoretical notion of 'drama' that finally derives from the conventions of the printed book, on the one hand, from the theatre and its performative conventions, on the other, conventions that largely remained *un*theorized during the period and which Renaissance writers struggled to reconcile with their neo-classical prescriptions for drama as a distinct mode of poetic art.[1] Once this reconceptualization of the object of inquiry has

---

[1] For the modern critic, of course, nearly all the surviving evidence for theatrical practice derives from early printed play texts, a state of affairs that goes a long way towards explaining the general persistence of a binarism between stage and page in drama criticism; see esp. De Grazia and Stallybrass (1993), demonstrating how close attention to the interpretative potential of the 'materiality' of the play text reveals theatrical traces that often frustrate modern expectations about dramatic structure, language, and meaning and undermine the metaphysical presuppositions that govern our evaluation of drama as a 'literary' form; Worthen (1997: 20–1, 151–91; 1998); Weimann (2000);

been adopted, furthermore—once the full complexity of 'drama' as a *practical* and *theatrical* form emerges into view—an adequate account of its specific conventions and of its social function (the enduring object of current historicist criticism) requires a corollary shift of attention beyond the fields that have conventionally informed modern scholarship.

In what follows, I argue that English playwrights working in the public theatres at the turn of the seventeenth century began to conceptualize problems of theatrical representation in terms that derived not simply from neo-classical literary theory, as is often presumed of playwrights such as Ben Jonson, nor simply from the legacy of medieval staging and the Tudor interludes, as is often argued about Shakespeare, but from contemporary developments in early-modern technology, applied mathematics, and pre-scientific thought. As Thomas Dekker observed in his *Old Fortunatus* (1599), performed both at court and at Philip Henslowe's Rose Theatre, playwrights might perfectly well disregard as irrelevant any 'lawes of Poesy', as Dekker put it, that audiences might have come to expect from reading romance or the arguments of Sidney or any number of Continental writers. In the 'Prologue' that he wrote for *Old Fortunatus*' public performance at the Rose sometime in December 1599 or early in 1600, Dekker seems to have in mind the claims for 'heroic' poetry that (among English writers) first Sidney and then Spenser, more recently, had advanced:

> Of *Loves* sweete war, our timerous Muse doth sing,
> And to the bosome of each gentle deare,
> Offers her Artles tunes, borne on the wing
> Of sacred Poesy . . . [2]

The epic invocations of the lines extend the separate 'Prologue at Court' that Dekker had written for the performance before Elizabeth on 27 December, where two elderly 'Pilgrims'—one from England, one from Cyprus—journey together to 'pay a whole yeeres tribute' to the 'Dread Queene of Fayries' (54–5):

1. Are you then travelling the temple of *Eliza*?

2. Even to her temple are my feeble limmes travelling. Some cal her *Pandora*: some *Gloriana*, some *Cynthia*: some *Belphœbe*, some *Astræa*: all by severall names to expresse severall loves: Yet all those names make but one celestiall body, as all those loves meete to create but one soule. (lines 1–6)

Kastan (2001: 5–9, 14–49); Chartier (1999, esp. 17–22, 28–46, 51–69); and J. S. Peters (2000, esp. 93–112, 122–5, 166–80, 181–200), demonstrating how much early-modern ideas about theatre derived from print; also McKenzie (1977), making similar arguments with respect to Congreve. Peters and McKenzie each illustrate a crucial point: 'theatre' and 'drama' increasingly converge as categories over the course of the 17th century; 'drama', we might say, is what 'theatre' comes to look like when it is considered from the perspective of the book; see Ch. 5, below; also Elam (2002: 2–3); Pavis (1982b: 18–19, 25–35).

  [2] Dekker (1953–61, vol. i, 'The Prologue', lines 1–4).

The several names for Elizabeth and the references to a hermeneutic theory of the Queen's two bodies all indicate that the immediate source for Dekker's 'lawes of Poesy' is almost certainly Spenser's letter to Sir Walter Ralegh prefaced to the 1590 edition of the *Faerie Queene* and, via the letter, Torquato Tasso's similar arguments concerning allegory in his *Gerusalemme Liberata* (1581). Both are fitting theoretical reference points for the peculiar mixture of romance, morality play, and masque that follows, in which the figure of Fortune offers Old Fortunatus, a Cypriot and the play's title character, a magic purse of infinite riches with which to travel through all of Asia and Europe and which he passes to his son upon his death. Like Christopher Marlowe's *1* and *2 Tamburlaine* (*c.*1587–*c.*1588) and *Dr. Faustus* (*c.*1588)—famous predecessors in the Admiral's Men's repertory that Dekker seems to have freshly in mind and which, in the case of *Faustus*, he may even have had a hand in revising—*Old Fortunatus* unfolds over a vast international geography; like Marlowe before him, Dekker adopts several different performative techniques in order to solve the mimetic, imaginative, and structural problems that an action of such scope and diversity implied.

In Babylon the Sultan describes to Fortunatus his collection of occult and mythological devices, from which he might choose in exchange for his magic purse

> the ball of gold that set all *Troy* on fire   (2.1.44)

>   a wheele of *Titans* carre,
> which dropt from heaven when *Phaeton* fir'd the world:
> Ile give thee (if thou wilt) two silver Dooves
> Compos'd by Magicke to divide the ayre,
> Who (as they flie)shall clap their silver wings,
> And give straunge musicke to the Elements   (2.1. 48–53)

Fortunatus, however, is interested only in the most precious device of them all, the magic hat of which the Sultan is especially proud:

> SOULD.   ... this clapt upon my head,
> I (onely with a wish) am through the ayre,
> Transported in a moment over Seas,
> And over lands to any secrete place;
> By this I steale to every Princes court,
> And heare their private councels and prevent
> All daungers which to *Babylon* are meant.
> By helpe of this I oft see armies joyne,
> Though when the dreadfull Alvarado sounds,
> I am distant from the place a thousand leagues,
> Oh, had I such a purse and such a Hat,
> The *Souldan* were, of all, most fortunate.   (2. 1. 86–97)

As the audience well knows from the allegorical masque of Virtue, Vice, and Fortune that has opened the play, however, it is Fortunatus who is the 'most fortunate', and in the matter of a few lines he easily outwits the simple Sultan:

FORTUNAT. Me thinkes, me thinkes, when you are borne o're Seas,
    And over lands, the heavinesse thereof
    Should waigh you downe, drowne you, or breake your necke . . .
SOULD. Fie, ya're deceav'd: trie it upon your head.
FORTUNAT. Would I were now in *Cyprus* with my sons.   *[Exit]*

                          (2. 1. 102–8)

'Would I were now in *Cyprus* with my sons—*Exit*': the play text records its own verbal charm, its technologos, as it were, to mark the magic of the theatrical gesture that could transport Fortunatus thousands of miles away simply by donning a cap and walking off the stage. How to explain the quasi-magical powers of a performance that could manipulate space, time, and the conventional properties of bodies so easily? How to defend, if necessary, the theatre against the scepticism of audiences, the disdain of critics, and the accusations of authorities? These were some of the most pressing questions facing Marlowe, Dekker, Shakespeare, Jonson, and their contemporaries: their livelihoods, their legacies, their very identities depended on the answers.

For Dekker the answer was surprisingly simple, and surprisingly modern: the stage is like a map, and the imaginative conventions of theatrical performance like the system of geometrical projection on which the map depended. In his separate Prologue written for *Old Fortunatus'* public performance at the Rose, Dekker makes his argument as explicitly as possible:

And for this smal Circumference must stand,
For the imagind Sur-face of much land,
Of many kingdomes, and since many a mile,
Should here be measurd out: our muse intreats,
Your thoughts to helpe poore Art, and to allow,
That I may serve as Chorus to her scenes,
She begs your pardon, for sheele send me foorth,
Not when the lawes of Poesy doe call,
But as the storie needes . . .

                (Prologue, 15–23)

To Dekker's mind, any 'lawes of Poesy' derived from a Spenser or a Tasso might always prove insufficient in a public theatre that was trying to claim an extraordinary authority and mimetic freedom for itself. Prompted by an 'Art' who worries that the sudden shifts of scene and the massive geographic displacements to follow—the sheer *simultaneity* of so great a space compressed in so little compass—will stretch the imagination to the point of implausibility, Dekker's Chorus steps forward only 'as the storie needs': successful performance requires not the rigorous application of theoretical principles but a flexible, adaptive, and improvisational approach that could accommodate the narratives and fantasies of a period to the conventions of a new representational medium: to the theatre and its platform stage.

A fuller explanation is perhaps best left to the play's own advocate:

> *Enter* Chorus
> CHORUS. The world to the circumference of heaven,
> Is as a small point in Geometrie,
> Whose greatnes is so little, that a lesse
> Cannot be made: into that narrow roome,
> Your quicke imaginations we must charme,
> To turne that world: and (turn'd) again to part it
> Into large kingdoms, and within one moment,
> To carrie Fortunatus on the wings
> Of active thought, many a thousand miles.   (2. 0. 1–9)

For Dekker's Chorus, the power of geometry resides in its magical 'as': in a wondrous analogical extension that facilitates comparisons among radically heterogeneous entities—here the terrestrial and celestial spheres—by means of purely formal and quantitative categories ('circumference', 'greatness'). Geometry is a fictional system that, like the stage, requires an infusion of imagination to make its fictions plausible. Indeed, geometry offered early-modern writers nothing less than an entire system of representation to rival that of language, whereby all bodies, places, and ideas, no matter how distinct, might be rendered conceptually equivalent to one another. As the smallest conceivable geometrical entity, the geometrical point functions as a primary structural element in a kind of Euclidean general linguistics, serving as a semiotic unit that 'marks', both literally and figuratively, the dialectical moment where matter sublates into form and form collapses into matter, and, at the same time, providing the foundation, along with other geometrical units such as the line and the figure, for a mathematical syntax of purely formal and proportional relationships. As a consequence, geometry may be described as a *tropic* discourse for early-modern writers, one in which quantitative rather than qualitative similarity among heterogeneous elements becomes a principle of 'turning': of revolving like a mechanical globe but also of mutation and transformation—of 'translation', in its Renaissance sense of 'changing form'. And as we shall see, geometry accomplishes this feat not, or not merely, through language and verbal argument but through showing, or the visual demonstration of its figures—like the theatre, in which objects, actions, and bodies exceed themselves to become ostensive, performative signs of something else.

By asserting a fundamental congruence between stage and map—by proposing geometrical projection as a kind of poetic projection that is somehow necessary to stage performance—Dekker's analogy, furthermore, is more than novel: it is typical in its novelty. Some ten years later, the surveyor Arthur Hopton would illustrate the title page of his *Speculum Topographicum; or, The Topographicall Glass* (1611), a practical compendium of military and civil surveying problems, with a

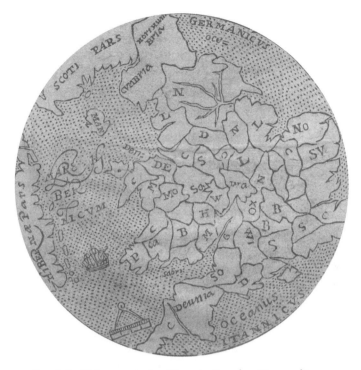

FIG. 1.1. Title page, Arthur Hopton, *Speculum Topographicum;
or The Topographicall Glasse* (1611)

remarkable image that translates Dekker's analogy into its exact cartographic equivalent (Fig. 1.1). If, as Kent van den Berg and John Gillies have observed, the stage—the 'Globe'—functions as a kind of atlas at the turn of the seventeenth century, for Hopton the surveyor's book becomes a mirror in which the entire world may be reduced to graphic form, according to the rules of an 'Art' that is nothing less than geometry itself.[3] In the verses that Hopton composed and prefaced to his reader, Geometry is invoked to authorize the 'show' that follows and to distinguish it from lesser illusions:

> Come you, whose eyes stand not in envious head,
> Whose tongue with Criticke humors is not fed,
> And in this Glasse, unto your comfort view,
> Such needfull workes that much may profit you.
> The grounds of Art have brought it forth for thee,
> Which we have suckt from famous Geometrie,

[3] Van den Berg (1985: 32–43); Gillies (1994); Helgerson (1992).

With Theorm's mixt and demonstrations rare,
Such as in hiddan Propositions are:
Heer's no vaine shew: illusions have no place,
No spirit confind, no hatefull painted face,
No eye-deceiving glasse, no Cristall brave,
Which from the frozen seas we often have.
But in a faire and most perspicuous light,
The earthy Globe lies subject to thy sight. . . .
This frame enough for all the world to view,
This Glasse layes in a small proportion true.
That like an Eagle towring up aloft,
Whole regions thou mayst view and review oft.
Discoursing now of Europe in particular,
And then of other Countries distant farre.
Now of *Jerusalem* that was before,
And then of *Rome*, by Tybers silver shore . . .
Learne here to bound the Alpes, *Spaine*, *France* and all . . .
America, the new found land beside,
And eke those Southerne parts yet undiscride.   (a2ᵛ)

Geometry delights, since it provides an artificial means whereby the viewer may see a series of particular places—remote in time as well as in space—that could never be grasped by the naked eye alone, even as it renders these heterogeneous places comparable and similar, much the way the stage could do. Jerusalem, Rome, Spain, France, America, mountains, rivers: all are reducible to the same set of mimetic conventions and all are juxtaposed within a single 'frame'. Marlowe's Tamburlaine invokes just this power of 'translation' as he asserts his will to conquest, proclaiming that he will literally redraw the world in his own image, as in a cartographic mirror:

I will confute those blind geographers
That make a triple region of the world,
Excluding regions which I mean to trace
And with this pen reduce them to a map,
Calling the provinces, cities, and towns
After my name and thine, Zenocrate.
Here at Damascus will I make the point
That shall begin the perpendicular.[4]

---

[4] Christopher Marlowe, *1 Tamburlaine the Great*, 4. 4. 73–80; cf. *2*, 5. 3. 126–60. The passages have been much cited in criticism on the geographical imagination of the early-modern period, but with little acknowledgement of its roots in practical modes of thinking; see esp. Seaton (1924, 1929); Greenblatt (1980: 193–221); De Somogyi (1996), citing *2 Tamburlaine*, 3. 2. 62–7, 68–82, and 3. 3. 41–53; Bartolovich (1997, with additional bibliography); Sullivan (1997); Gillies (1994: 52, 56–7, 1998: 203–29, esp. 205, 225); and now Cahill (2004), placing the play firmly in the context of military manuals and practical mathematics.

In effecting a similar imaginative translation, Hopton's Geometry also 'profits' the reader–viewer, since it represents these places truthfully and without conjuring or trickery, through theorems and demonstrations that silence any 'Criticke humours' which might doubt its authority. In Horatian language worthy of one of Jonson's stage inductions, in short, the verses claim for Geometry a very un-Jonsonian principle: the power to transport the viewer across vast distances through a single act of imaginative projection.

However loudly Jonson himself may have objected to contemporary performance conventions—foremost among them the very mimetic freedom that Dekker was claiming for the stage in his 'Prologue' to *Old Fortunatus*—he also recognized the limitations of classical precepts when confronted with the formal problems posed by stage representation. When, in the Induction to *Every Man Out of His Humour* (1599), the critic–spectator Mitis asks whether the playwright Asper will 'observe all the lawes of Comedie' in his play—'the equall division of it into Acts, and Scenes, according to the Terentian manner, his true number of Actors; the furnishing of the Scene with GREX, or CHORUS, and that the whole Argument fall within compasse of a dayes businesse' (Induction, 237–41)—his companion Cordatus offers a surprising demurral: 'O no, these are too nice observations . . . we should enjoy the same licence, or free power, to illustrate and heighten our invention as [the Ancients] did; and not bee tyed to those strict and regular formes, which the niceness of a few (who are nothing but forme) would thrust upon us.'[5] Obviously both Horace and Terence remained fundamental points of reference for Jonson throughout his career. But Jonson also owned several books on geometry, architecture, and practical mathematics and even lived for a brief period at Gresham College, a London institution founded with the express purpose of offering instruction in applied mathematics and many different technical fields to an urban audience of tradesmen and gentlemen alike, and the methods of practical thinking he encountered in these books form an important aspect of his approach towards theatrical representation that has been largely disregarded.

And Shakespeare, too, in *Henry V* (1599)—written in the very same year as Jonson's Induction and Dekker's Prologue, and perhaps even in imitation of Dekker's play[6]—was making nearly identical claims for the theatre's ability to whisk characters and audience alike overseas, from England to France, London to

---

⁵ Jonson (1925–52, vol. iii, Induction, 242–70); cf. *Discoveries*, viii. 641. 2555–65.

⁶ The chronology depends on whether 'the I parte of Forteunatus' revived by the Admiral's Men from 3 February to 26 May 1596 was originally written by Dekker and whether the Prologue and Chorus passages formed part of the later additions for which Dekker was paid a total of £9 during November–December 1599 for 'the hole history of Fortunatus' and 'the eande of Fortewnatus for the corte'; see Chambers (1923: iii. 291). If the passages were written during this later period (as many scholars presume, although on the basis of no conclusive evidence), then Dekker would seem to be imitating Shakespeare, since *Henry V* is likely to have been written sometime between January and June 1599.

Southampton to Dover to Harfleur, then back again to Calais, London, and Blackheath, and then again to France . . . 'things | Which cannot in their huge and proper life | Be here presented'.[7] Certainly it is possible to identify many complex and significant influences on Shakespeare's approach to theatrical representation that have little to do with technology or practical mathematics: here, for instance, the problem confronting the working playwright was one of accommodating diegetic or narrative sources and their logic ('Vouchsafe to those that have not read the story'; 5. 0. 1) to a very different mimetic or enacted mode. But the solution to this problem requires not simply an epic-heroic 'muse of fire, that would ascend | The brightest heaven of invention' (lines 1–2) but an act of mathematical calculation from the audience that is almost identical to the imaginative projection Dekker had also sought:

> . . . But pardon, gentles all,
> The flat unraisèd spirits that hath dared
> On this unworthy scaffold to bring forth
> So great an object. Can this cock-pit hold
> The vasty fields of France? Or may we cram
> Within this wooden O the very casques
> That did affright the air at Agincourt?
> O pardon: since a crookèd figure may
> Attest in little place a million,
> And let us, ciphers to this great account,
> On your imaginary forces work.
> Suppose within the girdle of these walls
> Are now confined two mighty monarchies,
> Whose high uprearèd and abutting fronts
> The perilous narrow ocean parts asunder.
> Piece out our imperfections with your thoughts:
> Into a thousand parts divide one man,
> And make imaginary puissance.

>   (*Henry V*, Prologue, 8–25)

The semiotic conventions of theatrical performance convert historical chronicle into a kind of mimetic bookkeeping, as stage wall and actor's body become quantitative units in a grand imaginative equation. And if the conventions of the theatre require a defence or an apology, it is because the peculiar mathematical logic of stage representation *divides* at the same time that it multiplies: the risk of stage mimesis conceived in mathematical terms is a conspicuous deflation of an event—'Agincourt'—whose epic grandeur and historical significance had become legendary in English culture.

---

[7] 5. 0. 4–6; for ease of reference, all citations are to the Norton Shakespeare, based on the Oxford text.

These two choric invocations of intellectual fields that would appear, at first glance, to lie at some distance from Renaissance poetic discourse are liable to seem somewhat less surprising when we consider that even earlier, in 1574—some twenty-five years before the rival passages of Dekker, Shakespeare, and Jonson, each written in the same year and each conspicuous in its attempt to justify the conventions of the platform stage—Gabriel Harvey was already naming Chaucer, Lydgate, Sidney, and Spenser in the same breath as writers whom we would certainly never describe as 'literary' figures and whose names we may no longer recognize at all: John Dee, Thomas Harriot, John Blagrave, and Leonard Digges, those 'mathematical practitioners', as E. G. R. Taylor has called them, whose knowledge of mathematics and expertise in early forms of technology made them increasingly sought after by men of wealth and power. And Harvey might well have added other names to his list: Robert Recorde, author of the first geometry textbook in English; Thomas Blundeville, author of a popular university logic textbook, of several books in applied mathematics and astronomy, and the translator of Italian treatises on horsemanship and history writing; John Norden, author of one of the period's most popular surveying manuals; Humphrey Cole, a maker of mathematical instruments who lived in London and collaborated with the instructors at Gresham College. All of these writers appear in Harvey's marginalia and correspondence alongside more familiar names such as Roger Ascham, Edmund Spenser, or George Gascoigne. When we examine Harvey's annotations alongside the work of writers as diverse as George Puttenham, Christopher Marlowe, Thomas Middleton, Sidney, Shakespeare, Dekker, and even Jonson himself, we find that Renaissance men of letters are beginning to regard poetics, and especially the theatre, as a distinctive way of coming to knowledge about metaphysical principles, about society, and about human action, and not simply as a matter of philology, grammar, and style. And they arrive at this new epistemological approach to poetics, surprisingly enough, not simply by reading classical authors but by comparing it to practical geometry, early-modern technology, and the mechanical arts that were flourishing around them. As Henry Peacham would argue some years later, praising geometry in his *Compleat Gentleman* (1622) as 'this most ingenious and usefull Art' and crediting it with 'the formes and draughts of all figures . . . the cunning working of all tooles, with all artificiall instruments whatsoever', including the theatre:

By the benefit likewise of Geometrie, we have our goodly Shippes, Galleies, Bridges, Milles, Charriots and Coaches . . . She also with her ingenious hand reares all curious roofes, and Arches, stately Theaters . . . first brought to light our clockes and curious Watches (unknowne to the ancients) . . . even to the wheele-barrow. Beside whatsoever hath artificiall motion either by Ayre, water, winde, sinewes or chords, as all manner of Musicall instruments, water workes and the like. Yea, moreover, such is the infinite subtiltie, and immense depth of this admirable Art, that it dares contend even with natures selfe, in infusing life as it were, into the sencelesse bodies of wood, stone, or mettall . . . (p. 73)

For Peacham, we may be surprised to find, the marvelous effects produced by geometrically derived devices in material objects are best compared to the inventions of the poets: 'If Mechanical Arts hold their estimation by their effects in base subjects,' he argues in his very next chapter, 'Of Poetry', 'how much more deserveth [Poetrie] to be esteemed that holdeth so soveraigne a power over the minde, can turne brutishnesse into Civilitie, make the lewd honest . . . turne hatred to love, cowardice into valour, and in briefe, like a Queene, command over all affections' (p. 80).

LITERATURE, SCIENCE, AND 'PRACTICAL KNOWLEDGE'

The causes for this 'geometric turn' and its consequences for our own modern sense of disciplinary categories are the subject of the book that follows. Each chapter describes a convergence between literary and scientific epistemologies in England, during a period when both fields were in a crucial moment of formation.[8] If we examine the distinctive habits of reasoning that preceded modern experimental method and the mathematical world-view of the seventeenth century, we find ways of thinking that would help to define the 'new science' in unexpected places: scattered throughout sixteenth-century poetic discourse; crowded into marginal annotations; mentioned casually in letters about the importance of moral philosophy; motivating simple manuals that sought to popularize geometry among new classes of readers. In the sixteenth century both poetics and geometry began to enjoy a new status as socially useful kinds of knowledge and seemed to offer insights into moral, social, or natural problems that more established epistemologies, such as the neo-scholasticism of the universities, were unable to provide; in their novelty, they were often regarded

---

[8] The relationships between 'literary' and 'scientific' epistemologies have been of particular interest to literary critics, but less so to historians of science, since C. P. Snow's (1964) seminal lecture on the 'two cultures'; Montagu (1946*a*) anticipates Snow's arguments and provides extensive bibliography from the 1930s and 1940s (most concerned with the 17th and 18th centuries). Bush (1950), Nicolson (1956, 1960), and Empson (1957) are notable early treatments of the problem, with particular reference to the poetry of Donne. Scholarship in the area developed significantly as of the 1990s; the following list is necessarily partial, but see esp. Paster (1993), Sawday (1996), and Hillman and Mazzio (1997), on the place of the body in 16th-century epistemology; Markley (1993) and Bono (1995, esp. 8 n. 6), on the relationship between philosophies of language and inquiry into nature; Svendsen (1956) and Martin (1996, 2001), on Milton; Albanese (1996) and Solomon (1998), on Bacon; Markley (1993), Reiss (1997, 2000, 2004), Albanese (2002), H. S. Turner (2002*b*), and Mazzio (2004), as well as the other essays collected by Glimp and Warren (2004), on mathematics, language, and literature; Rogers (1996), on the scientific and the political revolutions of the 17th century; Crane (2001), on the relevance of cognitive science to Shakespeare studies; Harris (2004), on the way medical discourse informed early-modern analysis of economic problems; Spiller (2004), on poetic fiction and experiment; Wolfe (2004), on humanism and machines; Saiber (2005), on Bruno's geometrical rhetoric; and Blair (1999), a concise survey of the topic.

with suspicion by contemporaries and gradually came to require more explicit and systematic justifications from those who cultivated them. In the fields of both poetics and geometry, furthermore, social groups who sought to enhance their personal status or the status of their activities did so by claiming an epistemological and a moral authority for them; in both fields, too, this claim to authority eventually required the subordination of long-standing practices and techniques to a self-conscious and explicit theoretical discourse that could be defended, circulated, and further refined.

As a distinct domain of cultural production, 'poesy'—and especially 'dramatic poesy'—developed defensively during the late sixteenth and early seventeenth centuries in England in response to ideological critiques from the pulpit and restrictions from legal authorities; it assumed a new coherence as of approximately 1580, when Sidney composed his famous *Defence* and concluded it with a survey of English poets, both medieval and contemporary. As a coherent epistemology with distinctive terminology, methods of inquiry, and institutional organization, the 'experimental science' of the Royal Society and the 'mathematical world-view' associated with Galileo, Descartes, Kepler, and Newton emerged not simply by refuting the neo-scholasticism of the universities but by subordinating older practical and craft traditions to systematic principles and by abstracting and generalizing data-gathering procedures so that they could be reproduced by others. Mario Biagioli (1993) has demonstrated how Italian court culture was fundamental to the legitimization of Galileo's new science, as well as to Galileo's own self-fashioning from mathematical practitioner to mathematical philosopher, while Steven Shapin and Simon Schaffer (1985) have shown how the emergence of 'experiment' also required publication—literally a 'making public'—in order to produce consensus among a larger audience of practitioners. In this way 'experiment' depended as much on a process of epistemological legitimization as it did on the novel definition of traditional natural problems or on greater technical refinement.

That a movement towards a recognizably modern 'scientific' mode of thinking occurs in sixteenth-century England, not only in practical geometrical handbooks but in treatises on rhetoric and dialectic and in the field of poetic discourse, has been largely ignored in scholarship on the history of science, which has tended to focus on developments within the fields of mechanics, natural philosophy, or astronomy (those fields of inquiry most continuous with modern science), and their implications for the empiricism and mathematical modelling of the seventeenth century.[9] Strictly speaking, of course, the modern notion of 'science' is an

[9] In addition to the works cited in n. 10 and Ch. 2, see the very full survey of the historiography of science offered by Cohen (1994); Lindberg (1990); Hall (1959); Barker and Ariew (1991); Crombie (1952, 1994, both with exhaustive bibliography); Dear (1997). On experimentalism, see Shapin and Schaffer (1985) and Gooding *et al.* (1989); on the increasing mathematization of natural philosophy, see Kuhn (1977) and Dear (1995, *passim*, esp. 210–16); on the mechanical world-view, see Dijksterhuis (1986); Laird (1986); and Gabbey (1990, 1993); on probability in 17th-century thought, see Shapiro (1983, 2000).

anachronism in the sixteenth century, and several recent studies in the history and sociology of science have considered the specific epistemological presumptions of those medieval and early-modern activities that promised insights into natural process or control over the natural world but which often remained of doubtful authority, their practitioners of dubious social reputation, and their methods closer to craft or to magic than to modern 'experiment'.[10] Extending this recent work, this book argues that several important aspects of both modern scientific method and Renaissance poetics may be traced back to the central place occupied in sixteenth-century English thought by ethical philosophy, the 'arts of discourse' that dominated the university curriculum, and the field of geometry as it was developing both inside and outside a university context.

Throughout the chapters that follow, I use the phrase 'practical knowledge' to describe a specific intellectual formation characteristic of sixteenth-century England, a pre-scientific epistemology that arose out of a convergence between humanist habits of reasoning inherited from classical rhetoric, dialectic, and prudence—Aristotle's *phronēsis*, or deliberation about human action—on the one hand, and a growing interest on the part of the educated gentleman in technology and the practical geometrical fields of building, surveying, engineering, and cartography, on the other. Once we recognize this intellectual formation as a distinctive feature of the period, we begin to realize how broadly it extended, across areas of early-modern intellectual and social life that today we are accustomed to regard as quite distinct from one another: from the university college to meadows, workshops, and harbour fortification projects; from textbooks to carpentry and cartography; from military strategy to poetic invention, stylistic experimentation, and techniques of theatrical performance. In this epistemological moment, and as a consequence of the new status that geometry and its associated fields enjoyed, we encounter new ideas about form and structure that would become central to poetic discourse, and a new vocabulary for these ideas; new presuppositions about the nature of language as a medium for representing the natural world and for representing human action, as well as a new interest in alternative codes for doing so; and new attitudes towards the imagination and its ability to invent, ingeniously and spontaneously, forms in which this knowledge might be communicated to others. Out of this same moment, too, we find new ways of thinking about the relationship between theory and practice; new modes of forming judgements about particulars, before these particulars become the 'facts' of experimental procedure; new methods of modelling, diagramming, and visualizing technical problems; and new attitudes about the importance of technology to the state, as well as to professional self-advancement.

One of the many consequences of this convergence between geometry and poetics, I argue, is that we must adjust our sense of the playwright's epistemological

---

[10] See esp. Long (1985, 1997, 2001); Vérin (1993); P. Smith (1994); Rossi (1968, 1970); Perez-Ramos (1988); Eamon (1994); Bono (1995, 2004*a*, *b*); W. R. Newman (1989); Grafton (1999).

presuppositions, as well as our accounts of his social position and uncertain professional status: he appears less as a modern 'author'—a category that was only beginning to emerge during the period, as several scholars have argued—than as a figure who is more similar to the contemporary surveyor, engineer, mason, and carpenter than we might expect. This shift in category is especially relevant when we consider the position of those playwrights, like Shakespeare and Jonson, who had themselves once been actors and who often worked directly in the theatres with other actors and stage managers as well as with other artisans of all types, rather than considering the playwright simply in his relationship to the printed book—the 'work' whose production, marketing, and rhetorical defences contributed so much to the formation of the modern category of the author and its legal protections, as well as to the larger concept of the 'literary' domain itself.[11] Like the mathematical practitioners of his period, the playwright found that his domain of expertise was still very much in formation and that it was often viewed with suspicion; for this reason he was at some level always in a defensive position as he attempted to formulate the defining categories and principles of legitimization for his field. Like the practitioner's activity, too, the work of the playwright was fundamentally collaborative and distributed among different centres of power, which he depended on for wealth, status, and legal protection but from which he always remained semi-autonomous.

Both of these aspects would become particularly clear to Jonson and Dekker in 1603–4, for instance, when they began an enforced collaboration with the joiner Stephen Harrison over *The Magnificent Entertainment* offered by the City of London to King James on the occasion of his accession to the English throne. Both Jonson and Dekker would appeal to the monarch and to City officials simultaneously, as they sought to position themselves to receive future commissions; for both writers, too, the event allowed them to display the poet's distinctive mode of intelligence to a powerful audience and to defend his compositional principles. Jonson, characteristically, adopts a defensive stance that he would continue to occupy throughout his career, distancing himself as much as possible from Harrison's arches, or 'the *Mecanick* part yet standing', in an attempt to formulate a de-materialized and classically derived notion of the poetic object. Dekker, in contrast, devotes considerable attention to the quantitative dimensions and the physical materials of the arches, reducing the significance of the monarch himself until he becomes one personage among many, a figure nearly overshadowed by the artisans who made the occasion possible.

The Magnificent Entertainment provides a particularly clear view of an exchange in concepts, terminology, and practical techniques that was taking place more

---

[11] Scholarship on the history of dramatic authorship in the period is much too extensive for a single note, but see Bentley (1971: 197–234, esp. 228–34), on collaboration; De Grazia (1991); Masten (1996, 1997), also on collaboration; Marcus (1996); Worthen (1997); Kastan (1999, 2001); Brooks (2000); Loewenstein (1985, 2002*a*, *b*); and Orgel (2002).

broadly at the turn of the seventeenth century between playwrights and mathematical practitioners, and particularly from the latter to the former. The precise nature of this exchange is the subject of the chapters that follow, and it is most clearly visible, I argue, in three areas: in the working methods of composition that writers used to generate ideas for poems and dramatic productions; in the vocabulary that playwrights employed to designate a concept of symbolic content—in short, what the performance would be 'about'—and in the shared semiotic conventions that made the 'delightful and measur'd lines', as Thomas Hobbes would later put it, of the poet, the playwright, the painter, the carpenter, the surveyor, and the engineer alike into meaningful mimetic units.[12] In the end, Jonson and Dekker were each attempting to come to terms with two distinct notions of 'form' that were characteristic of early-modern poets and practitioners, respectively: a qualitative, verbal, and rhetorical notion ultimately inherited from Aristotle, Cicero, and Quintilian, and a quantified, spatial, and geometrical notion derived from Euclid and from Neoplatonic and Pythagorean philosophy, one that was being modified by the practical geometrical manuals and disseminated more widely through English culture.[13] As we shall see, both notions of form would persist throughout their work for the public theatres, and Jonson, in particular, would expend considerable intellectual energy attempting to reconcile them with one another.

FORM AND METHOD: THE PROBLEM OF 'PLOT' IN THEATRICAL REPRESENTATION

By taking as more widely significant these aspects of Jonson and Dekker's work on *The Magnificent Entertainment*, I mean to advocate a return to the category of 'form' as fundamental to historical, cultural, and theoretical inquiry but as a category, too, that must be understood as a material, dialectical *process* and not as the ideal artefact imagined by New Criticism.[14] I have presumed, for instance, that any analysis of a play's content and relation to its historical moment must attend

---

[12] Hobbes (1650): 'Poets are Painters: I would fain see another Painter draw so true, perfect, and natural a Love to the Life, and make use of nothing but pure Lines . . .' (55. 17; cf. 61. 20–3); cf. a similar comparison in Ferrarius (1559: 90ᵛ).

[13] My argument is indebted to Trimpi (1983).

[14] I draw on Wolfson's (1997) discussion of American debates over form, esp. pp. 1–19; also the special issue of *Modern Literary Quarterly* (Mar. 2000) with much additional bibliography, esp. Wolfson (2000); Rooney (2000, esp. 26); Dubrow (2000); and Gallagher (2000, esp. 230–1 and n. 5). See also J.G. Harris (2002*a*); and De Man (1983): 'The idea of totality suggests closed forms that strive for ordered and consistent systems . . . Yet, the temporal factor, so persistently forgotten, should remind us that the form is never anything but a process on the way to its completion' (p. 31); 'the work changes entirely . . . depending on whether one considers it as a finished form (*forma formata*) or . . . as a form in the process of coming into being (*forma formans*)' (p. 43). I thank Caroline Levine for helping me to clarify my terms and arguments in this section.

to the specific ways in which that content has been selected, organized, and arranged; I have also presumed that this informing process is partly attributable to playwrights working within the specific intellectual and social contexts of the theatre and who made deliberate decisions about how given narratives might best be represented on stage. But it should perhaps go without saying that the process of 'giving form' is also a historical process that finally exceeds the work of any individual figure, and one of the purposes of this book will be to demonstrate how plays gave theatrical expression to the social and ideological tensions typical of the period—problems of citizenship, gender, forms of wealth, social class, and status, among others—partly through their characters, actions, locations, stories, and themes but partly also *as* form, as the very means by which this symbolic content was organized and communicated on stage to early-modern audiences.[15]

At this level of my argument, I understand the concept of 'form' in several distinct ways, all of which have determined my methodology in what follows. In the first place, and in a literary register that will be most familiar, I mean what Paul De Man has described as 'groupings from which the constitutive parts cannot be isolated or separated' (1983: 27). The definition is broad enough to encompass both aspects of De Man's later distinction between a 'constituting form' and a 'signifying form' (p. 232), but it is the first notion that remains primary here: an idea of form that never merely reproduces a prior experience or object of knowledge but organizes it and makes it thinkable as such.[16] The complexity arises when we consider precisely how this act is achieved, at the level of the formalized object, at the level of its reception, and in the dialectic between them. These problems become even more difficult in the case of 'dramatic form', since the 'form' of performance is of an entirely different order from the 'form' of a play when it is printed and read. At the same time, it is necessary to distinguish clearly between a concept of 'form' and a concept of 'genre': I have regarded 'form' as a principle that *precedes* genre, in so far as the parameters that structure theatrical performance as a distinct mode of representation (or 'form') may in turn accommodate many different types of play, each with its own internal differentiating features ('genres') and each employing the conventions of the theatre in distinctive ways.

---

[15] I draw especially on Jameson (1971, esp. 327–32; 1981), where he considers the problem of form in terms of narrative representation, specifically. Jameson's (1981) arguments require some modification in order to suit the conventions of theatrical performance; as I indicate in what follows, these modifications would include a more precise distinction between the concepts of 'form' and 'genre' beyond Jameson's 'semantic' and 'syntactic' or 'structural' notions of genre (pp. 107–8), since it is only in examining the particular mimetic conventions of theatrical performance as a 'form' that makes possible many different 'genres' that the full structural and theoretical importance of the boundary between onstage and offstage becomes visible.

[16] A notion of 'form' that finally derives from Aristotle, as I have discussed briefly in Turner (2001, with additional bibliography); see also Williams (1983) on 'formalism', emphasizing a second definition of 'form' as 'an essential shaping principle, making indeterminate material into a determinate or specific being or thing' (p. 138).

This notion of 'form' is at root a materialist one, and in this sense it supplements notions of form in New Criticism that would ignore the concrete physical conditions subtending representation. One of the enduring contributions of the so-called 'new New Bibliography', after all, has been to point out that in the era of print, the physical expanse of the page itself serves as another significant 'formal' medium of expression in the materialist sense I have adopted.[17] But this is precisely why it remains important to distinguish a notion of 'form' in the *theatre* from a notion of 'form' that the book makes possible, for several reasons. In the book we find bibliographic conventions of lineation and speech-prefixes, both of which allow a variety of interpretative arguments about the 'poetic' qualities of the play—distinctions between verse and prose; arguments about tropes and images; observations concerning characterization—that are assisted by arresting the text, hesitating over details and evaluating them by returning and comparing examples in other passages. In the book, too, we find bibliographic conventions of pagination and a distribution into Acts and Scenes that segments the action, allowing it to be coordinated into a larger conceptual whole (the 'Work') and making possible arguments about the 'structure' of the play. Obviously the early play texts are often inconsistent in these conventions, and this inconsistency accounts for much of their enduring interest: title pages accentuate different lines of action than we might expect or declare a generic affiliation that a later edition of the play revises. But whatever its inconsistency, the book makes the play thinkable in formal terms that are quite distinct from theatrical performance, where a different set of conventions, meaningful units, and interpretative responses are required. And of course the 'form' of the page also exerts itself in other areas of early-modern culture: the practical geometrical manuals I consider in Chapter 2, for instance, depend on several methods that are non-verbal and that exploit the possibilities of printed page format in critical ways. These methods include the use of diagrams to facilitate reasoning through analogy, similarity, and proportion or to make possible imaginative acts of 'making' and imitation, and English playwrights adapt these methods to their work in the public theatres—to a very different medium and 'form' of symbolic expression.

By expanding the category of 'form' so as to facilitate a more nuanced analysis of how representation occurs across very different kinds of documents, however, we encounter an additional set of theoretical problems, since most discussions of form have sought to define the distinctiveness of 'literary' writing and of aesthetic, especially poetic, expression. This isolation of poetic language has tended to foreclose an avenue of inquiry that remains fundamental to historicist criticism, which is the need to generate a mode of analysis that can account for the different degrees of conventionality, motivation, figuration, and structure

---

[17] See McKenzie (1977; 1986, esp. 7, 9–20); Chartier (1997: 81–9); De Grazia and Stallybrass (1993); Kastan (2001, esp. 4–5).

inherent in *all* semiological artefacts—literary or otherwise, non-linguistic as well as textual—and begin to correlate these more precisely with the institutional structures out of which these artefacts emerge.[18] As Susan Wolfson has observed in her discussion of formalism in Romanticism and American New Criticism, this task has largely been taken up by Marxist critics, and the prevalence of a notion of 'social formation' (Marx's *Gesellschaftsformation*) in Williams, Jameson, Althusser, Foucault, and many others demonstrates how pervasive the tendency to view social processes in formal categories has become. But the project was already implicit in the work of the Russian Formalists, as Wolfson points out: 'under the cover of the seemingly isolated literary figure, Russian Formalism theorized literary effect in terms with a potential beyond literary criticism, especially the display of constructedness and the obstruction of transparent apprehension. There were political applications as well for seeing how, in Shklovsky's description, convention "coated" perception "with the glass armor of the familiar."'[19]

As a mode of cultural analysis that extends beyond conventionally 'literary' texts to encompass broader problems of historical critique, politically motivated formalism arguably reaches a peak in the semiology of Roland Barthes, who maintained that 'the more a system is specifically defined in its forms, the more amenable it is to historical criticism. To parody a well-known saying, I shall say that a little formalism turns one away from History, but that a lot brings one back to it . . . [mythology] is a part both of semiology inasmuch as it is a formal science, and of ideology inasmuch as it is an historical science; it studies ideas-in-form' (1972: 112). The sociologist Pierre Bourdieu, too, has argued that 'a work is tied to a particular field no less by its form than by its content' and that 'form and the information it imparts condense and symbolize the entire structure of the social relation from which they derive their existence and their efficacy' (1991: 139, 80). Arguably the principle of form has here been generalized to a point of diminishing analytic value, and in general Bourdieu's analyses of Flaubert lack the subtlety that is so remarkable in Barthes.[20] Nevertheless, in furnishing a powerful statement of the irreducibly formalized, because structured, nature of *all* social fields, Bourdieu provides a valuable model for the way in which the category of form mediates between institutions, concrete practices, and any mode of symbolic expression, including literary writing but also types of highly conventionalized language or non-linguistic signifying expressions.[21] In this respect, Bourdieu's work provides an explicit articulation of theoretical problems that tend to remain implicit in the work of early-modern social and legal historians, for instance, where we find clear

[18] Cf. McKenzie (1986, esp. 4–5), redefining bibliography as 'the sociology of texts' (and, incidentally, invoking Peirce on pp. 1–2); also pp. 34–9, on the semiology of maps.

[19] Viktor Shklovsky as cited by Wolfson (1997: 7).

[20] It is one effect of the materialism that underlies Bourdieu's thought; he himself traces the mode of argument back to Durkheim, among others; see esp. Bourdieu (1991: 164–6).

[21] Cf. Bourdieu (1991: 70–1, 79, 137–59).

examples of how institutionally codified linguistic 'forms' both respond to and provoke changes in subjective perception and expression.[22]

Throughout the chapters that follow, I have employed the concept of 'form' in the more neutral heuristic sense that the work of both Barthes and Bourdieu makes available: as an analytic principle of particularization and specificity that I use to identify the basic protocols that organize any act of expression, 'literary' or otherwise. This notion of form permits the identification of reiterated patterns of arrangement in ideas, words, and other signifying units that occur in a relatively predictable way and that can be traced through the evidence of texts of all kinds: through lectures, letters, prefaces, textbooks, manuals, essays, commonplace books, and plays, but also through maps, diagrams, and other visual documents. For pragmatic reasons it will be necessary to specify *some* 'form'—some initial set of meaningful units and relations that obtain among them—so that individual texts may be differentiated from one another and their particular codes described with precision. This heuristic notion of form is necessary, too, however, so that broader patterns of arrangement may be identified that *exceed* any particular text and that appear to characterize an epistemology in general. After Foucault, we may call this a 'discursive' notion of form: I have assumed, in other words, that any domain of intellectual activity employs various habits of thought which, over time and through processes of transmission and legitimization that are themselves quite complex, become both more explicit and more conventional and which may be identified in the specific vocabulary of that domain, as well as in the 'form'—in the specific instantiation and structure—of that domain's arguments and mean-ingful units. These 'meaningful units', or 'statements' as Foucault has called them, will include both linguistic and non-linguistic units of representation such as images, gestures, objects, and other signifying elements. Together they constitute the epistemological threshold of any single domain by determining the questions that may be asked within it, the way in which these questions may be formulated, the methods that may be adopted to answer them, and the answers that are perceived to hold a truth-value for those who evaluate them.[23]

These statements, or 'structured and structuring' elements, to once again adopt the terminology of Bourdieu, must be sought *outside* the so-called 'literary'

---

[22] See, for instance, Rainey (1991) on Florentine sumptuary law, where the evidence includes acts that explicitly challenge legal designations, as in the case of the 14th-century Florentine woman who befuddled the notary charged with enforcing city ordinances by spontaneously renominating the buttons on her jacket: they were not *bottoni*, which were forbidden under the ordinances, but *coppelle*, since they corresponded to no buttonholes, as the ordinances specified (p. 225).

[23] See Foucault (1972), esp. his comments relating 'archeology' to the history of ideas, pp. 135–40, and my further comments in Turner (2001, 2002*a*). Among scholars in the history of science, Dear (1995) also takes a methodological cue from Foucault, although without detailed explanation; cf. also Poovey (1998, esp. 16–26), who shares my reservations about the 'rules' and limitations of Foucauldian discourse but who does not discuss the *Archeology* in particular; cf. her discussion of the concept of the epistemological 'domain' in Poovey (1995: 5–8).

field as well as inside it; indeed, one of the most important developments in sixteenth-century English poetics lies in the way that the field of dramatic poesy comes to constitute itself first by borrowing techniques, vocabulary, and basic epistemological assumptions from several fields of early scientific practice and then by gradually distinguishing itself from them.[24] Already this formulation of the problem proves inadequate, however, since 'exchange', 'borrowing', or 'convergence' between fields attributes a prior and separate coherence to each, when in fact this coherence is achieved—if indeed it is ever 'achieved'—dialectically through this very process of convergence or intersection. In this heuristic sense, then, the principle of 'form' always also describes *a principle of historical appearance*: it permits the identification of provisional structures, of repeated juxtapositions, associations, substitutions, or oppositions in both words and ideas, across domains that may appear quite distinct from one another, at the same time that these 'domains' themselves emerge into view and assume a new, albeit provisional, disciplinary stability.

A concrete philological problem will introduce the primary thread I have used throughout this book to organize my analysis of the larger dialectical convergence between poetics and geometry that I am describing and to demonstrate the significance of practical epistemologies for the development of English 'drama' as a performative form enacted in the public theatres. In English, the term 'plot' did not designate our familiar sense of 'arranged story' or 'action composed into artfully arranged episodes'—the translation of the Greek *muthos*, Latin *fabula*, Italian *favola*, or French *fable*, all of which had this meaning in the Renaissance period—until approximately 1600, with an explicit canonization of this modern literary-critical usage not appearing until John Dryden's *Of Dramatick Poesy: An Essay* of 1668.[25] During the sixteenth and early seventeenth centuries, the term 'plot' and its related terms 'plat', 'groundplot', and 'groundplat' derived from the field of geometry as it developed in a practical context, where they designated the schematic diagrams or working drawings used by the mason, surveyor, or carpenter; in its verbal form—'to plot', 'plotting', or 'platting'—the term described the act of measuring and reducing to a two-dimensional diagram or spatial pattern (Figs. 1.2 and 1.3). From the mid-sixteenth century these words are also closely linked to the stage, as an extension of this artisanal use: the *OED* cites a document from 1558–9 in which 'plat' is equivalent to 'platform' and is used to designate not a drawing but a three-dimensional structure, 'A stage . . . and in the same a square

---

[24] I draw on De Certeau (1984, esp. 45–60, 61–76); Bourdieu (1977, esp. 159–97; 1990, esp. 52–65; 1993: 29–73; 1998, esp. 1–13, 31–4).

[25] Several other scholars have remarked on the geometrical meanings of the terms 'plot' and 'plat', although without the same interest in practical knowledge as a distinct pre-scientific epistemology; see Robinson (1972: 122–8); Parker (1987); Hutson (1993, esp. 86–7; 1994: 91–114, esp. 105–11) Lupton (1993); Sherman (1995: 152–70, esp. 152–3); Sullivan (1994, rev. and expanded in 1998); Brückner and Poole (2002); Eriksen (2000: 1–24), making arguments similar to my own.

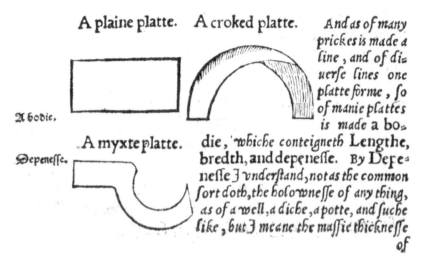

A plaine platte.   A croked platte.   *And as of many prickes is made a line, and of diuerse lines one platte forme, so of manie plattes is made a bo-*

A body.

A myxte platte.   *die, whiche conteigneth* Lengthe, bredth, and depenesse. By Depe-*nesse I vnderstand, not as the common sort doth, the holownesse of any thing, as of a well, a diche, a potte, and suche like, but I meane the massie thicknesse of*

Depenesse.

FIG. 1.2. The geometrical 'platte': Robert Recorde, *The Pathway to Knowledge* (1551)

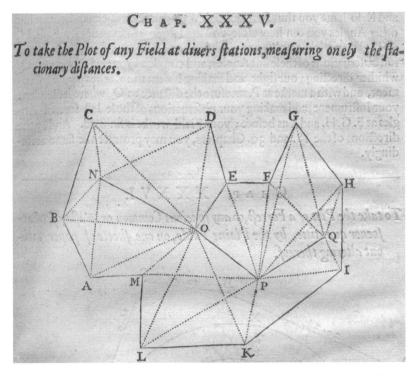

CHAP. XXXV.

To take the Plot of any Field at diuers stations, measuring onely the sta-cionary distances.

FIG. 1.3. Surveyor's 'plot': Aaron Rathborne, *The Surveyor in Four Books* (1616)

platte rising with degrees'. Similarly, an account book from the 1581–2 renovations of the Banqueting House at Whitehall records the 'Reringe of a platt with Shoores under the same enclosing upp thendes . . .', in this case a small stage.[26] By the 1590s the 'platt', or 'plot', has become a distinct form of stage property, a schema of stage action that is posted in the backstage area to subdivide the narrative action of the play into the entrances and exits of the actors, all within carefully ruled columns and boxes (Fig. 5.1).

At the same time, derived from the French *complot*, the term was being used in practical books of military strategy to describe a distinct mode of practical intelligence: a way of thinking about human action that was directly related to methods of deliberation about means and ends in classical prudence but which had been modified by the new sixteenth-century interest in practical geometry and the productive mode of knowledge that the mechanical arts made possible. This practical mode of emplotment constitutes an important innovation in early-modern dramatic form, one that builds on the dramatic structures of both Roman intrigue comedy and medieval drama but which modifies them by modelling methods of reasoning in which an intricate spatial disposition, or 'situation', of action is a critical aspect of the deliberative process.[27]

The specific geometrical meanings of the term 'plot' that were typical of the sixteenth century are liable to seem somewhat removed from the conventional uses of the term in modern literary discourse, where it designates two concepts that are essential to distinguish from one another. This is the difference between action and the *representation* of action: between a kernel of events considered in and of themselves and the way those events are selected, combined, and presented in any given form, whether this be dramatic, narrative, or cinematic. The distinction may be traced back to Aristotle's *Poetics*, which presumed, at least implicitly, a difference between the kernel of events that formed the *logos* of a play and the specific way those events had been arranged in an artful way into *muthos* or *praxis*, the two primary terms Aristotle used to designate the object of dramatic *poiēsis*, or 'making'.[28] This basic distinction between action and its formal manifestation has persisted in modern narratology, which has traditionally designated the former as *fabula, histoire,* or 'story' and the latter as *sjuzet, discours,* or 'plot'; conversational

---

[26] Cited by Orrell (1988: 39).

[27] Hutson (1993, 1994) was the first critic to discuss the practical and formal aspects of the term 'plot' in detail; although her arguments concerned prose narrative rather than the drama and did not extend to the broader field of geometric practice and discourse, her insights into the prudential nature of the term and its embeddedness in military strategy have been of great assistance to my argument about drama in what follows, and especially in Ch. 7, below.

[28] Both words came to encompass the various terms in the *Poetics* for story, action, or a summary of these; see *Poetics* 1447ᵃ1; 1450ᵃ15, ᵇ22; 1451ᵇ9–11, 27–9; 1455ᵃ34, ᵇ18; also Else's observations on matters of structure (Aristotle 1957: 242–3, 538); Fergusson (1949: 242–55); Knowles (1963: 156–202); P. Brooks (1984); Forster's (1927) somewhat different distinction between 'story' and 'plot' (pp. 83–103); Chatman (1978), who prefers the term 'discourse' to 'plot'; Bal (1997); Culler (1975, esp. 205–24); Pavel (1985).

use sometimes elides the distinction, in that we speak often of the 'plot' of a play, novel, or film when we mean to designate rather the simple story that is its subject. It is also true that since 'story' is understood to form a simple order or sequence of actions, this primary level is itself already abstracted or at one remove from the real and in this sense could be said to constitute a preliminary level of emplotment, as indeed would all modes of ordering perceived experience.

Peter Brooks has argued that the very distinction between story and plot inevitably breaks down when considered from the analytic and necessarily retrospective position of the reader, who grasps the 'story' that putatively exists prior to its representation in narrative only through the act of reading that narrative itself. For Brooks, 'plot' thus acquires an expanded meaning that captures the fully dialectical oscillation between action and events ('story') and the way these have been textualized in narrative discourse ('plot'), a dialectic that results from the reader's inherently temporal movement through the sequence of the narrative medium (the turn of the page) and with it the retention of an emerging sense of how events, characters, or themes are interrelated. This act of retention implies also one of protension or 'projection'—for a successful narrative arguably produces not simply a memory of events but also the anticipation of events to come—and the operation of both in tandem results in the reader's total apprehension of the narrative 'form'. In this broadest dialectical sense, therefore, the concept of 'plot' may be regarded as equivalent to the concept of form in general: it is the process through which events and experience are 'given form'.

On stage in performance, however, the 'emplotment' of a dramatic action—the selection of episodes from out of a larger potential continuum of events and their arrangement so as to produce probability, complexity, and interest—required a mastery of *space*, and not simply of time, as the mimetic medium in which that action took place. Above all, it required a playwright to manage the all-important boundary between onstage and offstage space, as this appeared in the entrances and exits of the actors or, more concretely, in the backstage wall of the theatre and the structural features that were associated with it. This process of showing and withholding is precisely what Dekker's description of the stage's 'smal Circumference', above, addresses most directly: in the theatre, the action that appears in the representational space of the 'scene' before the audience is *pure* plot, and the 'story', or the bare sequence of events that constitute the subject of the work, vanishes backstage behind the wall into an unrepresented space of invisibility and implication. Throughout the chapters that follow, I will argue that the techniques and spatial habits of thought that geometrical textbooks were disseminating through English culture were ideally suited to the formal requirements of the platform stage, itself the most highly spatialized mode of representation in the period. These 'habits of thought' include the very category of 'form' itself, which in the sixteenth century was *becoming* a distinctly geometrical and spatial concept and which was designated in the period by the words 'plot' and 'plat' in their practical geometrical senses. The linguistic evidence alone is remarkable: despite many specialized critical terms, in all the major scholarly languages of the period, to designate an idea of structural arrangement in a written or spoken work, English critics nevertheless eschewed these terms and eventually adopted the term 'plot'— a term they borrowed from the carpenter, the mason, the engineer, and the surveyor.

THE SPATIAL ARTS: ICON, DIAGRAM, WALL

As early as 1120 Hugh of St Victor had classified the theatre as one of seven 'mechanical sciences', and in doing so he posited a set of fundamental similarities between the world of artisanal culture and that of theatrical production—in perceived value, in working methods, in social and economic organization—that would endure through the production of the medieval mystery plays by craft guilds until well into the seventeenth century, when craftsmen and poets continued to collaborate over pageants, masques, and civic entertainments.[29] Johannes Ferrarius, defending artisans and the mechanical arts as necessary to the commonwealth in the fifth book of his *De Republica Bene Instituenda* (1556), still listed 'stage-plaiyng' last among the seven mechanical sciences, after husbandry, woolworking, carpentry, navigation ('labouring on the water'), hunting, and surgery.[30] By the mid-sixteenth century the 'mechanical sciences' had expanded to include many new technologies, such as mining, glass-making, and other forms of small industry; 'arte[s] of occupying of tooles or instrumentes', including masonry and surveying (80ʳ); and civil and military engineering projects of all kinds. Many, if not all, of these fields derived their basic epistemological assumptions and operating procedures from the field of practical geometry, and for this reason I will call them the *spatial arts*, with the understanding that the term 'art' is to be taken in its classical and more practical sense of *ars* or *technē*, rather than in its modern aesthetic sense. Since, in the fifteenth and sixteenth centuries, painting, sculpture, and architecture were often still closely associated with the classical mechanical arts, they may be included within the three-part division I have adopted in this book: the arts of spatial *structure* (carpentry, masonry, fortification, architecture),

---

[29] Hugh of St Victor (1961, bk. 2, ch. 2, p. 62, and chs. 20–7, pp. 74–9). Hugh himself wrote a treatise on practical geometry and made extensive use of analogies derived from masonry in both the *Didascalicon* and in his 'De Tribus Maximus Circumstantiis Gestorum' (*c.*1130), a treatise for students on the writing of history; see Carruthers (1993), whose arguments have been influential on my own, and (1990: 80–5, 92–3). Yates (1969) was among the first to argue for a direct relationship between the practical arts and theatre design; see also the concise and pointed discussion of Vitruvian theories by Cerasano (1989); Parker's (1996) notion of 'joining', esp. pp. 43–8; Yachnin's (1997) discussion of 'stage-wrights' and artisanal culture; Harris and Korda (2002); and J. G. Harris (2002*b*, esp. 37–41).

[30] English translation by William Bavande (1559, fo. 80ʳ).

the arts of spatial *movement* (navigation, ballistics, hydraulics), and the arts of spatial *representation* (surveying, mapping, painting, sculpture). The theatre—a built structure in which space itself became a pre-eminent medium of representation—encompassed all three aspects of the spatial arts, and for this reason it formed the ideal site for a convergence between the techniques of the carpenter, the surveyor, the engineer, and the playwright. As I discuss in Chapter 5, James Burbage, father of Shakespeare's famed contemporary Richard Burbage and one of the two entrepreneurs responsible for the Theatre, England's first public playhouse, was himself not simply a former actor in the Earl of Leicester's company but a professional joiner with the technical knowledge and the personal connections necessary to undertake the project. Even the anti-theatricalists recognized the proximity between the fields: 'The carpenter raiseth not his frame without tools, nor the devil his work without instruments; were not players the mean, to make these assemblies, such multitudes would hardly be drawn in so narrow room.' So wrote Stephen Gosson, the most famous sixteenth-century critic of the public stage and himself a former actor and sometime playwright.[31]

One of the most important overlaps between theatrical production and the spatial arts was the fact that, in both areas, problems of epistemology were inseparable from problems of representation, and especially of *mimetic* representation, or representation through imitation and showing: both playwrights and mathematical practitioners were concerned with the problem of how artificial constructions produced by the intellect—fictions, diagrams, images, figures—might either assist in the production of knowledge about the natural and social world or impede it. In both cases, too, this primary concern with the epistemological value of representation implied several additional semiotic problems, among them whether language offered an adequate medium for representing the natural world, how to understand the relationship between words and the things or concepts they designated, and how linguistic signifiers compared with other forms of signification such as images, diagrams, numbers, or other formalized methods of abstraction.

Theorists of stage performance, among them Patrice Pavis and Keir Elam, have characterized stage representation with a semiotic distinction drawn from the work of the American pragmatist and philosopher of science Charles Sanders Peirce, who distinguished the 'icon' as that type of signifier which implies an analogical, motivated, and referential relationship to its signified, as opposed to arbitrary, unmotivated, and more highly mediated forms of signification such as the symbol or language.[32] The icon sometimes overlaps or coincides physically with its signified, as in mimetic iconicity on stage, where a prop represents a

---

[31] Gosson, *The School of Abuse* (1579); cited by Ingram (1992: 163).

[32] Peirce (1931–58, vol. ii, paras. 247–9, 274–307). In using the term 'icon' to refer to this aspect of theatrical performance, I follow Elam (2002, esp. 17–24) and Pavis (1982*a*), who makes the observation that icon and symbol differ in Peirce's terminology not simply in terms of analogy or motivation but in terms of *reference*: in the icon the referent is materialized, 'actualized', or immanent, but in the symbol it is not (pp. 13–18).

fictional object of the same type, and sometimes does not, as in other uses of stage iconicity (a dance representing a swordfight; the body of the boy actor representing a fictional female body) or as in a photographic image, a diagram, or a metaphor, all examples of iconic representation for Peirce.[33] Onstage, the physical object—a wall, for instance—is a 'diagrammatic' representation of a fictive object in the sense that it corresponds to that object in structure but does not correspond at all points in detail to the fictive object that it represents: the backstage wall, after all, may serve as an iconic sign for many different kinds of fictional walls of different height, material, and connotative value, all of which are realized through language and the imaginative projection of the spectator.

I argue that this iconicity, fundamental to stage performance, is precisely what enables the theatre to become a practical epistemology: a way of coming to knowledge through representation, or, more precisely, through a mode of representation that is nothing less than a process of doing and making, one that generates a secondary level of semiosis through its enacted process and which, as a consequence, makes pure movement or living action into *significant* action that can be studied, analysed, and understood.[34] This performative, processual, and dialectical quality is also typical of the practical geometrical manuals that I discuss in Chapter 2, in which iconic diagrams assist the reader in reaching solutions to a series of specific problems, and the reader's knowledge of the fundamental principles that make geometrical representation possible is achieved through a reiterated process of enacting the solutions to these particular problems, which gradually assume a paradigmatic or generalized form. But the theatre and the manuals share more than a mimetic and performative process, since diagrams and images are themselves important forms of iconic representation for Peirce on the basis of the *analytic knowledge they make possible* because of their ostensive and visual aspect— their ability to reveal knowledge that has previously remained inaccessible to the eye and mind (Peirce 1931–58, vol. ii, paras. 277–83).

It is this analytic and ostensive quality of the icon, I argue, that also links theatrical representation and the sixteenth-century geometrical manuals most directly to the data-gathering procedures of modern experimental method. As Peter Galison, Bruno Latour, Steven Woolgar, and others in the history and sociology of science have shown, the analysis of natural objects and processes requires the generation of an extensive series of images, diagrams, and tables, all of which

---

[33] See Eco's (1976) critique of Peirce's notion of the icon on the basis of its perceived 'natural' similarity, motivation, or analogy with its signified, which denies the icon's highly conventional aspects. Despite his early suspicion of the 'referential fallacy' often presumed in accounts of the icon, Eco has more recently readmitted the importance of reference as an important conventional (rather than 'natural') feature of semiological communication and has revisited earlier debates; see Eco (2000, esp. 280–336, 337–92). Barthes (1964: 35–8) provides a helpful overview of semiological terms among different authors. I am grateful to Michael LeMahieu for helping me to clarify my ideas about semiotic reference; further discussion follows in Ch. 4, below.

[34] Cf. Lefebvre (1992: 135–6).

permit processes that are inherently invisible or inaccessible to be objectified, evaluated, and made the subject of theoretical principles.[35] These 'transcriptions', as Latour has called them, and the instruments that generate them play a fundamental rhetorical role in the constitution of coherent objects of inquiry and in the legitimization of methods and scientific arguments. No matter how various in their specific forms or in their contexts of production and use, all of these transcriptions have an iconic value in the sense that their referential and analytic gesture allows them to become meaningful to their communities and to be integrated into the process of scientific argument. From a semiological perspective, whether or not the transcriptions actually reproduce natural objects or phenomena in a perfectly mimetic way is beside the point: as authoritative and exemplary representations of phenomena, they come to enjoy a sufficient level of reference and thus enable higher-level operations. When the modern scientist translates the movement of astronomical bodies into a mathematical equation, for instance, he uses signs that are conventional and unmotivated, or arbitrarily assigned (there is no natural reason, except that established by convention, to use alphabetic characters as algebraic signs) to construct a mathematical statement that is governed by logical rules and that comes to stand *in toto* as an icon for the actual movement of the astronomical body in question. Once the relationship of reference and adequacy between the iconic equation and the body it designates has become conventional, we would be justified in saying that this reference is in fact produced by the equation and is really only to be found there: there is no physical contiguity, after all, between the algebraic equation and the rings of Saturn.

Much the same may be argued for social science: the subsequent development of the modern social sciences depends (among many other aspects) upon the adoption of iconic representational conventions—models, charts, diagrams, tables, equations—for the analysis of social life and social processes rather than natural objects and phenomena. Often, of course, the adoption of these objectifying methods implies a naturalizing and essentializing gesture: the extension of the category of 'Nature' to include human institutions and human action.[36] One of the significant epistemological consequences of sixteenth-century cartography, for instance, is that for the first time social as well as natural phenomena could be visualized and analysed in the form of static graphic abstractions; cartography is among the first fields of knowledge to use iconic modes of semiosis in order to

[35] I draw on Galison (1997); Daston and Galison (1992, esp. 85–7); Shapin and Schaffer (1985); Galison and Jones (1998); Lynch and Woolgar (1990), esp. Latour (1990), Lynch (1990), and Amann and Knorr Cetina (1990); also Latour (1987) and Knorr Cetina (1999); the analysis of instruments by Hackmann (1989) and by Schaffer (1989); of 'mimetic experimentation' by Galison and Assmus (1989); and Pickering (1989, esp. 276–7), correcting an excessive emphasis on the graphic or 'ostensive' features of scientific explanation; cf. also Bono's notion of 'technologies of the literal' (2004*a*, *b*).

[36] See Baker on Condorcet's mathematization of social science; S. Gordon (1991, esp. 100–10); Manicas (1987, esp. 7–23); Poovey (1995, 1998).

study the communal aspects of social life, in particular, in all their complexity and variety. Charts and other navigational tools might have recorded the natural features of the coastline, the depth of harbours, or tides and wind patterns, but they also indicated trade routes and territorial boundaries; in the form of chorography, cartography not only gave a spatial form to the classificatory and encyclopedic impulses of humanist natural history but joined them with a distinctly 'sociological' interest in designating groups of people according to family and status and then organizing them into geopolitical entities: communities of nation, region, or county, but also economic communities joined by patterns of exchange and historical communities oriented in time.

I suggest that in the sixteenth and early seventeenth centuries, when demography, statistics, economics, sociology, or political science did not exist in their modern disciplinary forms, the 'inventions' of early-modern writers provided a method for modelling large social processes, specifying categories and units of analysis, hypothesizing about cause and effect, and examining the principles of structural relationship that constituted a social totality. I propose that the theatre was particularly well suited to this epistemological project of social analysis not simply because of its semi-autonomous institutional position in London's cultural life, as Steven Mullaney, Jean-Christophe Agnew, and Douglas Bruster, among others, have argued, but because of the iconic nature of its mimetic conventions and the referential mode of semiosis that these conventions made possible. This is not to argue, however, that the embodied, materialized form of iconic representation in the theatre always achieves a seamless or perfectly mimetic mode of semiosis without remainder—quite to the contrary, and for two reasons. Theatrical iconicity is, first, a fetishistic mode of representation, based as it is on the substitution of one object or body for another object or body, and, furthermore, one that displays its own substitutive process as a series of immanent objects: actor's body projected onto character's body projected onto the connotations, associations, and ideas of the body furnished by the spectator and his or her culture, whether fictional, Symbolic, discursive, or ideological (an infinitely regressive or proliferating series). It is precisely the co-presence of these projections in a single particular body that is necessary for successful theatrical representation, whether this 'success' is measured as the spectator's engrossed absorption in the fiction or the spectator's knowing decoding of the stage's mimetic conventions. Both are necessary if the theatrical performance is to be meaningful in any sense or to generate knowledge of any kind, and the same is true of the icon in modern scientific representation, which exhibits similar fetishistic tendencies. Secondly, however, and perhaps even more importantly, theatrical iconicity is a *perforated* mode of representation: the (implied) presence of the offstage space always functions as a negatively determining limit, an unrepresentable invisibility behind the wall, the 'blink of the eye' that punctures theatrical representation as the spectator's phenomenological projection. It is here that the analytic purpose of early-modern performance is of most significance to the modern critic, for the opposition between onstage and offstage space may be granted a hermeneutic function and regarded as a mode of expression for a set of logical oppositions that can then be seen to structure early-modern culture more broadly.

TOWARDS AN ANALYSIS OF EARLY-MODERN TOPOGRAPHESIS

The crucial question that awaits further scholarly work on early-modern drama, therefore, is not *whether* the theatre operated as a site for refracting social and ideological contradictions of its moment but *how* specifically it did so, and how this process is itself determinative of English 'dramatic form' in fundamental ways. How theatrical representation occurs through separate semiotic elements such as word, gesture, prop, or wall and the iconic conventions on which they depended; the complexity of the overlapping semiotic codes that dispose and enable these separate elements to signify in different ways, such as the codes of language, of body, of object, or of architectonics; the major units of performative representation that language, body, prop, and wall combine to form, be these 'scenes' or character groupings or fictional locations—all of these formal questions must be considered in relation to the much broader discursive structures that organized early-modern culture *outside* the theatre and gave that culture meaning to early-modern people. Historicist criticism of the last twenty-five years has tended to preoccupy itself with this discursive or ideological level of analysis while at the same time impoverishing its critiques by largely ignoring structural and semiotic questions, and no doubt this is because the early-modern theatre's unusual representational conventions make the process of analysis particularly complicated.

In order to provide a model for how such an analysis might proceed, and in order to take seriously Dekker's analogies in *Old Fortunatus* between theatre and other modes of representation derived from the spatial arts, I pursue throughout this book case studies in what I call topographesis. If we define 'topographie' after Hopton's *Topographicall Glasse* (1611) as 'an Arte, whereby wee be taught to describe any particular place'[37] and *topographia* after George Puttenham as either the 'description . . . of any true place' or of any 'counterfait place' or fictional invention, 'which ye shall see in Poetes',[38] then we may define topographesis as the representation of place by texts of all kinds but also by maps, diagrams, paintings, or images, and even by built structures such as buildings and monuments, particularly when these are approached as 'texts' with a coherent semiotic structure and a communicative function and especially when they are described verbally or portrayed in visual, graphic form. As a distinct mode of representation, topographesis

---

[37] Hopton (1611, sig. B).
[38] Puttenham (1589: 246).

encompasses many different kinds of early-modern writing, both 'literary' and otherwise, and each chapter that follows considers how it functions in different modes and in a variety of social and intellectual contexts. Broadly speaking, Part I provides a detailed analysis of the intellectual background to the problem of topographesis, including its use in poetic discourse and in early-modern measurement and technology; Part II examines topographesis as a mode of dramatic composition, specifically, since it is in the theatre that the concept assumes one of its most complex forms. In Part II, I will be particularly interested in those plays that adopt a performative or theatrical model of semiosis rather than a textual one, and I have concentrated on plays that are unusually self-reflexive or that exhibit remarkable meta-theatrical elements. Here I mean the term topographesis to designate those plays in which the representation of location becomes the primary mode of giving structure and sequence to the symbolic content of the performance, be this a cause-and-effect model of dramatic action ('intrigue') or a rhetorical, emblematic, or 'poetic' content that is developed through a series of scenic units, as is often the case in Shakespeare, in Jonson's early comical satire, or in the public pageants.

It is important to emphasize that topographesis operates on two distinct levels simultaneously. It functions first at the level of symbolic form, the level of 'artfulness' or the aestheticizing impulse in the representation of place. Here the term topographesis describes the specific way in which any given text integrates the representation of place into the wide variety of interpretative conventions that were typical of different forms, genres, subject matters, or stylistic modes during the period. I consider several of these conventions in the chapters that follow: they include questions of vocabulary (register, tone, groups of associated terms, philology), questions of signification (the mimetic presumptions of reference and 'meaning', or of *how* different semiotic codes represent place in any given text and how they differ between a poem, a stage representation, or a prose narrative, for instance), and the analysis of larger-scale meaning-units such as the image (place as a particularly saturated element of meaning in a text; the use of multiple places to develop a larger 'theme' or argument).

As I discuss it in this book, topographesis depends on several different iconic techniques of objectification, abstraction, reduction, or idealization, all of which derive from practical geometry as a repository for diagrammatic representational conventions. They include gestures of framing and bordering, or the setting apart of a representational field from the object or world to which it is presumed to refer; a referential semiotic mode that posits as conventional a one-to-one relationship of correspondence between the signifier inside the frame of the iconic field and the object or world outside of it; a proto-empirical attitude, in which the communication of information about the world has become a significant component of the signifier's purpose; an emphasis on seeing or viewing as the privileged mode of apprehending this objective information about the world; and, at the same time, an analytic posture that explicitly relies on artificial projections to present information that could not be gained by the naked eye alone: i.e. of objects that are either too large (continents, seas, oceans), too small (crystalline or molecular structures), too distant (stars, planets), too hidden (mechanical elements or bodily organs, geological layers, interior rooms), or too abstract (social, economic, or physiological processes) to be apprehended directly by the reader and that assist in his or her act of comprehension of them. In the early-modern period, the development of cartography best exemplifies many of these topographic representational techniques, but they are visible, too, in many other kinds of documents, from technical drawings to prose utopias, poems, entertainments, and plays—taken as a whole, these texts indicate a veritable explosion of topographic modes of writing during the period.[39]

Secondly and more broadly, however, I mean the term topographesis to denote the way in which 'place' is represented by the larger discursive networks typical of a given society, categorized according to various institutional functions, or endowed with meaning and value: we may call this topographesis in its ideological mode. This level includes but extends beyond the semantic or symbolic level, since ideological representation always borrows from the more specialized formal conventions that give meaning to any given text and that endow certain places with a ready-made significance that may be confirmed, appropriated, or challenged. The elements and rules of combination that structure topographesis in its ideological mode are obviously quite complex and depend on the configurations of fields of power and knowledge in any given historical moment, as well as on the overdetermined relationship between any text and the society in which it was produced. Much of my discussion in Part II, particularly in Chapter 6, will be concerned with this ideological level: my purpose will be to examine how several early-modern plays used location not simply to structure their action or 'arguments' but also to refract the larger social logic that made these different locations meaningful in early-modern culture more broadly. Here topographesis describes a process in which 'place' is used to give form to the discursive scripts embedded in a play and which have, for many new historicist and materialist critics, come to constitute the drama's primary symbolic content. In the 'topographic' play, the fundamental images, symbols, 'ideologemes' (in Althusserian terminology), 'philosophemes' (that of Derrida), 'myths' (that of Barthes), or discursive 'statements' (that of Foucault) that characterized early-modern culture more broadly are articulated *through* the representation of place and become the primary way in which concrete places themselves emerge into representation. At this level of analysis, places become the vehicles through which problems of social class, political identity and belonging, status aspirations, modes of production and value,

---

[39] I have discussed these developments in more detail in Turner (2007); see also Mendyk (1988), Helgerson (1992, esp. ch. 3); Gillies (1994); Cormack (1997); Traub (2000); and the works cited below.

competing epistemologies about the social and political world, or attitudes towards urban order and urban experience can be scrutinized and dissected.[40]

PLOTTING EARLY MODERNITY

All of the concerns that touch on the problem of dramatic form and that are the subject of the book that follows were fundamental to the period scholars have come to call 'early modern', in its many economic, social, political, and cultural aspects. The proliferation of practical geometrical manuals was a direct result of changes in property management, ownership, and patterns of residence that followed the dissolution of the monasteries, changes that the manuals in turn accentuated and that began to transform the topography of both city and country and the social reality of those who lived there.[41] The geometrical manuals were sponsored also by the protracted colonial expansion of the Elizabethan state into Ireland, and by its commercial and political interests overseas in the New World or across the Channel on the Continent. Fear of invasion during the Wars of Religion prompted harbour fortification works that drew engineers from Italy and France, as well as from the fields at home. Demand for consumption goods encouraged speculation in a wide variety of early industries or 'projects', from mining and metallurgy to woad-growing, hop fields, and tobacco, all of which required the mastery of machines and the surveying of formerly waste land. Greater wealth brought with it more frequent building on a more elaborate scale, and thus an expanded labour market for the carpenter and mason.[42] Gradually, the practitioner began to establish a professional identity that was as distinct from the traditional craft guilds as it was from the men who consulted him; at the same time, applied mathematics began to appeal to the 'gentleman' who had little interest in exact working methods but who found in globes, maps, and instruments a

---

[40] I draw on Bachelard (1964); De Certeau (1984, esp. 117); Lefebvre (1979, 1991); Tuan (1977); Harvey (1996: 207–326, esp. 291–326); Gregory (1994); Barthes (1964, 1972, 1977*c*, 1988*b*); Deleuze (1988: 1–44, esp. 34–7, 44); and Foucault (1972, 1979, 1980, 1984, 1998), the last a relatively underdeveloped article in which Foucault calls these topographic networks 'emplacements'. In the more elaborated linguistic terms of the *Archeology* these networks could be said to form specific syntactic arrangements of topographic 'statements' which together form the topographic *langue* or grammar of early-modern culture. In early-modern studies, the work of both Tom Conley and Karen Newman has gone furthest towards what I am calling 'topographic' analysis, esp. Conley (1996, 1998*a*, *b*) and Newman's notion of a 'topographic imaginary' in Newman (2000, 2002); also Perkinson's early article (1936) on 'topographic' comedy, emphasizing the Restoration but considering several Jacobean plays; Marin (1984, 1988, 2001); Mullaney (1988); Helgerson (1992); Orlin (1994, 1995); Sullivan (1998); Brotton (1998); B. R. Smith (1999, esp. 49–95), on soundscapes; West (2001), pursuing arguments similar to my own; Reynolds (2002, esp. 95–155); Reynolds and Fitzpatrick (1999); Howard (2003, 2006); Gordon and Klein (2001).

[41] See also H. S. Turner (2002*b*) and Ch. 2, below.

[42] On early industry and the development of speculative 'projects' during the period see Thirsk (1978); for the increase in building, see Girouard (1983); Platt (1994); Orlin (1995).

new mode of acculturation and display, as well as a knowledge necessary to diplomacy and state service. This interest was itself part of a broader encounter between a humanist community defined around the study of Latin—its vocabulary, ideas, literary forms, and associated habits of reading—and a practical community whose activities were pursued in the vernacular, with the different semantic and conceptual associations this implied. It was an encounter made possible by the growing importance of the printed book: by the different kinds of knowledge print made available and the different modes of literacy (linguistic, pictorial) it required.

At the turn of the seventeenth century we find an alignment between poets, playwrights, and mathematical practitioners that was peculiarly 'early modern', an alignment made possible in a culture where geometry and poetics appeared to contemporaries to be more similar to one another in their methods and epistemological presuppositions than they do to us today, as we view them from the vantage point of what C. P. Snow bemoaned as the 'two cultures' of literature and science. Chapter 2 examines the habits of reasoning and of spatial representation that were typical of this pre-scientific moment and prepares the way for the arguments to follow in subsequent chapters: it is an epistemological moment in which particulars often remained heterogeneous from the rules, laws, and concepts that would seek to explain them; in which memory, imagination, and judgement were as important as reason, if not more so; and in which quick-witted cleverness and ingenuity—*ingenium*—was of pre-eminent value to the engineer, the orator, the statesman, the military captain, the surveyor, and the playwright alike. The chapter introduces the concept of 'practical knowledge' in order to supplement accounts of early scientific thought in sixteenth-century England, which have either looked only to developments outside the universities or have argued that advanced mathematical study occurred only within the interstices of the official curriculum. I maintain that average university students would have frequently encountered geometrical principles by reading commonplace rhetorical and philosophical texts such as Quintilian's *Institutes* or Aristotle's *Nicomachean Ethics*; I suggest, furthermore, that several key components of humanist thought informed the popular geometrical handbooks that began to appear in England with increasing frequency during the sixteenth century and help explain the distinctive epistemology that these books employed.

Sixteenth-century humanists, poets, and practitioners then developed these analogies even further in their writings and in the way they began to view expertise in applied mathematics as being of crucial importance to their public, political careers. The mathematical practitioner Thomas Blundeville occupies a central place in Chapter 2, for instance, because his work indicates a surprising breadth of expertise and crystallizes with remarkable specificity the combination of fields that were important for the pragmatically oriented humanist reader in the final third of the sixteenth century. My discussion of Gabriel Harvey in Chapter 3 then demonstrates how one prominent humanist looked to books by mathematical practitioners such as Blundeville and others as models for his own pragmatic philosophy of conduct: as sources for Harvey's ideas, practical mathematics and early-modern technology have gone almost entirely overlooked.[43] Even more importantly, however, Harvey's pragmatism, his interest in applied mathematics, and his avowed experience with mechanical problems was also shared by his more famous acquaintance Sir Philip Sidney, and one of my purposes in Chapter 3 is to examine the extensive evidence for Sidney's knowledge of geometry and the spatial arts and then to show how methods of practical reasoning and representation informed Sidney's conception of 'poesy' in his *Defence* as a distinct intellectual method concerned with the 'making' of the poetic image.

As in Harvey's case, these aspects of Sidney's social and intellectual life have been largely ignored, and yet they transform our understanding of his *Defence*: the essay should be regarded not simply as a treatise of literary theory but as a state-ment of epistemological method that refines and disseminates concepts funda-mental to early scientific thought. For Sidney, 'poesy' is a proto-experimental epistemology that 'coupleth the generall notion with the particular example' through the use of artificial constructions and 'inventions'; it is also an instrumen-tal mode of knowledge with the power to transform nature, man, and society.[44] Indeed, I propose that the *Defence* offers a justification for a much broader transi-tion in modes of producing 'scientific' knowledge about the world that was taking place during the early-modern period. This is a shift *from dialogue to icon*, or from a verbal and discursive method of analysis to a visual and diagrammatic one: one of the central problems that Sidney confronts in the *Defence* is how iconic meth-ods of representation derived from the spatial arts might be adapted to modes of *linguistic* expression and to textual analysis. In doing so, Sidney's essay makes explicit concepts that are crucial to later scientific thought and circulates them among social groups that would eventually submit them to further development. At the same time, however, his essay also produces the possibility of 'scientific' knowledge by exemplifying an epistemology that seventeenth-century practition-ers will need to *reject* in order to define their method: *poiēsis* as a method of know-ing truth through revelation or inspiration; *poiēsis* as nothing more than an imaginative 'invention' of the mind that disregards the world of Nature; *poiēsis* as an activity that is simply 'delightful' or pleasurable in and of itself and thus as an activity that at some level remains *non*-useful and *non*-productive, an ecstasy of

[43] But see now the work of Wolfe (2004), which reached me after I had concluded this project; many of my arguments, especially those concerning Harvey in Ch. 3 and practical thinking in the second section of Ch. 7, below, may usefully be read alongside the evidence and arguments presented in Wolfe's study.

[44] Spiller (2004, esp. 24–44) has recently reached a similar conclusion; readers interested in these aspects of Sidney's thought will want to consult her work.

'inventive' frenzy that is perpetually in need of defending. As Bacon would argue in *De Dignitate et Augmentis Scientarum* (1623):

There remain the Chances of Experiment. This form of experimenting is merely irrational and as it were mad, when you have a mind to try something, not because reason or some other experiment leads you to it, but simply because such a thing has never been attempted before . . . For the *magnalia* of nature generally lie out of the common roads and beaten paths, so that the very absurdity of the thing may sometimes prove of service.[45]

The dawn of scientific method, in short, rises on the *irrationality* of an inventive procedure that knows no hypothesis and produces nothing but further contrivance and accidental effects.

Sidney's *Defence* provides an important theoretical account of the relationship between practical thinking and 'poesy' as a distinct intellectual method, but it is necessary to consider how practical geometry informed English poetics in a genuinely *practical* way, at the level of actual compositional techniques and stylistic and narrative modes. I address this problem most directly in Chapter 4, where I examine George Puttenham's account of *poiēsis* in his *Arte of English Poesie* (1589) alongside debates concerning the nature of poetic language by George Gascoigne, Edmund Spenser, and, again, Gabriel Harvey. All four writers are concerned with specific technical points regarding the 'making' of poems and the management of patterned language, and in Puttenham's case we find a particularly clear example of how techniques of poetic composition owed a direct debt to the cognitive and mimetic procedures of practical geometry. The second section of the chapter then considers how practical geometrical methods were used during the production of pageants, masques, and entertainments, with particular reference to *The Magnificent Entertainment* for King James (1604). Jonson, Dekker, and Harrison all use the occasion to experiment with different iconic conventions for representing the city of London and the competing social hierarchies, interpretative communities, and power structures that organized urban experience, and for Dekker these techniques derive directly from the quantitative systems of measurement that were fundamental to the spatial arts.

Chapter 4 plays a transitional role in the argument of the book as a whole by marking several shifts in emphasis: from a theoretical and epistemological analysis of 'poesy' to a consideration of practical questions of composition and execution; from verse form to 'performative' form, or embodied, acted form—but not yet to the *theatre*. Part II then demonstrates how English playwrights developed practical habits of thought not simply through theoretical argument—for some, especially Jonson, this will be a significant mode of engagement—but exploring the theatre as a technology for analysing social life and by testing out, in practical ways, the mimetic conventions of the platform stage. My purpose throughout the final four chapters of the book is to direct critical attention away from an analysis

---

[45] Bacon (1861: ix. 82); cited by Eamon (1994: 287–8).

of 'drama' and towards an analysis of 'theatre', as well as to show how the relationship between these two poles of critical analysis was itself changing during the period. Each chapter concentrates on how the boundary between onstage and offstage space delineated what critics have come to regard as the early-modern theatre's most fundamental unit of representation—the 'scene'—and the way in which the 'scene' as a theatrical unit gradually became inseparable from a fictional idea of location, or 'place'.[46]

Chapter 5 opens this analysis by examining one of the most spectacular examples of the theatre as a spatial art: Shakespeare's *King Lear* (*c.*1605 at the Globe). The chapter approaches the play as a technical exercise in spatial representation, a demonstration piece that deliberately sets out to explore the mimetic possibilities and limitations of the platform stage and particularly of the boundary between onstage and offstage space, considered in its most abstract form as a formal limit to theatrical representation. Like all such demonstration pieces, the play exhibits virtuosity by adopting techniques that expose the limits of its representational medium and that, as a consequence, are calculated to impress; it also incorporates a level of self-awareness into its *praxis* by comparing stage technology to other possible modes of representation derived from geometry, such as mapping and perspective painting, over which it asserts itself. I then examine how *Lear*'s subsequent editors have overlooked the meta-theatrical argument of the play by imposing stage directions and neo-classical acts and scenes retrospectively, in order to achieve a modern critical notion of location and dramatic structure that is foreign to the Elizabethan theatre. By attending to the play's peculiar spatial 'cruxes', we may grasp the way it makes explicit a set of iconic semiotic problems that are larger than any particular author, problems that form part of the fundamental conditions of theatrical performance during the period and that open new categories for the social and ideological analysis of early-modern drama.

The remaining chapters of the book then turn to focus on the particular genre of play that most clearly exemplifies the influence of the spatial arts on theatrical representation and on changing notions of dramatic form: what M. C. Bradbrook, L. C. Knights, Brian Gibbons, and others have described as 'city comedy' and what Jean Howard has recently argued should more neutrally be designated as the

---

[46] Some readers may object that I have presumed a generic 'platform stage' that abstracts from the particularities of individual theatres, overlooking significant differences in performance techniques and in this way 'theorizing' the stage rather than recognizing its truly practical (because irreducibly particular) qualities. This is admittedly a risk. In the interests of length and clarity of demonstration, however, I have found it necessary to isolate common aspects of performance practice in order to clarify how the theatre may be viewed as a spatial art and to emphasize the structural and ideological problems posed by the boundary between onstage and offstage space. On the need for these reductions, cf. Van den Berg (1985: 23–5) and Chambers (1923: iii. 103–4). Many of the plays I discuss were adapted to performance on several different kinds of stages, either because of shifting company membership, revival, provincial tour, or a movement between the commercial theatres and the court, and this fact, too, seems to me to justify a certain degree of generalization.

'city' play.[47] These are plays in which action is tightly structured around locations that are represented in a highly realistic or denotative fashion and in which these locations open a representational space for non-aristocratic urban social groups (tradesmen, merchants, wives, apprentices, maids, servants, prostitutes, gentlemen courtiers) that do not conventionally appear in other genres or in Shakespearean romantic comedy.[48] Throughout Chapters 6, 7, and 8 I aim to shift the terms of analysis away from the satiric, moral, and didactic stance that is usually presumed to be typical of city comedy and to place it firmly instead on broader questions of form and theatrical performance, for in doing so it is possible to demonstrate two primary arguments.

In the first place, it allows us to see how a playwright such as Dekker draws on habits of reasoning and representation that were typical of the spatial arts to produce a series of plays that differ in their style, tone, and theoretical justifications from those of a playwright such as Jonson but which are ultimately no less critical in their overall form and use of performative conventions. As I argue in Chapter 6, the critical and analytic force of Dekker's 'city' plays lies not (or not simply) in their overt satiric tone or treatment of character but in their practical use of the backstage wall to create scenic units organized around locations and in the way that these topographic units are used to manage the problem of dramatic emplotment. The material changes associated with London's urbanization produced new conceptions of the city as a representational space, as several critics have begun to argue, and as a consequence they required new structures for the plays in which contemporary ideas about the city were to be most fully realized. I will show how the genre of the 'city' play not only emerged out of the larger social tensions that were being generated by London's urbanization during the period but how these 'deeper sources of conflict and change', as Gibbons has described them, were realized *as the fundamental form of the play itself in performance*, in a practical way that eludes any self-conscious theoretical formulations of the type that Jonson is so quick to provide.

My second line of argument, pursued over the final two chapters of the book, demonstrates how Jonson's so-called 'classicism' and distinctive critical voice is in fact *mediated through* the methods of practical reasoning and representation that

---

[47] See Howard (2000, 2001, 2002). In addition to the works cited in the chapters that follow, I draw especially on Knights (1951); Bradbrook (1955); Perkinson (1936); Gibbons (1980); Leggatt (1973); Barton (1978); Wells (1981); Paster (1985, esp. 150–77); Levin (1986); Hunter (1986); Leinwand (1986); McKluskie (1994, esp. 54–75), a consideration of civic history plays as well as comedies; Bruster (1992: 29–46), a useful survey of the difficulties inherent in constituting the genre; Haynes (1992, esp. 13–33); Manley (1995: 431–77).

[48] Notable exceptions, however, would include *The Comedy of Errors*, *The Merry Wives of Windsor*, and *Measure for Measure*, the last exhibiting a mode of 'topographic' emplotment that is most similar to the city comedies I discuss in Ch. 6; *The Comedy of Errors*, too, may be regarded as an early metatheatrical experiment in the nature of the 'scene' as a compositional unit, in which models of character grouping typical of Roman intrigue comedy compete with the use of location to define the scenic unit, and Shakespeare employs the backstage wall to complex and highly knowing effect.

were typical of the spatial arts and that were being employed by playwrights in the public theatres. Jonson's significance, I argue, is that he attempts to convert theatrical practice into a coherent theory of 'drama' by distancing the theatre from the mechanical arts, appealing to irrefutable classical authorities, and transforming the professional position of the playwright from a 'practitioner' of the theatre to a 'critic' who secures the drama's commercial value and its moral authority. Scholars have typically taken Jonson at his word and have regarded him as England's first neo-classical dramatist, a figure who both anticipates and makes possible the critical opinions of the Restoration. But it is all the more important to insist on the enduring influence of Elizabethan stage practice on a writer such as Jonson, who himself insisted so vehemently on deriving a set of structural and formal principles from classical authors.

A major purpose of Chapter 7 is to examine two distinct modes of scenic composition in Jonson's *Every Man Out of His Humour*, performed in 1599 at the Globe and perhaps the first play to be produced there. *Every Man Out of His Humour* demonstrates how Jonson borrows methods of reasoning that were typical of the engineer or the military strategist—a 'projective' analysis of human action in both space and time, or in 'situated' circumstances, that writers such as Gabriel Harvey or Sir Philip Sidney actively cultivated—and transforms them into a model for representing action on stage. The chapter opens a detailed analysis of Jonson's use of the scene as a unit of composition that I continue in Chapter 8; it concludes by demonstrating how the practical and projective mode of intelligence exemplified in *Every Man Out of His Humour* also informs comedies by other playwrights, plays in other genres, and plays performed in different playing spaces.

In Chapter 8 I argue that we must revise our accounts of Jonson's intellectual life and formal development in light of his demonstrated awareness of the cognitive and mimetic techniques that were typical of practical geometry, an awareness derived from his collaboration with the architect Inigo Jones, from his reading of Vitruvius, and from his own apprenticeship as a bricklayer, for which he enjoyed liveried membership in the Tylers' and Bricklayers' Company. The chapter examines Jonson's annotations to his copy of Vitruvius' *De Architectura* and then offers a brief analysis of *Volpone* (performed in 1605 at the Globe, in 1607 at Oxford and Cambridge, and revived both at court and at the Blackfriars during the 1620s and 1630s); it then turns to an extended reading of one of Jonson's greatest plays, *The Alchemist*, performed in 1610 at the Globe and almost certainly also at the Blackfriars, in which Jonson asserts the moral superiority of drama over the many practical epistemologies of his period—from alchemy to proto-industrial 'projects' and applied mathematics—that the play holds up to satire.

Jonson is among the earliest playwrights to combine the two sixteenth-century senses of the word 'plot'—one spatial, geometrical, and topographic; one strategic, deliberative, and pragmatic—to produce a usage that resembles the term's modern literary and structural meaning. After a brief appearance in *Every Man*

Out of His Humour, the term surfaces again in a passage in Jonson's *Discoveries* transcribed in approximately 1629, where it returns unambiguously in reference to a total dramatic action and forms part of an extended comparison between the process of literary composition and that of building taken from the Dutch neo-Aristotelian critic Daniel Heinsius. The term does so tentatively, however, and indeed in a literally marginal fashion—it appears as one of two alternative glosses on a key passage—and in this way *Discoveries* also illustrates the way in which working playwrights might subsume practical techniques derived from measurement and geometry within a system of theoretical precepts concerning art, formal arrangement, and spatial structure that were derived from other intellectual fields.

To all of these developments, each in some way characteristic of the 'early modern', we may add, finally, the erection of platform stages themselves by practitioners of the building trades: men, like Burbage and the 'rude mechanicals' of Shakespeare's *A Midsummer Night's Dream* (1595, at Burbage's Theatre), who were seeking to satisfy their audience's demand for plays that reflected its pleasures and fantasies.[49] The new commercial theatres experimented with novel forms of economic organization, such as the system of shareholding adopted by the Chamberlain's–King's Men; they created a place for encounters across the social spectrum, and thus also for the display of wealth or status and for the acquisition of new modes of acculturation. But the theatres also created a discursive space in which the many contradictions, fears, and desires of the period might be shaped, and this was to be the work of the playwright: jobbing dramatist, sometime actor, company shareholder, citizen bricklayer, City Chronologer, state informant, literary critic, contemporary observer, and maker of plots.

---

[49] The thesis of many critics too numerous to cite; see esp. De Grazia (1997); Agnew (1986); Mullaney (1988); Bruster (1992); Howard (1994).

PART I
DIAGRAM, IMAGE, ICON

2

Practical Knowledge and the Poetics of Geometry

It is difficult to decide between the two definitions of mathematics; the one by its method, that of drawing necessary conclusions; the other by its aim and subject matter, as the study of hypothetical states of things. The former makes or seems to make the deduction of the consequences of hypotheses the sole business of the mathematician as such. But it cannot be denied that immense genius has been exercised in the mere framing of . . . general hypotheses . . . Perhaps the answer should be that, in the first place, whatever exercise of intellect may be called for in applying mathematics to a question not propounded in mathematical form [it] is certainly not pure mathematical thought; and in the second place, that the mere creation of a hypothesis may be a grand work of poietic genius, but cannot be said to be scientific, inasmuch as that which it produces is neither true nor false, and therefore is not knowledge. This reply suggests the further remark that if mathematics is the study of purely imaginary states of things, poets must be great mathematicians, especially that class of poets who write novels of intricate and enigmatical plots.

Charles Sanders Peirce, 'The Essence of Mathematics'

The purpose of this first chapter will be to establish the outlines of 'practical knowledge' as a specific intellectual formation typical of sixteenth-century England, one that resulted from a convergence between the predominantly linguistic epistemologies of European humanism, on the one hand, and the quantitative and iconic modes of representation characteristic of the spatial arts, on the other. Stated most broadly, the 'practical knowledge' I will be discussing throughout this book derives from several distinct traditions that were concerned with methods of reasoning about particular instances and with the kind of knowledge that might be gained from particulars, before these had become the 'facts' of modern scientific method.[1] In the sixteenth century the methods of problem-solving

---

[1] On the invention of the 'fact', see Shapin and Schaffer (1985); Shapin (1994); Latour and Woolgar (1986); Shapiro (1983, 2000); Daston (1991); Poovey (1998); I draw also on Vérin (1993); Long (2001); Summers's (1987) account of 'the particular intellect': classical, medieval, and Renaissance philosophies of 'postsensory and prerational faculties of the human soul', or faculties

I will be describing often remained open-ended and provisional, and even non-verbal: ways of operating that were closer to craft, wit, and cunning than to theoretical thinking.[2] They derive from four primary areas concerned with the knowledge of changeable things, such as human action or the products of human 'art':

1. Philosophical accounts of the mechanical arts and of their relationship to mimetic arts such as poetry, painting, and theatre: in short, accounts of what Aristotle categorized as 'productive knowledge' or *poiēsis*, knowledge derived from making the particular thing.

2. The tradition of prudence: Aristotle's account of *phronēsis*, or 'practical intellect', in his *Nicomachean Ethics*, known to Renaissance writers through Cicero's *De Officiis* as *prudentia*. As J. G. A. Pocock, David Summers, Victoria Kahn, and Kathy Eden have shown, the central epistemological questions in the area of prudence from the classical period through to the Renaissance concerned the faculty of judgement as a mode of knowing about the world and above all in decision-making: in the process of deliberation or calculation about possible future action in time.

3. Greek and Roman philosophies of psychology, including questions about whether sensory perception itself constituted a form of knowledge and about the role of memory and imagination in retaining this knowledge and in generating models of future action.

4. The sixteenth-century study of rhetoric and dialectic, and particularly the accounts of invention, disposition, judgement, and probable reasoning found in these fields. Since rhetoric and dialectic have not appeared prominently in histories of early-modern technology and scientific thought, they occupy a central place in what follows.

The primary argument I will be pursuing is that several aspects of Aristotelian prudence and of humanist dialectic and rhetoric—notably the role of judgement in deliberation, disputation, and textual analysis, the role of *decorum* as a ratiocinative procedure, and classical definitions of *technē*, or 'art'—supplied methods of reasoning that could be used in the solution of contemporary practical problems concerning geometry, measurement, and spatial representation. After surveying how intellectual categories derived from Aristotle were adapted by sixteenth-century writers, I examine the development of geometry as a distinctly practical discipline in England and its place within the 'arts of discourse' that dominated the university curriculum. I then undertake a detailed analysis of several technical manuals devoted to surveying, building, and measurement and of the distinctive

that are 'subrational and opinionative' (p. 17); P. Smith (1994); Pocock (1975: 3–330, esp. 22–5, 49, 58–66); Kahn (1985).

[2] Cf. De Certeau (1984); Eamon (1994: 281–2, 289); Serres (1982, esp. 89–91); Rossi (1968: 136, 144–9, 152–60, 178–85, 186–214); Gilbert (1963, esp. pp. xxi–xxii).

methods of problem-solving these manuals employed. Once the lineaments of 'practical knowledge' as a larger intellectual formation have been established, we will have a clearer understanding of all that follows in this book: of Sidney's philosophical defence of poesy as a mode of knowing through 'making', doing, and pleasurable imitation (Chapter 3); of the distinctly practical exposition of poetic 'making' found in George Puttenham's *Arte of English Poesie* and of collaborations between playwrights and craftsmen in the production of dramatic entertainments (Chapter 4); and finally of how techniques of representation derived from the spatial arts were adapted by Shakespeare, Dekker, and Jonson to solve problems of dramatic composition and dramatic form in the theatre (Chapters 5 to 8).

ARISTOTELIANISM, ART, AND JUDGEMENT

Officially the curriculum followed by the student seeking the Bachelor of Arts degree at sixteenth-century Oxford, and to a somewhat lesser extent at Cambridge, still conformed to the traditional seven liberal arts of the *trivium* and *quadrivium*, with grammar, dialectic, and rhetoric occupying approximately the first two or three years of study and the 'higher' arts of arithmetic, geometry, astronomy, and music forming the focus of the student in his fourth or possibly third year and of those graduates preparing for the MA or higher degrees. Moral philosophy, too, in its three areas—ethics, or the study of the individual person's actions towards the Good; politics, or the study of communal action and forms of government; and *oeconomia*, the study of household management, or action in the domestic, 'private' sphere—was studied along with metaphysics and natural philosophy primarily by more advanced students and by those Bachelors proceeding to the Masters degree.[3] For all the breadth of their subject matter, the seven liberal arts and the three philosophies shared a long-standing method of reasoning that depended on the perceived natural logic of grammatical categories and that proceeded through the verbal formulation of grammatical propositions.[4] For the student of the thirteenth century as for that of the sixteenth, language was the preeminent medium in which reasoning was conducted, truth tested, and *scientia*, or certain knowledge, acquired; the academic term was punctuated by regular oral disputations, usually with more advanced students, and these disputations constituted the only formal method of evaluation of the student, who was expected to participate in them if he wished to advance to the next stage of his degree.[5]

---

[3] Gibson (1931); Boase and Clark (1885–9, 1, esp. 1–85); McConica (1986); L. Jardine (1974*a*, esp. 17–58; 1974*b*, esp. 32–3, 43–7; 1975, esp. 17, 19–20, app.); J. M. Fletcher (1986: 171–81, esp. 172–7); Kearney (1970).

[4] L. Jardine (1974*a*: 17–24; 1974*b*: 36–42, esp. 36–7); Ong (1958: 106–10).

[5] J. M. Fletcher (1986: 165–71, 181–98); Curtis (1959: 83–125); L. Jardine (1974*a*: 17–54; 1974*b*: 33).

Charles Schmitt has established the continued importance of Aristotle and neo-scholastic Aristotelian textbooks in nearly all areas of the Renaissance university curriculum, particularly in the last third of the sixteenth century and above all in the fields of ethical and natural philosophy.[6] The methods of inquiry employed by the student derived directly from Aristotle's writings as well as from the medieval commentary tradition that had accrued around them, and the structure of the BA and MA curriculum itself continued to reflect in broad outline the basic intellectual distinctions that Aristotle's work had established. All knowledge was of three kinds, speculative (*epistēmē* or *theōrētikē*), practical (*praktikē*), and productive (*poiētikē*).[7] *Epistēmē* dealt with unchanging things and their causes; it encompassed the subjects of the *quadrivium*, including all metaphysical inquiry, the study of mathematics, and all questions of natural philosophy: the nature of being, of substance and accident, geometrical proof and demonstration, problems of physical change and motion, or questions of astronomical and cosmological order. The method of reasoning in each of these subjects was fundamentally the same: in so far as 'knowledge' (*epistēmē*) was possible only of things 'not capable of being otherwise' (*NE* VI. 3. 1139^{b}21), these things were also 'necessary' and 'eternal', and knowledge of them depended on first principles rather than on the opinions of men. The method of achieving *epistēmē* was that of logical demonstration—'knowledge, then, is a state of capacity to demonstrate (*apodeiktikē*)' (*NE* 1139^{b}31)—the rules for which Aristotle had set out in his *Prior* and *Posterior Analytics* (I. 2. 71^{b}9–72^{b}5).[8]

Whereas metaphysics and natural philosophy inquired into universal categories and first principles, Aristotle's two remaining epistemological categories—*praxis* and *poiēsis*, or practical and productive knowledge, respectively—both encompassed knowledge of variable rather than unchangeable things, and for this reason the knowledge gained about them could only be probable rather than certain.[9] Since probabilistic reasoning involved questions of choice and opinion, it fell generally under the rubric of dialectic, which Aristotle had treated in his *Topics* and

[6] Schmitt (1975, 1983*a,b*, 1984); McConica (1979); Reif (1962, 1969); Kristeller (1979: 32–49); J. M. Fletcher (1986: 178–9, 195); Curtis (1959: 100); Perez-Ramos (1988); Ong (1958: 23–4, 131–45, 172–5, 214–20); Boutcher (1998); Kearney (1970); R. French (1994, esp. 51–9, 10–15); Struever (1992, esp. 134–42).

[7] In *Metaphyics* 1025^b–1026^a Aristotle uses *epistēmē* to denote all three modes of knowledge; cf. *NE* VI. 3. 1139^{b}22, where he uses the term as an equivalent to *theōrētikē*. Likewise *poiētikē* is the general term for all productive knowledge, but *technē* is more usual; see *NE* VI. 4. 1140^a and below; Peters (1967: 59–60, 162–3, 190–1).

[8] On Aristotelian *epagōgē* and the subsequent history of induction, see Perez-Ramos (1988: 201–85); N. Jardine (1988: 686–93); L. Jardine (1974*a*: 47–58, 63–4); Rossi (1968: 147–8, 152–7); Randall (1940). Cf. Blair's (1997) discussion of Bodin's method, pp. 98–9.

[9] See *NE* VI. 2. 1139^{a}25–30, where *theōrētikē* is opposed to *praxis* because it is neither concerned with action nor with production, and *NE* I. 2. 1094^{a}27–9, where politics is called *architektonikē* or a 'master art'; also W. D. Ross (1953: 154, 187–234, esp. 187, 216–21); K. Eden (1986: 25–61); Dehart (1995); Devereux (1986); Peters (1967: 60, 162–3, 190–1); Long (1997: 4; 2001: 16–45); P. Smith (1994, esp. 45–50).

which he distinguished from the logical reasoning of scientific demonstration in several ways: dialectic proceeded on the basis of opinion rather than on certain knowledge, since it concerned objects that vary according to time and situation; it relied on general principles that were for the most part true and which served to guide investigation into particular cases.[10] But of even more significance to the sixteenth-century university student than the *Topics* was the discussion of probabilistic reasoning to be found in the *Nicomachean Ethics*, which appears more frequently than any of Aristotle's other works in both institutional and private inventories of the period: more than one-third again as many times as the *Organon*, or logical treatises, the next most commonly owned work; nearly twice as often as the *Politics* or the *Physics*; more than three times as often as the *Rhetoric*; and more than four times as often as the *Topics*, as remarkable as this may seem given the importance of disputation in the curriculum.[11]

In the *Nicomachean Ethics*, Aristotle elaborates on his three-part distinction between theoretical, practical, and productive knowledge by distinguishing five modes of truthful knowing: art (*technē, ars*), knowledge or 'science' (*epistēmē, scientia*), practical wisdom (*phronēsis, prudentia*), philosophic wisdom (*sophia, sapientia*), and comprehension or understanding (*noūs, intellectus*).[12] In the five-part classification of the *Nicomachean Ethics*, *technē* forms a species of *poiēsis* and often refers specifically to the mechanical arts or to the manual activity of the artist, while *phronēsis* is a species of *praxis* and refers to all inquiry into deliberation, choice, and decisions regarding action or conduct. Here, too, Aristotle maintains a clear distinction between *praxis* and *poiēsis* as modes of knowing about variable things, a distinction that medieval commentators also observed: *praxis* refers to 'doing' or 'activity', and also to 'habit', while *poiēsis* is the general term for all actions of 'making' that produced an object.[13] *Praxis* is distinguished from *poiēsis*, Aristotle argues, by the fact that action contains its end in itself, while making finds its ends in its object (*NE* 1139^{b}1–5).

Aristotle's arguments throughout the *Nicomachean Ethics*, however, are complicated by the fact that he regularly invokes military, technical, and craft

[10] Cf. *Prior Analytics* I. 1. 24^{a}28–30; *Topics* I. 11. 104^{b}1–3, III. 1–4, 6. 119^{b}16–30.

[11] See the evidence for Cambridge University and individual college libraries compiled by Adams (1967), the Cambridge probate inventories in Leedham-Greene (1986), and the inventories collected and edited by Fehrenbach and Leedham-Green (1992–8), which correspond in proportion almost exactly to the evidence of the Cambridge inventories. Ker (1986: 509) describes what appears to be a concerted effort in 1601 at Christ Church, Oxford (Sidney's college, from February 1567/8 until approximately 1571) to assemble Aristotle's writings on natural philosophy, with assorted commentaries. For bibliographic information on the 15th-century editions of Aristotle, see Rath (1925–38: ii. 551–669, nos. 2334–2498); for the 16th century, Cranz (1984).

[12] Cf. *NE* VI. 4. 1140^{a}1–16, also VI. 3–13 and throughout books II–VI; W. D. Ross (1953: 20, 216–17, 270–1). The Latin translations of the Greek terms are commonplace; see Heiland (1580: 92). All English translations are from Aristotle (1984) unless otherwise noted.

[13] *NE* VI. 4. 1140^{a}1–20. Else observes in his edition of the *Poetics* (Aristotle 1957) that *poiētikē* is 'highly general and can refer to any kind of "making": the production of ships, buildings, knives, clothing, etc' (p. 2).

comparisons to develop his notion of *phronēsis*, or practical wisdom, and *phronēsis* and *technē* exhibit many similarities.[14] Both modes of knowing, for instance, are concerned with the knowledge that might be derived from particular instances, and especially with the problem of how particular instances might be accommodated to general principles—this relation constitutes one of the central epistemological problems of Aristotle's inquiry into both prudential and productive modes of knowledge. Both *phronēsis* and *technē* are quasi-empirical methods of reasoning, since they use the particulars gained by sense experience as the basis for their generalizations.[15] One of Aristotle's most common examples of *technē* is rhetoric, since it functions by setting forth general rules that must be applied and modified according to the exigencies of particular situations: rhetoric, Aristotle observes, is the art of evaluating the particular, 'the faculty of observing in any given case the available means of persuasion' (*Rhetoric* I. 1. 1355^{b}26–7).[16] The same is true of ethical inquiry: 'In demonstrations comprehension grasps the unchangeable and primary definitions,' Aristotle argues, 'while in practical reasoning it grasps the last and contingent fact' (*NE* 1143^{a}25–^{b}3). 'Nor is practical wisdom (*phronēsis*) concerned with universals only,' he insists; 'it must also recognize the particulars; for it is practical, and practice is concerned with particulars. This is why some who do not know, and especially those who have experience, are more practical than others who know . . .' (*NE* 1141^{b}8–18; cf. 1139^{a}5–16). Aristotle even compares those members of a political body who concern themselves with 'action and

---

[14] Cf. *NE* I. 1. 1094^{a}10–13 (horsemanship, strategy), 24 (archers), 1094^{b}13–15 (craft products), 1097^{a}20 (medicine, architecture), 1097^{b}29–30 (carpenter, tanner), 1098^{a}28 (carpenter, geometer), 1101^{a}2–5 (the good carpenter, the good shoemaker), 1103^{a}35, 1103^{b}9–12 (builders). Cf. Summers (1987: 266–75); Whitney (1990: 25 and n. 7, 32–6).

[15] Because it depended on general rules and operated with knowledge of them, the skill of *technē* was distinct from the skill that derived from mere experience and remained unsystematic; see *Poetics* 1. 1447^{a}20; Whitney (1990: 25, 32–6); Else (Aristotle 1957: 20–2, esp. n. 78); Atkins (1934: i. 73–4, 83–4). *Technē* thus implied the operation of reason, but because the principles, or 'rules', of *technē* were only generally true and remained subject to modification, they did not have the same epistemological status that certainty or truth had in the speculative fields (*Metaphysics* α. 1. 981^{a}5–7).

[16] See also *NE* I. 1. 1354^{a}1–11, 1355^{b}26–2, 1356^{a}25–35; *Topics* I. 3. 101^{b}55–9; Slawinski (1991: 73–4); Atkins (1934: i. 73–4, 136, 150); K. Eden (1986: 34–6); Devereux (1986: 498); Kahn (1985: 30–3). Aristotle understood poetry as a specialized form of rhetoric that also employs probabilistic reasoning: dramatic action should treat of universals instantiated in particular characters, and the poet or maker should set his action in a general outline; compare *Poetics* 17. 1455^{a}35–^{b}1 with *NE* I. 3. 1094^{b}19–23, II. 2. 1104^{a}1–9. Cf. K. Eden (1986: 34–5); Devereux (1986: 494, 498); Trimpi (1983: 50–8). The very term that Aristotle uses throughout the *Poetics* to refer to the object of poietic making—*praxis* or human action—is clearly meant to be understood in an ethical sense, since the people who are represented are *prattontas* (literally 'men acting') and it is their character, either good or bad, that is at issue (*Poetics* 2. 1148^{a}1–5; also 3. 1448^{a}30, where Aristotle traces the origin of the term 'drama' itself back to *drōntas*, or 'men acting', and 6. 1449^{b}31). The object–product of dramatic performance and dramatic art, therefore, is a structured and organized representation of ethical life that is achieved through the process of acting and doing: its *poiēsis* is itself a mode of *praxis*. See K. Eden (1986: 32–61, esp. 33–5, 53–4, 61); B. R. Smith (1988: 13); Else (Aristotle 1957: 69–82); Atkins (1934: i. 105). I discuss the place of the *Poetics* in 16th-century England in more detail in Ch. 3, below.

deliberation' to manual labourers, since they deal with particulars in relationship to legislation, which serves as the universal (*NE* 1141ᵇ28–9).[17]

Central to Aristotle's discussion of *phronēsis* are the concepts of 'deliberation' (*boulē*), the faculty of reasoning in preparation for choice, and 'calculation' (*logisteīa*), that of 'reckoning' or reasoning with number and quantity. Calculation is the same as deliberation, Aristotle argues, and both denote the mental process by which we reason about means towards ends, about possibilities for action, and particularly about a future action whose outcome is unforeseen.[18] Deliberation and calculation concern only changeable things, and for this reason they are distinctive of practical wisdom:

Now every class of men deliberates about the things that can be done by their own efforts (*praktōn*) . . . but not always in the same way . . . e.g. about questions of medical treatment and of money-making. And we do so more in the case of the art of navigation than in that of gymnastics, inasmuch as it has been less exactly worked out, and again about other things in the same ratio, and more also in the case of the arts (*technas*) than in that of the sciences (*epistēmas*); for we have more doubt about the former. Deliberation (*bouleūesthai*) is concerned with things that happen in a certain way for the most part, but in which the event is obscure . . . The subject of investigation is sometimes the instruments, sometimes the use of them . . . sometimes the means, sometimes the mode of using it or the means of bringing it about.[19]

Both deliberation and calculation relied on the faculty of 'judgement' (*krinōn*) in particular circumstances. Translated literally as 'to distinguish, discriminate, or separate', the faculty of judgement might describe all acts of thinking and knowing about variable and particular things.[20] In the words of David Summers:

The internal senses performed judgments, which were acts of distinction, comparison, association, and combination. These judgments and operations were literally prerational, although the syllogism, as the paradigmatic operation of reason, and therefore the paradigm of right thinking, seems to have provided the dominant model in attempts to characterize the peculiar structure and cogency of fantasy, memory, recollection, or quick-wittedness. (1987: 27)

By the sixteenth century, as Summers has demonstrated, Aristotle's somewhat unsystematic notion of the 'common sense' had developed into a full-fledged epistemology, in which sensation, perception, imagination, and memory joined with the higher judicative faculties of *estimativa* and *cogitativa* to form a constellation of 'inner senses' through which knowledge of particulars might be gained.[21] Thus Leonardo da

---

[17] Cf. Whitney (1990: 25–6 and n. 9).

[18] *NE* VI. 1. 1139ª10–15; 2. 1139ᵇ5–10; cf. VI. 5. 1140ª28–35; 7. 1141ᵇ12–15.

[19] *NE* III. 3. 1112ª30–ᵇ31; also VII. 8. 1151ª15–19, comparing the first principles of virtue to the 'hypotheses' in mathematics; cf. Rackham's glosses (Aristotle 1926); Heath (1949: 270–80); Lee (1935).

[20] Summers (1987: 21–8, esp. 24–5); K. Eden (1986) emphasizes the term's roots in classical legal theory.

[21] Summers (1987: 71–109, esp. 78–89); on Aristotle's theory of imagination, see Summers (1987: 25–6, 62–3, 80–1, 84–5, with additional bibliography).

Vinci, for instance, could draw on medieval arguments that visual perception was a form of 'judgement' (*guiditio*) by the eye in order to distinguish poetry and sculpture from painting and to establish the latter as a liberal art, and we shall see the importance of similar arguments to Sidney's defence of 'poesy' as a distinctive way of coming to knowledge about the natural and social world.[22]

Aristotle's writings thus provided a set of distinctions between theoretical, practical, and productive modes of knowledge that were of fundamental importance to sixteenth-century students; at the same time, his work suggested overlaps between rhetoric, prudence, and the productive arts, in both objects and methods of inquiry, that encouraged the student to collapse these distinctions, to compare the deliberative methods of one field with another, and even to extend these methods to fields that Aristotle himself had not considered. As the study of dialectic became increasing prominent in the sixteenth-century university, especially at Cambridge, the roles of 'invention' and of 'judgement' became especially important for the student to master.[23] As in rhetoric, dialectical 'invention' employed the topics, or commonplace headings, which furnished material for analysing the composition of a text, for making positive arguments, or for destroying the premises of an opponent. The faculty of judgement, in turn, might be equivalent, first, to the simple act of knowing through sensory perception, as Aristotle had argued and as the Ramist Abraham Fraunce explained in his *Lawiers Logike* (1588).[24] More commonly and technically, however, dialectical 'judgement' became the equivalent of rhetorical *dispositio*, that part of dialectic concerned with the effective organization of an argument.[25] In this sense, judgement was analytical and evaluative, resolving an opponent's argument into its component parts and assessing its coherence, truth, or falsehood. But it also served as what we may call a faculty of form and structure, arranging the matter of invention by deciding which type of argument to use and how to compose a total sequence. 'Invention finds matter,' wrote Thomas Blundeville in his *Arte of Logicke* (1599), while judgement 'frameth, disposeth, and reduceth the same into due forme of argument'.[26]

[22] Summers (1987: 71–5, 170–6).

[23] See Fraunce (1588: 4, 5–6, and 85); Ramus (1574: 17); Temple (1584: 11, 63), dedicated to Philip Sidney; see Ch. 3, below, nn. 56, 71; Seton (1572, A3ʳ). On distinctions in dialectic and rhetoric more generally, see L. Jardine (1974ᵃ: 31–47; 1974ᵇ: 41, 51–3; 1975: 27, citing Gabriel Harvey's *Ciceronianus* (1577)); Rossi (1968: 145, 157–60); Ong (1958); Howell (1961: 146–72); Mack (1996); Joseph (1962); McConica (1979: 301–2, 301 n. 4); Feingold (2001).

[24] 'For as Aristotle teacheth in the second of his demonstrations, every sensible creature hath a naturall power and facultie of judging, which is called sence; & this sence (2. Topic) is of him sayde to bee a certayne kinde of judgement: and without doubt, the sence is a most upright judge of suche thinges as are properly under his jurisdiction, as the sight of colours, the hearing of soundes, the smelling of smelles. (4. Metap.)' (Fraunce 1588: 91).

[25] Ong (1958: 112–16) notes that both Ramus and Milton eventually adopt *dispositio* over *iudicium* as a designation for the second part of dialectic (p. 114); also pp. 182–90, and 351 n. 56.

[26] Blundeville (1599: 1); on 'method', see Ong (1958: 153, 225–69, 171–213; also 123–6, 149–67; and 17–35 for the facts of Ramus' life and an overview of his career); Gilbert (1963); L. Jardine (1974ᵇ: 58); Grafton and Jardine (1986: 122–57); Reiss (1997: 86–95, 104–8; 2000); Feingold (2001).

Since the role of judgement was to mediate between the particulars of a given problem and the general categories of argument that the student had learned, it functioned by observing a principle of *decorum* that was identical to the methods of both rhetorical argument and prudential deliberation, as Victoria Kahn has argued.[27] For this reason, the concept of *decorum* had a central ratiocinative or *epistemological* function, as well as coming to constitute (in both Aristotle and Cicero) a *moral* norm, and in this function it increased the extension of judgement across as many different types of problems so as to render it as effective as possible. Humanists were especially convinced of the usefulness of dialectical judgement and presented it as applicable to any field of knowledge whatsoever, including literary analysis. As Fraunce wrote in his *Lawiers Logike*: 'Logic was deservedly called the Art of Arts, the instrument of instrumentes, the hand of Philosophie, because by the helpe therof, not onely the groundes of naturall reason are artificially put downe, but all other Arts also are made to be Arts . . .' (pp. 1–2). 'I will never call him a Musician that never sang; a Carpenter that never builded house; a Soldier that never fought,' Fraunce proclaimed, 'not withstanding the general speculation of the first in Music, of the second in building, of the third in fighting: no more will I think him worthy of the title & name of a Logician, that never put his general contemplation of logical precepts in particular practice . . .' (p. 115).

This extension of dialectic into an 'art of arts' on the part of the humanist reformers, however, also implied an outright rejection of traditional Aristotelian distinctions between demonstrative and probabilistic reasoning—only the latter was necessary to master.[28] When John Rainolds delivered his lectures at Corpus Christi, Oxford, on Aristotle's *Rhetoric* in approximately 1572—only one year after Philip Sidney had left Christ Church—he explicitly attacked Aristotle's distinction between demonstrative and probabilistic reasoning in order to broaden his claims for the value of rhetoric as a mode of textual analysis as well as of argumentation.[29] Such distinctions in types of reasoning are illegitimate, Rainolds argued, since so-called first principles cannot withstand the epistemological challenge posed by particulars:

Vives teaches that the sources of demonstration in Aristotle's account—'first propositions,' 'immediate propositions,' 'necessary propositions,' 'proximate propositions,' and 'causes of a conclusion'—are things so very uncommon, so farfetched and so nearly impossible . . . being men with wits enslaved to error, we scarcely know what might be 'first principles,'

---

[27] Cf. Kahn (1985 esp. 30–6, 199 n. 7, and 201 n. 20, emphasizing *decorum* as an epistemological principle common to both prudential deliberation and rhetorical argument); Ong (1958: 212–13); Struever (1992: 115); and Shapin's (1994) notion of 'epistemological decorum' (p. 209).

[28] Cf. Feingold (1997*a*: 280–1); L. Jardine (1974*b*), on Seton (pp. 55–6) and the Ramist William Temple (pp. 58–9); L. Jardine (1975: 23–4), on Valla; Blair (1997: 6, 82–95), on Bodin. Ong (1958: 55–63, 101, 156–7) traces the collapse back to the 13th century.

[29] Cf. Rainolds (*c*.1570: 153; also 219); on Rainolds, see Green's introd. in Rainolds (*c*.1570); Ringler's introd. in Dethick (*c*.1572); McConica (1979: 302–9).

'unmediated terms,' and 'necessary propositions' . . . 'necessary propositions, that is to say, 'those propositions which cannot be otherwise,' we must all but abandon those, since all universals are understood from particulars, and particulars are numberless, and the numberless cannot be ascertained, and one unascertained element makes a universal totter. And those 'universals' long acknowledged by us 'in the elements' and 'in the heavens,' either times or places have finally shown that they cannot be universally confirmed . . . Now then, to conclude, I believe that this division of the art of dialectic into demonstrative and probable is absolutely worthless and useless.[30]

'One unascertained element makes a universal totter': does not the entire future of scientific method, and indeed of all critique, resonate in this ominous phrase? Dismantling these distinctions permitted Rainolds to argue that the matter of rhetoric and dialectic was ultimately the same, and in this way he could place rhetoric on a par with dialectic as a 'universal instrument', citing both Vives and Agricola as authorities for his approach.[31]

Rainolds's arguments made sense in a university curriculum where the traditional medieval *trivium* had been stretched to accommodate new texts and topics: the histories, orations, letters, plays, and dialogues that typified the *studia humanitatis* and the problems of morality and duty, of governance and political organization, or of elegant style and effective legal argumentation that these texts had introduced. His lectures reflect the distinctly pragmatic attitude that reform-minded writers brought to their discussions of dialectic and rhetoric, partly as teachers concerned with the clear presentation of difficult ideas in the classroom and partly as humanists interested how students could use knowledge outside the university in the larger world. Their methods were ideally suited to the profession-ally minded young gentlemen who had begun to populate the colleges and lecture halls of the sixteenth-century university, many of whom would not stay to take a degree. For these students, the applicability of knowledge to many different social circumstances was more important than a sophisticated grasp of intricate philo-sophical distinctions. Even those students who did master the intricacies of the higher arts curriculum had come to view dialectic and rhetoric as practical modes of knowledge whose probabilistic mode of reasoning rendered it an instrument of universal application, effective for all kinds of texts and any variety of question.[32]

---

[30] Rainolds (*c.*1570 205–7). Ramus makes a similar point about particulars when he distinguishes between two kinds of 'method', the first used teaching a subject matter 'brought down from universal and general principles to the underlying singular parts', the second used in prudence, 'which advises about disposition according to the condition of persons, things, times, and places . . . *For, over and above the foregoing rule of wisdom, no arrangement of this infinite variety of things common to all persons, questions, places, and times, can be given. The nature of all persons is not the same: so many different heads, so many different senses, the state of affairs not the same for all, so that persons often completely change in a matter of minutes* . . .' (Ramus 1546: 83–4, 87–90, cited by Ong 1958: 245–6; my emphasis).

[31] Rainolds (*c.*1570: 259; also 225–7).

[32] On the pragmatic aspects of humanism, see esp. Ong (1958: 123–6, 128–30, 149–67, 193, 225–69); Grafton and Jardine (1986: 66–82, 122–60); L. Jardine (1974*a*: 17–58, esp. 25–9, 59–65; 1974*b*: 52–6; 1975, esp. 25); Rossi (1968: 146–7; Struever (1992: 97–8); Reiss (1997: 76–7, 79).

This distinctly practical orientation is evident in the annotations of Gabriel Harvey, careful Ramist and university lecturer in Rhetoric at Cambridge from 1573 to 1576, who observes that he prefers Cicero's *Topics* to Aristotle's 'for civil use . . . and for public application (*praxis*) of arguments'.[33] For Harvey the ideal orator is to be a 'prudent' man equipped with the intellectual 'instrumentes' necessary to make judgements in any question whatsoever, and particularly in those decisions that involve political action.[34] As Anthony Grafton and Lisa Jardine have shown, Harvey makes admiring comments in his marginalia about Tudor diplomats whose prudential acumen and oratorical ability carried the day in difficult circumstances, much the same way that the military captain conducted affairs in the field. Doctor Dale, Doctor Wotton, Sir Thomas Smith: all 'pragmatics' should imitate their examples, in their choice of texts but above all in their virtues and actions.[35] Harvey in fact calls his ideal orator an 'Artificum Artificem'—'a Craftsman of Craftsman, equipped and armed at all points with most of the Arts'[36]—and his interest in practical methods of reasoning extended beyond oratory to the mechanical arts and the work of actual tradesmen. 'He that remembereth Humphrey Cole, a mathematical mechanician, Matthew Baker, a shipwright, John Shute, an architect, Robert Norman, a navigator, William Bourne, a gunner, John Hester, a chemist, or any like cunning and subtle empiric,' Harvey wrote in 1593, 'is a proud man, if he contemn expert artisans, or any sensible industrious practitioners, howsoever unlectured in schools or unlettered in books.'[37] As we shall see in Chapter 3, Harvey's 'pragmatic humanism', as Jardine and Grafton have described it, has as one of its central components a nearly Baconian interest in the epistemological potential of mechanical instruments and applied mathematics: there is a fundamental congruence in his thought between the faculties of reasoning necessary to dialectic, rhetoric, and prudence and the kind of knowledge that might be gained in contemporary technical fields and then put to use in the political arena.[38]

[33] 'Ad ciuilem Topicorum vsum, forensemq[ue] argumentoru[m] praxim, malim Ciceronem topicum doctorem, quam ipsum Aristotelem . . .' (cited by L. Jardine 1986: 38, also 41); on Harvey and his reading habits, see Stern (1979), with chronology of Harvey's appointment p. 28 and n. 44); Grafton and Jardine (1986: 161–200); and Ch. 3, below.

[34] 'His *principall Instrumentes* ar Rhetorique, for Elocutio[n], and Pronunciation; and Logique, for Invention, Disposition, and Memory' (cited by Jardine 1986: 43).

[35] 'Sir Thomas Smyth, the Queenes principal secretarie; in his trauails in Fraunce, Italie, Spaine, & Germanie but especially in his ambassages in Scotland, Fraunce, & Netherlande; found no sutch use of anie autours, as I heard himself say, as of Liuie, Plutarch, & Iustinian . . . Not the most, but the Best; was his rule. And I am for Geometrical, not Arithmetic proportion . . .' (cited by Grafton and Jardine 1990: 54; see also 60–6). The final annotation suggests that Harvey has the *Nicomachean Ethics* and its geometrical definition of virtue directly in mind.

[36] Cited by Jardine (1986: 43); also by Jardine and Grafton (1986: 191).

[37] Cited by Taylor (1930: 161); Hill (1965: 16); see also F. R. Johnson (1937: 191–5 and Ch. 3, below.

[38] Cf. Harvey's annotations to his copy of John Blagrave's *The Mathematical Jewel* (1585), complete with *volvelle*: 'All sciences are founded upon perception and reason . . . Experience [is] the firmest demonstration and an irrefutable criterion. Give me ocular and rooted demonstration of every principle, experiment, geometric instrument, astronomical, cosmosgraphic, horologiographic, geographic, hydrographic, or mathematical in any way' (cited by Stern 1979: 167 and n. 54).

The increasing conceptual proximity between practical and productive modes of knowledge and the growing extension of deliberative thinking that we find in Harvey's annotations is also visible in other sixteenth-century dialectic textbooks, particularly those written in the vernacular such as Thomas Blundeville's *Arte of Logicke*. Blundeville observes Aristotle's definition of the five modes of intellect, 'Intelligence, Science, Prudence, Art, and Sapience', defining 'art' in a perfectly conventional way as 'an habite of knowledge consisting of assured and certaine rules, tryed and approved by experience, and learned by exercise' (p. 25). As he continues, however, Blundeville follows Aristotle in reducing these five modes of intellect to two—the practical and the theoretical—and in the process collapses the distinction between *praxis* and *technē*, grouping the mechanical with the liberal arts: art 'grows to comprehend teaching *to doe or to make* something that is profitable to man's behooffe, and Art comprehendeth all arts, both liberall and mechanicall, that is to say, handie crafts' (p. 25; my emphasis).[39]

Other dialectical manuals draw explicit analogies with the mechanical arts to explain the operation of dialectical judgement, especially in its structural and formal functions. Thomas Wilson, who departs from tradition by placing judgement before invention in his *Rule of Reason* (1551), defends the organization of his book by explicitly comparing it with the techniques of the craftsman:

And now some wil say, that I should first speake of the finding out of an argument . . . And yet notwithstanding, it is more mete that the ordring of an argument shoulde be first handeled: forasmuche as it shal no more profit a man to find out his argument, except he first know how to order the same and to shape it acordingly . . . then stones or Timber shal profite the Mason or Carpenter, which knoweth not how to work upon the same. (Bi[r–v])

Blundeville goes even further, using an elaborate cartographic analogy to explain 'method'—the broadest term for the procedures of dialectical inquiry, and a watchword of Ramism—by comparing it to the process by which a traveller finds his way from London to Norwich by way of all the towns in between.[40] 'Method

---

[39] A similar blurring of categories appears also in the work of a more conventionally Aristotelian writer such as the Oxford doctor John Case, who repeats Aristotle's five categories of knowledge but also frames them as part of a broader distinction between the theoretical and the practical parts of the mind: the 'contemplative' and the 'active' (or 'consultative', *consultatricem*) faculties, respectively, the former concerned with necessary propositions, axioms, and universal principles (consisting of *scientia*, *intelligentia*, and *sapientia*), the latter with particularities and contingent propositions (consisting of *ars* and *prudentia*). *Ars* may be liberal, if its end is action; mechanical, if its end is work or making (*opus*); see Case (1585, book VI, esp. chs. 3–7, pp. 250–64; 1596a, book I, ch. 34, pp. 99, 102; 1596b: 260, 264). Case distinguishes art from prudence, and yet they are proximate in their classification as types of knowledge and even overlap to some degree, as is evident in his discussion of *ingenium* and *solertia*, or cleverness; see Case (1596a, book I, ch. 34, question 7 p. 105), commenting on *NE* VI. 9. 1142ª30–1142ᵇ15 and 12. 1144ª25–30; on Case generally, see Schmitt (1983b).

[40] Compare Thomas Wilson's *Rule of Reason* (1551), where invention employs 'the store house of places wherein argumentes rest. . . . A place is the restyng corner of an argument' (Iiiiiᵛ). The process of invention Wilson compared to mining and hunting on Iv[r]–Ivi[r], partially cited by Ong (1958: 120), who emphasizes the growing spatialization of dialectic teaching on pp. 74–91; cf. his discussion of Agricola's 'place-logic' (pp. 104–12, 116–21); Ong (1962); Blair (1997: 65–9); Joseph (1962);

compositive', Blundeville argues:

is that whereby we compound the whole of his parts, beginning at the smallest, and so proceede from greater to greater, until we come to the chief end whereto we tend, which kind of order or Methode we observe heere in writing this Logike: for first we treate of words or tearmes, then of a proposition, and last of al a Syllogisme: so likewise he that will reach the nighest way from Norwich to London by order compositive will bidde himself goe to Windham, from Windham to Atleborough, from Atleborough to Thetford, from Thetford to Newmarket, from Newmarket to Barkway, from Barkway to Ware, from Ware to London. (*Arte of Logicke*, 55)

He illustrates method 'resolutive' in the same way. Dialectic, and Ramist method in particular, is in fact referred to as a 'mapp' in *The Pilgrimage to Parnassus* (*c*.1598), the Cambridge University play that openly lampoons Gabriel Harvey in part for his advocacy of Ramist ideas.[41] As we shall see, Harvey, Sidney, George Puttenham, and Ben Jonson all explain problems of linguistic and poetic representation in terms that derive not simply from rhetoric or ethics but from those spatial arts, like cartography, carpentry, masonry, and surveying, that derived their fundamental epistemological procedures from the field of geometry. To understand this aspect of their thought, we must now consider the development of geometry as a distinctly practical discipline in England and its uneasy place in the humanist curriculum, and then to the changing epistemological status of practical mathematics, the techniques of the measuring manuals, and the methods of spatial representation they disseminated in sixteenth-century English culture.

RHETORIC, PRUDENCE, GEOMETRY

The close proximity between practical and productive knowledge reflected in Harvey's annotations, his enthusiasm for craftsmen and technical instruments, the mechanical and spatial analogies that we find in logic textbooks such as Blundeville's *Arte of Logicke*: each is a small example of a growing interest in

Moss (1996); Crane (1993: 12–38); Eamon (1994: 269–300). Melanchthon also defined method as a route or itinerary; Ong (1958: 158, 237); L. Jardine (1974*a*: 28 n. 2). On memory, see Yates (1966) and Carruthers (1990); for Gabriel Harvey, see Stern (1979: 29); also Ong's discussion of memory in the Ramist system (1958: 194–5, 213); and Rossi (1968: 207–14), on Bacon's use of the memory tradition.

41 See *The Pilgrimage to Parnassus*, Act I, where Philomusus addresses Studioso, a figure for Harvey: 'But cann wee hit this narowe curious waie | Where are such by wayes and erronious paths? | Saye whats the firste Ile wee muste travell in?' and Studioso replies: 'The firste lande that wee muste travell in (as that | oulde Hermite toulde me) is Logique. I have gotten Iacke | Setons mapp to directe us through this cuntrie. This Iland | is, according to his discription, muche like Wales, full of | craggie mountaines and thornie vallies . . . '. John Seton's *Dialectica* (1545 and many subsequent editions) was a popular logic textbook favoured by Ramist reformers like Harvey; see Schmitt (1983*a*: 18 n. 17, 29–40); Howell (1961: 240); Ong (1958: 171). The Sot, meanwhile, says that he had read 'Ramus his mapp, *Dialectica est*.'

mathematics and the practical application of mathematical knowledge among
several distinct social groups, foremost among them ambitious young gentlemen
of property and court-oriented humanists like Harvey, Sidney, or Sir Thomas
Smith. Blundeville's work is especially significant, in that it served as a direct
bridge between the formal instruction of the university and more informal circles
outside the schools that surrounded powerful courtiers such as the Earl of
Northumberland and the Earl of Leicester: since Blundeville was one of several
writers who enjoyed Leicester's patronage in the 1560s and 1570s, the range of his
work suggests the interests and intellectual juxtapositions that Leicester's circle
cultivated. Blundeville's *A brief description of universal mappes and cardes* (1589),
for instance, offers instruction not simply in how to use maps but in how to *read*
them as semiotic documents with specialized conventions of graphic representation:
'I Daylie see many that delight to looke on Mappes, and can point to England,
France, Germanie, and to the east and West Indies, and to divers other places
therein described,' Blundeville writes, 'but yet for the want of skill in Geography,
they knowe not with what maner of lines they are traced, nor what those lines to
signifie, nor yet the true use of Mappes in deed' (A2ᵛ). His *Art of Logicke* uses
arithmetical and geometrical concepts of proportion to explain ratiocinative
procedures in logic and even illustrates them with geometrical diagrams, while
his *Exercises for Young Gentlemen* (1594, with six editions by 1638), a popular
compendium of practical treatises, explains to the gentleman and educated
layman the geometrical principles necessary to cosmography, and to the use of
maps, globes, and astrolabes, especially when solving navigational problems.

Born in Norfolk, Blundeville (*fl.* 1560–1602) has been comparatively ignored
by historians of science and technology: he seems to have been educated at
Cambridge, although without firm evidence or date of matriculation; he served
for a period as a private tutor in the household of Sir Nicholas Bacon; later he is
associated with Gresham College and the group that included Henry Briggs
(1561–1630), the first Gresham Professor of Geometry (1597–1620) and later
the first Savilian Professor of Geometry at Oxford (1620 until his death), William
Gilbert (1540–1603), Edward Wright (1558–1615), and William Barlow
(1544–1625), the latter two both instrument-makers who wrote on navigation.[42]
Along with his contemporaries at Gresham, Blundeville was one of several 'mathematical practitioners', as E. G. R. Taylor has called them, who often took up residence in London as they sought to make a living either through commercial

---

[42] On the details of Blundeville's life and works, see, in addition to the *DNB*, F. R. Johnson (1937:
206–8); E. G. R. Taylor (1954: 173); Hill (1965: 35–42, esp. n. 106); Alexander (1990: 166);
Rosenberg (1955: 46–53, 56, 62–4), a detailed account of Blundeville's activities that does not, however, discuss his mathematical works. Blundeville's *The theoriques of the seven planets* (1602) includes
a description of two instruments 'invented' by Gilbert, the 'Instrument of Latitude' and 'Instrument
of Declination', as well as an appendix by Wright, added at Gilbert's suggestion, and a table prepared
by Briggs.

publication, private instruction, patronage, consultation on state-sponsored projects, or instrument-making.[43] Blundeville demonstrates considerably broader range than other practitioners of the period, however, and in this he is somewhat atypical of technical writers; in addition to *A briefe description of universal mappes and cardes*, *The Arte of Logicke*, and the *Exercises*, his most popular book, he had already published several treatises on horsemanship, a treatise on counsel, and a treatise on the writing of history, all partially translated or adapted from the Italian.[44] As we shall see in Chapter 3, many aspects of Sidney's *Defence of Poesy* (*c*.1579) assume a new significance when read alongside Blundeville's work: the opening anecdote in praise of Pugliano's horsemanship, Sidney's many comments regarding the reading and writing of history, his survey of contemporary 'arts' and professions, his use of logical terminology, and his interest in practical mathematics.[45]

In the sixteenth century geometry still remained a pre-scientific mode of knowledge whose symbols, instruments, and calculations often associated it with magic and astrology; it continued to appear mysterious in a world where functional numeracy may have been relatively common but advanced mathematical training was comparatively rare. Many Elizabethans would have nodded along silently with Mason, the colleague of the notorious Friar Bacon in Robert Greene's play of the same title (*c*.1589), when he averred that:

> No doubt but magic may do much in this;
> For he that reads but mathematic rules
> Shall find conclusions that avail to work
> Wonders that pass the common sense of men.[46]

---

[43] On the mathematical practitioner, see esp. E. G. R. Taylor (1954: 173–4, 176); Cormack (1997); Johnston (1991); Biagioli (1989, 1993); Ash (2000); Harkness (2002); the related analyses of alchemists by P. Smith (1994); and the works cited in n. 47 below.

[44] Rosenberg (1955: 47–56, esp. 55–6) suggests that Cecil may have brought Blundeville to Leicester's attention, who employed him as a translator and epitomizer of Italian works; in published form several of these were dedicated to Dudley (made Earl of Leicester in 1564) in his capacity as Master of the Queen's Horse, a position he held as of 1559. These include *A newe booke containing the arte of ryding, and breakinge greate Horses* (1561), a partial translation and partial adaptation of an Italian work by Federico Grisone; followed by *The foure chiefest offices belonging to horsemanship* (1566, 1570, 1580, 1593, 1597, 1609), a much larger and more popular work that included an improved version of Grisone and three additional treatises, two of which were later published separately (*The Order of Dietynge of Horses* (1565) and *The Order of Curing Horses Diseases* (1566)) and all dedicated to Leicester. These technical books were followed by Blundeville's translation and abridgement of Fadrique Ceriol's Spanish book on counsel (from an Italian translation), *A very briefe and profitable Treatise declaring howe many counsells and what maner of Counselers a Prince that will governe well ought to have* (1570) and then *The true order and Methode of wryting and reading Hystories* (1574), a compilation and partial translation of two Italian works on the topic by Francesco Patrizi and Accontio Tridentino.

[45] Rosenberg (1955: 50) points out that Sidney recommended Grisone and Claudio Corte's *Il cavallerizzo* (1572, 1573) to his brother Robert in a letter in 1580, suggesting that he knew the works through his uncle and Blundeville; she also notes that Gabriel Harvey writes approvingly of Blundeville's work on horsemanship.

[46] Greene, *Friar Bacon and Friar Bungay*, 2. 72–5 (and cf. 4. 53); cf. Zetterberg (1980).

Recent studies of the university curriculum by Mordechai Feingold and Lesley Cormack have demonstrated that the study of mathematics did take place at both Oxford and Cambridge, and in this respect their work has offered a corrective to the long-standing view among an earlier generation of intellectual historians, among them F. R. Johnson, Edgar Zilsel, and Christopher Hill, that the sixteenth-century statutes at best disregarded and at worst inhibited mathematical and scientific thought.[47] At the same time, however, the evidence gathered by both Feingold and Cormack indicates that advanced training in mathematics was pursued by a small number of exceptional rather than average students, generally at the Master's level.[48] Although we now have a more accurate picture of mathematics *within* the university, the fact remains that significant developments continued to occur *outside* the schools and were only partially making their way into the curriculum, official or otherwise.[49]

Not surprisingly, students used the classic works of Euclid and Archimedes as well as textbooks by contemporary Continental authorities. But many owned books by Englishmen, directed specifically towards practical use or even written

[47] See esp. Westman (1980: 128–31); Gascoigne (1575, esp. 220–34); Alexander (1990: 165–71); F. R. Johnson (1937: 10–13, 169–73; but also 195–7); Hill (1965); Johnston (1991). Following a line of argument inaugurated by Leonardo Olschki in the 1920s (whose work did not extend to English sources), scholars such as Taylor (1930, 1934, 1954), Parsons (1968), Zilsel (1941, 1942*a*, *b*), Houghton (1941), Hall (1959, a critical account, esp. 14–23), Hill (1965); F. R. Johnson (1937, 1940, 1942), Wightman (1962: i. 82–3, 87–99, 129–47, esp. the qualified comments on 146), and Yates (1969) began to examine the English evidence for a practically oriented, vernacular literature of mathematics, measurement, navigation, engineering, and technology that was distinct from the universities. Not all these scholars refer to Olschki's work; for a survey of the tradition, see Long (2001); H. F. Cohen (1994, esp. 322–51); Hadden (1994); for medieval terms and distinctions, see Vérin (1993: 19–31, 43–74); Gille (1966); Ovitt (1987, esp. 107–36); Whitney (1990); Weisheipl (1965, 1978).

[48] Feingold (1984) singles out St John's, Cambridge, for its mathematical instruction; see esp. pp. 23–44, 45–85, 91–121; also Feingold (1991; 1997*b*, esp. 359–89 (on the 17th-century Oxford curriculum); (1999). Cormack (1997) places greater emphasis than does Feingold on the practical nature of mathematical instruction and provides an indispensable survey of actual book-ownership, on which many of my comments are based; she identifies seven colleges in which the study of mathematics was particularly active: Corpus Christi, St John's, and New College at Oxford, and Peterhouse, Corpus Christi, Trinity, and St John's at Cambridge; see esp. pp. 23–6, 34–47 (esp. 44), 105–28. See also Simon (1966: 252–3), who discusses the Cambridge statutes of 1549 (stipulating Pliny, Strabo, Ptolemy, Euclid, Cardano, and Tunstall) and emphasizes instruction at King's, Trinity, and Queen's; Wightman (1962: i. 87–99); Strong (1932); Curtis (1959: 87, 91–2 and n. 31, 94, 116–18, 120–2); McConica (1986: 34–5, 38); J. M. Fletcher (1986: 161, 172–4); Clulee (1988, esp. 23–6, 145–76); French (1972: 23–7). On mathematical instruction in English grammar schools, see Simon (1966: 119); O'Day (1982: 60–2); Thomas (1987); Bendall (1992: 127–9); Reiss (1997 esp. 34–5, 37–43, 83–5, and 138–44 (emphasizing European developments)).

[49] A point overlooked by many of Feingold's readers, but see the related comments by H. F. Cohen (1994: 207); Cormack (1997) observes that 'of the 178 men with some known interest in mathematical geography between 1580 and 1620, 117, or 66 percent attended university' (p. 117)—which means that fully one-third of them had no university connection at all. Recent scholarship on Thomas Harriot and the circle surrounding the Earl of Northumberland has uncovered further evidence for advanced mathematical study outside the university proper (although obviously by men with university degrees); see Shirley (1974, 1983); Clucas (1999); and the essays collected in Fox (2000), esp. Clucas (2000) and Bennett (2000).

by non-university men such as Robert Norman, the very 'navigator' commended by Gabriel Harvey and also a maker of nautical instruments and charts.[50] As late as the second decade of the seventeenth century, for instance, Blundeville's *Exercises* was still being used as a university textbook,[51] as were other practical manuals written by his contemporaries: Robert Recorde's book of geometry *The Pathway to Knowledge* (1551), the first in English, and Recorde's arithmetic *The Castle of Knowledge* (1556); Leonard Digges's *Prognostication* (1555), the first English mathematical treatise to endorse a complete version of Copernican heliocentrism; and Digges's *Tectonicon* (1554), a popular early work on measurement and surveying often reprinted during the sixteenth century. Such evidence as survives for actual methods of university instruction in mathematics also indicates an interest in its practical application: the notebooks of John Ramsey, who spent two years at Peterhouse, Cambridge, from 1601 to 1603, display a familiarity with a wide range of mathematical knowledge, including speculative university mathematicians such as Henry Briggs, private and public lecturers such as Blundeville and Thomas Hood, and practitioners such as John Norden, John Blagrave, and Elias Allen, all surveyors, the latter two also well-known makers of mathematical instruments.[52] The manuscript notes of Brian Twyne, a tutor at Corpus Christi, Oxford, from 1605 to 1623, include a diagram of a carpenter's rule and instructions on how to calculate both board and timber measure, as well as more advanced arithmetical calculations and lessons in astronomy.[53]

The practical focus of these manuals is evident from their title pages, prefaces, and dedicatory letters, many of which address the craftsman directly and, like

---

[50] St John's, Cambridge, and St John's, Oxford, are both notable in this respect; inventories from the latter include Norman's *Safeguard of Sailors* (1584) along with arithmetic books by Robert Recorde, Thomas Hill, and Humphrey Baker. Robert Norman (*fl.* 1560–96) was described as 'not learned, yet . . . a very expert mechanician' by Barlow; see E. G. R. Taylor (1954: 179, 318–19, 322, 330); Feingold (1984: 117).

[51] The account books of Joseph Mede, a fellow at Christ's College, Cambridge, from 1613 to 1638, record that in 1618 he gave money to students to buy new mathematical books in Cambridge bookstores or sold them copies from former students; Blundeville's *Exercises* was among them, as was Digges's *Prognostication* (1555). The *Exercises* was also used at Oxford, this time in the MA curriculum; the notebooks of John Goodridge (Balliol College, *c.*1600) make reference to it in a course of Aristotelian astronomy, while at Cambridge students owned Blundeville's *Exercises* along with Digges's *Tectonicon* (1554), Wright's *Certain Errors in Navigation* (1599), and Recorde's *The Castle of Knowledge* (1556). All cited in Feingold (1984: 96–7, 102).

[52] Feingold (1984: 100); E. G. R. Taylor (1954: 181, 198). Bendall (1992: 143–5) discusses surveying texts in private libraries. Henry Savile, along with Dee the period's foremost speculative mathematician, teacher of both Sir Philip and Robert Sidney, and founder of the Savilian Professorships in Geometry and Astronomy at Oxford in 1619, expressly stipulated that 'It will, besides, be the business of the Geometry professor, at his own time, (as shall seem convenient to himself, with the consent of the University), to teach and expound all arithmetic of all kinds, both speculative and practical; land-surveying, or practical geometry; canonics or music, and mechanics' (cited by Bendall 1992: 142); see also Hill (1965: 35–47 (39–40)); Westman (1980: 129–31); Cormack (1997: 28–9); Curtis (1959: 116–17); Goulding (1999, esp. 126); Feingold (1984: 125–6; 1999: 179–80; 2001: 74), emphasizing Savile's interest in speculative mathematics, citing his lectures from the 1570s; Johnston (1991: 342–3), also emphasizing Savile's disdain for practical mathematics.

[53] Cited by Curtis (1959: 120–2).

Harvey's comments on Norman and others, depart from a long-standing bias against the mechanical arts that extended back through the Middle Ages to the classical period. Some even question the authority of those, like Harvey, with university degrees: Norman's own *The Newe Attractive* (1581), for instance, which explained the use of the compass and the magnetic dip of its needle, maintains that 'mechanicians or mariners' have more authority than 'the learned in those [mathematical] sciences . . . in their studies amongst their books' and claims that 'there are in this land divers mechanicians that in their several faculties and professions have the use of those at their fingers' ends, and can apply them to their several purposes, as effectually and more readily than those that would most condemn them'.[54] Arthur Hopton address the preface to his *Speculum Topographicum; or, The Topographicall Glasse* (1611), a guide to civil and military surveying, 'to the Mathematicall Practizer' and maintains that 'I know divers great Scholers, deeply seene in the theoricall part, though in the active, meere novices: which is a cause that such, so learned, were never able to correct and amend many defects' (a1ᵛ).

Other books of geometry, of all sizes and formats, evince a similar commitment to vernacular exposition and advocate a distinctly practical mode of instruction that departs from the speculative tradition of Euclidean geometry. Edward Worsop sought to make geometry available to 'the understanding of every reasonable man' and complained that earlier works could not 'be understood by the common sort'.[55] Richard More's *A Carpenter's Rule* (1602) declares on its title page that it is 'Published especially for the good of the Companie of Carpenters in London, and others also; and is very necessarie for Masons, Shipwrights, Joyners, and others, using to measure Timber and Boord, and other superficies and sollids'.[56] Robert Recorde's *Pathway to Knowledge*, arguably the most 'Euclidean' of the manuals, explicitly directs itself to the practical application of its principles:

A Poynt or a Prycke, *is named of Geometricians that small and unsensible shape, whiche hath in it no partes, that is to say: nother length, breadth nor depth. But as this exactnes of definition is more meeter for onlye Theorike speculacion, then for practise and outwarde worke (consideringe that myne intente is to applye all these whole principles to woorke) I thynke meeter for this purpose, to call* a poynt or prycke, *that small printe of penne, pencyle, or other instrumente, which is not moved, nor drawen from his fyrst touche, and therfore hath no notable length nor bredthe. . . . But as they in theyr theoreikes (which ar only minde workes) do precisely understand these definitions, so it shal be sufficient for those men, whiche seke the use of the same thinges, as sense may duely judge them, and applye to handy workes if they understand them so to be true, that outwarde sense canne fynde non erroure therein.* (Aiʳ⁻ᵛ)[57]

---

[54] Norman (1581, Aiiiᵛ, Bi–iᵛ), cited by Hill (1965: 20–1).
[55] Cited by Hill (1965: 21).   [56] More (1602, A3ʳ).
[57] Compare Billingsley's (1570) English translation of Euclid: 'Here must you consider when there is in Geometry mention made of pointes, lines, circles, triangles, or of any other figures, ye may not conceyve of them as they be in matter, as in woode, in mettall, in paper, or in any such lyke, for so is there no lyne, but hath some breadth, and may be devided: nor points, but that shal have some partes, and may also be devided, and so of others. But you must conceive them in mynde, plucking

Even as Recorde repeatedly justifies the study of geometry from a speculative point of view, he is savvy enough to realize that practical application will most interest the reader and includes a declaration, in verse, of all the tradesmen who will benefit from it.

By publishing books of applied mathematics, practitioners such as Blundeville, Recorde, Norman, and their contemporaries were undertaking a twofold project. In the first place, they were gathering traditional techniques that had been developed by unlettered artisans in workshops, meadows, and shipyards and were beginning to systematize them for the strategic and economic benefit of the commonwealth. In this way their manuals disseminated practical techniques through a wider range of social agents and status positions; over time, they contributed to the more gradual transformation of those methods into a legitimate mode of *scientia* that might command a new measure of social respect and political influence for the practitioner, even if it did not always produce immediate financial gain. But, by doing so, practitioners were also attempting to give to the field of mathematics, and especially to geometry, a new coherence and legitimacy in the eyes of educated gentlemen such as Sidney, who might provide patronage or facilitate political employment for a practitioner who had demonstrated his expertise in these new fields. To assert expertise in a field, after all, requires such a field-defining gesture: for a practitioner such as Blundeville, the strategies of disciplinary definition and social self-positioning were inseparable.

John Dee's 'Mathematicall Preface' to Henry Billingsley's English translation of Euclid's *Elements* (1570), one of the earliest vernacular translations of Euclid's work in Europe, attempts just such a field-defining project: the preface is primarily concerned with *defending* the study of geometry by universalizing its appeal and pointing out its usefulness to political life. The 'Common Artificer' along with 'the Common and Vulgar Scholer', 'unlatined people, and not Universitie Scholars', 'the Gramarian', and the 'many good and pregnant Englishe wittes, of young Gentlemen', Dee writes, 'will be hable . . . to finde out, and devise, new workes, straunge Engines, and Instrumentes: for sundry purposes in the Common Wealth'.[58] Although Dee distinguishes between a de-materialized, speculative geometry that pertains to philosophical study and an applied geometry that is necessary to practitioners of all types, the purpose of the preface is to draw both together into a larger intellectual formation—*mathēsis*—and to defend its epistemological status:

A Mechanicien, or a Mechanicall workman is he, whose skill is, without knowledge of Mathematicall demonstration, perfectly to worke and finishe any senseible worke, by the

them by imagination from all matter, so shall ye understande them truely and perfectly, in their owne nature as they are defined' (Bii'). Cf. Clucas (1999).

[58] Dee (1570, Aiii'–Aiiii'); the last is cited by Hill (1965: 18); see also Strong (1932: 204–13); Clulee (1977; 1984; 1988, esp. 1–4, 36–7 (emphasizing the distinctly Aristotelian aspect to Dee's early productive period), 61–3, 145–76, esp. 146, 154–62); Yates (1969); P. French (1972: 160–77); Sherman (1995); Harkness (1999: 91–7); Clucas (1999).

Mathematicien principall or derivative, demonstrated or demonstratable. Full well I know, that he which inventeth, or maketh these demonstrations, is generally called A *speculative Mechanicien*: which differreth nothyng from *a Mechanicall Mathematicien*. So, in respect of diverse actions, one man may have the name of sundry artes: as, some tyme, of a Logicien, some tymes (in the same matter otherwise handled) of a Rhetoricien. (aiiir–v)

In Dee's argument, the difference between *scientia* and *ars* is reduced to one of procedure, while the knowledge produced by both is shown to be qualitatively the same. Significantly, he makes his point by drawing a comparison with the arts of the *trivium*, using arguments very similar to those that John Rainolds was using at the same moment, as we have seen: logic and rhetoric work in different contexts and to different ends, but both treat the same kind of subject matter and employ similar methods of reasoning.

As an effort of justification as well as of definition, Dee's 'Preface' displays the insecure position that geometry continued to occupy within a humanist curriculum that emphasized the linguistic arts of the medieval *trivium*— grammar, rhetoric, dialectic—and joined them to the study of politics and civil behaviour.[59] In *The Pathway to Knowledge*, Record addressed this very problem as directly as possible: not only do both logic and rhetoric, the foundations of the humanist curriculum, depend on geometry for their essential principles, but Aristotle himself frequently uses geometry to illustrate difficult philosophical problems:

But now to procede with learned professions, in Logicke and Rhetorike and all partes of phylosophy, there neadeth none other proofe then Aristotle his testimony, which without Geometry proveth almost nothinge. In Logicke all his good syllogismes and demonstrations, hee declareth by the principles of Geometrye. In philosophye, either motion, nor time, nor ayrye impressions coulde hee aptely declare, but by the helpe of Geometrye as his woorkes do witnes. Yea the faculties of the minde dothe hee expresse by similitude to figures of Geometrye. And in morall philosophie he thought that justice coulde not wel be taught, nor yet well executed without proportion geometricall. (3 iᵛ)

In the *Nicomachean Ethics*, Aristotle indeed defines *phronēsis* by comparing it to the kind of perception that distinguishes a geometrical figure, and his more detailed discussion of perception in the *De Anima* includes many small but precise

---

[59] Cf. the synopsis of the undergraduate arts curriculum in BL, Harl. MS 3230, fos. 172–184ʳ, a commonplace book from 1583 (dated fo. 175ʳ), consisting of separate tabular analyses of arts subjects, as follows: 'Art' in general (fo. 172ʳ), Dialectic (fo. 173ʳ: 'Descriptio Dialect. Guhelmo Adolpho Scribomo authore'), Grammar and Rhetoric (fos. 177ʳ–179ᵛ), Arithmetic (180ʳ–ᵛ), Music (181ᵛ: 'Typus Musica ex ffrederica Beurhusio'), Natural Philosophy (182ʳ–ᵛ: 'Physicae adumbratio methodica'; 'ex ffrederica Beurheusio, et Adolpho Gul. Scribomo' crossed out), Medicine (183ʳ–ᵛ: 'Medicinae adumbratio methodica; authore Timotheo Brighto Cantabrigiensi'), and Ethics (184ʳ: 'Methodica adumbratio Ethica. et primo Quaestio translata: virtutem esse in rebus expetendis: Guillemo Tempello Cantabrigiensi authore'). Geometry appears on fo. 181ʳ but has, notably, been left entirely blank: an indication, perhaps, of its uncertain position in the curriculum. Many of the authors indicated here are key points of reference for Harvey and Sidney; see Ch. 3, below, esp. nn. 28, 56, 71; cf. Struever (1992: 135, 138).

technical examples drawn from geometry to illustrate his points.[60] Indeed, geometrical concepts and definitions featured throughout many of passages in the *Nicomachean Ethics* that sixteenth-century readers found most significant, among them the discussion of distributive and rectificatory justice and the famous analysis of money and of value in exchange.[61] In the case of both distributive and commercial justice, 'geometrical' proportion provides a method of evaluating equal relationships among heterogeneous people and objects: how else will it be possible to make commensurable the shoes of the shoemaker and the house of the builder? Geometry here founds an entire philosophy of justice but also a definition of the urban community as a tissue of commercial exchanges given spatial form. 'This sort of justice does hold men together—reciprocity in accordance with a proportion and not on the basis of equality,' Aristotle comments, 'for it is by proportionate requital that the city holds together.'[62]

Each of these passages reveals a further point overlooked both by the first generation of scholarship on the history of mathematics in the English university curriculum and by more recent revisionist accounts: the average sixteenth-century undergraduate was far more likely to encounter discussion of geometrical definitions and concepts in his reading of texts that were foundational to the humanist curriculum but which ostensibly had nothing to do with mathematics, such as Aristotle's philosophical writings or Quintilian's *Institutes*, than he would have by reading actual mathematical textbooks. Quintilian, for instance, had repeatedly recommended knowledge of geometry, in both its speculative and practical forms, as his primary example of the breadth of knowledge necessary to the orator:

[Geometry] soars still higher in the consideration of the system of the universe: for by its calculations it demonstrates the fixed and the ordained courses of the stars, and thereby we

---

[60] See esp. *NE* VI. 8. 1142ª23–30 (the perception of a triangle); *De Anima* 402ª22 (starting points of inquiries), 402ᵇ18–20 (necessity of knowing the essential nature of substances), 403ª12–15 and ᵇ18 (definition of the affections), 409ᵇ4–6 (examples of movement and the generation of surfaces and lines), 413ª17–20 (examples of insufficient definitions). He also compares finding the mean in moral excellence to finding the middle of a circle (*NE* II. 9. 1109ª25); soon he points out that this requires that we resist our own worst impulses and 'drag ourselves away to the contrary extreme . . . as carpenters (*poioūsin*) do in straightening sticks that are bent' (*NE* II. 9. 1109ᵇ5). 'Carpenters' is Rackham's translation of *poioūsin*; cf. *NE* 1106ᵇ6–15 and *Rhetoric* I. 1. 1354ª25 ('It is not right to pervert the judge by moving him to anger or envy or pity—one might as well warp a carpenter's rule (*poiēseie*) before using it') and *NE* I. 7. 1098ª30, where Aristotle distinguishes between the carpenter (*tektōn*) and the geometer (*geōmetrēs*), both of whom 'look for right angles in different ways; the former does so in so far as the right angle is useful for his work (*poīon*), while the latter inquires what it is or what sort of thing it is; for he is a spectator (*theatēs*) of the truth'. On the place of mathematics in Aristotle's thought, esp. in the logical treatises, see Heath (1949); Strong (1932: 19–27); Funkenstein (1986: 303–7). Ong (1958) discusses the importance of geometry to Ramus and other 16th-century reformers; see esp. pp. 74–91, 131–48, 156–67, 175–6, 179–81, 240; also Gilbert (1963: 81–92); Reiss (1997: 95–6, 108–11, 114–17, 120–5 (on Ramus), and 110–14, 118–20, 146–54 (on mathematics and philosophical thought more generally)).

[61] *NE* V. 3, esp. 1131ª30–ᵇ15; also V. 4. 1132ª20–ᵇ10.

[62] *NE* V. 5. 1132ᵇ–1133ᵇ35; cf. II. 2. 1104ª17; cf. Harvey's comments about Smith cited in n. 35; also Kaye's study of geometrical models of proportion in the *Nicomachean Ethics* and its importance to medieval philosophical, scientific, and economic thought.

acquire the knowledge that all things are ruled by order and destiny, a consideration which may at times be of value to an orator . . . From this we may conclude that if . . . an orator has to speak on every kind of subject, he can under no circumstances dispense with a knowledge of geometry.[63]

As an example of the kind of expertise an orator might need, Quintilian includes a detailed discussion of a surveying problem that he characterizes as 'easy even for those who have no knowledge of geometry' (I. 10. 40–9): the need to calculate the area of a field on the basis of its dimensions, a problem very like those found in sixteenth-century student notebooks. Rainolds, too, arguing, for the universal applicability of rhetoric within a year or two of Dee's 'Mathematicall Praeface', invoked geometry, specifically, as his example of a field that rhetoric already encompasses:

Aristotle defines rhetoric as the power or faculty of seeing what may be probable in any situation. Rhetoric, he says, does not create (*facit*) probabilities, but instead perceives (*videt*) them . . . If so, *then all arts belong to rhetoric, just as all drugs belong to medicine. Nay more, medical practice itself will become a part of rhetoric, as already is that silent investigation of bodies, lines, and numbers, and the entire art drawn with sand and rod.*[64]

For Aristotle, as we have seen, the purpose of rhetoric's breadth of application was 'to deal with such matters as we deliberate upon without arts or systems to guide us . . . For it is about our actions that we deliberate and inquire, and all our actions have a contingent character' (*Rhetoric* I. 2. 1357ᵃ2–25). And in book III of the *Nicomachean Ethics* he explicitly compares the faculty of deliberation and calculation—of *logisteīa*, the faculty of reasoning about choice but also of numerical reasoning—with the technique of the geometer: 'The person who deliberates', he remarks, 'seems to inquire and analyse in the way described as though he were analysing a geometrical construction' (*NE* III. 3. 1112ᵇ20–5).

In undertaking the epistemological project of defining, defending, and disseminating practical geometry, therefore, practitioners such as Blundeville and his contemporaries encountered an arts curriculum that repeatedly invoked geometry and the mechanical arts as a way of explaining the practical nature of prudence and rhetoric but which did not offer extensive instruction in solving mathematical problems of any complexity. Encouraged by their tutors, a few advanced students had begun to take an active interest in mathematics—but most students, if they thought about mathematics at all, only realized that they *ought* to take such an interest. I propose that the methods of reasoning typical of rhetoric, dialectic, and

---

[63] *Inst. Orat.* I. 10. 49; cf. I. 10. 2–7, 34–40.

[64] Rainolds (*c.*1570: 161; my emphasis). Approximately three years later Sir Thomas Smith would use similar language when he endowed two mathematical lectureships at Queens' College, Cambridge, in 1573, stipulating that 'the which two lectures are not to be redd of the reader as of a preacher out of a pulpit, but *"per radium et eruditum pulverum,"* as it is said, that is with a penn on paper or tables, or a sticke or compasse in sand or duste to make demonstracon that his schollers maie both understand the reader and also do it themselves and so profit' (cited by Feingold 1984: 39); on Smith's interest in mathematics, see F. R. Johnson (1937: 88–90), citing Richard Mulcaster's testimonial.

prudence—methods that formed the epistemological core of the arts curriculum and that *all* students were required to master—provided coherent paradigms for thinking about the kind of technical problems that might plausibly confront the politically ambitious or propertied young gentlemen when he left the university and which were *already* confronting the surveyor, the engineer, the carpenter, or the military captain, who worked outside the university in social and political circumstances very like those in which the gentleman might find himself.[65] As Aristotle had argued, *phronēsis* 'does not aim at theoretical knowledge' (*NE* II. 2. 1103^{b}26) because particulars 'do not fall under any art or set of precepts, but the agents themselves must in each case consider what is appropriate to the occasion, as happens also in the art of medicine or of navigation' (*NE* II. 2. 1104^{a}4–9). Quintilian had made a similar point about rhetoric:

let no one however demand from me a rigid code of rules such as most authors of textbooks have laid down . . . most rules are liable to be altered by the nature of the case, circumstances of time and place, and by hard necessity itself. Consequently the all-important gift for an orator is a wise adaptability since he is called upon to meet the most varied emergencies. What if you should instruct a general, as often as he marshals his troops for battle, to draw up his front in line, advance his wings to the left and right, and station his cavalry to protect his flank? This will perhaps be the best plan, if circumstances allow. But it may have to be modified owing to the nature of the ground, if, for instance, he is confronted by a mountain, if a river bars his advance, or his movements are hampered by hills, woods or broken country.   (II. 13. 1–4)

It has always, therefore, been my custom not to tie myself down to universal or general rules . . . For rules are rarely of such a kind that their validity cannot be shaken and overthrown in some particular or other . . . I do not want young men to think their education complete when they have mastered one of the small text-books of which so many are in circulation, or to ascribe a talismanic value to the arbitrary decrees of theorists. The art of speaking can only be attained by hard work and assiduity of study, by a variety of exercises (*plurimus experimentis*) and repeated trial, the highest prudence and unfailing quickness of judgment. (II. 13. 15–16)

Quintilian's term for 'wise adaptability' is *consilium*—the art of the courtier as well as of the surveyor, military captain, or engineer, and thus of *praxis*, or prudential reasoning, as well as of persuasion. As in the art of war, Quintilian concludes, so in rhetoric: 'there are no subjects in which, as a rule, practice is not more valuable than precept' (II. 5. 14–15).

   Rhetoric, prudence, and dialectic each offered ways of understanding practice and theory as distinct epistemologies and for synthesizing them in a dialectical fashion, for using probable reasoning to evaluate particular instances in a

---

[65] I draw especially on P. Smith (1994); Long (1997, esp. 21–39; 1985; 2001); Vérin, whose (1993) study of Renaissance engineering has inspired much of my analysis; Rossi (1968, 1970); Gille (1996); C. Smith (1992); Kristeller (1990); Heidegger (1977); Ong (1958, esp. 131–48); Keller (1976); Merriman (1983). Reiss (1997, 2000, 2004) also emphasizes the linguistic aspects of the *trivium* and the eventual displacement of rhetoric and dialectic by mathematics as a primary epistemological tool of discovery, questioning the importance accorded to visual and spatial thinking in the period.

proto-inductive, calculative way, independently of any first principles, and for arriving at knowledge through a process of doing and making rather than through deductive argument and logical demonstration. For this reason, I propose that all three fields provided mathematical practitioners with a legitimate philosophical framework in which to consider working methods long associated with the mechanical arts. For although traditional Aristotelian philosophy had difficulty accounting for artificial, 'made' objects and tended to refuse them a significant epistemological status—as changeable things they were inherently unknowable in certain terms and thus outside the realm of *scientia* properly conceived—this same philosophy had elaborated a method of inquiry suitable to human action, speech, choice, and opinion, despite the fact that as objects of knowledge these, too, depended on a knowledge of particular instances and occasions, were changeable, and were as a consequence unknowable in certain terms. I propose that it is precisely because the field of mathematics was still in formation and had not yet acquired the institutional, social, and epistemological frameworks that would come to canonize it as 'scientific' in the seventeenth century that a transfer of intellectual categories and ratiocinative methods could take place in the work of practitioners such as Blundeville and his contemporaries. In order to suggest how this transfer in habits of reasoning occurred, I will now examine several aspects of the manuals in more detail before turning in subsequent chapters to examine how their methods were appropriated in poetic discourse and adapted to theatrical representation. In what follows I will be concentrating on specific questions of vocabulary and technique in order to illustrate as clearly as possible the manuals' distinctive cognitive procedures, specifically the place of graphic, diagrammatic, or iconic representation in the solution of problems involving the arrangement of objects and bodies in space.

THE ART OF GEOMETRICAL POIĒSIS

Not yet 'experimental' in a seventeenth-century sense, the practical mode of knowledge employed in the geometrical manuals allows both for informal, improvised solutions and for a multiplicity of solutions: the books describe a series of independent geometrical operations that are to be implemented and modified as necessary, offering mathematical principles as general guides to action rather than as precepts or laws. The practitioner operates much like the orator or courtier, observing a geometrical *decorum*, a deliberative or calculative procedure that matches appropriate procedures to individual problems.[66] Geometry as *gnōsis*, or abstract knowledge, is reformulated into geometry as both *praxis*, or prudential knowledge, and *poiēsis*, or productive knowledge: the practitioner is being taught how to *use* his knowledge in an effective way by means of the imagination, which

[66] Cf. Vérin (1993: 45–6); also Lachterman (1989: 32–49 (esp. 32–3, 37), 71–2, 122).

is itself understood to be an instrumental or technical organ.[67] In general, the manuals attempt to be effective in their teaching rather than exact, and for this reason they are best regarded as new permutations on earlier practical traditions rather than as radical departures from them. To conflate theoretical and practical mathematics into a single field (the 'mathematical sciences') or to insist only on authors' attempts to legitimize the study of arithmetic or geometry risks overlooking the curious mixture of methods that is the manuals' most distinctive feature. Dee's 'Preface', for instance, certainly attempts to 'mathematize' the procedures of the carpenter or seaman, but his preface is closer to what we might call a 'defence of *mathēsis*'—it is *not* a manual, as Edward Worsop complained in 1581.[68]

As Francis Johnson has observed, 'with the possible exception of Italy, England saw more original work of significance in the history of science printed in the vernacular than any other country', and the decisive importance of print is the first feature of the manuals' practical epistemology that I wish to emphasize— many of their most important characteristics depend on it.[69] Given the shortage of fellowships and permanent positions in the universities, the aspiring graduate practitioner might decide that publishing a book could grant him some authority in the field; for the non-university man, publication was often the only recourse to reach a larger audience.[70] Printing technique itself, furthermore, may be regarded as an important mode of practical knowledge that remains materialized in the text but which remains, at least until the works of Joseph Moxon (1683–4), outside direct discursive consideration.[71] Type-founders, map-engravers, and instrument-makers all relied on the same skills and raw materials; as Stephen Johnston has shown, engravers and instrument-makers formed part of an

---

[67] Cf. Lachterman (1989: 121–2, and 25–125, esp. 26–9, 61–91); Crombie (1996*b*), on the geometrical constructions of Kepler and Descartes; Dear (1995, esp. 30–1, 36–43, 55–62, 211–22); Homann (1983); Perez-Ramos (1988: 56–7); Funkenstein (1986: 296–327), on the place of geometrical construction in the emergence of a practical, instrumental mode of knowing through doing; Peirce (1957: 260–1).

[68] 'His mathematical preface unto these Elements is a work of such singularity and necessity to all students of the Mathematicalls, *that I wish them to make it a manual*' (cited by E. G. R. Taylor 1930: 178; my emphasis). Cf. Clucas (1999); Strong (1932, esp. 92–3, 94–5, 106–7), who in my view overlooks the distinctly practical aspects of the English manuals.

[69] F. R. Johnson (1937: 3); Eisenstein (1979: ii. 520–74); Johns (1998, esp. 6–28).

[70] See, for instance, the dedicatory letter to More's *Carpenter's Rule*, A3ʳ. As Johnston has argued, however (1991, esp. 327–30), Thomas Bedwell refrained from publication lest it compromise his authority, exclusivity, and control of the dissemination of his knowledge; Long (1997) shows that technical knowledge did not necessarily need print to flourish and that manuscript writers also presented themselves as authorial figures making a distinct contribution to applied mathematics.

[71] Moxon's *Mechanick Exercises on the Whole Art of Printing* (1683–4) was intended to form part of a series of works devoted to the mechanical arts, including smithing, joinery, carpentry, turning, and bricklaying; the work's preface explicitly situates printing within the tradition of mathematics and architecture and invokes Dee to do so. Moxon specialized in printing technical manuals (including an edition of Edward Wright's *Certain Errors in Navigation* (1657)) but was known by contemporaries primarily as a maker of mathematical instruments and an engraver of maps, particularly of 'sea plats'. See Davis and Carter's introduction to their edition of the *Mechanick Exercises*, esp. pp. xix–xxii.

immediate commercial circle that included printers, publishers, and lecturer practitioners like Thomas Hood.[72]

Most of the manuals are slim quartos printed in black-letter, with rudimentary woodcut illustrations and tables of measurement, and many formatting aspects suggest their specific pedagogical orientation.[73] Typography sometimes guides the reader by highlighting important definitions and concepts. John Norden's *Surveiors Dialogue* (1608) includes tables and charts that obviate the need for actual mathematical calculation, providing conversions for measurements or informing the reader how long a field must be to constitute an acre in area if only its breadth is known—the exact exercise that Quintilian had also considered (I. 10. 40–9). Leonard Digges's *Tectonicon* provides definitions for customary standards of measurement and provides exact numerical equivalents for each half-unit, rather than relying on the reader's ability to perform even basic division. As in Norden's work, a reader need know only the ten integers, which he may enter into a table of conversions explicitly designed for 'them that bee voide of Arithmeticke' (7[r]; also 10[v]). Another table includes ready-made square-foot measurements for pieces of board or glass. Tables and charts were also common in books of navigation or trigonometry, such as Wright's *Certain Errors*, Norwood's *Seaman's Practice*, and Norwood's *Trigonometrie; or, The Doctrine of Triangles* (1631), where they extend for many pages and provide figures pertaining to latitude, compass variation, and logarithms.[74]

Several of the manuals integrate actual paper instruments into their pages: these *volvelles* were especially characteristic of astronomical books and books on navigation. Blundeville's *Exercises* is a notable example; the 1594 edition includes, in addition to many geometrical diagrams and illustrations, a 'Marriner's Card', or chart with compass directions, and an 'instrument of tides', a true *volvelle* in the form of a rotating paper wheel anchored to the page with knotted string. The 1613 edition adds a 'Mariner's astrolabe'—a double-disc wheel—along with the tide wheel. Blundeville's *Theoriques of the seven planets* (1602) includes an even more complex four-disc rotating wheel (the 'theorique of the moon') modelled on an instrument designed by William Gilbert.[75] In many cases the *volvelle* enhances the expertise of the practitioner by advancing his claims to the invention of a particular instrument, which is usually presented as indispensable to accurate

---

[72] Johnston (1991: 337–41); also G. L'E. Turner (1983: 95), on Humphrey Cole, the instrument-maker, engraver of dies for the Royal Mint, and also associated with the new Company of Mineral and Battery Works created by royal patent in 1568; Harkness (2002: 147–51).

[73] Cf. Bendall (1992: 119–24, esp. 120–2).

[74] Cf. E. G. R. Taylor (1947: 126–9); on the use of tables, see Swan (2002: 122–31); Blair (1997: 30–40).

[75] See the *Exercises* (Blundeville 1594: 325, 350); and *Exercises* (1613), BL, 1608/2472, pp. 676, 744. Complete information on the use of *volvelles* in English books is provided by Luborsky and Ingram (1998); cf. Clucas's (1999) discussion of Dee's 'device' affixed to Billingsley's Euclid (1570: 154–5), and Stern (1979: 167), who observes that Harvey's copy of Blagrave's *The Mathematical Jewel* (1585) included moveable paper instruments.

measurement.[76] Digges's *Tectonicon* promotes his version of the carpenter's square, rule, scale, and the cross-staff; his *Pantometria*, published posthumously by his son Thomas in 1571, describes even more sophisticated surveying instruments. Both Hopton's *Topographicall Glasse* (1611) and More's *Carpenter's Rule* (1602) provide detailed illustrations of their instruments. Ralph Agas, in his *Preparative to the Platting of Landes* (1596), urges the theodolite on his reader:

> I tell you truly the same Ingine carrieth in it selfe Euclide, Pithagoras, Archimedes, Architas, and the rest, with their points, Draughtes, Lines, Theoremes, Theoricks, Propositions, Figures, and Mathematicall conclusions, not in Elements, shewes, speculations, and demonstrations, but in the work & operation itself . . .

But these devices are really *between* tools and instruments: no longer the familiar object that assists in a series of habitual tasks, the device is also not yet the mark of absolute measure and the embodiment of principle that it will become in modern science.[77] The device has not yet achieved the status of indispensability, ubiquity, or sheer obviousness that characterizes the scientific instrument: the 'Theodolite', 'Circumferantor', 'Glasse', etc. is proposed only as the best alternative among a range of other possible devices, whose claim to accuracy, convenience, and durability its inventor must refute.

The use of diagrams to illustrate problems of spatial relationship forms the basis for an entire mode of pedagogy based on reasoning by similarity of structure or by analogy, by immediate intuition, and by 'doing' and 'making', rather than on deductive logic or the application of theoretical precepts. William Bedwell introduces his translation of Ramus' *Via Regia ad Geometriam* (1636) by emphasizing that the 'end of Geometry will appear much more beautifull and glorious in the use and geometricall workes and practise then by precepts' (pp. 1–2); Leonard Digges concludes his *Tectonicon* with a similar sentiment, wishing 'where my grosse writing seeme to bee obscure, that I were present the Instructer: for truely a lively voyce of a meane speculator somewhat practised, furthereth tenne fold more in my judgement, than the finest writer' (26ᵛ, G4ᵛ). 'Demonstration' in the classical Euclidean sense as a procedure of geometrical proof cedes to a looser meaning in which 'demonstration' describes the mimetic re-enactment of actual measuring procedures by the reader. Ralph Agas claims to have refrained from publishing a full-size treatise because his 'clients' 'shall the better understand and carrie, what hereafter may be written' once they have been 'first trained and taught therein by briefe, apt and lively demonstrations' (1596: 1). Richard More promises that he 'will not stand to demonstrate this or any thing else in this booke geometrically,

---

76 On instruments, see esp. G. L'E. Turner (1983, 1991); Johnston (1991); Bennett (1986, 1987, 1991*b*, 2000); Hackmann (1989); Schaffer's (1989) analysis of Newton's experiments with prisms; Latour's (1987) notion of the 'black box': those instruments whose contingency has been eliminated and whose precise workings are accepted without further scrutiny.

77 Cf. G. L'E. Turner (1991: 313); Bennett (1986: 2).

because it is beyond the common capacitie', and instead advises that 'you may perceive the greatnes of this error, *onely by beholding* this figure A. where I have made a square with prickes, in the circle' (1602: 8; my emphasis). Other problems, More asserts, 'are better taught by an example then by a precept', and are accompanied by the requisite figure inserted in a box in the text (p. 21). Still others are 'far sooner wrought then spoken, and [are] better explained by an example, then taught by a rule' (p. 31). The reader will better understand the operations if he reproduces them himself:

But how round Timber is to be measured is taught in the sixt chapter of the second part, and in the ninth chapter of the third part of this booke: which when you have *learned and tryed*, then you will tell your selfe, that in measuring round Timber after the former way, is very erronious and intolerable. (p. 9; my emphasis)

How much this losse is, doth not appeare by this demonstration. But in this figure (if you will take my word) there is lost a sixt part full. But I had rather you would trie the losse your selves, by the rule taught in the fift chapter of the second part of this booke, then to beleeve me in this case. (p. 12)

Chapters 2 and 5 provide even more detailed examples of the same procedure.

These diagrammatic geometrical figures are referred to as 'plats' or 'plots' throughout the manuals, and the use of the term marks their practical focus. Recorde provides the standard English definition:

Platte formes . . . have *both* length and bredth, but yet no depenesse. *And* the boundes *of everie platte forme are lines: as by the examples you maie perceive.* (Aii^v; Fig. 1.2)

The *platte* is the minimal material representation of an ideal geometrical form. The terms 'figure', 'form', and 'shape' Recorde defines as:

that thyng that is inclosed within one bond or manie bondes . . . to speake properlie, a figure is ever made by platte formes, and not of bare lines unclosed, neither yet of prickes. Yet for lighter forme of teaching, it shall not be unsemely to call all such shapes, formes and figures, whiche ye eye maie discerne distinctly. (Aiii^r)

The terminology has been taken from the workshop: the schematic working drawings used by the mason, carpenter, and surveyor are called 'plats' or 'ground-plats' in building contracts as early as the second decade of the sixteenth century.[78] By mid-century the terms 'plat' and 'plot' begin to overlap with one another in meaning: in general, the Elizabethans speak of 'plats', while Jacobeans refer to 'plots'.[79] By the later sixteenth century this technical meaning is extended to

---

[78] Salzman (1952: 5, 15–22) cites several examples from 1513, *c.*1522, and 1539, and cites William Horman's Latin–English phrase book *Vulgaria* (1519: 18). In 1586 similar technical drawings are referred to as 'plottes' in a Sussex contract (Salzman 1952: 15). Orrell (1988: 58–9) cites several other documents from the late 16th and early 17th century (1588, 1613, 1618); the works of both Merriman (1983) and Schofield (1987) provide many additional uses.

[79] See Robinson (1972: 122–8); Hutson (1993, esp. 86–7; 1994: 91–114, esp. 105–11); Sherman (1995: 152–70, esp. 152–3); H. S. Turner (2002*b*).

designate any spatial system for classifying or arranging a body of knowledge, even if this system is a mental one and not literally graphic. Recorde, for instance, also uses 'platte' in the dedicatory letter to his reader to describe the organization of his treatise as a whole (¶ii˅), where the term designates Recorde's attempt to arrange the rules of geometry in an orderly fashion. Approximately twenty-five years later, in 1570, Dee will repeat this use of 'platte' in his 'Preface', to which he attaches a chart, now termed a 'groundplat', that outlines the hierarchical division of the mathematical sciences (Fig. 2.1).

Throughout the manuals, these 'plats', or iconic diagrams, are often accompanied not with integers or units of measurement but with letters, which are keyed to the textual exposition; in each case, the illustrations form what Luce Giard has called a 'vocabulary of images as signs', in which 'a series of visual prompts . . . participate in the construction of meaning'. Like a rhetorical device, the diagrams display:

a grammar of rules concerning their use, a system of scales governing the relationship between a body in space and its representation on the printed page. The language of graphics and representation was thus legitimized as a language of knowledge, alongside the language of words. . . . The eye learns to move between two systems of signs; images are now an integral part of a knowledge which language alone can no longer contain.[80]

The diagrams guide the reader through a step-by-step series of operations or provide several alternative methods for reaching a single conclusion; like the tables, they are occasionally used to demonstrate how exact quantitative measurements are unnecessary. In these cases, the diagrams illustrate problems in an approximate way, one that is suitable for those readers who are presumed to have no formal geometrical understanding. Hopton's *Topographicall Glasse*, for instance, addresses the reader directly as though he or she is standing in a field, and the field itself is already imagined to be like a two-dimensional geometrical figure. Hopton illustrates several paradigmatic situations—an island surrounded by water or marsh (chapter 8), and thus inaccessible; woodland (chapter 10); reducing irregular lands to regular forms (chapter 31), and many other kinds of land—although he generalizes his examples to a greater extent than previous surveying treatises. In several cases, the same diagram is used repeatedly to illustrate separate problems, and many of the problems do not involve actual quantities but rather letters and proportions (Fig. 2.2).

By converting actual measurements into abstract proportions, manuals such as Hopton's present a series of idealized forms whose structural relationships are meant to stand as general *models* for any possible empirical situation that might arise. Hopton coordinates each diagram with a different instrument, such that

---

[80] Giard (1991: 29–31); see also Crombie (1996*b*: 320); Robinson (1972: 75–87); Conley (1992).

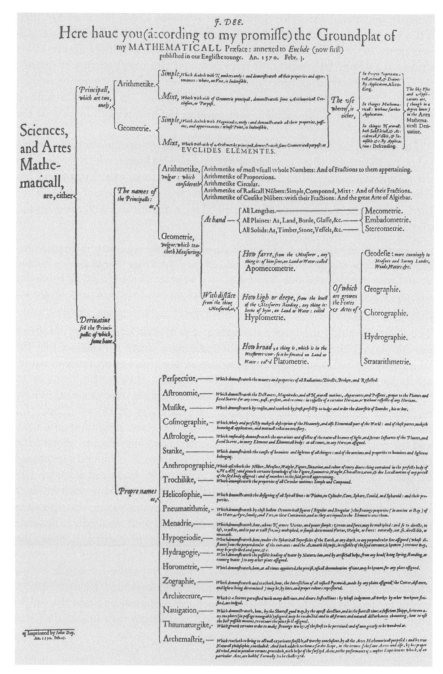

FIG. 2.1. 'Groundplat' of the mathematical sciences: John Dee, 'The Mathematical Preface' to Henry Bilingsley's English translation of Euclid's *Elements* (1570)

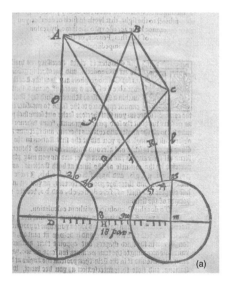

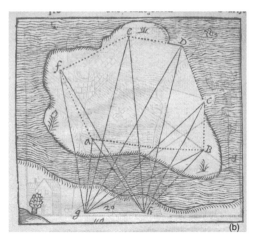

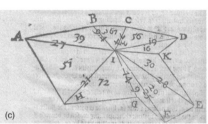

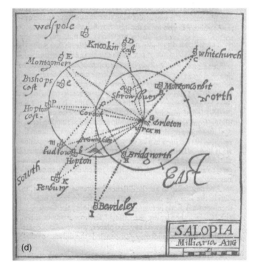

Fig. 2.2. Letters, proportions, models: Arthur Hopton, *Speculum Topographicum; or, The Topographicall Glasse* (1611)

every problem may be solved in a variety of ways: a field may be 'platted' from one position, from two, by measuring the circumference, or by measuring angles. In some cases the reader may 'see' the entire field, in others only parts of it. The same method is followed by Aaron Rathborne in his more elaborate *The Surveyor in Four Books* (1616). Agas's pamphlet uses 'module' twice as a verb, noting how difficult it is for the unskilled surveyor 'to module, & imbosse their books, after the nature of the ground' (1596: 7) and promising in the future to provide instruction not simply in surveying and mapping but for 'moduling' building plans (p. 14).

Both A. C. Crombie and Hélène Vérin have identified the use of models, whether actual material objects built to scale, two-dimensional diagrams, or mental constructs, as a crucial aspect of early modern technology and pre-scientific thought.[81] As model, the diagram displays a set of rules that are presumed to encompass a wide variety of particular objects or occasions, and it transposes these rules into an operational form that can be held and manipulated, allowing the practitioner to move between knowledge that is already possessed and knowledge that has not yet been discovered. It provides a semi-permanent surface (a paper image) or a three-dimensional construction (a model in the more usual architectural sense) that may be modified and adapted as necessary, making possible a revision of the operative protocols that drive the project. Finally, the model legitimizes these protocols by allowing them to be shared with or reproduced by others, such that a given set of assumptions and methods gradually becomes conventional. As Vérin describes the modelling procedure in her study of Renaissance engineering:

In those situations where the project demands recourse to complex mechanical devices (*dispositifs mécaniques*), it becomes necessary to appeal to the engineer. In fact, it is necessary to think ahead, to 'project' ('*porpenser*'), to conceptualize the task, to evaluate it in advance, to anticipate through calculations. *Ingenium*, 'esprit' as the French say, this sagacity that facilitates the discovery of appropriate choices, becomes a factor that is indispensable to success. These choices must be adequate to the situation *created by the project*, which means that they depend on those which have not yet been made, that they derive from those which have already been set in motion, that they may be re-evaluated in the process of elaborating a solution, or even in the course of implementation.[82]

As both Crombie and Vérin have argued, the fundamental mode of reasoning used in modelling is analogical: it seeks to establish a generality on the basis of a similarity in quality, form, structure, movement, or cause that is recognized in any two or more objects. For early-modern students, the most enduring example of this mode of analogical reasoning was furnished by geometry, since *analogia* was, as Quintilian pointed out, the Greek term for 'proportion' and was most useful in 'the testing of all subjects of doubt by the application of some standard of comparison about which there is no question'.[83] Analogy is only effective as a technique

---

[81] See Crombie (1996*b*, esp. 301–2; also 1996*a*, esp. 102–6; and 1994 (identifying modelling as one of six distinct 'styles' of scientific thought)). Vérin (1993) is less quick than Crombie is to assimilate modelling and analogical thinking to later scientific thought, retaining a practical sense; see esp. pp. 43–8. Cf. Serres (1982) on the notion of 'model' and 'module' in Greek geometry, esp. pp. 85–6.

[82] See Vérin (1993: 43–4, my translation; also 66–7, 106–11).

[83] *Inst. Orat.* I. 5. 3–4. See Lachterman's (1989) discussion of analogy and proportion, pp. 29–49, esp. 45–6; Crombie (1996*b*) cites Kepler: 'we must use the geometrical languages of analogy, for indeed I greatly love analogies, the most trustworthy of my instructors, the confidants of all the

of argumentation, Quintilian cautions, if it is employed with 'critical judgment' (*iudicium*; I. 6. 1–4), since 'we must remember that analogy cannot be universally applied, *as it is often inconsistent with itself*' (I. 6. 12; my emphasis). For this reason analogical reasoning can never be theorized about: 'For analogy was not sent down from heaven at the creation of mankind to frame the rules of language, but was discovered after they began to speak and to note the termination of words used in speech. It is therefore based not on reason but on example, nor is it a law of language, but rather a practice which is observed, being in fact the offspring of usage' (I. 6. 16).

Arguably the model plays its more generative role precisely where the pertinent theoretical principles remain inaccessible or only partially so: while authors like Recorde, Serlio, Hopton, Digges, or even the carpenter Richard More display considerable knowledge of speculative geometrical principles and are seeking to widen their application, they do not presume that this knowledge will be available to their readers. Confronted by a series of objects, the practitioner employs the diagram to move 'horizontally' from particular case to particular case rather than 'up' or 'down' according to the usual processes of deductive argument. At each moment he uses his judgement to evaluate and compare these isolated objects on the basis of their structural similarity to one another and then to accommodate them within a larger system of general rules, which he learns dialectically: in part these rules derive from prior knowledge (and have often been set out in early sections of the book in hand), in part they derive from use and operation. Although geometrical precepts are often *represented*—through rhetorical injunction, through bibliographic format and the sequence of the book—as governing all possible effective practical operations, these latter operations are in fact elaborated in the gaps formed by limitations in mathematical knowledge or by the vagaries of empirical situations, such that they remain rigorously unsystematizable and finally exceed or transform the very precepts that are putatively one of their fundamental enabling conditions.

The distinct method that the practitioner is expected to follow appears in the organization of the manuals themselves. Recorde divides his treatise into three major parts: basic geometrical definitions; followed by 'the practike workinge of sondry conclusions Geometrical', which teaches the reader how to 'make' simple constructions (the term is Recorde's); and finally an entire second book devoted to geometrical theorems. Here Recorde apologizes for omitting rigorously deductive proofs in favour only of brief verbal discussions of the theorems accompanied by diagrammatic illustrations. The work thus provides two distinct methods of

secrets of nature: especially to be esteemed in geometry' (p. 332). See also Arber (1946); Clucas (1999) on Dee and Billingsley's Euclid and on Harriot, esp. pp. 150–1, 155–6, 161–3, 166, 171. For Aristotle, all inductive reasoning was fundamentally analogical; see Perez-Ramos (1988: 204 and n. 8, 218–19; 260–3 and 267–9 (on Bacon's use of analogy); and 185 (on Locke)); Jardine (1974*a*: 159–68).

geometrical instruction: learning by definition, axioms, and the immediate visual perception of images, but also learning by exercise, or by making and doing those figures on the page in a material fashion. Hopton's *Topographicall Glasse* follows a similar organization to that of Recorde, as does Robert Peake's 1611 English edition of Sebastiano Serlio's *Tutte l'opere d'architettura et prospettiva* (1584), which promises to avoid theoretical explanations in favour of simple text and images (B1ʳ). The second book warns that even geometrical diagrams may be insufficient, since 'it is very difficult and troublesome to set downe in writing . . . the body, or modell of things, which are drawn out of the ground' (II, A1ᵛ). 'Friendly Reader,' he continues, 'you must not be weary to bee long in learning this Figure, or in *making* it often times; untill you can doe it perfectly and understand it well' (II, C1ʳ; my emphasis). In all the manuals the geometrical diagrams become a fulcrum between practical operation and theoretical knowledge: they supplement the verbal exposition of a particular problem by guiding, in outline, the actual physical gesture—'mechanicall and bodily exercises', to quote Norwood's *Sea-Man's Practice* (B2ʳ)—that will produce its solution. Paradoxically, this gesture reveals the larger rules that govern its action but that remain immanent until the gesture has been completed: it is only through the act of physical mimesis that the speculative principles will have become understandable and the workman will have come to a self-conscious and retrospective understanding of what he has been doing habitually all along.

Practical geometry thus requires the ceaseless iteration of figures, lines, and units, and in this way it is not simply deliberative, calculative, mimetic, or poietic, in their primary etymological senses: it is a *performative* mode of knowledge. 'Perform' is in fact the term used in the treatises to denote the procedures of the geometrician: Recorde uses it only once, in his seventh conclusion ('And so have you performed th'intent of this conclusion'; C4ᵛ), but by the early seventeenth century it is commonplace.[84] Rathborne uses the term repeatedly to designate a series of alternative techniques (1616, Book II, part 1, problems 3, 6, 20, 23, 24); John Norden's *Surveiors Dialogue* uses it to describe the operation of the instrument by the surveyor in the field (pp. 129, 131); and Richard More uses it to designate the solution to problems of timber measurement (1602: 18, 24). Hopton employs the term to refer to the very operation of the 'excellent Geometritian' who must 'performe' a 'peece of work' through 'the very habit, and perfection of the Arte' (1611: A4ʳ); Ralph Agas's *Preparative to the Platting of Lands* uses the term in a similar way to describe the act of 'platting', or reducing to two dimensions, itself: 'with sundry necessarie points in perspective, for setting out of your plats besides Arethmeticke, and Geometrie for the performance of the premisses' (p. 14).

---

[84] See Crane's (2002) survey of terminology during the period, esp. pp. 172–9, pointing out that the term 'perform' encompassed a broad sense of 'doing' and 'making'; theatrical performance was itself designated by terms like 'play', 'use', or 'exercise' (the latter two also commonplace terms in the practical manuals).

THE PROFIT AND PLEASURE OF
GEOMETRY

Having set out the epistemological similarities between prudence, rhetoric, dialectic, and practical geometry, we may turn to one final aspect that links all four kinds of knowledge: the technical manuals all make the somewhat surprising claim that geometrical operations should be delightful in and of themselves, as well as useful, productive, or 'profitable'. In short, they describe a knowledge of pleasure as well as of 'commoditie': John Dee suggests that the 'Common Artificer' may consult geometry not simply 'for sundry purposes in the Common Wealth' but also 'for private pleasure' (1570: Aiiii^r) and Blundeville, Recorde, Serlio, More, Norwood, Digges, Agas, and Rathborne all use the term in similar ways. Here we rejoin the most salient aspect of Renaissance poetics— the Horatian precept that art must both profit and delight—and thus also a mode of geometrical knowledge that appeals to a new class of reader: the humanist gentleman and statesman, for whom practical geometrical knowledge had more to do with personal conduct, property management, civic duty, and codes of male friendship than with productive manual labour. For while the conventional Ciceronian and Horatian notions of 'pleasure and utility' or 'delight and profit' had become so generalized as to apply to almost any topic, in the technical manuals this same language has a direct connection with economic practices that were central to the growing capitalization of the English countryside.[85] At the same time, practical mathematical knowledge was itself becoming a source of cultural capital and offered a way of preserving power or gaining access to it. Practitioners may have come from many backgrounds, from the most humble to the propertied and privileged, but each sought to advance his position through an expertise in applied mathematics. As Stephen Johnston has argued, Thomas Bedwell attempted to create a distinct professional identity by positioning himself as a social and intellectual intermediary between masons, carpenters, statesmen, and gentlemen; on some occasions—notably during state-sponsored engineering projects such as the fortification of Dover Harbour in 1582–3—he seems to have functioned as a general manager or coordinator of skilled craftsmen.[86] On at least one occasion, we shall see, Philip Sidney was invited to play a similar role.

---

[85] The literature on the relations between the agrarian roots of English capitalism, surveying, and early-modern English writing is growing by the day; see H. S. Turner (2002*b*) for bibliography and many of the works cited in previous notes. The surveying of tenements in the city has not yet received the same attention, although the work of Schofield on Ralph Treswell (1987) and on London houses (1994) has done much to prepare the way; see Orlin's (2000*b*) recent study of Treswell and the article by Schofield (2000) in the same collection; I consider Treswell's urban surveys briefly in Ch. 6, below. Agas's *Preparative* (1596) advertises his skill in urban and not only rural surveying.

[86] See Johnston (1991: 321–2, 325–6, 327, 340–1), arguing that the more widespread interest in the mechanical arts did not necessarily translate into any change in status for the workman; Biagioli (1989), arguing that men engaged in the same activities with knowledge of the same

But the greatest opportunities were to be found in London: the diverse population in the city, both 'foreign' and 'stranger', the close proximity of the court and thus of patronage channels, the concentration of the craft guilds, all meant that London was more congenial to the mathematical practitioner than Oxford or Cambridge. The foundation of Gresham College in 1597 by Sir Thomas Gresham, the London merchant, was instituted explicitly as an alternative to the two universities, with the express purpose of making practical mathematical knowledge available to a population of urban merchants, tradesmen, seamen, and gentlemen. The college was surrounded by an elaborate network of lecturers, private tutors, booksellers, instrument-makers, and courtiers, all of whom made London a centre for applied mathematical activity.[87] Having been thwarted by the London College of Physicians in his attempts to pursue a career in medicine, Thomas Hood, the son of a London merchant tailor, turned to chart-making, selling instruments, and publishing manuals to make a living. With the support of Sir Thomas Smith, Hood delivered public lectures on mathematics, geography, and navigation at the Stapler's Chapel, Leadenhall. 'When I call to mind the great commoditie,' Hood began, in terms that both Recorde and Dee had inaugurated, 'that wil henceforth arise unto our Realm in that day there is a *platforme laied* for the better increace of the Mathematical science . . . I triumph indeed and leape for joy'. Of all those gathered he repeatedly commends the 'Citizens of London' in particular, 'careful of the Citie' during the recent Armada crisis, which had left many more convinced than ever of the need for public instruction in mathematics and its application to problems of navigation.[88]

traditions nevertheless perceived status differences depending on the *site* of their activity and their social contacts. Norman was a sailor, Bourne a port official and innkeeper, Agas a rector and estate agent for an absentee farmer, and Leonard Digges a landed gentleman from Kent; see Bendall (1992: 77–138) and the brief biographical notes in E. G. R. Taylor (1954); P. Eden (1983). Agas sought to defend the 'certaine, perfect, and true' profession of surveying from the 'plumber' or 'painter', who 'are termed Surveighors, if they but once shewe forth a plaine table', even as he was left to argue for his own expertise largely on the basis of experience in the field and not from theoretical knowledge; see Agas (1596: 7–8 (7 paginated incorrectly as 11)); cf. Bennett (1991*b*, esp. 345–8). Like Agas, Norden's surveyor distinguishes himself from 'mechanical men and country fellows' (Norden 1618: 15) who are illiterate and innumerate.

[87] Henry Billingsley, Euclid's English translator, was an alderman and later Lord Mayor of London; John Dee was closely associated with the merchant companies of the city and advised the Muscovy Company in matters of navigation, as did many other practitioners; see Sherman (1995); Yates (1964, esp. 1–41); E. G. R. Taylor (1930: 75–139). On London as a mathematical center, see Harkness (2002); P. French (1972: 171–2); Cormack (1997: 203–23); Simon (1966: 385–92); on Gresham College, see Ward (1740); Feingold (1984: 166–89), an account that attempts to identify a prototype for the modern scientific community, emphasizing theoretical rather than practical questions; Ames-Lewis (1999); Hill (1965: 33–5); Cormack (1997: 203–7); F. R. Johnson (1937: 196–205, 263–7; 1940; 1942).

[88] Hood (1590*a*), in F. R. Johnson (1942: 95; my emphasis); see also F. R. Johnson (1937: 196–205), correcting chronology (198 n. 91); Johnston (1991: 300–41); Hill (1965: 18–19, 32, 63–4).

Hood's books were sold at the site of his lectures, along with other practical manuals, and in this way publication also functioned as a direct form of advertisement: the books indicated Hood's London addresses as precisely as possible so that interested readers might seek him out.[89]

As the sixteenth century came to a close, practical books of geometry began to appeal more overtly to the wealthy gentlemen who were becoming frequent consumers of geometrical instruction. These men, sometimes possessed of university degrees but often having left the university after only partially completing the arts course, sometimes studying at the Inns of Court, and sometimes resident in London for a season of plays and society, possessed both the disposable wealth and the leisure to attend public lectures, hire private tutors, or acquire an assortment of globes, instruments, maps, charts, and illustrated books.[90] Often, as William Bourne complained in his *A Regiment for the Sea* (1573), these 'masters' did not understand how to use the instruments they owned.[91] To interest his auditors in astronomy and make it 'pleasurable' as well as 'profitable', Thomas Hood recounted many of the 'poetical fables' associated with the constellations, maintaining that

the Poets in setting forth these fables had this purpose, to make men fall in love with Astronomie: For many times it falleth out so among us, that albeit we are not willling to give eare unto a matter, or to reade a discourse because it is profitable, yet will wee give eare unto it, and take paines to read or heare it, because it is pleasant. . . . They saw that Astronomie being for commoditie singular in the life of man, was almost of all men utterly neglected: Hereupon they beganne to set foorth that art under these fictions, that thereby such as could not be perswaded by the commoditie, might by the pleasure be induced to take a viewe of these matters, and thereby at the length fall in love with them.[92]

The gentlemen of the realm who were attending mathematical lectures, hiring tutors, and purchasing technical books were doing so in part because a knowledge of practical mathematics was becoming a mark of gentlemanly status. A 1572 proposal (never implemented) by Humphrey Gilbert, for an 'Achademy in London for education of her Majesties Wards, and others the youth of nobility and gentlemen', had included instruction in applied mathematics as part of a larger attempt to provide an exclusive environment in which noble and gentle children might be trained to assume their places among the political and cultural

---

[89] E. G. R. Taylor (1954: 330, 179); Johnston (1991: 335 nn. 65 and 66, 337); and F. R. Johnson (1937: 196–205), noting that Hood dedicated his English translation of Ramus' geometry textbook *The Elements of Geometry* (1590) to Sir John Harte, Lord Mayor, and to the Aldermen of the City of London (p. 198 n. 91).

[90] On the cultural capital of maps and instruments, see Morgan (1979); Cosgrove (1988); Helgerson (1983: 114); Bendall (1992: 141–50); Mukerji (1983); Feingold (1984: 191–205).

[91] Cited by E. G. R. Taylor (1930: 158).

[92] Hood (1590*b*: 23ʳ⁻ᵛ), partially cited by S. Johnston (1991: 335 (and 335–7)); cf. Quintilian, *Inst. Orat.* I. 4. 4.

elite. Gilbert stipulated that

there shalbe placed two Mathematicians, And the one of them shall one day reade Arithmetick, and the other day Geometry, which shalbe onely employed to Imbattelinges, fortificacions, and matters of warre, with the practize of Artillery, and use of all manner of Instruments belonging to the same. And shall once every moneth practize Canonrie (shewing the manner of underminings) and tryne his Awditorie to draw in paper, make in modell, and stake owt all kindes of fortifications . . .

The other Mathematician shall reade one day Cosmographie and Astronomy, and the other day tend the practizes thereof, onely to the arte of Navigacion, with the knowledge of necessary starres, making use of Instrumentes apertaining to the same; and also shall have in his Schole a shippe and gallye, made in modell, thoroughly rigged and furnished, to teache unto his Awditory as well the knowledge and use by name of every parte thereof, as also the perfect arte of a Shipwright, and diversity of all sortes of moldes apertaining to the same . . .

Also there shalbe one who shall teache to draw mappes, Sea chartes, &c. and to take by view of eye the platte of any thinge, and shall reade the growndes *and* rules of proportion and necessarie perspective and mensuration belonging to the same.[93]

In addition to mathematics, students were to pursue an exhaustive programme, including grammar, logic, and rhetoric; Greek, Latin, and Hebrew; French, Italian, Spanish, and 'the highe Duche tongue' (either Dutch or German); natural philosophy, political philosophy, and military strategy; civil and common law; divinity; medicine and surgery; horsemanship and the use of hand weapons, music, dancing, vaulting, and heraldry—in short an utterly comprehensive education for the aspiring courtier.

The growing interest in the practical arts among elite readers is made evident by Robert Peake's 1611 English translation of Sebastiano Serlio's *Five Books of Architecture*: a thick folio illustrated profusely with geometrical illustrations and detailed ground plans of classical buildings, the book is in almost every respect the bibliographic opposite of the technical manuals by Hopton, More, Digges, and others.[94] The work is dedicated to Prince Henry, at whose court university-trained mathematicians such as Edward Wright, William Barlow, and Thomas Harriot might encounter instrument-makers, lecturers, and the Privy Counsellors who could implement large engineering projects and offer patronage.[95] But Serlio's work suggests another trajectory for practical geometry: having opened with a book devoted to geometrical definitions, diagrams, and problems of construction, the work closes with a chapter dedicated to how they may be employed in the building of a *theatre*. Practical geometry here founds an entire *technē* of representation: to read and imitate the geometrical diagram is to participate in a performative mode of knowing that functions through ostension and visual

---

[93] Gilbert (1972: 4–5), cited by Shirley (1983: 78–9).
[94] Its black-letter, however, suggests its practical orientation; see Field (1999: 199).
[95] See Cormack (1997: 207–23), on Henry's court.

demonstration.[96] As the terms 'plot' and 'plat' move out of the workshop or meadow and into the playhouse, we shall see how poets and dramatists adapted a practical knowledge of geometrical form to the realm of aesthetic form, using the methods, habits of thought, and even the economic formations of these technical fields to produce a device—a *theatron*, or 'beholding place', as George Puttenham would put it—that produces utility, profit, and 'pleasure' of many different kinds.

[96] See Serres (1982, esp. 93).

3

Sir Philip Sidney and the
Practical Imagination

When the question of the construction of a port at Ostia came up for discussion, had not the orator to state his views? And yet it was a subject requiring the technical knowledge of the architect . . . Will he not deal with measurements and figures? And yet we must admit that they form part of mathematics. For my part I hold that practically all subjects are under certain circumstances liable to come up for treatment by the orator.

(Quintilian, *Institutio Oratoria* II. 21. 18–20)

For to what purpose should our thoughts be directed to various kinds of knowledge, unless room be afforded for putting it into practice, so that public advantage may be the result, which in a corrupt age we cannot hope for?

(Philip Sidney to Hubert Languet, 1 July 1578)

The relative scarcity of literary criticism in sixteenth- and early seventeenth-century England is remarkable when compared to the many Continental writings of the same period devoted to an analysis of the poetic arts. Before the publication of John Dryden's *Of Dramatick Poesie: An Essay* in 1668, the English critical landscape had been fragmented, occasional, and defensive: attempts by Spenser, Harvey, and others to establish the importance of vernacular English as a poetic language; rejoinders between Campion and Daniel over the value of rhyme; strident anti-theatrical polemic from Northbrooke, Stubbes, Gosson, and Prynne, among other examples. Discussion of dramatic poesy, in particular, had suffered from the Puritan attacks on the public stage, such that the development of a systematic critical discourse on the drama was hindered by the need to justify the very existence of public theatres and players in the first place. Both Sir Philip Sidney's and Thomas Heywood's famous essays are, of course, 'apologies' or 'defences' of poesy, and as such both primarily address the ethical status of poetics, as was typical of their contemporaries.[1]

---

[1] G. G. Smith (1904, vol. i, pp. xi–xcii); Spingarn (1924); Atkins (1951); Barish (1981: 80–131); Howard (1994: 22–46); Burrow (1999); Scodel (1999).

It has become conventional to regard as synonymous the two titles under which Sidney's essay was eventually published in 1595, but 'the defence of poesie', as the William Ponsonby edition was entitled, promised a somewhat different essay from 'an apologie for poetrie', the book published by Henry Olney in the same year.[2] The reader of the Olney edition opened a polite treatment of a specific kind of writing that she or he may have been inclined to regard as frivolous, perhaps scandalous, or even outright pernicious. 'Poetrie' gestured towards a distinct group of texts and writers that the essay promised to re-evaluate and to excuse. The reader of the Ponsonby edition, in turn, confronted a spirited, even polemical, defence of an entire way of thinking, a process rather than a product: 'poesie' suggested methods, categories, and aims typical of a mode of thought that had somehow been called into question.[3] Where the 'apologie for poetrie' announced a classificatory argument and emphasized the stylistic and generic concerns of the latter half of Sidney's essay, the 'defence of poesie' signalled an argument about epistemology addressed most explicitly in the first half of Sidney's essay and cast it as an intervention in a broader debate about the value of invention, judgement, and the imagination in generating knowledge about the world.

It would be difficult to say which essay was more important to the constitution of the 'literary' field in sixteenth-century England: the canonizing, institutionalizing essay or the essay that provides a forceful statement of the method and ends of poetic discourse. Finally, of course, the two remain inseparable, and modern editions have made the choice unnecessary in any case. Sidney defines 'poetrie' by invoking classical precedents, singling out English writers, both medieval and contemporary, and by comparing poetry with other kinds of writing that the educated gentleman or gentlewoman consumed, especially history and philosophy. But the larger purpose of his essay, I suggest, is to promote a clearer understanding of 'poesie' as a distinct intellectual method, and one that Sidney defends in two primary ways, albeit playfully and sometimes at the risk of contradiction.

In the first place, his essay defends poesy as a specifically *linguistic* epistemology and does so, I will argue, as a response to the contemporary emphasis on dialectic and rhetoric as intellectual instruments in the production of knowledge that was typical of the university curriculum when Sidney was himself a student at Oxford and when he composed the *Defence* in approximately 1579–80. Secondly, his essay attempts to defend mimesis, or 'imitation', as the primary method used by poesy as an epistemology, and so the essay defends poesy as a mode of knowing through *formal representation*—what Gabriel Harvey will call an 'iconic' mode of representation, as we shall see—in a way that dialectic or rhetoric were not. Because of this emphasis on iconic representation, I propose, poesy achieves a

[2] Sidney (1922–6, vol. iii, pp. v–vi); for dating, see Sidney (1973: 59–63, 65–70) (all citations are from this edition); Woudhuysen (1996: 232–5).

[3] Shepherd in Sidney (1965: 152 n. 18) observes a similar distinction, as do Duncan-Jones and van Dorsten (Sidney 1973: 189 n. 77. 21); Heninger (1989: 514–15 n. 5) disagrees, but notes a similar usage in Jonson.

proto-'scientific' quality for Sidney: in his essay we may observe a shift from the neo-scholastic understanding of *scientia* as certain knowledge of metaphysical causes to an empirical meaning that anticipates several modern scientific presuppositions. Poesy has an analytic value rather than merely a prescriptive, moral one: it assists in the understanding of human action—its motivations, means, ends, and general models or patterns—and in this way Sidney positions poesy as an extension of ethical philosophy and even of what we would today call political science.

My primary purpose in what follows is to show how Sidney derives key arguments about the nature of poetic invention and the poetic image from methods of reasoning that were typical of 'practical knowledge' and the spatial arts, as I have described them in Chapter 2. As I have argued, this tradition was Aristotelian in important ways, and so my discussion begins by reassessing what way English literary theory, and Sidney specifically, may be called 'Aristotelian'—for Sidney is Aristotelian in a *literary* way only in a limited sense, and it is necessary to establish clearly how familiar he and his contemporaries were with key Aristotelian texts and thus also with the fundamental epistemological categories to be found there. The chapter thus opens my examination into how practical knowledge directly informed English ideas about poetic form, poetic representation, and poetic purpose; the relationship of practical knowledge and the spatial arts to actual habits of poetic composition, and particularly to working techniques of *theatrical* composition and production, is taken up in the chapters that follow.

SIDNEY AND ENGLISH 'ARISTOTELIANISM'

The genuineness of Sidney's *respect* for Aristotle's *Poetics* is not in question (cf. 88. 8–9, 109. 16–17): the doubt lies in how extensively he actually knew the work, by what means, and how immediately it influenced his analysis of the means and ends of the poetic image. He invokes Aristotle as a specifically literary authority seven times during the course of his essay in ways that suggest an awareness of several sections of the *Poetics*, notably those concerning imitation (79. 35–80. 2 and 92. 24–7), the relationship between poetry and history as one of the universal to the particular (87. 34–88. 9), the ideal length of tragedies and their mode of presenting a story (113. 9–12, 114. 1–6), and the purpose of laughter in comedy (116. 2–9). He points out the derivation of 'poet' from the Greek *poiēin*, or 'maker' (77. 31–8), and he organizes a central aspect of his analysis around the concept of mimesis that he seems to take directly from the *Poetics*: 'Poesie therefore is an arte of imitation, for so *Aristotle* termeth it in his word *Mimesis*, that is to say, a representing, counterfetting, or figuring foorth: to speake metaphorically, a speaking picture: with this end, to teach and delight' (79. 35–80. 2). But the definition is 'Aristotelian' only in the broadest sense and is equally Ciceronian, Horatian, and Neoplatonic; as such it reflects the more immediate influence of Continental critics such as Scaliger and Minturno, whose own discussions of poetics had been formatively shaped by these traditions and from whom Sidney has in fact taken most of his discussion in these passages.[4]

Even these limited references, however, whatever their immediate source, would distinguish Sidney as exceptional in an English literary culture where the *Poetics* was even less influential than it was elsewhere in Europe. Marvin Herrick names him along with Sir John Cheke, Roger Ascham, and, somewhat surprisingly, Thomas Blundeville as the only sixteenth-century English writers possibly acquainted with the *Poetics* directly, although in each case the evidence finally remains inconclusive.[5] As Herrick, Bernard Weinberg, and Joseph Spingarn have established, rhetorically inflected readings of Horace's *Ars Poetica* continued to dominate critical investigation into the purpose and formal requirements of the poet's art even after the first major commentaries on the *Poetics* began to appear in the mid-sixteenth century. Despite the fact that Aristotle's work provided the terms for an internal, *structural* analysis of dramatic form that was quite distinct from the external and ethical relation between work and audience privileged by the Horatian tradition—addressing the proper arrangement of episodes, distinguishing constituent parts, both qualitative (plot, character, diction, thought,

---

[4] Cf. Shepherd's excellent notes to his edition (Sidney 1965); Smith (1904: i. 158. 5–9; esp. i. 386). Among others, Heninger (1974, esp. 291–4, 301–2, 322 n. 42, 315; 1988) argues that Sidney's notion of mimesis and *poiēsis* is Platonic rather than Aristotelian and describes the mimesis passage as 'screamingly eclectic' (1974: 301), although Heninger (1989, esp. 238–54, 286–306) emphasizes the Aristotelian aspects, as does K. Eden (1986). Hardison (1988) follows Myrick (1935) and argues that the rhetorical organization of Sidney's *Defence* situates it as part of a 'pre-Aristotelian phase of Renaissance criticism', noting its similarity to Barnadino Daniello's *Poetics* (1536) (p. 46); like Heninger, Hardison regards Sidney's notion of *poiēsis* as Neoplatonic rather than Aristotelian (p. 50); nor does Sidney follow Castelvetro in his discussion of comedy and tragedy, Hardison argues, but Donatus and perhaps William Baldwin's introduction to the *Mirror for Magistrates* (1559) (p. 52); see also p. 57, however, where Hardison recognizes the debt to Castelvetro in Sidney's discussion of place and time. Atkins (1951: 116–38) provides a clear discussion of the Platonic and Aristotelian elements in Sidney's work and maintains that Sidney 'was well acquainted' with Continental theory (p. 127); Weiner (1978: 34–50) stresses the distinctly Protestant (especially Calvinist) aspects to Sidney's arguments; Trimpi (1999), the Ciceronian and Senecan elements and the possible influence of Proclus.

[5] Herrick (1930: 8–34, esp. 24–9). Cheke's *De Pronuntiatione Graecae* (1555) includes what is thought to be the first reference to Aristotle's *Poetics* in English, but little discussion of the work; Herrick (1925: 134–5; 1926: 250); Atkins (1951: 86–91). In *The Scholemaster* (1570) Ascham mentions how he, Thomas Watson, and Sir John Cheke 'had many pleasant talkes togither, in comparing the preceptes of Aristotle and Horace *de Arte Poetica* with the examples of *Euripides*, *Sophocles* and *Seneca*' (Smith 1904: i. 23–4), but the few structural terms that follow (*Protasis*, *Epitasis*) derive from Donatus and Terence rather than from the *Poetics*, and in other passages it is Aristotle's *Topics* that Ascham singles out for praise, in very similar terms; see esp. Ascham (1570: i. 20. 29–21. 14). Ascham's notion of 'imitation' (as I discuss below) differs significantly from Aristotle's notion of mimesis in the *Poetics*; in defining the term he cites neither Aristotle nor Horace but rather the third book of Plato's *Republic* and later mentions Aristotle only in passing (Ascham 1570: i. 13. 7). Blundeville's claim rests on *The true order and Methode or wryting and reading Hystories* (1574), but here, too, there is little that is specifically Aristotelian and the work is not original to Blundeville (see Ch. 2 n. 44, above). Finally, Harvey notes in his copy of Gascoigne's *Certayne Notes of Instruction* (1575) that Gascoigne 'doth prettily well: but might easely have dun much better, both in the one, & in the other: especially by the direction of Horaces, & Aristotle's Ars Poetica' (Harvey 1913: 168); nevertheless, Herrick (1930: 20–2) doubts that Harvey actually knew the *Poetics*, since it never appears in his other works or annotations.

spectacle, and melody) and quantitative (prologue, episode, exode, choral song, but also the more vague 'beginning', 'middle', and 'ending')—critics used Aristotle's work to continue lines of inquiry that their reading of Horace and the Roman rhetoricians had already established, emphasizing questions of etymology, *decorum*, generic prescription, the grammatical or stylistic qualities of poetry, and its didactic ends.[6] Ben Jonson exemplifies the critical tendency: he translated the *Ars Poetica* not once but twice, after his first effort burned in a fire, and, as I shall show in Chapter 8, his turn to Aristotelian categories came late in his career, remained at second hand, and never fully displaced the Roman literary and rhetorical tradition with which he was more immediately familiar. It is worth pointing out that the first Latin translation of the *Poetics* to be printed in England appeared only in 1623, relatively late by Continental standards, while the first *English* translation did not appear until 1705—nearly forty years after Dryden's *Essay*, as surprising as this may seem.[7]

Cambridge University and college library records, furthermore, confirm the strongly ethical orientation of English Aristotelianism more generally, as I have observed in Chapter 2: here we find approximately four times as many copies of the *Nicomachean Ethics* and *Rhetoric* as we do of the *Poetics* and nearly twice as many of the *Politics*, including commentaries, epitomes, and manuals of various kinds.[8] Evidence from probate inventories for private book-ownership during

---

[6] Weinberg (1963, esp. i. 71–2, 349–52); Spingarn (1924); Herrick (1930, 1946); Atkins (1951); B. R. Smith (1988, esp. 12–58). A brief comparison with Henry Dethick's *Oratio in Laudem Artis Poeticae* is instructive, since it was composed as part of a disputation exercise during the period 1569–72 at Corpus Christi, Oxford, almost exactly the years when Sidney was an undergraduate at Christ Church (1568–71). The work provides an excellent sense of the range of authorities that an advanced student was expected to know, and yet, as William Ringler has emphasized, 'not a single statement in the *Praise of Poetry* can be traced directly to [Aristotle's *Poetics*] or to any other work of Aristotle. Even the one vague reference that might be to the *Poetics* is so overlaid with Renaissance accretions that it obviously comes from some intermediate source' (Dethick *c.*1572: 17); see also pp. 69–70 and 16–17, esp. n. 33, on other sources, and p. 19: 'The Italian critics, whose influence some scholars have so greatly magnified, are conspicuously absent. The works of the ancients, such as Aristotle's *Poetics*...are ignored.' Ringler mistakenly attributed the *Oratio* to John Rainolds; see Dethick (*c.*1572) and Binns (1975).

[7] Herrick (1926: 247) observes that although Erasmus had included the *Poetics* and the *Rhetoric* in his Greek edition of Aristotle's works (Basle, 1531) he never took systematic account of either text; cf. Atkins (1951, esp. 50–1, 66, 216–18, 222–3, 239), who quotes Vives: 'the *Poetics* contained little good fruit, being occupied entirely with the consideration of old poems and with those niceties in which the Greeks are so tiresome...and inept' (p. 50).

[8] The number of possible editions to include the *Poetics* is quite few, the number of *definite* editions fewer still; see the evidence for Cambridge University and individual college libraries compiled by H. J. Adams (1967, nos. 1730–50 (various *Opera* editions); 595, 1463, 1775–6, 1901–8, 1909, and 1951 (individual editions and translations)). We find only eight separate editions of the *Poetics* either alone or with other rhetorical works, including scattered copies of the translations and commentaries by Francesco Robortello (1548), Bernardo Segni (1549), and Ludovico Castelvetro (1570). Antonio Minturno's *De Poeta libri sex* (1559) appears only twice; Scaliger's *Poetices libri septem*, however, appears fourteen times, in three editions (1561, 1581, 1586), and Scaliger is by far the most closely studied source behind Sidney's own essay, despite his own occasional departures from Scaliger's arguments. The Bodleian *Catalogue* published in 1605 lists at least one possible *Opera* edition (and possibly incomplete; that of Casaubon (*Opera*, Lyon, 1590) is too late for Sidney), an

the period show a similar pattern: here, too, the *Nicomachean Ethics* was by far the most commonly owned work of Aristotle, and it is remarkable that here, in contrast to the institutional records, no separate editions of the *Poetics*, either alone or with the rhetorical writings, appear at all, nor do any of the commentaries and treatises of Robortello, Scaliger, Minturno, or Castelvetro.[9] Anyone seeking to follow the trail of the *Poetics* into private libraries, and from there into English literary culture more broadly, is bound to conclude that it quickly runs cold.

In contrast, Sidney is known to have translated two books of Aristotle's *Rhetoric*, although they no longer survive;[10] his correspondence to Hubert Languet cites the work in some detail,[11] and another letter to Languet written from Padua affirms his interest in such a project, although this time in reference to Aristotle's *Politics*:

> As for Greek, I should wish to absorb only enough to understand Aristotle well; for although several translations appear every day, I still suspect that they do not express the author's ideas distinctly and exactly enough; and besides, I am utterly ashamed to be following the stream, as Cicero says, and not go to the fountain head. Of Aristotle's works, I think that one must read his *Politics* in particular . . .[12]

A letter to his brother Robert, meanwhile, opens by praising 'Aristotle's Ethicks . . . you knowe it is the begyning, and foundacion of all his workes, the

'opuscula Italicè 1549' (likely to be Segni's Italian translation), and 'Averr. In Poeticam Arist. Ven. 1515' (probably the *Rhetorica Aristotelis* with Colonna's commentary and the *Poetics* in Valla's translation, with Averroes's commentary). The *editio princeps* of Aristotle's complete works in Greek by Aldus (Venice, 1495–8, 5 vols; *Gesamtkatalog*, no. 2334) included neither the rhetorical writings nor the *Poetics*, nor are they included in any of the Latin *Opera* editions to be published during the 15th century (*Gesamtkatalog*, nos. 2335–42); for further information, see Weinberg (1963: i. 349–423, esp. 352–67).

[9] See Leedham-Greene (1986). As of 1579, editions of the *Rhetoric* might include Antonio Riccobono's translation of the *Rhetoric* and the *Poetics* published by Paul Meiettus at Venice, relevant to four of the Cambridge inventories collected and edited by Fehrenbach and Leedham-Green (1992–8): Roberts (1579/80), Collet (1588), Perne (1589), and Tillman (1589/90). Since the inventories do not indicate exact titles or editions, we will never know how widely owned Riccobono's translation was among English students; if Sidney knew the *Poetics* directly, this seems to me to be the most likely edition. Buxton asserts that although Sidney 'does not refer to the *Poetics* in his letters . . . he knew the book well, and probably heard Zabarella, Professor of Logic at Padua, lecturing on it' (1954: 72) but provides no evidence for the claim; aside from Osborn's (1972) and Stewart's (2000) discussions of this period, Sidney's stay in Padua remains a fascinating but undocumented episode in his intellectual biography.

[10] John Hoskyns comments in his *Directions for Speech and Style* (c.1599) that 'The perfect expressing of all qualities is learned out of Aristotle's ten books of moral philosophy; but because, as Machiavel saith, perfect virtue or perfect vice is not seen in our time, which althougether is humorous and spurting, therefore the understanding of Aristotle's Rhetoric is the directest means of skill to describe, to move, to appease, or to prevent any motion whatsoever; whereunto whosoever can fit his speech shall be truly eloquent. This was my opinion ever; *and Sir Philip Sidney betrayed his knowledge in this book of Aristotle to me before ever I knew that he had translated any part of it. For I found the two first books Englished by him in the hands of the noble studious Henry Wotton*' (p. 41; my emphasis); see Coogan (1981: 255); Buxton (1954: 146); Payne (1990).

[11] Pears (1845: 121); the original letter is printed in Sidney (1922–6: iii. 118); see Feuillerat's comment on p. v, n. 1; Duncan-Jones (1991: 76, 84); Herrick (1926: 256–7).

[12] Sidney to Languet, 4 Feb. 1574, in Sidney (1922–6: iii. 84–5); trans. Osborn (1972: 144).

good ende which everie man doth & ought to bend his greatest actions';[13] a letter to Edward Denny written in May 1580 similarly recommends 'Aristotles Ethickes' first among works of moral philosophy, although Sidney acknowledges that Aristotle is 'somethinge darke and hath need of a Logicall examination' and that Cicero's *De Officiis* should be Denny's 'foundation' next to the 'foundation of foundations ... I meane the holy scripture'.[14]

   As several scholars have recognized, the most clearly Aristotelian passages of the *Defence* are overtly ethical in nature and define the core of Sidney's analysis of both the means and ends of poesy as an epistemology. If poetry is defined, according to familiar Ciceronian and Horatian dicta, as a mode of writing that moves men through its 'Delightful teaching' (81. 37–8, 91. 7–11), then the knowledge and learning that results is valuable only in so far as it accomplishes two final ends, which Sidney presents in both sacred and secular terms. The first is fulfilment of man's postlapsarian spiritual potential ('to lead and draw us to as high a perfection as our degenerate souls, made worse by their clayey lodgings, can be capable of'; 82. 14–16; cf. 82. 25–7), a Christian and Neoplatonic aspect of his argument that occasionally moves at odds to the empirical and Aristotelian orientation of his arguments about the ends of poetic 'making'. This second, Aristotelian end is the achievement of man's political and practical potential in the social world:

all these [fields of knowledge] are but serving sciences, which, as they have each a private end in themselves, so yet are they all directed to the highest end of the mistress-knowledge, by the Greeks called *architectonike*, which stands (as I think) in the knowledge of a man's self, in the ethic and politic consideration, with the end of well-doing and not of well-knowing only—even as the saddler's next end is to make a good saddle, but his further end to serve a nobler faculty, which is horsemanship, so the horseman's to soldiery, and the soldier not only to have the skill, but to perform the practice of a soldier. So that, the ending end of all earthly learning being virtuous action, those skills that most serve to bring forth that have a most just title to be princes over all the rest. (82. 33–83. 9)

and later:

For, as Aristotle saith, it is not *gnosis* but *praxis* must be the fruit. And how *praxis* cannot be, without being moved to practise, it is no hard matter to consider. (91. 13–16)

Here Sidney obviously has books I and VI of the *Nicomachean Ethics* directly in mind, as well as the *Rhetoric* and, more distantly, the *De Anima*, as both Kathy Eden and Victoria Kahn have argued.[15] Indeed, the invocation of the saddler and the art of horsemanship in the first passage I have just quoted returns us to the opening anecdote of his essay regarding Pugliano, which we can now grasp as an extended analogy for the philosophical stakes of Sidney's entire essay—if one

   [13] Sidney (1922–6: iii. 124–7), dated May 1578 by Osborn (1972).
   [14] Sidney to Denny, 22 May 1580, printed in Osborn (1972: 537–40 (537–8)); cf. Elyot (1531: i. 91–2).
   [15] Kahn (1985, esp. 188–90); K. Eden (1986); Doherty (1991); Ferguson (1983: 137–62); Worden (1996: 3–22).

rereads the opening paragraphs of the *Nicomachean Ethics* alongside the opening paragraph from the *Defence*, one sees immediately that Sidney has simply redacted them as an argument about poetics. For if horsemanship is simply one example of a productive art that is similar to the even more important practical art of politics, as Aristotle repeatedly argues throughout the *Nicomachean Ethics*, and Sidney is, playfully but also earnestly, a kind of Pugliano in his avocation of his own 'unelected vocation' (73. 31) as a poet, then poesy is indeed a form of *architektonikē* as Sidney argues. The anecdote not only confirms the fundamentally prudential Aristotelianism that underlies Sidney's *Defence* and thus marks the *Nicomachean Ethics* as his primary point of reference among Aristotle's writings: it also aligns poesy with the mechanical arts, since Sidney indicates by analogy that he understands poesy to be a productive art like saddle-making, shipbuilding, carpentry, or shoemaking, the other examples of productive arts that Aristotle often invokes. This is true not simply in epistemological terms but in terms of social status, which is in part why acting in the 'vocation' of the poet requires a 'defence' from a man in Sidney's position, who in writing poems has found himself masquerading as a kind of artisan, or 'maker'.[16]

Sidney broaches his defence of poetic making in an 'interdisciplinary' fashion by comparing poesy to the other liberal arts that currently configure English intellectual life in its institutional form, as we have seen in Chapter 2: the *quadrivium* and the three philosophies of the Master ('the astronomer... the geometrician and arithmetician... the musician... the natural philosopher... the moral philosopher... the metaphysic'; 78. 5–20) and the *trivium* of the Bachelor ('the grammarian... the rhetorician and logician'; 78. 13–18), with the professions thrown in for good measure ('the lawyer... the physician'; 78. 12, 18). But he will develop this argument into a defence of the different methods of knowing that characterize each of the arts and of the unique mental operations necessary to the act of making the poetic image. 'Poetry'—individual works studied illustratively for grammatical, stylistic, and moral purposes, a 'rhetorical' definition typical of his period—may play an increasingly prominent role in the reformed humanist curriculum, the implicit argument runs, but *poesy*, as a mode of generating knowledge about the natural and social world, deserves further attention. It is a representational way of coming to knowledge: it gives a provisional form to action so that it may be analysed according to available systems of thought and then modified as necessary.

Certainly this view of poesy is compatible with Aristotle's analysis of drama in the *Poetics*. But if we look more closely at the *Defence* and consider it in light of contemporary book inventories, Sidney's own private correspondence, his reading

---

[16] Sidney probably has in mind the work of Federico Grisone, translated by Thomas Blundeville (see Ch. 2 nn. 44 and 45), since he recommends 'Grison' for horsemanship to Robert in his letter of 18 October 1580 and specifically distinguishes between a theoretical and a practical reading of the work (Sidney 1922–6: iii. 133); cited and discussed by Osborn (1972: 81–2); cf. Stewart (2000: 132–3).

habits, and his social contacts, it becomes obvious that he has arrived at his analysis of poesy by way of his formation *first* in the ethical, rhetorical, and dialectical tradition rather than from a foundational immersion in the *Poetics*, a text that he knew less well than he did Aristotle's *Rhetoric* and *Nicomachean Ethics*, Horace, Cicero, Quintilian, Livy, or even contemporaries such as Jean Bodin. His references to the *Poetics* are typical of his 'apologetic' mode of writing, which joins classical authorities to contemporary ones—and in 1580 Aristotle, particularly the Aristotle of the *Poetics*, was both—in an attempt to *define* poesy as well as to defend it, and to do so with as much variety as possible. By employing an etymology and a concept of mimesis that he traces directly to antiquity, and by conspicuously invoking Aristotle as the author of the *Poetics* rather than of works that would have been more familiar to his readers, Sidney is in fact attempting to *legitimize* a much more complex and innovative epistemology derived from the changing attitudes towards nature and the mechanical arts that were increasingly common among his contemporaries. 'Aristotelian' literary discourse—authoritative, international, up to date—was itself a field of inquiry that was still very much in the process of cohesion; for this reason it was an ideal point of insertion for Sidney's more unusual epistemology of poetic invention as 'making' and one that allowed him to reconcile his approach to the poetic image with the dialectical, rhetorical, and prudential categories of thought he had inherited. However much Sidney tries to associate this new 'poietic' epistemology with Aristotle, it is one that he has adapted from other sources—books, people, activities—that are more proximate and contemporary to him, and it is to these sources that I now turn.

POET AS PRACTITIONER

Sometime during a five-month period between October 1576 and February 1577—only a few years before the composition of the *Defence of Poesy* is thought to have taken place—Sidney met with Gabriel Harvey to read a text that Sidney himself valued above all others: Livy's Roman history. Harvey's edition of the book survives, along with extensive annotations from the Sidney reading and at least three later ones; his notes after the session with Sidney emphasize that their focus was 'qualities of actions', and he has turned to Livy in the first place, he writes later, at Sidney's recommendation.[17] Lisa Jardine and Anthony Grafton have shown how Harvey and Sidney used history to reflect upon their own political circumstances and to digest the principles of humanist political thought. A crucial component of their interest, and one that warrants further study, lay in methods of practical reasoning: in the role of judgement, imagination, and memory in

---

[17] See the passages cited by Grafton and Jardine (1990: 36, 55, and 36–7 (for the immediate historical context for the reading)); on Harvey's use of the term 'pragmaticus', see L. Jardine and Sherman (1994, esp. 115–16).

accommodating general principles to particular examples, in the instrumentality of these intellectual faculties, and in the working methods that were typical of the mechanical and spatial arts.

This practical attitude is evident, for instance, in the very collative practice that Harvey and Sidney used when approaching classical texts, as described by Ascham in his famous chapter on 'imitation' in *The Scholemaster*. The student, Ascham recommends, would ideally read Cicero:

> at the same tyme as diligently *Plato* and *Xenophon* with his bookes of Philosophie, *Isocrates* and *Demosthenes* with his orations, and *Aristotle* with his *Rhetoricke*, which five of all other be those whom Tullie best loved and specially followed, and would marke diligently in Tullie where he doth exprimere or effingere (which be the verie proper wordes of Imitation) . . . and not onelie write out the places diligentlie, and lay them together orderlie, but also to conferre them with skilfull judgement by those few rules which I have expressed . . . (1570: 17. 34–18. 11)

The purpose of Ascham's method is to use judgement to match particular examples with general rules, much as he notes that Aristotle has done in his *Topics*: 'right judgement' consists in 'the applying of those examples' that have been collected and which must be organized under 'a certaine fewe fitte preceptes' (17. 16–21), and the purpose of the commonplace book is to organize the particular matter of different authors under these more general categories. The 'tools and instruments' or 'skill and judgment' (8. 6–8) necessary to 'imitation' are distinctly spatial faculties in Ascham's view; the student is to examine 'the shape and forme' of Plato's books (11. 30)—i.e. the dialogue—whose 'Paterne' Cicero has followed in his *De Oratore*, rather than 'invent some newe shape him selfe' (11. 15–16); he is to 'joyne together' the two texts (8. 32) so that he may observe 'This he ordereth thus, with placing that here, not there,' 'This he altereth and changeth, either in propertie of wordes, in forme of sentence, in substance of the matter . . .' (9. 18–21), or the 'use of right forme, figure, and number, proper and fitte for everie matter' (23. 16–17). Those authors who have already written books on 'imitation' 'be no more but common porters, caryers, and bringers of matter and stuff togither', Ascham maintains: 'They order nothing. They lay before you what is done: they do not teach you how it is done. *They busie not them selves with forme of buildying. . . . onely Sturmius is he, out of whom the trew survey and whole workmanship is speciallie to be learned*' (18. 35–20. 20; my emphasis). Ascham consistently describes his reading method by means of craft analogies and an artisanal vocabulary: even 'ignorant Artificers' are more skilled in 'gayning a small commoditie', Ascham complains, than students are in analysing texts (10. 11) and 'the meanest painter useth more witte, better arte, greater diligence, in hys shoppe' than students at the university (10. 12–16).

In some readings, as with Sir Thomas Smith in 1571 or with Sidney several years later, Harvey's annotations focus on individual figures who employ a practical, pragmatic mode of deliberation to give form to their action in a particular context. Hannibal, Scipio, Marcellus, or Fabius Maximus are admirable for the mental acts of judgement, cunning, or wit that they used not merely to respond to particular circumstances but to transform them; both Marcellus and Fabius are 'worthy men, and judicious', Harvey writes during the reading of Livy with Smith focused on strategy and military affairs, 'Marcellus the more powerful; Fabius the more cunning. Neither was the latter unprepared, nor the former imprudent: each as indispensable as the other in his place.'[18] Harvey himself cannot decide whom to emulate more: 'there are times when I would rather be Marcellus, times when Fabius'.[19] For Harvey, Livy offers concrete examples of the kind of intelligence that Machiavelli, too, would consider as an imposition of the will upon the circumstances of fortune or that first Aristotle and later Lorenzo Valla would consider in their discussions of 'wit' and 'cleverness' as modes of practical, deliberative thinking.[20] For Harvey, the importance of Machiavelli was that he mediated between the individual actions of particular historical figures and the philosophical tradition of Aristotelian prudence, as he indicates in another annotation:

There is no specialist in political, or economic, or ethical axioms drawn from histories and poems to match Aristotle in his Politics, Oeconomics, Ethics. But how much greater would he have been had he known histories that were so much greater—especially Roman history? Machiavelli certainly outdid Aristotle in observation of this above all, though he had a weaker foundation in technical rules and philosophical principles. Hence I generally prefer Aristotle's rules, Machiavelli's examples.[21]

In his annotations Harvey imagines a new kind of reader—perhaps himself—who surpasses both Aristotle and Machiavelli by converting the insights gained through textual inquiry into a new set of theoretical precepts:

I want a politician who fixes the adamantine basis on deeper foundations, and illustrates the best precepts with the best examples—and thus outdoes Aristotle himself in weight of principles, Machiavelli in choice of histories...Then to leave nothing unexamined or unexplained in the subtlest school doctors or deepest worldly pragmatics, which could improve or enlarge the principles.[22]

If Harvey's comments sound familiar, it is because they are remarkably similar to Sidney's arguments in the *Defence* concerning the limitations of the philosopher and the historian: we could replace Harvey's 'politician' with the word 'poet' and the passage would describe almost exactly the sentiment that seems to motivate these sections of Sidney's essay.

---

[18] Cited by Grafton and Jardine (1990: 40).   [19] Cited ibid.
[20] Cf. *NE* VI. 9. 1142^{a}30–^{b}15 and 12. 1144^{a}25–30; for Valla, see Kahn (1985: 78), citing his *Dialecticae dispuationes*, where deliberation is called a kind of technical skill or cleverness (*sollertia*); also Ch. 7, below.
[21] Cited by Grafton and Jardine (1990: 61); also p. 55, citing Harvey's comments on Caesar, who surpasses all men, even those 'exceedingly beholden to Machiavel'. Cf. also Curtis (1959: 128 and n. 7; also 126–48); Stern (1979: 41–2, 162–3); and Ch. 7 nn. 20 and 23, below.
[22] Cited by Grafton and Jardine (1990: 62).

But Harvey derived elements of his 'pragmatic' philosophy not simply from classical prudence, Roman history, or the new attention among some English readers to Machiavelli's writings: he developed it, too, from his interest in technical instruments, craft practices, and applied mathematics. As Harvey was surely aware, Cicero counselled that the orator sometimes requires experience in the art of war (*rei militaris usu*) and that, conversely, skill in speech was often useful in many areas, including natural science, mathematics, or architecture and fortification (*De Oratore* I. 14). Quintilian, as we have seen in Chapter 2, explicitly recommended the study of geometry, in both its speculative and practical forms, to the orator, citing Cicero as his authority, and he made frequent allusions to the mechanical, productive arts in order to explain rhetoric as a distinctly practical epistemology. Not only does rhetoric deal with any subject matter, Quintilian argues, but it is definitively an 'art' like building, weaving, or 'moulding vessels from clay' (*Inst. Orat.* II. 17. 1–4); rhetoric, like all arts, is useful and instrumental, 'a power reaching its ends by a definite path' (II. 17. 41–3); the 'speech' is the work (*opus*) of the orator just as the statue is the work of the sculptor, for both speeches and statues 'require art for their production' (II. 21. 1); art originates in nature and is based on 'experiment' (*experimentis*), since 'experience is the best of all schools', as we find in medicine or in the arts of building (II. 17. 9–13). In other passages he compares oratory to navigation (II. 17. 24–5) and to military science (II. 17. 34) and argues that although rhetoric is definitively a practical mode of knowledge, it partakes of the productive arts (II. 18. 1–5).

Harvey himself owned and annotated several works by English practitioners, including Thomas Blundeville, Leonard Digges, John Blagrave, William Bourne, and Thomas Hood; many were personal friends who introduced him to the world of London instrument-makers, which he seems to have known intimately. 'Schollars have the books,' he writes in Blagrave's *Mathematical Jewel* (1585), '& practitioners the Learning' (Harvey 1913: 213), noting the recent publication of Blagrave's *Familiar Staffe* (1590) and observing:

The Instrument itself, made & solde by M. Kunvin, of London, neere Powles. A fine workman, & mie kinde frend: first commended unto me bie M. Digges, & M. Blagrave himself. Meaner artificers much praised bie Cardan, Gauricus, & other, then He, & old Humfrie Cole, mie mathematical mechanicians. As M. Lucar [author of a popular surveying treatise] newly commendes Jon Reynolds, Jon Read, Christopher Paine, Londoners, for making Geometrical Tables, with their feet, frames, rulers, compasses, & squires, M. Blagrave also in his Familiar Staff, commendes Jon Read, for a verie artificiall workman. Mr. Kynuin selleth ye Instrument in brasse.[23]

[23] Harvey (1913: 211–12); on London instrument-makers, see E. G. R. Taylor (1954); Harkness (2002: 147–51). In addition to Blagrave's *Mathematical Jewel*, Harvey owned and annotated Blundeville's *The four chiefest Offices belonging to Horsemanship* (1580), William Bourne's *A Regiment for the Sea* (1592) and his *Treasure for Traveilers* (1578), and Thomas Hood's *The Marriners Guide* (1592), but his marginalia reveal his familiarity with the work of Digges, Recorde, Cunningham, Robert Tanner's *Mirrour for Mathematiques* (1587), Euclid, Tycho Brahe, Ptolemy, Copernicus, and Gemma Frisius; see Harvey (1913: 173, 213); Stern (1979: 159, 165–71); and nn. 26 and 58

'A man is commonly, as his cumpany, and Instruments ar,' Harvey writes in his commonplace book (Harvey 1913: 105); in several annotations he admonishes himself to turn his mathematical reading to advantage in the civil sphere, since mathematics prepares the intellect for the kind of deliberative procedures that are necessary for success at court or in diplomatic affairs:

Above all one ought to be utterly prepared in the Arithmetics of Ramus and Recorde, along with an ever-sharp wit, solid judgement, an invincible and focused mind, a pragmatic skilfulness in all things, a ready and pliable tongue, and an amiable and favourable countenance. This makes a great difference. Always keep it in mind, and always act this way.[24]

In his commonplace book he writes:

In studdy: præsent Meditations, & particular impressions, orderly disposed & digested for ever, only available with effect. In actions, instant occasions ar resolutely, & most industri-ously to be solicited, importuned, & dispatched for lyfe. other raunging and transcending generalityes in abstracto & contemplativo, & in ye Clowdes, nothing but idle & vain speculations. Idle Heddes ar allway in yr transcendentibus, & in nubibus: politique Witts, evermore in concreto activo. omnis theoria puerilis, sine virili praxi.

All A mans Actions woold be Expeditous, to be steepid in quick sylver, or Mercury precipitate, not in cowld water, or heavy booyling leade. A resolute hedd: An active Hand: an Invincible Hart: A plyable Tongue; rather well spoken, & temperid with quick discretion, and reason, then vainely curious with the lest spyce of apparent Affectation . . .[25]

These passages, and others like them, describe a delicate art of personal conduct in which mathematics, mathematical instruments, and even alchemy model how knowledge might be strategically deployed in fleeting moments of opportunity, sometimes in the service of state or public interests but more often as a means to personal advancement, public recognition, and financial reward.[26] In a 1598 letter to Sir Robert Cecil, son of Lord Burghley and his recent successor as the

---

below. A note in his Quintilian includes both Blundeville and Digges among 'the most famous wits of England' (*illustriora Anglorum ingenia*), along with Chaucer, Sidney, and Spenser; see Harvey (1913: 122); Stern (1979: 149; also 143–4 n. 21 (on Blundeville's *Exercises*)).

[24] 'Oportet præterea in Arithmeticis, Rami et Recordi esse promptissimum, cum ingenio semper acuto; iudicio solido; animo præsenti, et inuicto; pragmatica in omnibus dexteritate, lingua expedita, et flexanima; vultu amabili, et gratioso; quantùm interest. Hoc cogita semper, et hoc semper Age' (Harvey's annotation to Joannis Foorth, *Synopsis Politica* (London, 1582); cited in Harvey 1913: 189).

[25] Both cited in Harvey (1913: 199, 87), the first from Harvey's 'Commonplace Book', the last from his copy of Foorth; see also Grafton and Jardine (1986: 161–200, esp. 188–96).

[26] Other relevant passages include Harvey (1913: 90–1 ('Ower litle Hubert'); 124 ('An especiall regard to be had of Decorum'); 175 (in R. Grafton, *A brief treatise conteinying many proper Tables* (London: John Waley, 1576): 'One of mie York pamflets 1576. then fitt for mie natural & mathematical, studies, & exercises in Pembrooke Hall'—further evidence for the pursuit of mathematics at Cambridge); 208 (commending the radius of the 'Jacob's staff' as the 'most excellent and profitable' geometrical instrument and citing Ramus' *Geometry*); and 212–13 (Harvey's many annotations in Blagrave concerning 'instrumenti Geometrici' and the 'Principia Geometria', 'after which nothing is difficult in mathematics or mechanical instruments, or experiments')).

Queen's Secretary, Harvey pleaded his case for a Mastership of Trinity Hall, Cambridge, by alluding to his own 'manie...Traicts & Discourses, sum in Latin, sum in Inglish...sum in Mathematiques, in Cosmographie, in the Art of Navigation, in the Art of Warr, in the tru Chemique without imposture...& other effectual practicable knowlage.... For I can in one yeare publish more, then anie Inglishman hath hetheto dun.'[27]

To his acute dissatisfaction, Harvey continued to occupy a 'professional' academic position very different from Sidney's more active and courtly role. But this was precisely what led him to seek in mathematics and the mechanical arts a model for what he hoped to become: a 'pragmatic' orator who might some day conceivably take his place at court alongside men like Sidney, for whom a knowledge of these practical fields was a political necessity. As an undergraduate at Christ Church, Oxford, from February 1567/8 until approximately 1571, Sidney was in the company of many men who would become crucial to the cultivation of mathematics in England;[28] outside the university his friendships extended across many fields of practical, pre-scientific endeavour, including medicine, navigation, and alchemy.[29] John Dee's library at Mortlake was near to Barn Elms, home to Sidney's father-in-law, Sir Frances Walsingham; Thomas Moffet, physician to the Earl of Pembroke and one of Sidney's earliest biographers, records that Sidney and his friend Edward Dyer studied chemistry with Dee at Mortlake, perhaps some-time in 1576–7, when Dee's diary records that the two men visited with the

---

[27] Cited in Stern (1979: 125); cf. Harkness (2002: 150–1).

[28] He may have studied with Thomas Allen, one of the few tutors in mathematics at Oxford during the period of Sidney's matriculation; Allen was probably the mathematician who cast a sixty-two-page horoscope for Sidney in 1571. Elsewhere at Oxford were Walter Ralegh, at Oriel College; Henry Savile was already teaching mathematics as a Fellow at Merton; see Ch. 2 n. 52 above; Buxton (1954: 40–1, 143–4); M. W. Wallace (1915: 107–11); Cormack (1997: 59–66). The wide range of books dedicated to Sidney throughout his life suggests his enthusiasm for practically oriented works, from the dedication by Hakluyt (see below) to Timothy Bright's edition of Adophus Scibonius' medical textbook for students, *In Physicam G. A. Scriboni* (1584) (also a favourite work of Harvey's), William Blandy's *The castle of pollicye* (1581), and Nicholas Lichefild's English translation of *De Re Militari* (1582) by Gutierres de la Vega, a book on the art of war that included diagrams of battle formations used by the Spanish; see Duncan-Jones (1991: 229, 271). P. French (1972: 132) cites Greville's comment that Sidney would have distinguished himself 'even in the most ingenuous of Mechanicall Arts'—posthumous claims, to be sure, but significant ones nonetheless.

[29] Richard Hakluyt was with Sidney at Christ Church, where he lectured on geography using globes, maps, and other instruments; the dedication to Sidney of Hakluyt's *Divers Voyages touching the Discoverie of America* (1582), very near the time of the composition of the *Defence*, suggests that the two men shared an interest in navigation and exploration. They certainly shared an interest in colonial expeditions, since on several occasions Sidney invested in searches for the north-west passage and actively pursued the formation of a company devoted to the settlement of plantations in the New World; M. W. Wallace (1915: 195–6, 284–7); Duncan-Jones (1991, esp. 116–17, 142, 229–30, 273–4), who cites Greville's portrait of Sidney as 'a man fit for conquest, plantation, reformation, or what action soever is greatest and hardest among men' (p. 229). Cf. Sidney's letter to Languet dated 1 October 1577, in which he writes enthusiastically of Frobisher's voyage (Pears 1845: 118–20); Sidney (1922–6: iii. 116–17); also Stewart (2000: 156–7, 191–2, and 265–76 on Sidney's involvement with Drake's voyage to the West Indies in 1585).

Earl of Leicester on state business.[30] In London, Sidney was acquainted with the merchant and cartographer Michael Lok, the man who, with Dyer, coordinated the analysis of ores that Martin Frobisher had brought back from a trip in search of a north-west passage by a series of English and foreign alchemists living in the capital.[31] His Continental friendships and acquaintances were extensive, including Peter Ramus, Giordano Bruno, the botanist Charles de L'Ecluse, the printers Andreas Wechel and Henri Estienne, and, most famously, the humanist and diplomat Hubert Languet.[32]

Sidney's letters to Languet indicate the central place that geometry, especially in its practical or applied forms, had in his own private curriculum and the reading habits of his circle. While in Venice during December 1573 he wrote that he was 'learning the sphere, and a little music' (Pears 1845: 8), and Languet commends his interest:

You are right to pay attention to astronomy; without some knowledge of it, it is impossible to understand cosmography; and he who reads history without a knowledge of this, is very like a man who makes a journey in the dark. (Pears 1845: 20)

About Sidney's plans to study geometry itself, however, Languet is more cautious:

You were quite right to learn the elements of astronomy, but I do not advise you to proceed far in the science, because it is very difficult, and not likely to be of much use to you. I know not whether it is wise to apply your mind to geometry, thought it is a noble study and well worthy of a fine understanding; but you must consider your condition in life, how soon you will have to tear yourself from your literary leisure, and therefore the short time which you still have should be devoted entirely to such things as are most essential. I call those things essential to you, which it is discreditable for a man of high birth not to know, and which may, one day, be an ornament and a resource to you. Geometry may, indeed, be of great use to a man of rank, in the fortification or investment of towns, in castramentation and all branches of architecture, but to understand it sufficiently to make it useful would certainly require much time, and I consider it absurd to learn the rudiments of many sciences simply for display and not for use . . .[33]

---

[30] Dee (1842: 2); Duncan-Jones (1991: 115–17, 248); Buxton (1954: 87); Stewart (2000: 169). P. French (1972: 126–59) provides the most extensive treatment of Dee's relationship to the Sidney circle, discussing the purported 'chemistry' instruction on pp. 127–9 and noting that Aubrey describes Mary Sidney as a 'great chymist, and spent yearly a great deale in that study'. Mary employed Adrian Gilbert as a 'laborator' at Wilton; he was the brother of Humphrey Gilbert, the navigator, adventurer, and projector of the 'Academy' for Queen Elizabeth that I have discussed in Ch. 2; both brothers knew Dee. Clulee provides circumstantial evidence for a direct connection between Sidney and the occult aspects of Dee's activities when he points out that it was Sidney who brought Albrecht Laski to visit Dee at Mortlake: a Polish prince with keen interests in alchemy and other occult philosophies, Laski eventually persuaded Dee and his scryer Edward Kelly to leave England so that they could pursue their alchemical experiments and angelic conversations in Cracow and Vienna; Clulee (1988: 197–8); Harkness (1999: 53).

[31] Harkness (2002: 151–4).

[32] On Sidney's Continental contacts, see Buxton (1954); M. W. Wallace (1915, esp. 298–302, on Bruno); Osborn (1972); van Dorsten (1962).

[33] Pears (1845: 25); see also Osborn (1972: 136–7, 142–3).

In response Sidney seems to have decided to forgo further study in both astronomy and geometry:

I am glad you approve of my intention of giving up the study of astronomy, but about geometry I hardly know what to determine. I long so greatly to be acquainted with it, and the more so because I have always felt sure that it is of the greatest service in the art of war; nevertheless I shall pay but sparing attention to it, and only peep through the bars, so to speak, into the rudiments of the science. (Pears 1845: 28)

The fervent tone of the letter is striking, and Sidney is obviously reluctant to give up the study of a field that both he and Languet, not to mention Quintilian and Cicero, finally regarded as 'essential' to a man of his position.

Sidney's letters are significant, too, because they indicate the larger, predominantly Aristotelian intellectual formation in which his interest in practical geometry was embedded: in his letters to Languet, Sidney moves immediately from declaring his love of geometry to asserting his desire for Greek in the next sentence, the better to read Aristotle's *Politics*, in the passages I have quoted above. The same letter to Robert that opens by praising 'Aristotle's Ethicks . . . you knowe it is the begyning, and foundacion of all his workes, the good ende which everie man doth & ought to bend his greatest actions' concludes by passing Languet's advice on to his brother, encouraging him to 'take delight likewise in the mathematicalls', and recommending Henry Savile to him repeatedly as one who 'is excellent in them':

I thinke yow understand the sphere, if yow doe, I care little for any more astronomie in yow. Arithmatick, and geometry, I would wish yow well seene in, so as both in matter of number and measure yow might have a feeling, and active judgment I would yow did beare the mechanicall instruments wherin the Dutch [blank in MS].[34]

'Active judgment' is the critical term here, since the skill Sidney would have his brother cultivate by handling instruments is one of practical, prudential deliberation rather than actual material production. Geometry is meant to supplement his reading in other subjects—Aristotle, but also history-writing—for the benefit of his own ethical and political education.[35] An even more remarkable letter from

---

[34] Sidney (1922–6: iii. 132).

[35] Sidney (1922–6: iii. 130); cf. Clucas (2000: 106–11), who observes the 'essentially . . . Aristotelian' aspect of the Earl of Northumberland's *Advices to his son* (1594), which recommends 'all the . . . major areas of the Aristotelian corpus' alongside astronomy, navigation, military strategy and engineering, and geometry—in which, the Earl argues, 'is comprehended a great part of our knowledge' (cited by Clucas 2000: 110); also the letter prefaced to Richard Haydocke's translation of Lomazzo's *Trattato dell'arte della pittura* (*A Tracte Containing the Artes of Curious Paintinge, Carvinge, and Buildinge* (Oxford, 1598)) by John Case, the noted Oxford tutor, physician, and commentator on Aristotle: '*Geometricians* heere-hence for Buylding may take their perfect Modelles. *Cosmographers* may finde good arte to make their Mappes and Tables. *Historians* cannot heere want a pencell to overshadow mens famous Actes, Persons, and Morall pictures. *Princes* may heere learne to builde Engines of warre, and ornaments of peace. For *Vitruvius* (who writeth of Building to *Augustus* the Emperour) saith, that all kinde of warlike Engines were first invented by Kings and Captaines, who were skilfull in the Arte of Painting and carving. One thing more I adde above all the rest . . . that in reading your booke I finde therein two notable images of Natural and Morall Philosophie, the one so

Sidney to Edward Denny, written only five months before the letter to Robert, provides an extraordinary glimpse of the place that practical geometry occupied in Sidney's own intellectual habits. Denny was about to depart for Ireland in service to Lord Grey, who had been appointed Lord Deputy Governor; Edmund Spenser would be one of his companions. In response to Denny's request for a curriculum to prepare for his new position, Sidney advises the reading of the Scriptures, Aristotle, Cicero, and Plutarch, as well as the study of history, geography, and cartography. 'Bend yourself to souldiery,' he advises, in terms that echo his *Defence*:

what bookes can deliver, stands in the books that profess the arte, & in historyes. The first shewes what should be done, the other what hath bene done . . . but this I thinke if you will studdy them, it shall be necessary for you to exercise your hande in setting downe what you reed, as in descriptions of battaillons, camps, and marches, with some practise of Arithmetike, which sportingly you may exercise . . . For historicall maters, I woold wish you before you began to reed a litle of Sacroboscus Sphaere, & the Geography of some moderne writer, wherof there are many & is a very easy and delightfull studdy. You have allready very good judgement of the Sea mappes, which will make the other much the easier; and provide your selfe of an Ortelius, that when you reed of any place, you may finde it out, & have it, as it were before your eyes; For it doth exceedingly confirme, both the judgement, & memory.[36]

He concludes:

But nowe may you ask me: what shall I doe first? Truly in my opinion, an hower to your Testament, & a peece of one to Tullyes offices, & that with studdy. Plutarkes discourses you may reede with more ease. For the other maters allott yourself an other howre for Sacroboscus & Valerius, or any other of Geography, and when you have satisfied yourself in that, take your history of England, & your Ortelius to knowe the places you reed of; and soe in my conceit, you shall pass both pleasantly and profitably. Your books of the Art of Souldiery must have an other hower, *but before you goe to them you shall doe well to use your hande, in drawing of a plotte, & practise of Arithmetike. Whether nowe you will doe these by peecemeale, all in a day, or first goe thorow with one, yow must be your owne judge, as you find your memory best serve. To me, the variety rather delights me, then confounds me.*[37]

shadowed with precepts of Nature, the other so garnished [with] the best colours of Vertues; that in mine opinion, I never found more use of Philosophie, in any booke I ever read of the like theame and subject. And truly had I not read this your Auctor and Translation, I had not fully understoode what *Aristotle* meante in the sixth booke of his Ethickes, to call *Phidias* and *Polycletus* most wise men; as though any parte of wisdeome did consist in Carving and Painting; which now I see to be true . . .' (cited by Schmitt 1983*b*: 132, 244–5). Case had been a contemporary of Sidney's at Oxford (BA 1567, MA 1572, both from St John's; MD 1589) and, like Thomas Blundeville, formed part of the Earl of Leicester's broad circle of patronage.

[36] Osborn (1972: 535–40 (539)).

[37] Osborn (1972: 539–40; my emphasis). More than half a century later, Milton would still recommend Sacrobosco as a guide to astronomy for his nephew Edward Phillips; see H. S. Turner (2007). Harvey certainly knew of Sidney's advice to Denny, as he notes in his copy of Sacrobosco (with inscription dated 1580, near the date of the composition of the *Defence*); see Grafton and Jardine (1990: 38). There seems no reason to assume, however, as they suggest (p. 39), that Harvey actually wrote the letter to Denny, since the advice it offers is consistent with Sidney's letters to his brother Robert and with the advice that he himself had received from Languet.

It would be difficult to find a clearer confirmation of the fundamental compatibility Sidney perceived among moral philosophy, history-writing, and the spatial arts: the letter indicates that he moved laterally from one subject to another in the pursuit of 'delight' or pleasure, training his 'judgement' and 'memory' by juxtaposing the study of Cicero with the practice of drawing actual geometrical diagrams and then moving on, perhaps, to consult his edition of Ortelius alongside popular histories by Richard Grafton or John Stow, to calculate distances in military situations, to write a letter to his mentor Languet, or even to engage in literary composition.[38]

There is reason to suppose, furthermore, that Sidney was recommending a conjunction of exercises that was commonplace among gentlemen of his position. The title page of Thomas Blundeville's *A brief description of universal mappes and cardes* (1589) addresses itself to 'those that delight in reading of histories: and also for Travelers by Land or Sea'; the letter to the reader declares the reading of history 'halfe lame, and . . . neither so pleasant, nor so profitable, as otherwise it would be' with a knowledge of geography (A2ᵛ). In *The Governor* (1531), too, Sir Thomas Elyot had recommended that the student be trained in both 'painting and kervinge' so that he is 'equall to noble artificers':

the feate of portraiture shall be an allective to every other studie or exercise. For the witte therto disposed shall always covaite congruent mater, wherin it may be occupied. And whan he happeneth to rede or here any fable or historie, forthwith he apprehendeth it more desirously, and retaineth it better . . . by reason that he hath founde mater apte to his fantasie . . . Experience we have therof in learnynge of geometry, astronomie, and cosmographie, called in englisshe the discription of the worlde. In which studies I dare affirme a man shal more profite, in one wike, by figures and chartis, well and perfectly made, than he shall by the only reding or herying the rules of that science by the space of halfe a yere at the lest . . . (Elyot 1531: i. 43–5)

Children should read history alongside 'the olde tables of Ptholomee, where in all the worlde is paynted', Elyot recommends, 'havynge firste some introduction in to the sphere . . . [and] there is none so good lernynge as the demonstration of cosmographie by materiall figures and instrumentes, havynge a good instructour' (i. 76). Richard Mulcaster's *Elementarie* (1583), published only three years after Sidney's letter to Denny and also dedicated to the Earl of Leicester, included drawing along with reading, writing, singing, and playing music in his influential curriculum for the young student. Drawing, Mulcaster believed, was useful to 'manie good workmen' who pursue 'architectur, pictur, embrodierie, engraving, statuarie, all modelling, all platforming . . . besides the learned use thereof, for Astronomie, Geometrie, Chorographie, Topographie and som other such' (p. 58). Mulcaster's curriculum

---

[38] Both M. W. Wallace (1915: 304) and Duncan-Jones (1991: 174) point out that the letter to Denny was written from Wilton during the period when Sidney was engaged in writing the *Arcadia*, carrying with him on hunting trips a small 'table book' in which he would jot down ideas for his romance.

might also have had a directly political purpose, since, as Lisa Jardine and William Sherman have shown, these were precisely the areas of knowledge that would be most useful to the 'intelligencer' who sought patronage from powerful statesmen.[39]

This pragmatic application of mathematical knowledge is nowhere more evident that in Sidney's own involvement with the fortification works in progress at Dover Harbour, which he had begun to supervise in 1584 in the capacity of Master of the Ordnance, a position to which he was officially named in 1585.[40] His appearance in the State Papers concerning Dover during 1584 associates him closely with one of the most important sites for applied mathematical activity in England, and his official appointment suggests at least a sufficient grasp of technical problems to direct the projects then under way.[41] Sidney seems to have served primarily as a social and intellectual intermediary between statesmen such as Walsingham and Burghley and practitioners such as Thomas Bedwell and Thomas Digges, the son of Leonard Digges and himself a mathematician of some reputation.[42] In at least one case Sidney was asked to report to the works in person to adjudicate in the long-simmering disputes over designs: a communication from Digges to Walsingham, dated 8 June 1584, asking Sidney to come to Dover indicates that he was regarded by all parties as capable of making a final decision regarding the course the works should take, and that his experience with 'plats' was crucial to the process.[43]

[39] Using a phrase very similar to that of Sidney in his letter to Denny, Henry Wotton notes in his commonplace book that 'in reading of history, a soldier should draw the platform of battles he meets with, plant the squadrons and order the whole frame as he finds it written, so he shall print it firmly in his mind and apt his mind for actions'; in a letter dated 20 November 1590, Wotton offers to send Lord Zouche, for whom he was acting as a foreign correspondent and 'intelligencer' from Vienna, a 'model' of Rudolf II's 'lust-house' and to provide him with the price of mathematical books. See L. Jardine and Sherman (1994: 103–7, esp. 104), citing Wotton's letter to Zouche on p. 103 and his commonplace book on p. 107; cf. Heninger (1989: 73–5).

[40] M. W. Wallace (1915: 289–90, 306–7, 319); Stewart (2000: 252–3, 269–70).

[41] On plans for Dover's fortification in the years immediately preceding Sidney's involvement, see Ash (2000); also Colvin (1982: 729–68). Stewart notes that Sidney visited fortification works outside Strasbourg in the spring of 1573 (2000: 100).

[42] On Bedwell, see Ch. 2, above. Bedwell had been involved in the works since at least 1582, when both he and Thomas Digges submitted proposals for clearing the mouth of the harbour, along with Fernando Poyntz and a group of Flemish engineers. Although Poyntz eventually received the initial commission, Bedwell profited from the occasion to draw Walsingham's attention to his own expertise in related projects; see *Calendar of State Papers Domestic, Elizabeth, 1581–90* (hereafter *CSPD*), vol. cliii, no. 27 (p. 52), Apr. 1582. As Poyntz's project foundered and he sought excuses in bad weather and a perceived conspiracy among the workmen, Bedwell was quick to write to both Walsingham and Burghley with a vigorous condemnation of his work; see *CSPD*, vol. clvi, no. 14 (p. 78), no. 22 (p. 79), and nos. 23 and 24. In 1589 Bedwell himself was appointed Keeper of the Ordnance, and Johnston suggests that he used the store of *matériel* to perform experiments in ballistics, which he then circulated in manuscript (S. Johnston 1991: 324). On 22 April 1582 Digges proposed his own plan privately to Walsingham, over one proposed by yet another candidate (*CSPD*, vol. clxx, no. 46 (p. 173)). Digges would accompany Sidney into the Low Countries in 1586 as muster-master, charged by Sidney with inspecting the Dutch fortification works; Stewart (2000: 278).

[43] The National Archives, State Papers Domestic Series, SP 12/171/13: 'And if it might please your Lordship to write a letter unto Sir Thomas Gros and the rest of the commissioners ther, to attende on Sir Philip Sidney for finall resolutions of all matters, ther is no doubte of very good successe . . .'. The 'plat' was a regular component of the proposals; see *CPSD*, vol. clii, nos. 25, 33, 87, 96; clii, nos. 15, 57, 60, 64.

Although a later document suggests that Sidney was finally unable to visit the works as Digges requested and that engineers from the Low Countries were sent instead, his position at court and his general reputation for learning seem to have endowed him with an authority that practitioners such as Digges or Bedwell somehow lacked.[44] In the field, Digges and Bedwell adapted the theoretical principles of geometry to solve a variety of individual problems, wielding the plat as a device to make these principles concrete and accessible to powerful men who had no technical expertise of their own. At the same time, a gentleman practitioner like Sidney had the requisite familiarity with technical details to explain that a proposed solution was feasible and legitimate, using his general knowledge of practical mathematics and his position in a court hierarchy to help further the project at a political level.[45] His advice to Denny and Robert epitomizes the values of the gentlemen courtiers who felt the need to cultivate an active interest in practical mathematics, both for their usefulness to civil and military projects but also as a mode of knowledge leading to political advancement. Their interest in mathematical instruments or in geometry in general was limited to a perceived effectiveness and potential for application rather than an attention to accuracy, principles of design, or theoretical consistency, Languet's opinions notwithstanding: geometry was above all a polite and useful field of learning that distinguished them as men of sound judgement and productive civil action.

INVENTION, IMAGINATION, AND
THE POETIC IMAGE

Some of Sidney's sharpest arguments in his *Defence* concern the nature of the poetic image: in its living detail it exceeds the 'thorny argument', 'bare rule' (85. 11), and 'wordish description' (85. 28) of the metaphysician and compels the imagination far more effectively than the 'mouse-eaten records' (83. 31) and foolish antiquarianism of the chronicler, who remains mired in the dull particulars of remote ages. However much Sidney now seems to depart from his own advice to his brother Robert—to whom he continued to recommend the reading of history above all other kinds of writing—he has in fact simply transposed to the domain of poesy the same techniques he used in reading history with Harvey and the same interest in theory and practice, the general and the particular as fundamental epistemological categories in the analysis of human action.[46] Whereas for Harvey, the 'politician' mediated between Livy on the one hand and Machiavelli and

---

[44] *CSPD*, vol. clxxii, no. 12 (p. 189).

[45] Cf. P. Smith (1994: 67–92, esp. 72–3; 82–3 and n. 83, 87–9 (on 'judgment' as an epistemological activity)).

[46] See especially the letter to Robert dated 18 October 1580 (Sidney 1922–6, vol. iii, no. 42, pp. 130–3), where Sidney describes the historian in terms similar to his discussion of the poet in the *Defence*; cf. M. F. Wallace (1915: 237); Herman (1989).

Aristotle on the other, for Sidney the poet has come to perform the same intellectual function that Harvey's 'politician' once did: the poet 'coupleth the general notion with the particular example' (85. 25–6), precisely the intellectual operation that neither the philosopher nor the historian are able to execute. His images are, of course, images of military virtue like those to be found in Livy and Machiavelli: moral abstractions of valour, courage, strength, and fortitude personified in the particular examples of Cyrus—one of Machiavelli's favourite examples—and other heroes. For Sidney, as for Harvey, these figures exemplify a pragmatic philosophy of action rooted equally in the philosophical tradition of prudence and in the deliberative thinking of military tacticians. 'Heroic' poetry—epic and romance—is the genre in which a reader may best study the deliberative process by which action is undertaken.

Moreover, the intellectual faculties that Harvey and Sidney admired in the Roman captain were precisely those that were necessary to the poet, as Lorna Hutson (1993; 1994: 91–114) has argued, and as I discuss in more detail in Chapter 7. Caesar, in Harvey's estimation, is gifted with a particular kind of intelligence that he terms 'conceit' and that is the source of his facility in managing strategic action; the 'plats', designs, and diagrams that rival engineers submitted during the fortification process at Dover are specifically called 'inventions' and 'devices' in other documents, terms that were, of course, commonly used to describe poetic compositions and other visual designs, as we shall see in Chapter 4.[47] Juan Huarte's *The Examination of Men's Wits* (Spanish, 1575; English, 1594), a study of psychology in terms of Galenic humours and a work that Harvey certainly knew, classifies the imagination as necessary for

all the Arts and Sciences, which consist in figure, correspondence, harmonie, and proportion: such are Poetrie, Eloquence, Musicke, and the skill of preaching: the practise of Phisicke, the Mathematicals, Astrologie, and the governing of a Common-wealth, the art of Warfare, Paynting, drawing, writing, reading, to be a man gratious, pleasant, neat wittie in managing, & all the engins & devises which artificers make: besides a certain speciall gift, whereat the vulgar marvelleth, and that is, to endite divers matters, unto foure, who write togither, and yet all to be penned in good sort. (p. 103)

Later Huarte cites 'platforming, and building, which belong to the imagination' (p. 108) and observes that 'all that which may be tearmed good figure, good purpose and provision, comes from the grace of the imagination, as are merrie jeasts, resemblances, quips, and comparisons' (p. 131). It is also true, Huarte remarks, that 'Such as I have marked to be good practitioners, do all piddle somwhat in the art of versifieing, and raise not up their contemplation very high' (p. 182).

---

[47] *Acts of the Privy Council of England*, NS (hereafter *APC*), 1575–7, ix. 344, a letter to 'Lord Cobham and others' dated 13 May 1577 'touching *some devise* for the repaireng of the haven of Dover', and *APC* 1580–1, xii. 161, another letter to the same parties dated 15 August 1580 referring to 'two severall plottes drawen for the repairing of Dover Haven, thone by William Burrough with the advise of some skilfull persons of Dunkerke, thother by one Drew' and twice recommending 'the *invention* of Drew' (my emphases).

Because the imagination excels in problems of figure and proportion, it is a distinctly spatial faculty; this is evident in Huarte's discussion of the art of war but no less so in his account of the orator, for whom the imagination functions, like judgement in the dialectic textbooks, as a faculty of form or structural arrangement. The imagination shows the orator how to 'dispose his matter, placing everie word and sentence in his fit roome, in sort that the whole may carrie an answerable proportion, and one thing bring in another... This property of ordering and distributing, is for certaine a worke of the imagination, since (in effect) it is nought else, but figure and correspondence' (p. 134). For Huarte the most important function of the imagination in oratory is to move to action: this is why Huarte can group the orator with the captain, and his account is, again, almost exactly like Sidney's poet or Harvey's 'pragmatic'. Through the imagination, orators 'give a being and life to the things which they speake, and with the same do move the hearers, and supple them to beleeve how that is true which they go about to persuade... action (for certaine) is a worke of the imagination, for all that which we have uttered thereof, maketh figure, correspondence, and good consonance' (p. 135). Huarte's orator requires 'much invention... a swift imagination' as he seeks out arguments that are convincing and pleasing to his audience. Invention and imagination, he argues, 'hunt and bring the game to his hand, and when he wants what to say... devise somewhat as if it were materiall' (p. 131). That Huarte understands this 'devising' to be a kind of artificial making is clear from a further comment: when the orator can discover no further arguments, 'this imagination hath force not onely to compound a figure possible with another, but doth joyne also (after the order of nature) those which are unpossible, and of them growes to shape mountains of gold, and calves that flie' (p. 132).

Sidney's account of 'invention' and the role of the imagination in generating the poetic image in his *Defence* resembles Huarte's discussion of the orator's purpose and skill so closely as to invite the question as to whether he may have seen the Spanish edition of *Examen des Ingenios* (1575) before Richard Carew's 1594 translation into English—since Harvey refers to Huarte's Spanish work briefly in his marginalia, it is entirely possible that he brought it to Sidney's attention.[48] For Sidney, the poet's capacity for 'invention' is what most distinguishes him from scholars in other fields of inquiry, and it is in the shifting meanings of this word that the transitional, 'early modern' nature of his essay emerges most clearly. Many details indicate that he has borrowed the term directly from the *trivium*, and he opens his defence by invoking familiar analogies with the arts of discourse, offering poesy as an intellectual instrument of unusual extension, much the way Rainolds or Blundeville understood rhetoric and dialectic to be.[49] Like dialectic

---

[48] '... ye new French politique discourses of Vocation: & ye Spanish Examen de Ingenios', in Harvey's copy of Erasmus' *Parabolae* (Basel, 1565) (Harvey 1913: 137).

[49] Cf. his repeated mention of 'Tully', Demosthenes, and familiar rhetorical maxims ('art, imitation, and exercise'; 112. 3); his reference to 'all virtues, vices, and passions so in their own natural *seats* laid to the view' (86. 29; my emphasis), using terms common to the memory tradition; his references to the 'imaginative and judging power' (86. 6–7), and to the 'purifying of wit... enriching of

and rhetoric, poesy is not limited to one discrete area of inquiry in the way of philosophy, history, or theology.[50] At the same time, his definition of 'art' in a famous passage—'There is no art delivered to mankind that hath not the works of Nature for his principle object' (78. 1–2)—seizes on an empirical, practical, and quasi-experimental attitude visible in the rhetorical handbooks that allows him to broaden his approach to invention and to depart from the conventional procedures of academic disputation. Whereas the 'rhetorician and logician . . . give artificial rules, which still are compassed within the circle of a question according to the proposed matter' (78. 13–18), and whereas 'all other arts retain themselves within their subject, and receive, as it were, their being from it', the poet, in contrast, 'only bringeth his own stuff, and doth not learn a conceit out of a matter, but maketh matter for a conceit' (99. 5–9). Both dialectic and rhetoric, in other words, however broad their application in theory, always remain in practice limited to a particular case or question: both employ invention and judgement to find 'matter' for a suitable argument by turning to the commonplaces and assessing their relevance and effectiveness to the point at hand, which has been posed externally either by historical circumstance (deliberative or judicial rhetoric) or by arbitrary choice (encomiastic rhetoric or formal disputation). The 'matter' of the poet, in contrast, need not conform to any prior existing particular case or question but only to that 'conceit' which the poet himself has 'made'. He may use conventional invention from the topics to do so, but as Sidney makes clear in *Astrophil and Stella* 1, 3, or 15, for instance, the cleverness of the poet's invention will be measured by how far it seems to depart from commonplace comparisons and cliché.

The complexity of Sidney's discussion of 'invention' in these passages depends partly on the meaning of the term 'matter', which is most obviously an English rendering of the Latin *res*, the 'matter' or 'subject' in question in verbal disputation but which both S. K. Heninger and John Ulreich have interpreted in a directly philosophical sense as further evidence for a Neoplatonic (and thus hylomorphic) attitude towards matter and form.[51] It is typical of Sidney's allusive and playful style to draw on the resonance of both meanings simultaneously, since the poet is not simply a 'discourser' but an 'artificer' (79. 7) who fashions conceits out of 'stuff' much the way the sculptor works bronze or the builder raises a house.

---

memory, enabling of judgment, and enlarging of conceit' (82. 11–12). On the *topoi, loci,* or commonplaces necessary for 'invention', see Lechner (1962); Ong (1958, esp. 104–12, 116–21); Mack (1996); Blair (1997, esp. 65–9); Moss (1996); on the relevance of the commonplaces to 16th-century poetic composition and notions of the poetic image, see Tuve (1947, pt. II, *passim*, esp. pp. 331–55; 1968); Joseph (1962); on 'invention' specifically, see Langer (1999) and Heninger (1974: 294–5 and n. 30).

[50] John Carter's commentary on book I of John Seton's popular *Dialectica* (included in the 1572 and all subsequent editions) defends rhetoric and dialectic in ways that are very similar to Sidney's defence of poesy, adducing arithmetic and geometry as two examples of circumscribed forms of knowledge (dealing with numbers and magnitudes, respectively) that are both served by rhetoric and dialectic, neither of which are themselves limited to any circumscribed matter (Aiii^v).

[51] Heninger (1974: 306); Ulreich (1986: 148); cf. my discussion of matter and form in H. S. Turner (2001).

Similar metaphors had already been used by Ascham, Rainolds, Agricola, Quintilian, and Cicero to describe the act of 'imitation' or the relationship between the orator and his speech, as we have seen, and comparisons between the poet and the carpenter or mason were frequent among Sidney's contemporaries, as we shall see in Chapter 4.[52] I suggest that Sidney's conception of poetic invention throughout these crucial passages is best understood as an example of what Antonio Perez-Ramos, in his study of Bacon, has described as a 'maker's knowledge' of natural objects and natural processes and which Pamela Long, Pamela Smith, William Newman, William Eamon, and Paolo Rossi, among others, have also identified in the practice of alchemy and in many other areas of early-modern technology.[53] Indeed, the degree to which sixteenth-century poetic discourse is absent from recent historiography of scientific thinking is surprising, despite the obvious similarities between Sidney's discussion of poesy and the publications of sixteenth-century artisans such as Bernard Palissy, hermetic philosophers, astrologers, and natural magicians such as Dee, Giambattista Della Porta, Henry Cornelius Agrippa, or Giordano Bruno, seventeenth-century alchemists such as Johann Becher, or, more immediately, Bacon himself.[54]

Sidney, for instance, sarcastically dismisses an automatic, unreflective process of 'invention' that simply collates familiar material but fails to produce a genuinely novel comparison or insight: such poets are indiscriminate in their selection and arrangement of material, since they depend too much on memory—or worse, rely only on the book as a substitute for memory—and give no thought to the role of judgement in the composition or analysis of discourse, and therefore in the larger process of acquiring knowledge (118. 13–22). Bacon's objection to 'similitudes' in dialectical argument are nearly identical to Sidney's, as Shepherd has observed.[55] But of even greater interest are Bacon's comments on traditional dialectical and rhetorical invention, which he was seeking to reform in order to formulate an improved method of inquiry that might discover a truly new knowledge of nature

---

[52] Rainolds (*c.*1570: 219): 'materiam enim ex illis delibatam orator vt artifex informat'; Agricola's definition of rhetorical matter is 'like the statue on which the artist works' (cited by Ong 1958: 98). Heninger (1989) emphasizes the importance of artificial 'making' to Sidney's notion of invention, esp. pp. 15–58, drawing parallels between 'fiction' and *fingere* (pp. 60–1).

[53] On Renaissance alchemy, see Rossi (1968: 11–22, 22–35); P. Smith (1994, esp. 8, 207; and 260–2 on 'invention'); Silver and Smith (2002: 41); W. R. Newman (1989, 1997); W. R. Newman and Grafton (2001); Eamon (1994: 116–18); Harkness (2002: 151–5), on English and foreign alchemists living in London.

[54] Compare Giambattista Della Porta's *Magia Naturalis* (1558, 1560): 'Art being as it were Nature's Ape, even in her imitation of Nature, effecteth greater matters than Nature doth. Hence it is that a Magician begin furnished with Art, as it were another Nature, searching thoroughly into those works which Nature doth accomplish by many secret means and close operations, doth work upon Nature, and partly by that which he sees, and partly by that which he conjects and gathers from thence, takes his sundry advantages of Nature's instruments, and thereby either hastens or hinders her work, making things ripe before or after their natural season, and so indeed makes Nature to be his instrument' (cited by Eamon 1994: 217, from the 1658 English translation of *Natural Magick*; Eamon's entire discussion of magic is relevant, esp. pp. 218–19).

[55] Shepherd (Sidney 1965: 230), observing that Bacon draws on *NE* VI. 3 for his argument.

and which argue in terms that are nearly identical to Sidney's in the *Defence*: 'The invention of arguments is not properly an invention,' Bacon objected, 'for to invent is to discover that we know not, not to recover or resummon that which we already know.'[56] Bacon's account of the imagination, too, as a mediator between judgement and sense is almost identical to Sidney's account of the imagination in several passages, although it partly for this reason that Bacon will dismiss 'poesy (which in the beginning was referred to imagination)' as 'being to be accounted rather as a pleasure or play of wit than a science'.[57]

It would be more accurate, however, to say that Bacon's formulation *effects* a categorical distinction between 'poesy' and 'science' that is as yet less evident in Sidney's essay. Nor is the distinction fully operative in Harvey's annotations: to Harvey's mind, knowledge of mathematics, astronomy, astrology, and alchemy were necessary not simply to the orator but *especially* to the poet. He singles out Chaucer, Lydgate, and Sidney ('Astrophilus') for their astronomical knowledge, but also John Blagrave, John Dee, Thomas Harriot, and Thomas Digges—the very Thomas Digges with whom Sidney had collaborated at Dover—as men who excel in the kind of knowledge that the poet requires:

Others commend Chawcer, & Lidgate for their witt, pleasant veine, varietie of poetical discourse, & all humanitie: I specially note their Astronomie, philosophie, & other parts of profound or cunning art. Wherein few of their time were more exactly learned. It is not sufficient for poets, to be superficial humanists: but they must be exquisite artists, & curious universal schollers.[58]

In a separate annotation in the same volume, Harvey complains that contemporary poets are ignorant of astronomy and notes that although Spenser 'does not consider

[56] Bacon (1861: ix. 83–4); compare Sidney: 'Exercise indeed we do, but that very fore-backwardly: for where we should exercise to know, we exercise as having known; and so is our brain delivered of much matter which never was begotten by knowledge. For there being two principal parts, matter to be expressed by words and words to express the matter, in neither we use art or imitation rightly' (112. 5–10). See also Rossi (1968: 152–7); Perez-Ramos (1988, esp. 221–3, 231–2). L. Jardine (1974*a*) cites the same passage from Bacon (p. 69) and suggests that the work of William Temple, the Cambridge Ramist, may have informed Bacon's approach (pp. 59–60; also 62–5, 68–9). Temple may also be a source for Sidney's ideas: in 1584 Temple dedicated his edition of Ramus' *Dialecticae* to Sidney and wrote a Ramist analysis of the *Defence of Poesy*; in 1585 he became Sidney's secretary and would attend him on his deathbed in 1586. See n. 71, below; Duncan-Jones (1991: 271–2, 301).

[57] Bacon (1861: ix. 61–2); also ix. 115, where Bacon calls poesy a 'luxuriant plant, that comes of the lust of the earth, without any formal seed. Wherefore it spreads everywhere and is scattered far and wide—so that it would be vain to take thought about the defects of it'; also L. Jardine's (1974*a*) discussion of the imagination in Bacon, esp. pp. 91–2.

[58] All from marginalia to Harvey's edition of Dionysius Periegetes, *The Surveye of the World…englished by T. Twine* (1572), transcribed in Harvey (1913); the quotation above is from pp. 160–1; references to Chaucer and Lydgate appear throughout pp. 159–62, with 'Astrophilus', Spenser, and Blagrave mentioned on p. 162, Digges on pp. 161 and 163, and Harriott and Dee on p. 163. Stern (1979: 126 n. 144) dates the annotations to approximately 1574; see also Harvey's extensive mention of contemporary surveyors, 'fine Geometricians & greater artists', 'notable mathematicall practitioners, & polymechanists', in his copy of Luca Gaurico's *Tractatus Astrologicus* (1552), including Dee, Harriot, Digges, Blagrave, Richard Benese, Cyprian Lucar, and Valentine Leigh, among others (cited by Stern, p. 168).

himself completely ignorant of globes and astrolabes', he is 'inexperienced in his astronomical rules, tables, and instruments' (Harvey 1913: 162–3). 'Give mee the astrological descriptions in anie language', Harvey enthuses, 'that from the pictures of the heavens appeare most visible, livelie, flourishing, & admirable' (p. 162). In their vivacity and accuracy, these verbal 'pictures' or 'descriptions' are nothing less than *icons*, according to Harvey: 'Divini Iconismi, et coelestes Picturae', he writes admiringly in one annotation, 'divine descriptions and heavenly pictures' (p. 162).[59] Harvey takes particular delight in Chaucer's many 'descriptions' in the *Canterbury Tales*: 'of the hower of the day: in the Man of Lawes Prologue. In the tale of the Nonnes preist. In the parsons prologue'; 'of a cunning man, or Magician, or Astrologer, in the Franklins tale'; 'the discoverie of the counterfait Alchymist, in the tale of the Chanons Yeman' (p. 160). All these, too, he calls 'icons': 'Eccè etiam personarum, rerumque Iconismi', Harvey marvels ('Look at such lively descriptions of persons, and of things!'; p. 160). And of Chaucer's description of spring in the General Prologue, Harvey writes that these iconic descriptions are simply the finest example of the poetic art—of 'poesy': 'Pöesie, a livelie picture: and a more flourishing purtraiture, then the gallantest Springe of the yeare' (p. 159).

Sidney, too, explains the vivacity of poetic imitation—that 'perfect picture' (85. 26)—by comparing it with the naturalistic depiction of flora, fauna, and marvellous animals by northern European painters, as well as to the use of visual illustration in building and fortification:

Now doth the peerless poet perform both: for whatsoever the philosopher saith should be done, he giveth a perfect picture of it in someone by whom he presupposeth it was done, so as he coupleth the general notion with the particular example. A perfect picture I say, for he yieldeth to the powers of the mind an image of that whereof the philosopher bestoweth but a wordish description, which doth neither strike, pierce, nor possess the sight of the soul so much as that other doth. For as in outward things, to a man that had never seen an elephant or a rhinoceros, who should tell him most exquisitely all their shapes, colour, bigness, and partic- ular marks or of a gorgeous palace, an *architector*, with declaring the full beauties might well make the hearer able to repeat, as it were by rote, all he had heard, yet should never satisfy his inward conceits by being witness to itself of a true lively knowledge; but the same man, as soon as he might see those beasts well painted, or the house well in model, should straightways grow, without any description, to a judicial comprehending of them: so no doubt the philosopher with his learned definition ... replenish the memory with many infallible grounds of wisdom, which, notwithstanding, lie dark before the imaginative and judging power, if they be not illuminated or figured forth by the speaking picture of poesy. (85. 22–86. 8)

Both painting and 'model' provide analogies for the distinctive qualities of the poetic image, whose vivacity and visual quality make possible an act of knowledge in which reason, in the form of judgement, acts instantaneously. The passage (and 104. 14–23) recalls not simply a rhetorical notion of *enargia* or a Senecan notion of *exemplar* but Sidney's own experience with the spatial arts of painting, drawing,

[59] Cf. Elyot (1538) and Cooper (1578), both of whom define *iconismus* as 'description' in Harvey's sense.

and engineering, as well as Dürer's famous engraving of the rhinoceros that had passed as a royal gift from India to Spain, an animal that Dürer himself had never seen but which he sought to represent as accurately as possible in accordance with a new interest in empirical observation that characterized sixteenth-century still-life painting and the early-modern *studiolo* or *kunstkammer*.[60] And we know from a conversation reported by the painter Nicholas Hilliard that Sidney took an active interest in the practical techniques of perspectival rendering:

[Sidney] once demanded of me the question, whether it weare possible in one scantling, as in the length of six inches of a littel or short man, and also of a mighty bige and taulle man in the same scantling, and that one might well and apparently see which was the taule man, and which the littel, the picture being just of one length. I showed him that it was easely decerned if it weare cunningly drawne with true observations, for ower eye is cuninge, and is learned without rulle by long usse, as littel lads speake their vulgar tonge without gramour rulls. But I gave him rules and suficient reasons to note and observe.[61]

Sidney seems to have asked Hilliard whether the proportions among the parts of the human body in a painting will be enough to distinguish two figures of different absolute size, even if they are painted according to a scale and a perspective that makes them appear to be of the same stature, i.e. as if the larger man were placed at a greater distance from the viewer than the shorter. Hilliard's reply assumes an awareness of practice and theory as two completely distinct epistemologies of artistic representation and, remarkably, goes on to compare the difference between the two with an analogy drawn from Sidney's own field of expertise: the distinction between the daily, unstudied use of the vernacular and the theoretical system of grammar that structures it, organizes it, and constitutes it as a formal language.[62]

When we consider Sidney's analysis of the poetic image in light of these references and alongside Harvey's annotations, we see that his arguments depend on mimetic

---

[60] Sultan Muzafar II of Cambaia, India, had given the rhinoceros to Alfonso d'Albuquerque, Governor of Portuguese India in 1515, who in turn gave it to Don Manuel I, King of Spain; see P. Smith and Findlen's (2002*b*) discussion of the gift and Dürer's painting, pp. 1–19, and of the role of naturalistic painting and illustration in fostering an empirical attitude; also Alpers (1983); Kaufmann (1993, esp. 11–48, 175–94); Findlen (1994); Bredekamp (1995). Blair's (1997) discussion of Bodin's natural philosophy, esp. pp. 65–81, and the role of the commonplace book in producing natural facts is also relevant, esp. p. 5; cf. Heninger (1974: 299–302; 1989: 91–110, on poetry and painting more generally). Stewart (2000) notes that the Frankfurt fair, which Sidney attended in March 1573, included sideshows of live elephants (p. 95).

[61] From Hilliard's *Treatise concerning the Arte of Limning*, cited by Buxton (1954: 151). Elyot (1531) had told a similar (although less flattering) story about a conversation between Alexander and Apelles, which he took from Pliny (ii. 403–4 and n. a).

[62] In this respect, Hilliard's response confirms the arguments by Elkins (1994, esp. 45–80) that 'perspective' described a loosely related series of practices and methods rather than a formal, codified and unified theory (see Ch. 5, below). Quintilian, too, had defended the orator against the very charges of deception that Sidney now found directed against poesy by comparing him to the painter who uses perspectival techniques to create an illusion of three dimensions: this does not make his art deceptive, Quintilian argues, as people charge; see *Inst. Orat.* II. 17. 21, and compare II. 17. 38 with Sidney: 'The astronomer, with his cousin the geometrician, can hardly escape [being liars], when they take upon them to measure the stars' (102. 19–21).

presuppositions that will become distinctive features of experimental inquiry in the next century. Foremost among these is the notion that sensory experience offers a legitimate mode of knowing particulars and that the deficiencies of the senses can be corrected by an visual, artificial construction—an 'icon'—that frames perception and even makes evident processes that the senses alone might not perceive.[63] Of course the 'inventions' of Sidney's poesy are verbal constructs meant to exemplify moral virtues and not mechanical devices of the type that Bacon would employ to produce knowledge of natural objects and operative control over them.[64] Nor is the union of particular and universal that characterizes the poetic image an exact analogue for seventeenth-century experimental method: the 'fact' as the fundamental epistemological unit of the experiment is not yet visible in Sidney's essay, nor does he provide a model in which specific hypothetical propositions might be tested and revised. But his account of poetic making can be seen as 'experimental' in the specific medieval and early-modern sense of the term: artificially constructed conditions in which knowledge might be produced.[65]

For Sidney, after all, poesy does more than 'imitate', 'assist', or supplement nature: it departs from nature and improves upon it, in this way conjoining natural and artificial processes in a way that violated traditional Aristotelian distinctions but which was also typical of other instrumental arts such as alchemy or natural magic and which was crucial to Bacon's later epistemological reforms:[66]

Only the poet, disdaining to be tied to any such subjection [to nature], lifted up with the vigour of his own invention, doth grow in effect another nature, in making things either better than nature bringeth forth, or, quite anew, forms such as never were in nature, as the Heroes, Demigods, Cyclops, Chimeras, Furies, and such like: so as he goeth hand in hand with nature, not enclosed within the narrow warrant of her gifts, but freely ranging only within the zodiac of his own wit. Nature never set for the earth in so rich tapestry as divers poets have done; neither with pleasant rivers, fruitful trees, sweet-smelling flowers, nor whatsoever else may make the too much loved earth more lovely. Her world is brazen, the poets only deliver a golden. (78. 22–34)

---

[63] Cf. Bacon's observation on the role of experiments in supplementing that natural deficiencies of the senses in Bacon (1861: ix. 70–1); cf. Heninger (1974: 308).

[64] Cf. Bacon (1861: ix. 69); Perez-Ramos (1988: 231–2).

[65] Cf. Clulee (1988: 174); Eamon (1994: 55–8). Similarly, his insistence that 'the skill of the artificer standeth in that *Idea* or fore-conceit of the work, and not in the work itself' (79. 7–8) can be understood not only as invoking a Neoplatonist and Mannerist strain of Continental art theory but as supplying a legitimate philosophical justification, in 16th-century terms, for a distinction between the 'scientist' and the 'technician' that will become an intellectual and a social distinction crucial to the development of experimental method; see Shapin and Schaffer (1985); Shapin (1994).

[66] Cf. Heninger (1974: 301–2, 306–7), who reaches a position similar to my own; also pp. 287–324. On the art and nature distinction in classical thought and its increasing occlusion in the mechanical arts, see Rossi (1970, esp. 137–45); Eamon (1994, esp. 38–90); C. Smith (1992: 41–6); P. Smith (1994, esp. 207, 263–5); W. R. Newman (1989, 1997), who argues that artificial and natural categories had begun to blur in medieval alchemical texts long before Bacon's work, a point overlooked by scholars such as Rossi and Perez-Ramos; Blair (1997: 40–8); in reference to Bacon, see Perez-Ramos (1988: 144–8, 159–60, 235); Rossi (1970: 138–9).

Like the astrologer, the poet penetrates metaphysical mystery and harnesses the power of the universe; like the alchemist, the poet as 'maker' studies minute natural processes in order not simply to reproduce them but to perfect them into a 'golden' form. The power of the poet lies partly in his capacity to reproduce nature's own processes and apply them to things that nature never intended. But it lies also in his ability to 'invent' an iconic model in which the workings of nature might be studied, a set of artificial or hypothetical conditions that correspond or 'imitate' reality but which have been deliberately constructed to reveal causes and general principles. Here 'invention' describes not simply the intellectual capacity of the poet but the vivid artificial construct—the image—that he produces, which, through attentive reading and analysis, in turn enables further knowledge and an active intervention in the natural and social world. For Sidney poesy furnishes insight into natural *processes* that have hitherto lain undiscovered: poesy is a fully analytical mode of knowledge because the vivacity of its images allows us to discern the principles of a *natura naturans* that lie secret and inaccessible, much the way Greek philosophers 'did exercise their delightful vein in those points of highest knowledge, which before them lay hid to the world' (75. 6–8).

Throughout these passages, Sidney is claiming for 'poesy' the same instrumental potential and metaphysical authority that his contemporaries had claimed for geometry, alchemy, or astrology: Dee, Harvey, Bruno, Agrippa, men Sidney knew personally or whose work he had read.[67] In the place of Dee's defence of *mathēsis*, he has offered a defence of *poiēsis* in which an Aristotelian notion of 'architectonics'— politics, or the 'master science'—has been substituted for Dee's more occult concept of 'archemastrie'.[68] By defining poetic 'invention' or 'making' as finally a mode of *praxis*, or virtuous political action, Sidney attempts to purge poesy of any occult connotations and in this way seeks to annex the power of these new epistemologies to a Christian humanism rooted in Aristotelian and Ciceronian prudence. For Sidney poesy is valuable because it links secular ethical and political insights to a redemptive Christian project, such that participation in public life is the most appropriate course of action for the Protestant humanist, and poesy is saved from the challenges of more extreme Puritan attacks. But an important

[67] See P. French (1972, esp. 145–7 and 89–105 on Dee and the possible influence of Agrippa on both Dee and Sidney). According to several biographers, Sidney himself disliked astrology, although his uncle the Earl of Leicester regarded it as a quasi-medicinal science and perhaps encouraged Sidney to consult the mathematician Thomas Allen, for whom he acted as patron; see n. 28 above and Osborn (1972: 18, 517–22); Duncan-Jones (1991: 50–1); Buxton (1954: 39–43). P. French (1972) argues that Sidney was sympathetic to both 'mathematical' and 'judicial' astrology, as the foretelling of future events was known, citing *Astrophil and Stella* 26 as evidence; he points out that Sidney's horoscope not only registers his talents in grammar, rhetoric, dialectic, natural philosophy, and ethics but claims that Sidney is 'intended by nature for the study of the mathematicals, and by birth for learning celestial philosophy', observes that he shows an 'eager and ardent' (*studiosa et ardens*) interest in astronomy, and notes that he can discuss *mathēsis* (*Mathesi*) intelligently (p. 131). On the place of astrology in English thought more broadly, see Clulee (1977; 1984; 1988, esp. 21, 39–73); also Harkness (1999: 195–214); on Bruno in England, see Yates (1964: 178, 205–11); Weiner (1980); and Yates (1966: 252–3), linking Sidney's discussion of the poetic image to Bruno's theory of memory.

[68] Cf. Clulee (1984; 1988, esp. 152–3, 175).

effect of this broader ethical orientation is that Sidney begins to extend the meaning of 'nature' to include human action and forms of *social* organization as well as natural objects and processes, in this way using the terms and categories of sixteenth-century humanism to frame a set of philosophical questions that Hobbes or Locke would refine in the next century, and Vico after them.

'AN IMAGINATIVE GROUNDPLAT OF A PROFITABLE INVENTION'

Sidney has expanded the meaning of the term 'invention' in order to distinguish his concept of 'imitation' from a naive realism that produces no new knowledge (the 'meaner sort of painters'; 80. 30–1) and the rote copying of literary models (the humanist pedagogue and the bad poet). The hermeneutic relation is crucial to Sidney's defence of poesy on the grounds of its ultimate ethical purpose—obviously the text must be read and interpreted if it is to move the reader towards action in the world—and given his careful attention to particular reading methods with Harvey or in his letters to Robert, it is somewhat surprising that he never addresses more directly how the reader is meant to approach the poetic text. The image moves the reader, as he repeatedly emphasizes, and his analogy to painting and diagrams provides some indication as to how this moving occurs through the faculties of judgement and imagination. It often seems as though for Sidney the reader's prudential imitation is inseparable from the act of interpretation itself: by 'imitating' the poetic model, in other words, the reader intuitively imitates also the very deliberative process that was constitutive of that model in the first place and that continues to reside within it.[69] As he emphasizes, the act of poetic making is 'not wholly imaginative, as we are wont to say by them that build castles in the air' (79. 11–12) but works '*substantially*... not only to make a Cyrus, which been but a particular excellency as Nature might have done, but to bestow a Cyrus upon the world to make many Cyruses, if they will learn aright and how that maker made him' (79. 12–16; my emphasis).

Later in the essay, however, Sidney offers a more explicit analogy for the act of interpretation that distinguishes between what the reader takes from history and what he or she takes from poesy, specifically. The allusion is a brief but telling one, as Sidney attempts to defend poesy against the charge that it is a mode of 'lying':

and therefore as in historie looking for trueth, they may go away full fraught with falshood: So in *Poesie*, looking but for fiction, they shal use the narration but as an imaginative groundplat of a profitable invention.[70]

Sidney's use of the technical term 'groundplat' (or 'ground-plot', as the Olney edition reads here) provides perhaps the clearest indication in the essay that he has

---

[69] Kahn (1985: 39).

[70] I cite from the original spelling of Ponsonby's edition (Sidney 1922–6: iii. 29); editors emend 'groundplat' to 'ground-plot' on the authority of the Olney edition without noting the fact.

the practical spatial arts directly in mind as a model for the hermeneutic response to poetic fiction.[71] The act of reading as Sidney understands it implies the use of the imagination not simply in its capacity to 'make' mental images but in the distinctly spatial capacity that it had acquired for early-modern writers. Reading is an act of mental diagramming, one that arranges material in both a geometrical, logical formation and a linear, progressive movement through a series of textual instances, much the way Sidney had advised Denny to read Livy alongside Ortelius, adopting a method of reading that combined an eye for narrative progression with a topographic literacy, or the way Robert was to follow the lead of Henry Savile, England's foremost geometrician, and 'sett downe such a Table of Remembrance to your selfe' when he read Tacitus, Livy, or Plutarch.[72] The circumstances, situations, agents, and events that constitute the poetic 'narration' have been composed by the poet to demonstrate universal principles in particular examples and to model actions and deliberative procedures. The role of the reader is to treat these artificial images like the 'models' or 'groundplats' that they are: to reconstruct from the methods of reasoning that they demonstrate, using the imagination to vivify the image on the page and judgement to produce action in the substantial world. One suspects, in fact, that there is nothing inherently wrong with history itself, so long as it is not read naively or without 'method' but the way that Sidney and Harvey themselves did—in the same way that they read poetry.[73]

---

[71] Robinson (1972: 88–96, 122–8), was the first to trace Sidney's use of the term back to practical mathematical authors such as Recorde and Dee, but without mention of Sidney's own personal involvement in engineering projects or his wider reading; on 'groundplot', see Ong (1958: 38, 302); Tuve (1947, esp. 331–55); Osborn (1972, esp. 51 n. 44); Gilbert (1963: 81–92, esp. 85); Trimpi (1999: 197 and n. 15 (connecting the metaphor to Aristotle's notion of the 'dramatic hypothesis' in *Poetics* 17. 3; see Ch. 2 n. 16, above); 1983, esp. 50–8); K. Eden (1986: 158–60); Heninger (1974: 296). We have seen in Ch. 2 how Dee himself had called his table of the mathematical sciences a 'groundplat'; P. French (1972: 31, 59–60, 142–5, 167–71) has discussed Dee's relationship to Ramus and the similarity of practical purpose in both men's work, especially concerning mathematics. Sidney had met Ramus during his trip to Paris and continued to correspond with several of Ramus' students, among them du Plessis Mornay and Théophile de Banos (Buxton 1954: 45–7; Osborn 1972: 51; Duncan-Jones 1991: 70, 81); he maintained relationships with several English advocates of Ramism, including Harvey, Abraham Fraunce, and William Temple (see n. 56 above). Sidney supported Fraunce at St John's and received the dedication of a manuscript by Fraunce treating Ramist logic and emblems (*c.*1581); see Buxton (1954: 46, 146–8); Duncan-Jones (1991: 155). On Harvey's Ramism, see Ch. 2 above, and Grafton and Jardine (1986: 184–96); he, too, uses a variant of the term 'groundplat'—in this case, 'platforme' (Harvey 1913: 155–6)—to designate a pattern for his personal philosophy of conduct.

[72] Cf. Sidney's letter to Robert of 18 October 1580, recommending an approach to history reading based on Bodin's *Methodvs ad facilem historiarum cognitionem* (1566, 1572) (Sidney 1922–6: iii. 130–2); also the *Arcadia* of 1590, as Strephon, gazing at the spot where Urania departed, declares to Claius: 'here we finde, that as our remembrance came ever cloathed unto us in the forme of this place, so this place gives newe heate to the feaver of our languishing remembrance. . . . as this place served us to thinke of those thinges, so those thinges serve as places to call to memorie more excellent matters' (Sidney 1922–6: i. 6–7).

[73] Cf. most famously Spenser's 'Letter to Ralegh' appended to the 1590 edition of the *Faerie Queene*, where he uses 'history' and 'historical fiction' to explain the prudential purpose of the poem in ways that are close to Sidney's arguments; also Elyot's (1531) several defences of history; i. 81–91, ii. 385–401, esp. 397.

But Sidney's usage of the 'groundplat' figure, we should recall, concerns not merely poetic or prose 'inventions' but the use of the imagination necessary to successful *theatrical* representation, specifically, and he invokes the theatre, too, when he defends poesy as a practical epistemology by comparing it to the disciplines that currently define the university curriculum.[74] All 'arts', as intellectual artefacts abstracted and organized into a coherent, teachable body of knowledge, are performative imitations of nature, or 'actors and players, as it were, of what nature will have set forth' (78. 4–5). Although he observes that 'the mathematician might draw forth a straight line with a crooked heart' (82. 30–2) and thus render geometry suspect as a mode of moral instruction, Sidney later invokes geometry as a way of defending the often scurrilous nature of comedy on stage, the very institution that Stephen Gosson had attacked in his *School of Abuse* (1579) and, perhaps unwisely, dedicated to him: 'Now, as in geometry the oblique must be known as well as the right, and in arithmetic the odd as well as the even, so in the actions of our life who seeth not the filthiness of evil wanteth a great foil to perceive the beauty of virtue' (96. 2–6). For Sidney as for many of his contemporaries, the theatre is valuable because it provides a way of coming to knowledge about nature, the self, and the social world: it gives symbolic form to human action in a medium that is itself a spatialized mode of *praxis*; it distances, organizes, and abstracts, allowing for the modelling of ethical behaviour or social processes that are so large as to be inaccessible to the naked eye. We may identify this as a proto-'experimental' method; we may call it 'critique'; we may, as early-modern authors did, call it 'satire'. This is the value of the theatre and of dramatic poesy, a value that was not lost on Sidney or on the playwrights of the period, whose task it would be to produce the 'imaginative groundplats' of a civic architecture.

[74] On the 'theatre' as a pervasive metaphor in Renaissance humanist thought, see W. West (2002); Blair (1997, esp. 153–79).

4

Noun, Foot, and Measured Line

A Line is a right consecutive imagination in length, beginning at a poynt, and
endeth also at a point, but it hath no bredth.

(Sebastiano Serlio, *The Five Books of Architecture, 1611*)

Since Bacon, the recurring dream of the scientist has been not simply of comprehensive classification and taxonomy, nor of technological mastery over the world
and its objects, but a dream of mimesis: a dream of *representing* natural phenomena,
accurately and in the fullness of their objectivity, in the service of theoretical
abstraction, reason, and absolute law. For Bacon himself, conventional linguistic
representation finally proved inadequate to the project: 'words are imposed
according to the apprehension of the vulgar', he complained in 1620 in his
Novum Organum, 'and therefore the ill and unfit choice of words wonderfully
obstructs the understanding...words...throw all into confusion, and lead men
away into numberless empty controversies and idle fancies'.[1] Scholars should
imitate 'the custom and wisdom of the mathematicians (*ex more et prudentia
mathematicorum*)' when establishing the definitions of their words and names, so
as to avoid useless disputes; in 1623 Bacon called for a 'grammatica philosophica'
in addition to '*grammatica literaria*' that would 'diligently inquire, not the analogy
of words with one another, but the analogy between words and things, or reason'.[2]
Despite the objections of later seventeenth-century anti-Platonists such as Samuel
Parker that 'the use of Words is not to explaine the Natures of Things, but to stand
as signes in their stead'—an opinion more suited to our own post-Saussurean
attitudes—the search for a universal and artificial language to rival that of Adam
persisted, in which there might be a perfect 'harmony', to use Johannes
Comenius' terms, 'between things and the concepts of things...everything in our
new language must be adapted to the exact the perfect representation of things'.[3]

[1] Bacon (1861: i. 252; cf. i. 262); Padley (1985–8: i. 331). On the universal language projects of
the 17th century, see Padley (1985–8: i. esp. 325–81); Slaughter (1982: 85–186); Knowlson (1975,
esp. 3–11); Stillman (1995); Markley (1993: 63–94, with additional bibliography); Bono (1995, esp.
199–246 (on Bacon), 247–71 (on Mersenne and Descartes)).

[2] Bacon (1861: i. 262, ii. 414–15, ix. 111–12).

[3] Both cited by Padley (1985–8: i. 333, 346); cf. Knowlson (1975: 39); Slaughter (1982:
114–15).

For many of the seventeenth-century language projectors, mathematical symbols, whether arithmetic, geometric, or algebraic, seemed to offer the most natural and most promising precedent for an unmediated and perfectly referential mode of representation that might form the basis of a universal 'character'.[4] Comenius believed that his system of characters could 'express all concepts and all things in their special characteristics' much more effectively than Latin, since like a mathematical instrument 'its individual names will be made to match the numbers, measurements, and weights of things themselves'.[5] Thomas Sprat's *History of the Royal Society* (1667) argued that in all scientific investigation it was necessary to 'return back to the primitive purity, and shortness, when men deliver'd so many things, almost in an equal number of words ... bringing all things as near the Mathematical plainness, as they can: and preferring the language of Artizans, Countrymen, and Merchants, before that, of wits, or Scholars'.[6] Descartes, too, based his few comments about the prospects of a universal language on a mathematically derived 'method' for human understanding:

I believe ... that it would be possible to devise a further system to enable one to make up the primitive words and their symbols in such a language so that it could be taught very quickly. Order is what is needed: all the thoughts which can come into the human mind must be arranged in an order like the natural order of the numbers. In a single day one can learn to name every one of the infinite series of numbers, and thus to write infinitely many different words in an unknown language. The same could be done for all the other words necessary to express all the other things which fall within the purview of the human mind.[7]

Seth Ward, Savilian Professor of Astronomy at Oxford, followed Descartes in turning to the symbolic conventions of algebra, finding there a model for the formation of a universal, international, and truly philosophical language in which the nature of all things might be expressed:

When I first fell from that verbose way of tradition of the Mathematicks, used by the Ancients ... into the Symbolical way, invented by Vieta, advanced by Harriot, perfected by Mr. Oughtred, and Des Cartes: I was presently extreamly taken with it ... it did presently occurre to me, that by the helpe of Logick and Mathematicks ... all discourses [might be] resolved into sentences, those into words, words signifying either simple notions or being resolvable into simple notions ... it is manifest, that if all the sorts of simple notions be found out, and have Symboles assigned to them ... the reason of their composition easily

---

[4] On the mathematical aspects of universal language projects, see Knowlson (1975: 17–27, esp. 22, 91, and 108–9, citing Leibniz in a 1677 letter: 'if we had [this universal character] as I conceive it, we would be able to reason in metaphysics and in ethics [*morale*] more or less as in Geometry'); Slaughter (1982: 87, 119–20, 125, 127–30, 137–8); Padley (1985–8: i. 336); Markley (1993, esp. 66–9); Bono (1995: 193–8, 264–71); Reiss (1997: 110–14, 118–22, 128).

[5] *Via Lucis*, cited by Knowlson (1975: 91).

[6] Sprat (1667: 113), cited by Knowlson (1975: 40–1).

[7] Descartes to Mersenne, 20 Nov. 1629 (1984–91: iii. 12). On Descartes's theories of a universal language modelled on a universal mathematics (*mathēsis*), see Slaughter (1982: 127–8; Padley (1985–8: i. 336); Knowlson (1975: 48–51, 65–6, 91); Bono (1995: 264–71).

known . . . and yet will represent to the very eye all the elements of their composition, and so deliver the natures of things . . .[8]

In his *Il Saggiatore* (1623), Galileo argued famously that the book of philosophy is quite unlike the 'book of fiction created by some man, like the *Iliad* or *Orlando Furioso*—books in which the least important thing is whether what is written in them is true':

Philosophy is written in this grand book—I mean the universe—which stands continually open to our gaze, but it cannot be understood unless one first learns to comprehend the language and interpret the characters in which it is written. It is written in the language of mathematics, and its characters are triangles, circles, and other geometrical figures, without which it is humanly impossible to understand a single word of it; without these, one is wandering about in a dark labyrinth.[9]

Galileo's comments emblematize the role that geometry had come to play in the new philosophy of nature by the early seventeenth century, providing a model for a rigorously deductive logical method and for defining distinct classes of objects of knowledge but serving, too, as an entire system to representation to rival that of human language, one through which mathematical practitioners and natural philosophers as diverse as Leonardo da Vinci, Copernicus, Tycho Brahe, Nicolo Fontana de Brescia (Tartaglia), Geramolo Cardano, Simon Steven, Descartes, and Galileo himself could reconceptualize traditional problems in astronomy, optics, or mechanics and develop new methods of demonstration.

This tendency to conceptualize in mathematical and geometrical terms not merely language or the natural and cosmological world but all reasoned, analytic thought in general is also visible in Thomas Hobbes's *Leviathan* (1651), where nouns or 'names' are units of signification that may be set upon things in the world—'imposed' is the word Hobbes uses—and then set beside one another in a relationship of extension and spatial commensurability. Using quantitative analogies to describe the relationship between 'common' or 'universal names' and the things they signify, Hobbes presents philosophical thought itself as nothing less than a grand mental act of conceptual measurement:

. . . *man, horse, tree*, every of which, though but one name, is nevertheless the name of divers particular things, in respect of all which together it is called an universal . . . One universal name is imposed on many things for their similitude in some quality or other accident; and whereas a proper name bringeth to mind one thing only, universals recall any one of those many . . . And of names universal, some are more, and some of less extent, the larger comprehending the less large; and some again of equal extent, comprehending each other reciprocally. As for example, the name body is of larger signification than the word

---

⁸ *Vindiciae Academiarum* (1654), cited by Slaughter (1982: 138–9).
⁹ *The Assayer* (Galileo 1623: 183–4); cf. Crombie's (1952: ii. 131–74) discussion of developments in 17th-century mechanics (citing the same passage on ii. 151); Bono (1995: 193–8).

man, and comprehendeth it; and the names man and rational are of equal extent, comprehending mutually one another.[10]

As Hobbes continues to discuss the process of thinking, he begins to convert the noun from a qualitative unit to a purely quantitative one: that which is 'subject to names', he writes, 'is whatsoever can enter into or be considered in an account, and be added one to another to make a sum, or subtracted one from another and leave a remainder'.[11] The act of reasoning itself Hobbes calls 'reckoning', by which he means a logical process of adding or subtracting these nominal units, which are now simultaneously qualitative *and* quantitative:

When a man *reasoneth*, he does nothing else but conceive a sum total from *addition* of parcels, or conceive a remainder from *subtraction* of one sum from another; which (if it be done by words) is conceiving of the consequence of the names of all the parts to the name of the whole, or from the names of the whole and one part to the name of another part . . . These operations are not incident to numbers only, but to all manner of things that can be added together and taken one out of another. For as arithmeticians teach to add and subtract in *numbers*, so the geometricians teach the same in *lines, figures* (solid and superficial), *angles, proportions, times,* degrees of *swiftness, force, power,* and the like; the logicians teach the same in *consequences of words*, adding together *two names* to make an *affirmation*, and *two affirmations* to make a *syllogism*; and *many syllogisms* to make a *demonstration*; and from the *sum*, or *conclusion*, of a *syllogism* they subtract one *proposition* to find the other . . .

Out of all of which we may define (that is to say determine) what that is which is meant by this word *reason*, when we reckon it amongst the faculties of the mind. For REASON, in this sense, is nothing but *reckoning* (that is, adding and subtracting) of the consequences of general names agreed upon for the *marking* and *signifying* of our thoughts . . . (I. v. 1–2)

Hobbes regards the process of thinking in language as a simple mathematical syntax—nouns are units arranged in a linear sequence of either accretion or diminution—and this syntax is not simply arithmetic or numeric but is explicitly one of extension, spatial positioning, and placement. This is evident from the first passage I have cited and the analogy with geometry above, but also from Hobbes's definition of 'truth':

truth consisteth in the right ordering of names in our affirmations; a man that seeketh precise *truth* had need to remember what every name he uses stands for, and to place it accordingly, or else he will find himself entangled in words . . . And therefore in geometry (which is the only science that it hath pleased God hitherto to bestow on mankind) men begin at settling the significations of their words; which settling of significations they call definitions, and place them in the beginning of their reckoning. (I. iv. 12)

If in 1651 geometry has become a model for Hobbes not simply of scientific method but of 'signification' in general, conceived in a systematic, scientific way, and the noun has become a quantitative, spatial unit with size and extension that can placed upon, or 'imposed' upon, its object and then arranged in a sequence

---

[10] Hobbes, *Leviathan*, p. I, ch. iv, 'Of Speech', paras. 6–8.
[11] *Leviathan*, I. iv. 14; cf. I. iv. 10; cf. Reiss (1997: 115), on similar analogies in Ramus.

seriatim, a way of measuring equivalency that is nothing less than the act of reasoning itself—what then was the conceptual relationship between measurement and language at the beginning of the seventeenth century, fifty years before it had become a foundation of scientific thought? Is it possible to identify a poetics or rhetoric of measurement that is not yet fully rational, universal, or theoretical and which flourishes not in the mind of the philosopher but under the frenzied pen of the poet?

DELINEATING: GEORGE PUTTENHAM'S *ARTE OF ENGLISH POESIE*

From the opening sentence of his *Arte of English Poesie* (1589), George Puttenham defines *poiēsis* in terms that are nearly identical to those that Sidney had established; despite the fact that his book was published before Sidney's essay actually appeared in print, the influence of Sidney's ideas are everywhere visible in Puttenham's arguments and definitions, from the very first sentence.[12] Like Sidney, Puttenham takes pains to distinguish the poet's mental act of genuine 'making' from mere 'imitation', although unlike Sidney he accords a certain distinction to poets who excel in the latter mode. For Puttenham, too, 'imitation' describes an act of observing and copying from nature that also formed an important part of Sidney's notion of the poetic image: he is simply taking note of several distinct critical traditions that were already present in Sidney and in Continental writing on poetics and hesitating to choose between them.

This 'empirical' approach to poetic production is consistent with Puttenham's larger emphasis, like Sidney, on poesy as a distinct epistemology—a way of coming to knowledge about the world through representation—even though much of his book is concerned with cataloguing tropes and also presents itself as a manual of style. Poesy offers a coherent 'method' for arriving at knowledge 'gathered by experience' (p. 21), and it is in this sense that it is best compared to rhetoric or dialectic. It is in this concluding chapter on art and nature where Puttenham's 'scientific' approach to poetics becomes most evident. Like 'Grammer, *Logicke*, and *Rhetorick*' (p. 311), poesy not only 'imitates' natural principles but even improves on nature and alters its products. In this sense the poet is most similar to the physician who administers medicine, the lens-maker who grinds spectacles, the gardener who prunes, fertilizes, or cross-breeds plants, and the alchemist who fabricates gold (pp. 308–10). The skilful poet 'need no more be ashamed thereof than a shoemaker to have made a cleanly shoe, or a Carpenter to have buylt a faire

---

12 'A poet is as much to say as a maker. And our English name well conformes with the Greeke word: for of *poiein* to make, they call a maker *Poeta* . . .' (Puttenham 1589: 19); all citations are to the facsimile edition ed. Arber; cf. Heninger (1974: 302–6).

house' (p. 308), writes Puttenham—indeed, this is the most marvellous use of art, for it is also the most completely synthetic:

Finally in another respect arte is as it were an encounterer and contrary to nature, producing effects neither like to hers, nor by participation with her operations, nor by imitation of her patternes, but makes things and produceth effects altogether strange and diverse, and of such forme and quality (nature always supplying stuffe) as she never would nor could have done of her selfe, as the carpenter that builds a house, the joyner that makes a table or a bedstead, the tailor a garment, the Smith a locke or a key . . . (p. 310)

Puttenham's direct association between the craft of the poet and many other early modern forms of technological intelligence is remarkable: he describes a quotidian culture of experiment, in which every meal or every keyhole conceals within itself a creative act of human intellect that borders on the occult.

As for Sidney, for Puttenham this supreme act of poetic 'making' consists in a 'devise' and 'an excellent sharpe and quick invention', which proceeds from 'a clear and bright phantasie and imagination' (p. 312), which Puttenham regards as an instrumental or productive organ; as Juan Huarte had argued, so Puttenham claims that this type of imagination is shared among poets, the 'politique Captaine', the 'witty enginer or cunning artificer'; as for Harvey, for Puttenham the poet's quickness of thought is typical of the 'law maker or counselor of deepe discourse' (p. 34): 'of this sorte of phantasie are all good Poets, notable Captaines stratagematique, all cunning artificers and engineers, all Legislators Polititiens and counsellours of estate, in whose exercises the inventive part is most employed and is to the sound and true judgment of man most needful' (p. 35). A certain defensiveness about foreign words and inkhorn terms, meanwhile, has provoked Puttenham to clarify his choice of words at the opening of the book by invoking terms reminiscent not simply of Sidney or Aristotle but of no less an authority than John Dee, as we have seen in Chapter 2:

These be words used by th'author in this present treatise, *scientificke*, but with some reason, for it answereth the word *mechanicall*, which no other word could have done so properly, for when hee [Puttenham himself] spake of all artificers which rest either in science or in handy craft, it followed necessarilie that *scientifique* should be coupled with *mechanicall*: or els neither of both to have bene allowed, but in their places: a man of science liberall, and a handicrafts man. . . . (p. 158)

Like Dee, Puttenham regards the terms 'scientificke' and 'mechanical' as synonymous, since both words are appropriate adjectives to describe types of 'artificers'; at the same time, his later explanation indicates that he recognizes a distinction between each position that the poet seems in some way to transcend. This is the distinction between theory and practice, the very distinction that Dee, too, was seeking to resolve by gathering the practical measuring techniques of the carpenter and surveyor into the coherent and epistemologically viable intellectual field of *mathēsis* founded on the rules of Euclidean geometry.

Puttenham, too, will look to the methods of geometry as a model for the poetic intelligence: on the one hand, he will affiliate poesy with ideal geometrical proportions, musical harmony, speech, hearing, and the dimension of time, a chain of Neoplatonic and Pythagorean associations that runs throughout his essay and lends to it its self-consciously theoretical aspect. On the other hand, he will continue to conceptualize the act of poetic composition as a mode of material 'making' that derives directly from the geometrical manuals and the representational techniques they employed, as I have discussed in Chapter 2. The distinctly practical orientation of the *Arte* is most visible in those moments where Puttenham shifts from a rhetorical or philosophical account of poesy to a series of illustrative and pedagogical techniques that depend on the use of iconic diagrams and the active imitation of models integrated on the two-dimensional space of the page itself. It is here that the fundamental similarity between Puttenham's 'art of English poesie' and the art of geometrical *poiēsis* visible in the technical manuals of his period emerges most clearly. Even Homer, Puttenham asserts, must have been a 'Surveyour in Court' to describe with such detail and accuracy the 'order and array of battels . . . the sieges and assaults of cities and townes . . . the order, sumptuousnesse, and magnificence of royal bankets, feasts, weddings, and enterwewes' (p. 20). '*Amphion* and *Orpheus,* two Poets of the first ages . . . builded up cities, and reared walles with the stones that came in heapes to the sound of his harpe' (p. 22).

The 'art' of the poet is 'a skill appertaining to utterance' (p. 21), and poetic utterance is distinguished from rhetoric and from common speech alike by being 'contrived into measures' (p. 24) that are arranged in 'proportion' (p. 78). With a sweeping set of analogies drawn from 'such as professe the Mathematicall sciences' (p. 78), Puttenham argues that 'proportion' is either musical, arithmetical, or geometrical (p. 78). 'Proportion in measure' (p. 81) provides Puttenham with the smallest unit of analysis: he invokes the Greek and Latin etymology of the term (*metron* and *mensura*) and observes that in classical poetry 'quantity' refers to duration of the syllable, whereas in contemporary English usage the term denotes simply the number of the syllables in each 'verse' (p. 81). Puttenham here joins a long-standing debate, initiated by Ascham and flourishing in the 1580s between Spenser, Harvey, Sidney, Dyer, and Greville, over the need to reform English poetry along a classical model: to create a native system of quantitative prosody that will rival that of the ancients and bring artful order to the English verse line by reducing it to a series of formal, abstract, and purely interchangeable units, each of which can be added to one another or resolved together into a larger unit, or 'foote' (p. 81).

Spenser, Sidney, Dyer, and Greville attempted a solution to the problem, at least for a time, while Harvey and Puttenham remained unconvinced. Spenser's famous expostulation that English writers should enjoy 'the Kingdom of oure owne Language', in which a metrical system might be developed that 'measure[s] our Accents by the sounde, reserving the Quantitie to the Verse', provoked only reluctance from Harvey.[13] 'Is there no other Pollicie to pull downe Ryming and set

[13] Spenser to Harvey, G. G. Smith (1904: i. 99. 6–10).

'uppe versifying', he responded:

> but you must needes correcte magnificat: and against all order of Lawe, and in despite of Custome, forcibly usurpe and tyrranize uppon a quiet companye of wordes that so farre beyonde the memorie of man have so peaceably enioyed their several Priviledges and Liberties, without any disturbance or the laste controlement?... never heard I any that durst presume so much over the Englishe...as to alter the Quantitie of any one sillable, otherwise than oure common speache and generall receyved Custome woulde beare them oute. (117. 16–34)

The key, Harvey insists, 'eyther for the assured and infallible Certaintie of our English Artificall Prosodye particularly, or generally to bring our Language into Arte and to frame a Grammer or Rhetoric thereof', requires 'first of all universally to agree upon ONE AND THE SAME ORTHOGRAPHIE, in all pointes conformable and proportionate to our COMMON NATURAL PROSODYE' (102. 17–23). Harvey's professed expertise in 'industrious practis, or Method, the two discovering eies of this age' (cited by Stern 1979: 125) and his reluctance to adopt the 'rules and precepts' of quantitative prosody that so enthused Spenser reflect a distinctly practical method of reasoning that recognizes the multiplicity of particular instances and only tentatively offers general precepts or laws. Several passages in his correspondence over questions of prosody are overtly philosophical and display a nearly Baconian grasp of induction or reasoning by analogy.[14] Asked by Spenser to send 'the Rules and Precepts of Arte, which you observe in Quantities' (99. 23–8), Harvey responds:

> I dare geve no Preceptes, nor set downe any CERTAINE GENERAL ARTE; and yet see my boldnesse. I am not greatly squaimish of my PARTICULAR EXAMPLES, whereas he that can but reasonably skil of the one wil give easily a shreude gesse at the other, considering that the one fetcheth his original and offspring from the other.... But to let this by-disputation passe, which is already so thoroughly discoursed and canvassed of the best Philosophers, and namely ARISTOTLE, that poynt us, as it were with the forefinger, to the very FOUNTAINES AND HEAD SPRINGES of Artes and Artificiall preceptes, in the ANALITIQUES and METAPHYSIKES...(102. 35–103. 28)

> Wherein nevertheless I grant, after long advise and diligent observation of particulars, a certain uniform Analogie and Concordance being in processe of time espyed out, sometime this, sometime that, hath been noted by good wits in their ANALYSES to fall out generally alyke, and, as a man woulde saye, regularly, in all or most wordes: as Position, Dipthong, and the like: not as firste and essentiall causes of this or that effecte (here lyeth the point), but as Secundarie and Accidentall Signes of this or that Qualitie. (121. 10–19)

The passages not only confirm Harvey's remarkable intellectual breadth and adventurousness but again indicate the relevance of contemporary English literary debates to the development of later scientific method: we see clearly the importation of technical language from a neo-Aristotelian university context and

---

[14] Cf. Curtis (1959: 255–6), on similarities between Harvey and Bacon's thinking.

analogical methods of reasoning typical of practical thinking brought to bear on a question of everyday pronunciation and how it might be systematized and transposed into poetic form.

Indeed, the entire English debate over orthography and prosody can be regarded as an extension of contemporary complaints among mathematical practitioners that the quantitative units of *spatial* or artisanal measure need to be standardized and correct measuring procedures disseminated more widely. Both poets and geometers sought to reconcile an artificial, standardized, and quantified measure with a series of heterogeneous objects, the infinite particularity of which was understood to derive from their naturalness, their use, or their custom.[15] In a letter to Harvey in 1579, Spenser puns on this precise overlap: 'And nowe requite I you with the like, not with the verye best, but with the verye shortest, namely with a fewe *Iambickes*: I dare warrant they be precisely perfect for the feete (as you can easily judge) and varie not one inch from the Rule.'[16] 'It is not either Position, or Dipthong, or Diastole, or anye like Grammer Schoole Device', Harvey responds, 'that doeth or can indeed either make long or short, or encrease, or diminish the number of sillables, but onely the common allowed and received PROSODYE, taken up by universall consent of all, and continued by a generall use and Custome of all' (121. 10). 'In good sooth,' proclaims Harvey, 'and by the faith I beare to the Muses, you shal never have my subscription or consent (though you should charge me wyth the authoritie of five hundreth Maister DRANTS) to make your *Carpēnter*, our *Carpenter*, an inche longer or bigger than God and his Englishe people have made him.'[17]

Turning to Richard More's *The Carpenter's Rule* (1602), we may observe a similar trend taking place in the practical manuals, in that More sets out to homogenize different customary standards of measurement into standard units while also exposing the errors in contemporary measuring techniques and offering new methods that are more accurate. 'Let us either have just measure, if we buy by measure,' More maintains (in rhyme), 'or els let us buy it by gesse. For it is a shame to pretend to measure truly, and yet doe nothing lesse' (A4[r]). At the same time, George Gascoigne's *Certayne Notes of Instruction Concerning the Making of Verse or Rhyme in English*, originally published in 1575 but reprinted in 1587 as part of his *Whole Woorkes*, only two years before Puttenham's treatise, complains of a similar inconsistency in *poetic* metre and urges the poet to maintain one continuous measure throughout a poem.[18] Gascoigne goes so far as to provide a simple diagram of two different kinds of metre, which he positions above the relevant verse line like a 'rule' so that the reader (and writer) may arrange the sounds and the duration of spoken syllables in a regular fashion (Smith 1904: i. 50–1; Fig. 4.1).

[15] On the problem of measurement and 'custom' in the period, see Sullivan (1997).
[16] Spenser to Harvey, G. G. Smith (1904: i. 90. 19–23).
[17] Harvey to Spenser, G. G. Smith (1904: i. 117. 11–16; also 98. 29–30, 119. 20–5).
[18] 'The commonest sort of verse which we use now adayes ... I know not certainly howe to name it, unlesse I should say that it doth consist of Poulters measure, which giveth xii. for one dozen and xiij. for another' (Smith 1904: i. 57. 4–9; also 49.1–17).

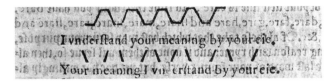

FIG. 4.1. Verse 'rule': George Gascoigne, *Certayne Notes of Instruction Concerning the Making of Verse or Ryme in English* (1575)

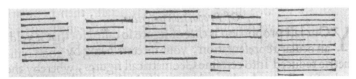

FIG. 4.2. Verse lines and stanzaic forms: George Puttenham, *The Arte of English Poesie* (1589)

Rather than the 'foot', however—the singular unit of measure—it is the structural and geometrical notion of the 'line' that dominates the central chapters of Puttenham's treatise. Chapter 21, on 'Proportion by Situation', begins by discussing the aural effects of poetry but immediately resorts to spatial analogies. Each verse is grouped in an artful pattern according to a set of geometrical principles, which are first simply perceived by the ear and are then fully realized *as a pattern* by the synthetic mental operation of the hearer (pp. 97–8). This synthesis takes a geometrical shape and is best understood, Puttenham argues, by 'an occular example, because ye may the better conceive it' (p. 98; Fig. 4.2). Puttenham continues to designate each of the kinds of 'proportions', or possible groupings of lines—'quadrein', 'sizeine', 'distick', and so forth—which are the aural equivalent of the definitions of multi-sided figures in the geometrical manuals. The exact correlation finally emerges in Puttenham's chapter devoted to 'proportion in figure', in which 'your meeters [are] by good symmetrie reduced into certaine Geometricall figures' (p. 104). Here the verbal units of 'verse' are realized pictorially as lines, in gestures that reproduce exactly the expository and practical techniques of the geometrical manuals that I have examined in Chapter 2. Puttenham again interrupts his discourse to provide a series of templates or figural examples, which are 'filled' with the lines that the poet, in turn, will 'fill' with his verbal content (Fig. 4.3). A subsequent section then provides a verbal exposition of the material, along with examples of actual shaped poems.

Having explained the arrangement of verses either by concord (rhyme) or distance and set out, in both illustration and verbal description, their possible permutations, Puttenham then draws the reader's attention to the small curved lines which unify the separate verses and mark their concord. These graphic marks represent the idea of structural relation itself, which he again illustrates

FIG. 4.3. Templates
and shaped poems:
Puttenham

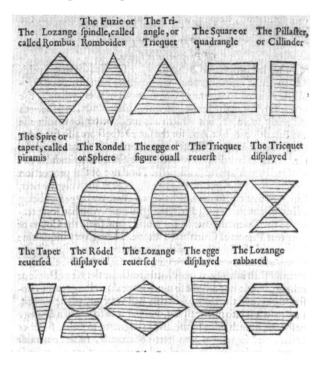

FIG. 4.4. Compass
strokes and 'concord':
Puttenham

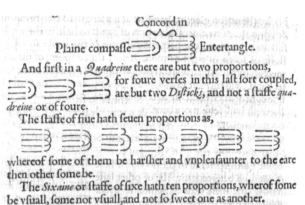

with a diagram (see Fig. 4.4):

Now ye may perceive by these proportions before described that there is a band to be given every verse in a staffe, so as none fall out alone or uncoupled, and this band maketh that the staffe is sayd fast and not loose; even as ye see in buildings of stone or bricke the mason giveth a band, that is a length to two breadths, & upon necessitie divers other sorts of bands to hold in the worde fast and maintaine the perpendicularitie of the wall: so, in any staffe of seven or eight or more verses, the coupling of the moe meeters by rime or concord is the faster band, the fewer the looser band ... (p. 102)

Puttenham then extends the comparison with the practical techniques of the building trades, as well as with their commercial and legal mode of organization, by proposing a small test for the aspiring poet:

To finish the learning of this division, I will set you downe one example of a dittie written extempore with this devise, shewing not onely much promptnesse of wit in the maker, but also great arte and a notable memorie. Make me, saith this writer to one of the companie, so many strokes or lines with your pen as ye would have your song containe verses; and let every line beare his severall length, even as ye would have your verse of measure. Suppose of foure, five, sixe, or eight, or more sillables, and set a figure of everie number at th'end of the line, wherby ye may knowe his measure. Then where you will have your rime or concord to fall, marke it with a compass stroke or semicircle passing over those lines, be they farre or neare in distance, as ye have seene before described. And bycause ye shall not thinke the maker hath premeditated beforehand any such fashioned ditty, do ye your selfe make one verse, whether it be of perfect or imperfect sense, and give it him for a theame to make all the rest upon. If ye shall perceive the maker do keepe the measures and rime as ye have appointed him, and besides do make his dittie sensible and ensuant to the first verse in good reason, then may ye say he is his crafts maister. (pp. 103–4)

Puttenham positions the reader as a kind of poetic artisan who is taught not a set of rules or precepts—not a *theory* of poetry—but is guided through a set of practical techniques according to the methods of the workshop: diagrammatic illustration, a quantitative imagination, a tool or instrument, a blank page on which to inscribe the figure, and the trained gesture necessary to perform the exercise. The geometrical manuals by Robert Recorde and Arthur Hopton illustrate nearly identical problems (Figs. 4.5 and 4.6).

Puttenham's exercise illustrates a 'parallel' quality in the verses that will be perceived by the ear and the eye simultaneously, a proportionate conversion made possible, he maintains, because the eye and ear both perceive a similar kind of harmonic form (p. 89). Puttenham designates this total synthesis with a technical term drawn from the procedures of the meadow and workshop—it is the poet's 'plat':

But now because our maker or Poet is to play many parts and not one alone, as first to devise his *plat or subject*, then to fashion his poeme, thirdly to use his metricall proportions, and last of all to utter with pleasure and delight ... it is not altogether with him as with the crafts man, nor altogether otherwise then with the crafts man, for in that he useth his metricall proportions by appointed and harmonicall measures and distances, he is like the Carpenter or Joyner, for borrowing their tymber and stuffe of nature, they appoint and

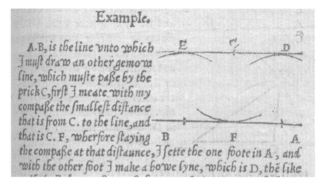

FIG. 4.5. Compass stroke and parallel: Robert Recorde, *The Pathway to Knowledge* (1551)

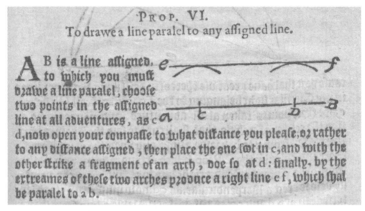

FIG. 4.6. Compass stroke and parallel: Arthur Hopton, *Speculum Topographicum; or, The Topographicall Glasse* (1611)

order it by art otherwise then nature would doe, and worke effects in apparance contrary to hers. . . . (pp. 312–13; my emphasis)

Like Sidney's use of the 'groundplat' metaphor, Puttenham's use of the term 'plat' in this passage conjoins two distinct notions of form—one spatial and diagrammatic; one temporal and linguistic—that the entire format of his book also displays, the first third devoted to geometrical figures and the second two-thirds to rhetorical figures of *speech*, the verbal ornaments of artful discourse delivered in a courtly context. The graphic layout of the text makes evident the degree to which Puttenham has derived his definition of form as a *literary* category from an entire epistemology of measurement and spatial representation that the practical geometrical manuals were defusing through many levels of English culture.[19]

[19] I have treated this question in more detail and with many individual examples in Turner (2007); cf. Menon's penetrating discussion of geometrical and rhetorical 'figure' in Puttenham (1589: 20–2).

A similar usage is visible in Gascoigne's earlier treatise, which included the following warning to those who would let rhyme lead them away from their original conceit:

Many writers, when they have *layed the platforme of their invention*, are yet drawne sometimes (by ryme) to forget it or at least to alter it, as when they cannot readily finde out a worde which maye rime to the first ... (G. G. Smith 1904: i. 51–2; my emphasis)

The appearance here of techniques and vocabulary derived from the measuring manuals is all the more significant, in that 'invention' is both the single most important aspect of poetic production for Gascoigne but also the very thing that resists theoretical generalization: in terms that are strongly reminiscent of Quintilian, Gascoigne admits that 'the rule of Invention, which of all other rules is most to be marked', is also 'hardest to be prescribed in certayne and infallible rules' because 'the occasions of Inventions are (as it were) infinite' (Smith 1904: i. 48. 5–26). It must be illustrated with practical methods of working through a problem, whereby the very rules which provide organization and form to the project are discovered only through their actualization by the operations of the maker.

As we now begin to chart the development of terms in English literary discourse that could designate a notion of *dramatic* form, specifically, it is important to distinguish the various connotations that conventional words like 'plat', 'invention', 'conceit', 'device', or 'argument' communicated. Of the five, only 'plat' and its variations provides a distinctive sense of structured content, if by 'structure' we mean the clarification of the parts of a poetic object as well as the relationships among these parts and among parts and whole: relationships of hierarchy, arrangement, or positioning, of logical priority or temporal sequence, of cause and effect, of similarity or difference.[20] 'Conceit', 'invention', and 'device' all indicate *what* content is represented rather than *how* representation occurs and emphasize the mental aspect of the compositional process, which produced an idea, a concept, or an 'imagination'. To borrow a metaphor that Ascham had used in his chapter on imitation, as we have seen in Chapter 3, terms such as these 'order nothing. They lay before you what is done: they do not teach you how it is done. They busie not them selves with forme of buildying' (18. 35–19. 1). We shall now see how appropriate Ascham's metaphor really was.

MAKING: THE REVEL'S OFFICE

The early Stuart masque and other occasional entertainments of the period provide some of the best examples in which to examine the semantic differences among these different terms more closely, since as performative events they

---

[20] Cf. Heninger (1974: 296, with a useful discussion of 'conceit' and 'invention' on 294–6 and nn. 28, 30, with additional bibliography).

occupy an intermediate point on the continuum between the verbal 'conceits' and extended analogies of the sonnet or lyric, the simultaneously verbal and visual 'conceits' or 'devices' of the emblem, and the represented action or (eventually) the 'plot' of a play. The masque, for instance, contains little 'action' in a narrative sense; nor is it entirely accurate to describe the masque as a 'drama of ideas', since its performance consisted simply in the replacement of one emblematic scene for another in a simple binary structure of alternation, rather than, as in a play, a progressive structure in which paradigmatic substitutions have a transformative function by determining subsequent possibilities of substitution and action.[21] And indeed the guiding theoretical vocabulary for the masque was in fact not 'structural' at all: terms such as 'invention' or 'device' appear throughout the masques in their conventional rhetorical senses, 'invention' designating, as D. J. Gordon has argued (1975: 81, 94–5 and n. 22), both the process of choosing a topic and the topic itself. In this latter sense, 'invention' was synonymous with the equally rhetorical term 'argument', since both described points of departure or premisses to be worked through in an organized fashion. Here the 'argument', like the invention, designates a kind of motto or single controlling idea, but brief manuscript summaries of several masques also survive as an 'argument' in the more usual dramatic sense (as we shall see in Chapter 7), a sketch of the major characters, elements, and sequence of the masque, which may have been drawn up to assist in the preparations for the event.[22] In this more technical function the 'argument' also approximates a stage 'plot' or 'platt', as we shall see in Chapter 5, although it lacks the graphic, schematic nature of these documents. To 'invent' a masque required less that the poet present a completely original idea than it meant translating the desires of a royal patron into a suitable conceit, usually drawn from classical models. 'To which limits, when I had *apted* my invention', Jonson wrote in *The Masque of Beauty*, and other similar comments indicate that this adaptation was a standard procedure—the desires of a Queen were irresistible.[23]

'Device' is somewhat more complex than the other terms in the range of its possible meanings; Gordon has identified it with the tradition of heraldry and the emblem, but the term may also be traced to the technical milieu of theatrical production, like the related terms 'plot', 'plat', and even, on occasion, the term

[21] I draw on Reyher (1909); Campbell (1923: 99–115, 161–94); Chambers (1923: i. 106–212, esp. 149–212); Cunningham (1955, esp. 108–9, 112); Orgel (1965, esp. 16–17 and his comments contrasting *Queens* with *Oberon*, 138–41; 1975); Welsford (1962, esp. 247–9, 254–6); Wickham (1959–81: ii/1. 206–75); Orgel and Strong (1973, esp. i. 1–14, 21); and D. J. Gordon (1975), particularly influential on my own discussion; also Ch. 8, below.

[22] Jonson (1925–52: vii. 318–19); D. J. Gordon (1975: 81); Loewenstein (2002*a*: 178 n. 93); also the examples from an entertainment offered to Elizabeth in 1562, discussed by Wickham (1959–81: iii. 81) and printed as app. D, pp. 267–70. A similar use reappears in the anti-masque to *Neptune's Triumph* (1624), as the Poet enters 'on the *STAGE*, to disperse the Argument' (Jonson 1925–52, vol. vii, line 7); also Ch. 7, below.

[23] 181. 9, my emphasis; cf. *Blacknesse*: 'Hence (because it was her Majesties will, to have them *Black-mores* at first) the invention was derived by me, and presented thus' (Jonson 1925–52, vii. 169. 21–2); Welsford (1962: 256); Cunningham (1955: 109–10).

'invention' when used in a diagrammatic sense.[24] Because the planning of royal entertainments required the involvement of both the Revels Office and the Office of the King's Works—where Inigo Jones would be Surveyor as of 1616—the production of these entertainments should be seen as an important occasion for the dissemination of practical techniques of geometrical representation, much like Dover Harbour in the 1580s, where, as we have seen in Chapter 3, both 'device' and 'invention' were used to describe technical solutions to engineering projects. Evidence from the Revels Office indicates that within a practical milieu the term 'device' could designate simultaneously an idea, invention, or conceit; the actual show or entertainment itself; and finally the sketch, 'outline', or plat that was used in the process of realizing the conceit in its material, mechanical form. A document from *c.*1572 proposing a reorganization of the office speaks at different moments of the expenses to be rendered of various 'Devices and shewes' and their materials; of 'devises as might be most agreable to the Princes expectacion'; and of Sir Thomas Cawarden, first Master of the Revels, as 'beinge skilfull and delightinge in matters of devise', a man 'such as for creditte pleasaunte witte and habilitye in learnyng' might be well suited to his office.[25]

The subsequent description of the office's actual working procedures indicates the technical complexity of the term, first in the question of 'airings' and inventory:

It is very convenyent the stuffe be layed abroade and eayred and that the officers in tyme of Eayringe be present to see to the safetye of it and to gather upon the layinge of it abroade certain devises from tyme to tyme howe thinges translated or amended maye serve afterwardes to good purpose where otherwise it is not possible for the officers to carye in memorye the forme of thinges they be so manye and of such diversitye which manye tymes maye serve aswell to purpose as if the Quenes Maiestye shoulde be at charge to make newe . . . (Feuillerat 1908: 8. 1–8)

Here the 'device' describes a kind of table or pattern book, a graphic depiction of various objects, raw materials, and their uses in different elements as well as suggestions for how they might again be adapted to new occasions in the future. The officers are to refer to these pattern books as they plan new shows in case they cannot 'carye in memorye the forme of thinges'. Tabular documents similar to these types of inventory survive from the Revels Office and record the passage of cloth, thread, or other decorative materials into a representational or symbolic form, which in turn moves through a variety of subsequent forms and generates a non-symbolic, valueless leftover. 'Translation' appears here in a specific technical sense to describe the mutation of materials from one shape to another, according to the informing, creative techniques of the hand of the workman—we are

---

[24] D. J. Gordon (1975: 81); Wickham (1959–81: ii/1. 206–36, 239, 244, 280–99; iii. 65–155).

[25] The document, originating from the Revels Office itself, has been printed in Feuillerat (1908: 5–15); it was recast several years later as a separate 'platte of orders' or table of provisions, which Feuillerat has also reprinted as table I (pp. 16–17); cf. Wickham (1959–81: ii/1. 264); Campbell (1923: 104–5). The citations above are at 7. 19, 6. 9–10, 6. 23–4, 6. 7–8.

reminded of Bottom's 'translation' in *A Midsummer Night's Dream*, where the usage recalls this artisanal meaning.

Conceiving a symbolic idea, recording it for others, and then putting it into act depended on an intuitive fluency with these approximate, and constantly evolving, patterns or drawings. These are also called 'plattes' in several documents. Once the device or show has been decided upon—or perhaps after its performance and before its subsequent dismantling and 'translation'—a record should be made for future reference: 'So sone as anye Maske or other devise ys finished the patterne and platte of the same shalbe Drawne and putt in collers by A painter aswell for witnes of the worcke, as for presidente to the office, to induse, Devise, and shewe, Difference, of that is to come frome that ys paste.'[26] 'To induse, Devise, and shewe, Difference': the document is a remarkable transcription of working methods in process, of materials suspended between different states of physical transformation and simultaneous temporalities, of performances fading into memory and leaving an archive of diagrammatic traces, painted drawings that will determine the shape of delights projected as yet to come.

So far we have remained within the methods of the Revels Office itself. But a similar procedure occurred also at the other side of the production process: the royal consultation. The Master should meet the Queen 'to receyve her highnes pleasure from tyme to tyme attendaunt in the Courte and . . . delyver the same over by speache or platt to one such as followeth'. The Queen dreams, or muses, or signals, or dictates; the Master takes notes and sketches quickly. These he takes back to the workshop and passes on to:

A serjaunte of the Revelles learned and skilfull howe to execute the devise receyved or to invente a newe meete and necessarye with the allowaunce of the master whiche Serjaunte is thoroughly to followe the devise in the office of the Revelles from the begynnynge to the latter ende. (Feuillerat 1908: 8. 15–17)

The Sergeant and Master together study the digestion of the Queen's conceit, adjust it slightly, and maybe even invent anew according to resources. The Serjeant will supervise the work; perhaps he will consult with others, over a platt that had been drawn out of the existing inventory, according to various ideas:

which Platt devised to be drawen and sett fourthe in payntinge by some connynge Artificer in that Arte and to be considered of by all the officers[.] And the best devise that canne be to serve the Prince according to the devisors invencion with lest charge to the Prince as aforesaid may by used as shall seeme meete to the Master of the said office. (11. 25–9)

Then the labour of production itself begins, and the Sergeant oversees its appropriate division:

ffor if a platte be never so well devised yf it be not aswell followed it will never come to his perfeccion whiche said Serjaunt after the devise of the master is to bende him selfe wholye

---

[26] Cited in Wickham (1959–81: ii/1. 295), transcribed from Revels Office accounts in BL, Lans. MS 83, fo. 155.

to devise and to see everye man to woorke according to his devise whiche will occupye him sufficientlye and thoroughlye and this will muche ease the Master who cannot alwayes wayte upon the Queenes pleasure and upon the devise and all the workemen | forthereunto may belonge devise upon devise[.] The Serjaunt besides is with the Master and the reast of the officers to be at the rehersall of playes, he is to conceyve the Masters opynyon to correcte and chaunge the matter after the Masters mynde to see wrought and sett fourthe anye devise that belongeth thereunto that ought to be followed for matter or learning and devise. (8. 15–31)

As the use of the term 'device' multiplies in the passage almost to the point of confusion, so also the scribe of the document moves downwards through the hierarchy of production: from the 'platte' or 'devise' drawn by the Master to the Sergeant who implements the plan, either by consulting the tables and pattern books and 'platts' drawn in-house or by generating new drawings of specific parts and distributing these among the different workmen, each of whom is coordinated 'devise unto devise', all while the Master attends to his many other obligations, checks in occasionally on the project, and mediates between the workshop and the Queen. That this procedure continued all through Elizabeth's reign and even into the 1620s is suggested by several references to 'devices', 'plotts', 'patternes', and 'models' throughout account books from the Revels Office and the Office of the Works pertaining to all aspects of dramatic production, down to the smallest, most precise details: buttons, flowers, edging for a cap, paper leaves, hinges for doors, carved mulberries, spangles and snowballs, 'repayringe lainge abroode turninge sowinge mendinge tackinge Spunginge wypinge brushinge makinge cleane foldinge and lainge up'—an abundance of delicate gestures 'translated' into the stuff of royal fantasy.[27]

Glynne Wickham has demonstrated how nearly identical production techniques were used outside the court in the planning of the city of London's annual mayoral pageants well into the seventeenth century, when poets and carpenters consulted together with the committees charged with supervising the choice of programme.[28] The consultations took place around schematic plots that both artists contributed in their bids to secure the rights of composition, in a process that is very similar to the consultations over 'platts', 'inventions', and 'devices' at Dover Harbour between Digges, Sidney, Bedwell, and others. In 1556 the painter John Leedes contracted with the Merchant Taylors' Company to

[27] 'Greenecloth & ffor the Clerke[:] Thomas Blagrave, esquier Clerke of this office for his Greene Cloth, with paper, Ink, Cownters, & such other Necessaries as to his office appertayneth & is incident to the devices plottes orders, Bills, Reckonings, & Bookes, by him devysed, framed, sett owte, compiled, conferred, cast upp, concluded & preferred for this whole yeare . . .' (1571/2; Feuillerat 1908: 143. 10–14); 'patternemaker[:] Robert Trunkye alias Arras for patternes by him made and plottes for sundry devices requizite in this office & and at this tyme employed in all' (1572; Feuillerat 1908: 157. 11–13); 'Necessaries for the clerk.[:] The Clerk of thoffice for his ordinary Greene cloth, Paper, Ink, Cownters Tooles and Necessary Implementes for the Making & conserving of Bills Bookes Plottes & Modells' (1574/5; Feuillerat 1908: 247. 22–4); 'Emptions and Provisions[:] Case of Iron plate to kepe plotte[s] in' (1622/3; Wilson and Hill 1977: 34; also Feuillerat 1908: 181. 12).
[28] Wickham (1959–81: ii/2. 239–44); also Bergeron (1971: 245–72).

devise a pageant 'accordying to a patern broughte in by the said Le[e]des'; in 1560
the Drapers' Company consulted 'touching the devise of a p[ageant] upon the
Shew of a paper drawen by one C[larke] being his devise onely the ordring therof
was [referred] unto the lord mayor elect to have his advice'.[29] In 1629 Thomas
Dekker collaborated with the carver and painter Garret Christmas to produce
London's Tempe for the Ironmongers' Company, illustrating the structure of the
entire show with

> a plott wherein was contayned 6 severall Pageants
> Namely   A Sea Lyon
>
>   for the Water
>
>   2 Sea Horses:
>   An Estridge
>   Lemnions forge
>   Tempe or the ffeild of hapines
>   7 Liberall Sciences

> ffor the accomplishing whereof they demaunded 200[li], w[hi]ch
> theis present conceived to be an overvalue, and thereupon
> offerred them 180[li] w[hi]ch they accepted of for the making
> and finishing of the said Pageants to be furnished w[i]th
> Children and Speakers and their apparell and necessaries thereunto
> belonging . . .[30]

As the shows became larger in scale, the craftsmen came to exercise greater influence on the poet's device, and in this sense the relationship between poet and
craftsman is parallel to that between Jonson and Jones, although it was certainly
more amiable.[31] Indeed, the increasingly acrimonious (and increasingly public)
debates between Jonson and Jones over the relative authority of 'poet' and
'architect' in masque production during the late 1620s and early 1630s provide
some of the clearest evidence we have for the way in which the fields of literary
production and the practical spatial arts were beginning to redefine themselves
and seek new principles of legitimization, in part by appealing to principles of
design that were explicitly structural and classical in their orientation. I will
return to the role of the Jonson–Jones quarrel in provoking this transformation
in Chapter 8. But the trend is visible, too, in an earlier collaboration between

---

[29] Robertson and Gordon (1954: 39) (cited by Wickham 1959–81: ii/1. 239 n. 89); also 40, 41,
42–4 (speeches and description of the device for a pageant by Merchant Taylors), and 45 (Grocers, for
which the Lord Mayor himself submits a device)).

[30] Robertson and Gordon (1954: 115), cited by Wickham (1959–81: ii/1. 239–40); see all of
Robertson and Gordon (1954: 114–19, esp. 117–18), 'The explanac[i]on of the Shewe'.

[31] See Thomas Heywood's generous acknowledgement of Christmas in *Londini Artium* (1632) as
'the Artist, the Moddellor and Composer of these severall Peeces' (cited by Wickham 1959–81:
ii/1. 243); also John Taylor's praise of Robert Norman in his *The Triumphs of Fame and Honour*
(1634), Robertson and Gordon (1954, pp. xxxvi–xxxvii). Bergeron (1971: 250) suggests that this
Norman may be the author of *The New Attractive* (1581), the same mathematical practitioner praised
by Gabriel Harvey and others.

poet and architect: *The Magnificent Entertainment* offered to King James in honour of his accession by the City of London in 1604, for which both Jonson and Dekker had been commissioned to contribute the 'invention' and verses.

BUILDING: *THE MAGNIFICENT ENTERTAINMENT* FOR KING JAMES

As an exercise in composition, *The Magnificent Entertainment* would be similar both to the smaller-scale *Entertainment at Althorpe* that Jonson would write for Queen Anne and Prince Henry's arrival into England in June of 1603 and to the masques that he would soon compose with Jones, as well as to the Lord Mayor's shows that Dekker would eventually produce. Both Jonson and Dekker would be working closely with Stephen Harrison, a joiner who had been given the authority to design and build the arches that would serve as stages for the speaking actors and as a built frame for the emblematic programme, to which Jonson and Dekker would each contribute. In a departure from the usual court entertainment, each poet would be responsible only for a portion of the total work: Jonson would write for arches one and seven, Dekker would provide the material for arches four, five, and six, and the Italian and Dutch merchants were each responsible for the design, financing, and erection of arches two and three. To these were added the 'Pageant in the Strand', produced by the city of Westminster and the Duchy of Lancaster with speeches written by Jonson; Dekker graciously notes also that Thomas Middleton contributed the speech of Envy at the sixth 'New World' arch in Fleet Street (line 1469–72). From the poet's perspective, each element remained relatively distinct from the others and could be handled as such, and both Jonson and Dekker published separate accounts of the event in 1604. Harrison, meanwhile, published a third account that provided engravings of the seven arches by William Kip and accompanied them with speeches drawn from both Dekker's and Jonson's texts.[32]

Since surviving accounts from the Revels Office indicate that city artisans who were not permanently affiliated with either the Revels Office or the Office of the Works usually executed the technical work for the production of the royal entertainments, it is safe to presume, first, that the working methods for

---

[32] Jonson's (1925–52) portion appears in vii. 83–109; Dekker's (1953–61) in ii. 253–303; Harrison's as *The Arch's of Triumph* (1604), the plates of which are reproduced as plates 2–8 in Bergeron (1971). Nichols (1828: i. 328–401) reproduces Dekker's and Jonson's accounts in full, Harrison's description of the first arch at Fenchurch Street, his dedication to the Lord Mayor, Sir Thomas Bennet, Dekker and Webster's dedicatory poems, and Harrison's conclusion to the work, along with assorted contemporary documents pertaining to the event. Bowers's 'Textual Introduction' to Dekker (1953–61: ii. 246–7, n. 1) provides a comprehensive account of the circumstances of publication; see also Jonson (1925–52: vii. 67–79, x. 386–7); Wickham (1959–81: ii/1. 239, and i. 51–111, on the pageants in general, esp. 82–3, 86–7); Robertson and Gordon (1954, pp. xiii–xlv); Bergeron (1971: 65–89); Manley (1995: 212–93); Loewenstein (2002a: 170–2, 175–6).

The Magnificent Entertainment under Harrison's supervision would be much the same as those of the masque that I have discussed above and, secondly, that these techniques were already familiar to craftsmen of all types working in the city because they were widely used. Harrison himself published his 'plottes' and 'moddells' for the arch designs at the order of the City (and at its expense), in part to serve as a pattern book and reference in the planning of future events, much as 'plottes' and 'devices' functioned within the Revels Office for its inventories and 'airings.'[33] Dekker's account of *The Magnificent Entertainment* alludes directly to these methods of design when he describes the first arch at Fenchurch Street as bearing up 'the true modells of all the notable Houses, Turrets, and Steeples, within the Citie' (Dekker 1953–61: ii. 259. 215–16). Jonson and Harrison both refer to the same structure as a 'pegme' or 'scene', a usage that tends to classicize the production and in this way to associate it with a more explicitly theoretical system of design principles and structural vocabulary. Dekker, as we shall see, retains a very different set of representational techniques more closely associated with the practical spatial arts.

Dekker and Jonson each display very different attitudes towards the occasion: both writers are sharply aware of their commemorative role and adopt a self-consciously distanced position regarding the event, but the texts they eventually produced differ significantly both in their audience and in their formal presuppositions. In every respect Jonson's contribution is a study for his subsequent work with Jones on the masque: its mythological conceit, general metaphysical orientation, detailed description of costume, use of verse, and—perhaps most importantly—its page format all declare it to be a work of properly rhetorical 'invention' (line 675), the 'soule' (line 680) of the entertainment that has been 'apt[ed]' to the 'bodie (being fram'd before)' (lines 679–80), i.e. made to fit with the arches as Harrison had designed and built them. In the original Quarto, Jonson was quick to adopt a defensive stance vis-à-vis Harrison's work and rushed to anticipate any possible aspersions that 'the *Mecanick* part yet standing' might cast upon his own contribution.[34] Typically, he includes a brief defence of his work that distances his invention from the mechanical arts by appealing to an emblematic tradition of design:

The nature and propertie of these Devices being, to present alwaies some one entire bodie, or figure, consisting of distinct members, and each of those expressing it selfe, in the owne

---

[33] On 27 May 1604, following *The Magnificent Entertainment*, the City ordered that: 'the Com[m]ittyes appointed for managing and ordering of the causes concerning the pageante[s] and other shewes made by this Cittye at the Kinge[s] majesties passage through the same Cittye shall consider of the paines and travell taken by Stephen Harrison Joyner in drawing of certaine plottes and moddells of the same pageante[s] and putting them in print in a booke to bee kept by Mr. Chamblen to the Cittyes use, and to make unto the said Harrison such consideracon and allowaunce for doing the same as they shall think reasonable' (Robertson and Gordon 1954, p. xxxiii n. 2).

[34] 'Thus hath both Court- Towne- and Countrey-Reader, our portion of devise for the Cittie; neither are we ashamed to professe it, being assured well of the difference betweene it and Pageantry. If the *Mecanick* part yet standing, give it any distaste in the wrye mouthes of the Time, we pardon them; for their owne ambitious ignorance doth punish them inough' (cited by Herford and Simpson in Jonson 1925–52: vii. 104).

active spheare, yet all, with that generall harmonie so connexed, and disposed, as no little part can be missing to the illustration of the whole: where also is to be noted, that the *Symboles* used, are not, neither ought to be, simply *Hieroglyphickes, Emblemes,* or *Impreses,* but a mixed character, partaking somewhat of all, and peculiarly apted to these more magnificent Inventions: wherein, the garments and ensignes deliver the nature of the person, and the word the present office. Neither was it becomming, or could it stand with the dignitie of these shews (after the most miserable and desperate shift of the Puppits) to require a Truch-man [interpreter], or (with the ignorant Painter) one to write, *This is a Dog*; or, *This is a Hare*: but so to be presented, as upon the view, they might, without cloud, or obscurities, declare themselves to the sharpe and learned: And for the multitude, no doubt but their grounded judgements did gaze, said it was fine, and were satisfied. (Jonson 1925–52: vii. 90. 247–91. 267)

As in the masque, the iconography of the arch is associative in its poetic logic and compresses the act of interpretation to an immediate moment of apprehension or understanding. The act of semiosis as Jonson presents it here is very similar to that imagined by later language projectors of the seventeenth century: each signifying element reveals instantaneously a chain of metaphysical ideas, all of which saturate the particular expressive vehicle to the point where its physical properties evaporate into the signified content to which they refer.[35] After Peirce, we may call it an iconic mode of semiosis in so far as the 'device' and its elements are perceived to have a direct analogical and diagrammatic relation to the ideas that they communicate and, in Jonson's eyes at least, retain a relationship of perfect reference and adequacy to the ideas they express: no meaning escapes from the emblem, as long as judgement has been appropriately calibrated to it.[36] Jonson opposes this overdetermined and connotative model of iconic expression to a mimetic realism of simple, denotative prose sentences that would refer not to ideas but to concrete objects, a process that Jonson parodies in a ridiculous way but nevertheless links to 'the ignorant Painter' and to the 'grounded judgements' of the multitude. The passage is similar to a later moment of self-justification in the *Masque of Queens* (1609), in which Jonson finds it necessary to defend the structure of his composition: the witches enter in sequence and are questioned by their Dame, he claims, because

if it had bene done eyther before, or other-wise, had not bene so naturall. For, to have made themselves theyr owne decipherers, and each one to have told, upon theyr entrance, *what they were, and whether they would*, had bene a most piteous hearing, and utterly unworthy

---

[35] Cf. Ashworth's comments on the 'emblematic worldview' of natural history (1990, esp. 306); Bergeron (1971: 273–308), on the pageant's emblematic conventions.

[36] Peirce (1931–58, vol. ii, paras. 247–9, 274–307) and my discussion of these terms in the Introduction above. It should perhaps go without saying that I distinguish a post-Saussurean analysis of the sign, in which the question of the referent is either of no importance (since meaning is determined at a purely structural or syntactic level) or the question of adequation is suspect (since no sign is ever entirely adequate to its referent) from that of Jonson and his contemporaries (for whom the promise of the emblem is precisely its fullness and adequacy to its signified, even if this signified initially remains obscure or concealed).

any quality of a *Poeme*: wherein a *Writer* should always trust somewhat to the capacity of the *Spectator*, especially at these *Spectacles*; Where Men, beside inquiring eyes, are understood to bring quick eares, and not those sluggish ones of Porters, and Mecanicks, that must be bor'd through, at every act, wth Narrations. (Jonson 1925–52: vii. 287. 100–10)

In both passages Jonson pretends to cede interpretative authority to the spectator but in fact claims it for himself by articulating a self-conscious and deliberate principle of design, and one that again depends on differentiating his audience into categories that are simultaneously intellectual and social, the courtly and the 'mechanical' intelligence. The former apprehends meaning visually and graphically, through inference and association; the latter requires explicit description and a severe reduction in semiotic reference. As we shall see in Chapter 8, Jonson will continue to lean on these same distinctions in his attacks on Jones and in his late plays, where he begins to assemble a rhetoric of self-conscious dramatic composition that might rival the geometric principles of painting and architecture, which Jones had been putting to such spectacular effect.[37]

Jonson has made every attempt to distance his contribution from the contingency of actuality: his verses convert the concrete circumstances of the occasion into a poetic celebration of the essential and timeless nature of legitimate sovereignty. James's arrival is at one moment recognized as a unique and irreducible event with the absolute power to sponsor Jonson's conceit and in the next moment is negated as a *mere* circumstance or accident that is immediately subsumed within the larger historical trajectory that it completes:

> Time, Fate, and Fortune have at length conspir'd,
> To give our Age the day so much desir'd.
> What all the minutes, houres, weekes, months, and yeares,
> That hang in file upon these silver haires,
> Could not produce, beneath the Britaine stroke,
> The Roman, Saxon, Dane, and Norman yoke,
> This point of Time hath done.   (lines 270–6)

In this temporal succession, the city has a place only as a transitory staging ground that must be passed over and through, since it, too, is gathered into the silent space of the printed text where the 'showtes' and 'cry' that would 'cleave all the ayre . . . as thunder' (lines 282–4) are reduced only to silent semantic units within Jonson's verse line and are subordinated to the order of his measure and couplet. 'Thronging joy, love, and amazement' (line 281) are generalized into universal

---

[37] Jonson may also be trying to distinguish himself from other dramatic writers; Orgel (1965: 132–3), Goldberg (1983: 58), and Loewenstein (1991) all read the *Queens* passage as a response to Samuel Daniel. The comment corresponds also to his later 'Induction' to *The Magnetic Lady*: '*Probee*: Not the *Faeces*, or grounds of your people, that sit in oblique caves and wedges of your house, your sinful sixe-penny Mechanicks—*Dam*. But the better, and braver sort of your people! Plush and Velvet-outsides! that stick your house round like so many eminences—*Boy*. Of clothes, not understandings?' (Jonson 1925–52, vol. vi, Induction, 31–8); also *The New Inn*: 'These base Mechanicks never keepe their word, | In any thing they promise' (Jonson 1925–52: vi. 2. 1. 8–9).

qualities without mouths or bodies, an abstract 'multitude' gazing in stupefied delight. The 'Genius' and 'Tamesis' speak from a world of myth and classical iconography, gesturing outside the tableau to designate the Lord Mayor, who stands mute before the King's entrance; Jonson sequesters his historical identity *as* Lord Mayor, and with it the potentially competing authority that his office implies, in a marginal notation, much the way he positions him off-centre within the performance of the pageant itself.

Whereas Jonson imagines a drama of kingship gathered up in a display of iconography and poetic conceit—a display so detailed and mannered that it threatens to eclipse the royal figure at its centre—for Dekker, the King is only one of many concrete personages who enable the entire pageant. The King's is a privileged movement, to be sure, an organizing axis that links each discrete element to the larger whole and provides an ordering principle for Dekker's narration. But Dekker's account admits of a scene that is broader in physical extent and more finely stratified in its social make-up, and in this way he addresses a very different centre of power than Jonson does: the aldermen, common councillors, and company masters who made up the City's governing institutions rather than the circles of court, university, Inns of Courts, and the Society of Antiquaries populated by nobility and educated gentlemen. Social reality, indeed, makes little or no appearance on Jonson's page, which establishes instead a hermetic, internal hierarchy that finally refers as much to its own process of self-legitimization as to the authorities it cites. Dekker's account, although equally aware of itself as a textualized artefact, gestures constantly beyond the limits of its own textuality to the historical present that it endeavours to represent.

An early passage in Dekker's text is surely addressed directly to Jonson's penchant for self-display—the poets' war over *Poetaster* (performed 1601, Q 1602) and *Satiromastix* (performed 1601, Q 1602) had only recently subsided, and both writers seem to have kept a studied distance during their enforced collaboration:

To make a false flourish here with the borrowed weapons of all the old Maisters of the noble Science of Poesie, and to keepe a tyrannicall coyle, in Anatomizing *Genius*, from head to foote, (only to shew how nimbly we can carve up the whole messe of the Poets) were to play the Executioner, and to lay our cities houshold God on the rack, to make him confesse, how many paire of Latin sheets we have shaken and cut into shreds to make him a garment. Such feates of Activitie are stale, and common among Schollers, before whome it is protested we come not now (in a Pageant) to Play a Maisters prize. (Dekker 1953–61, vol. ii, lines 55–64)

Much as in his Prologue to *Old Fortunatus*, Dekker is impatient with a classical and theoretical tradition of poetic discourse. His address is far more inclusive than Jonson's: 'the multitude' still remains distanced and depersonified, but they are viewed sympathetically as 'our Audience, whose heads would miserably runne a wooll-gathering, if we doo but offer to breake them with hard words' (lines 65–7).

Dekker's scene opens to include the entire process of civic preparation in all its tasks and locales, and in this preparation the poet, painter, and artisan are coordinated in a genuinely collaborative effort towards one single end:

By this time Imagine, that *Poets* (who drawe speaking Pictures) and *Painters* (who make dumb Poesie) had their heads and hands full; the one for native and sweet Invention: the other for lively illustration of what the former should devise: Both of them emulously contending (but not striving) with the proprest and brightest Colours of Wit and Art, to set out the beautie of the great *Triumphant-day*. (lines 139–45)

Although Dekker casts this collaboration, too, as a relationship between soul and body, neither pole is hierarchically opposed to the other in the way that Jonson will later develop the analogy in the prefatory comments to *Hymenaei* (1606) and *The Masque of Queens* (1609), with their metaphysical distinctions between the 'soul' of Jonson's verse and the 'carkasses' or 'bodily part' of Jones's scenes. For Dekker, the process of pageant-making is a collective and fully civic effort that seeks only to equal the majesty of the occasion and to figure forth, above all, the dignity of the city itself and its trades. London has become 'the onely Workhouse wherein sundry Nations were made' (lines 188–9):

Many dayes were thriftily consumed, to molde the bodies of these Tryumphes comely, and to the honour of the Place: and at last, the stuffe whereof to frame them, was beaten out. The Soule that should give life, and a tongue to this *Entertainment*, being to breathe out of Writers Pens. The limmes of it to lye at the hard-handed mercy of Mychanitiens.

In a moment therefore of Time, are Carpenters, Joyners, Carvers, and other Artificers sweating at their Chizzells . . . Not a finger but had an Office: he was held unworthly ever after to *sucke the Honey-dew of Peace*, that (*against his comming, by whom our Peace weares a triple Wreathe*) would offer to play the Droane. The Streets are surveyed; heigthes, breadths, and distances taken, as it were to make *Fortifications*, for the *Solemnities*. Seaven pieces of ground, (like so many fieldes for a battaile) are plotted foorth, uppon which these Arches of Tryumph must shew themselves in their glorie. . . .

Even children (might they have bin suffred) would gladly have spent their little strength, about the *Engines*, that mounted up the Frames: Such a fire of love and joy, was kindled in every brest. (lines 152–74)

The corporate, collaborative spirit that Dekker celebrates extends to his own efforts in narrating and publishing his account, since rather than describing the artistic programme of the several arches in detail he defers to Harrison's own forthcoming work, lists the names of the primary painters, and provides an inventory of the many different craftsmen who contributed to the project.

It is evident that for Dekker the working methods associated with surveying, building, and other mechanical arts were indispensable to the production of the civic pageants, and this awareness accounts for one of the most striking aspects of his account: his tendency to integrate into his narrative not simply the emblematic elements of the pageant and a wide range of civic participants but also a detailed description of the built elements themselves: their measurements, dimensions, and structural details. Whereas Jonson's contribution had aggressively sought to position an idealized, de-materialized, and emblematic mode of semiosis as central to the 'poetic' composition, Dekker's text, in contrast, displays a struggle for representational authority between a poetic language of emblematic symbolism and a purely denotative language of reference and objective description, one that he has modelled on measurement as a semiotic system.

How can measurement be said to function as a mode of semiosis? Drawing on the passages from Hobbes that I have cited at the beginning of this chapter, and recalling also the conventional three-part classification of the sign into signifier, signified, and referent, we may grasp how individual units of measure can be classified as signs in so far as they consist of a graphic mark whose signified 'content' is a concept of discrete and quantified spatial extension, a 'portion' of space, as it were, that has been abstracted or idealized out of the material body that is being measured and to which the unit of measure is presumed to refer or to 'translate'.[38] Since, as a practical matter, measurement is always used to measure *something*, it implies an act of reference as much as it implies an act of signification; indeed, the 'meaning' or 'content' of the act of measurement is, strictly speaking, nothing other than its referential gesture, its ability to bring an object into representation mediated through the categories of quantity and extension, and even to reify an 'object' that remains invisible, abstract, or purely hypothetical (the movement of planets, for instance) until the act of measurement, which reduces the object to empirical form by translating it into a quantitative system. In measurement, this referential premiss is achieved by reducing the object to only one of its primary qualities—size or spatial extension, and perhaps also its position, in so far as this follows closely on spatial categories—to the exclusion of its other qualities: its colour, texture, activity or passivity, and so forth. Perhaps more accurately, the unit of measure 'presences' the object by making it thinkable *as* a category of quantity, size, and extension; the 'mathematical world-view' so often ascribed to Western science depends on the recognition that quantity forms an essential aspect of the thing, in practice and in theory, since it can be assessed empirically through measurement. As a mode of representing the object and referring to it, therefore, the unit of measure is direct and unmediated, and this because of a tautology: measurement defines the thing that it refers to in the terms it uses to refer to it, and the triumph of the so-called mathematical world-view is that this tautology has been naturalized or suppressed.

---

[38] Wittgenstein (1958, vol. i, para. 53) has famously demonstrated the unmotivated or conventional relationship between signifier and signified in the 'language game' of measurement, but the point is equally evident from the early-modern debates over the standardization of measurement that I have considered above or from many other historical examples. Wittkower (1974*b*), for instance, has shown the difficulties that Palladio encountered when he was forced to convert the measurements of his drawings into the different practical systems used by regional builders and how the pressure of this conversion produced an approximate, particularized, or 'fudged' series of proportional measurements in his diagrams that are, conceptually speaking, entirely different from the absolute, Pythagorean proportions usually ascribed to 'Palladianism'.

For this reason measurement, too, may be described as a mode of iconic representation, according to the three primary ways in which Peirce defines the icon: the (always conventional) *referential* gesture that constitutes measurement as a 'meaningful' system is founded on a (conventional) relationship of *likeness* and *analogy* with its object. In a woodshop, for instance, the graphic designation '12 feet of timber' is presumed to correspond exactly to a body of identical dimension; more accurately, the graphic measure is a perfect translation of the material body, just as the noun 'timber', when used in the same woodshop and with the same body as referent, is presumed to correspond to, or to 'translate', the wood to which it refers. This is all the more visible when graphic measurement is translated into language: in the phrase '12 feet of cloth', for instance, the unit of measure not only refers to the material body in the same *manner* that the noun 'cloth' refers to the material body, but the unit of measure ('foot') has itself become a noun that now acts as a diagrammatic verbal abstraction at a small scale.[39] At the same time, the act of measurement performs an *analytic* function—Peirce's third criterion—by revealing qualities of the thing that remain occult or invisible and, in doing so, by making possible further knowledge about the object beyond the knowledge needed to represent it.[40] To measure an object, in other words, I must accept the conventional scientific premiss that it can be reduced to quantity and that this reduction is essential; once I have measured it, however, I may manipulate it, combine it, study it, and discover other aspects that I have not intended or foreseen. The reduction to quantity permits the formulation of new codes on the basis of this primary substitution, and in this way measurement forms the first step in an analogical abstraction that is typical of the icon and which Peirce finds fully realized in the algebraic equation, which can express with maximum efficiency an extremely complex series of heterogeneous relationships. 'The reasoning of mathematicians will be found to turn chiefly upon the use of likenesses,' Peirce writes, 'which are the very hinges or the gates of their science. The utility of likenesses to mathematicians consists in their suggesting in a very precise way, new aspects of supposed states of things . . .'.[41] In this sense, the algebraic equation is the emblem of modern science, and mathematics is its master code.

Dekker's account exemplifies mathematical realism as a literary style: his text is repeatedly punctuated by shifts in attention towards the surface of the built

---

[39] In Peirce (1931–58: ii. 286, 305) Peirce discusses the 'yard' as a mode of *indexical* sign, since he regards it as a sign not of an object but of the standard 'yard' existing in a specific place (London); he emphasizes its 'real connection' to the standard and groups it with other examples of 'natural' signs (such as the barometer's response to atmospheric pressure or the weathercock's response to wind direction). It is true that any individual yardstick is indexical in relation to a standard yard serving to anchor the language game of English measurement. But when considered in relation *to the object that it measures* (where there is no 'natural' relation whatsoever), the unit of measure has an iconic rather than an indexical value for the reasons I have argued above. Here Eco's critique of the presumed 'natural' relation or analogy or reference in Peirce's account is most relevant.

[40] Peirce (1931–58: ii, esp. paras. 277–83).

[41] Peirce (1931–58: ii. 281; cf. ii. 279–82, 305).

structures, as the narrative 'eye' lingers over the arch and adopts, momentarily, a denotative mode of narration that purports to link word with object in a one-to-one, referential correspondence. Consider the following passages; in the first, the narrative has arrived at Fenchurch, the first of the seven arches:

It was an upright Flat-square, (for it contained fiftie foote in the perpendiculer, and fiftie foote in the Ground-lyne) the upper roofe thereof (on distinct *Grices* [flights of stairs, a heraldic term]) bore up the true moddells of all the notable Houses, Turrets, and Steeples, within the Citie. The Gate under which his Majestie did passe, was 12. foote wide, and 18. foote hie: A Posterne likewise (at one side of it) being foure foote wide, and 8. foote in heigth: On either side of the Gate, stood a great French Terme, of stone, advanced upon wodden Pedestalls; two half Pilasters of Rustick, standing over their heads. (lines 213–22)

Or the description of the 'Italians' Pageant':

The building tooke up the whole bredth of the Street, of which, the lower part was a square, garnished with foure great Columnes: In the midst of which Square, was cut out a fayre and spacious high Gate, arched, being twenty seven foot in the perpendicular lyne, and eyghteene at the ground lyne . . . (lines 293–8)

Or that of the Dutchmen:

The Foundation of this, was (as it were by Fate) layd neere unto a royall place; for it was a royall and magnificent labour: It was bounded in with the houses on both sides the street, so prowdly (as all the rest also did) did this extend her body in bredth. The passage of State, was a Gate, large, ascending eighteene foot high, amply proportion'd to the other lymmes, and twelve foot wyde, arched; two lesser Posternes were for common feet, cut out and open'd on the sides of the other. (lines 448–55)

In each of the passages, Dekker adopts a language of pure quantification that exists alongside other possible modes of description such as analogy (the royal site is *like* the heroic effort to erect the gate), personification ('prowdly'), or metaphor ('lymmes'). The discursive shift recognizes that the process of measurement itself operates as a highly specialized semiotic system, one in which the specific qualities of the physical object are presumed to appear as fully and as accurately as possible. The 'foot' is a purely empty signifier whose meaning is determined by its relative position within a larger scale of measurement and whose content is filled only by the object it designates at any given moment. Dekker then appropriates the semiotic potential of measurement for his own descriptive language, an incorporation registered by the transition from pure numeral (18, 8, 8) in the first passage to the literal spelling out of this numeral with its verbal equivalent ('eighteen') in the second and third. 'Eighteene', 'twelve', and 'twenty seven' thus function as *both* verbal and arithmetic units simultaneously, establishing a homology between measurement and prose description as two complementary systems of representation: units of measure have become adjectival constructions that elaborate the physical qualities of a body in purely quantitative terms.

The fundamental proposition implied by this act of linguistic translation—that the essential attributes of physical bodies can be grasped in their fullest ontological sense only through numbers and quantitative units of measure—is the founding premiss of all scientific epistemology, but for Dekker this proposition derives not from scholastic logic (as it might have in the fourteenth century), nor from neo-classical architectural theory (as it might have in fifteenth- and sixteenth-century Italy), nor from empirical experiment (as it will in the seventeenth): it derives directly from the techniques of practical measurement and geometry of his period, which both Puttenham and Sidney had already integrated into their accounts of poetic composition and interpretation. These techniques are represented as constituting the very conditions of possibility for the entire entertainment: a significant portion of Dekker's account records the clearing out of absolute, quantifiable space from the fabric of the city and the conceptual appropriation of this space as the underlying field for poetic and artistic discourse. The process appears in his earlier description of the 'seaven pieces of ground . . . plotted forth', in which the techniques of the surveyor map out the largest structural component of the pageant, its progression from site to site; it appears also in Dekker's direct allusion to Harrison's work and the instruments of his profession:

I could shoote more Arrowes at this marke, and teach you without the Carpenters Rule how to measure all the proportions belonging to this *Fabrick*. But an excellent hand being at this instant curiously describing all the seven, and bestowing on them their faire prospective limmes, your eye shall hereafter rather be delighted in beholding those Pictures, than now be wearied in looking upon mine. (lines 222–9)

By adopting an empirical language modelled on mathematics, Dekker offers his text as a supplement to Harrison's carpenter's rule: blank 'squares' and 'tables' are first delineated by prose description and then filled with allegorical figures or verse inscriptions; each arch is dissected into its component measurements, the precise units delineating the empty space that fills the centre of the structure beneath the arch, whose commemorative potential will suddenly be animated by the King's instantaneous act of passing under and through. The narration shifts its point of view easily, showing both the front and the back of the arch with a mere redirection of the imagination (lines 358–63), inviting the reader to 'clime up to the upper battlementes' (line 602) or to 'walke into the *Mart*' (line 588) that the Dutch have painted on its surface. It lays down sight lines, parallels, and perpendiculars in the field of vision—'The opposite body to this (on the other side, and directly over the other *Portall*)'; 'From whome, leade but your eye, in a straight line, to the other side, (over the contrary Posterne)' (lines 507–8, 519–20)—in this way establishing relations of situation and composition among elements:

Above the upper edge of this large square Roome, and over the first Battlement, in another Front, advanc'd for the purpose, a square Table was fastened upright, in which was drawne the lively picture of the King, in his Imperial Robes, a Crowne on his head, the Sword and Scepter in his handes . . . (lines 486–9)

Here the exact image of the King is nearly irrelevant, 'royal' in generic way and granted a minimum of iconography so that it can be identified as such. Where Jonson would have specified the image with antiquarian rigour, Dekker uses his narrative to survey the surface of the structure like a technical instrument. Each prepositional phrase accumulates upon the next to form a single but articulated line of description that delineates a representational space by moving from terms of purely relative position ('above', 'upper') to terms that *substantiate* relative position ('edge') and then passing to simple, denotative adjectives of magnitude and shape ('large', 'square').

This is not to deny the many overt moments of metaphorization in Dekker's description of the arches or to minimize his interest in recording the details of their symbolic content. But the emphasis of his account is nevertheless on the purely abstract *form* of that content, since he integrates the arches into his commemoration of the event primarily as built artefacts—even as mechanical devices, 'Engines' that discover themselves (line, 292)—and only secondarily as emblematic vehicles. Like Jonson, Dekker describes his invention as a 'device', but in his case the term establishes a direct link between the script and workshop: his text is itself a working 'plat' for the pageant that is meant to complement Harrison's technical illustrations. This genealogy is particularly visible in the description of the Garden or 'Arbor' near the Cross in Cheapside, where the King is intercepted by the figure of Sylvanus and Dekker embeds into his own narration of the event a working drawing of the arbour that someone, presumably Harrison, has provided (lines, 1036–48). Throughout the *Entertainment* the King advances as the words themselves unfold on the page, creating a one-to-one correspondence between the linear dimension of Dekker's sentence and the royal movement through city space:

Wee have held his Majestie too long from entring this third Gate of his court Royall; It is now hie time, that those eyes, which on the other side ake with rolling up and downe for his gladsome presence, should injoy that happinesse. Beholde, hee is in an instance passed thorough; The Objects that there offer themselves before him, being these . . . (lines 558–63)

The descriptive or 'measured' mode of narration that Dekker adopts allows him to narrate the entire event in sequence as an action or movement, imaginatively re-creating the King's point of view while at the same time exploiting the freedom of narrative to shift that perspective at will, speaking now from the mind of the multitude, now from the mind of James, now from a third, more distanced narrative position, which is that of the poet. Later the King continues to move as Dekker stops to translate a Latin speech at the Dutch arch and then hastens to catch up (lines 705–71), finally reaching him as he is greeted by the City authorities:

let us followe King *James*, who having passed under this our third gate, is by this time, graciously receiving a gratulatorie Oration from the mouth of Sir *Henry Mountague, Recorder* of the Citie, a square lowe gallorie, set round about with pilasters, beeing for that purpose erected some 4. foote from the ground, and joyned to the front of the Crosse in

Cheape; where likewise stood all the Aldermen, the Chamberlaine, Town-clarke, and Counsell of the Citie. (lines 937–44)

As in all royal performances, the King becomes both subject and object of the event, a figure whose smallest movement is worthy of notation and who 'by tarrying... give[s] honor to the place' (lines 290–1) but a figure whose own progress is finally subject to the freedom of Dekker's own narrative discourse. His iconic mode of narration has the effect of reducing the entire event of the pageant to a homogeneous objective field, in which the categorical or qualitative difference in status that traditionally adheres to the monarch literally becomes *equivalent to* the more local authorities of the City, all of whom are distributed like so many points in a formal hierarchy of power.

Framed within the purely quantified volume of the arch, the civic administration of the city appears in an analytic view whose closest analogue is the topographical survey or architectural cut-away, in which different structural elements are isolated while the principles and forces of their interrelationship can be studied in detail. In this sense Dekker's description of the pageant is a perfect complement to Harrison's illustrations of *The Arches of Triumph*, each of which offers two views of each pegme, or 'scene', as he terms it, the largest in 'upright' and the smaller in 'ground plot' (see Fig. 4.7). Each view invites the reader to perform a distinct intellectual operation, the first emblematic and hermeneutic, the second iconic and analytic. The 'upright' reproduces the arch's surface or representational space; it offers a semantic view that is meant to be decoded visually alongside Dekker's and Jonson's verbal descriptions. The 'ground plot' reduces the arch to its physical outline and purely formal space of representation; it is a structural view that reveals dimensions and volumes and principles of interrelationship. Harrison then coordinates these two views with one another by omitting particular measurements so as not to 'call either [the reader's] skill or judgement in question' (Nichols 1828: i. 329), referring him instead to the scale he has provided so that he may generate the five-part system of 'commensurable proportions' (ibid.) out of which the work has been constructed. As a tool of translatability, the scale always tends to reveal the conventional nature of measurement as a semiotic mode, since it consists of an arbitrary set of rules designed to allow the conversion of one spatial relationship (or several) into another form, always while preserving the identity of relationship (which remains, of course, purely theoretical and abstract). In this sense, the scale is the graphic and spatial form of the (verbal) metaphor, since it permits the comparison of two heterogeneous qualities and even their immanent conversion, through a formal vehicle in which difference and similarity can be sustained simultaneously with one another.

In Part II, I will demonstrate how both Dekker and Jonson adapted the practical techniques of composition that they had encountered while working on the pageants to the formal conventions of the public theatres, where, in their own ongoing experiments in comedy, they were developing their own practical

Fɪɢ. 4.7. Stephen Harrison, *The Arches of Triumph* (1604)

solutions to the problems of dramatic emplotment on stage. There is some evidence, for instance, that a mode of composition by 'plot' similar to the collaborative methods used in generating devices and in winning civic commissions may have extended to the public theatres from the late 1590s until at least the second decade of the seventeenth century. A letter from Nathaniel Field to the theatre manager Philip Henslowe dating from approximately 1613 reports that 'M^r. Dawborne and I, have spent a great deale of time in conference about this plott, wh[ich] will make as beneficiall a play as hath come these seaven yeares' and goes on to reassure Henslowe of speedy delivery, while also mentioning casually that another company has expressed interest in the work.[42] Several entries in Henslowe's *Diary* indicate that playwrights, and Jonson in particular, were regularly paid according to this procedure: on 3 December 1597 Jonson was lent 20 shillings for a play in progress, of which he had 'showed the plotte unto the company', while on 23 October 1598 George Chapman was lent £3 for 'ii actes of a tragedie of bengemens plotte'.[43] Taken in the context of the other usages of the term that I have been examining, the entries suggests that each dramatist contributed a segment of the dramatic action—probably a brief prose summary or tabular outline—adding onto the sketch that had been provided to him much the way Jonson and Dekker had produced their respective portions of *The Magnificent Entertainment* or the way the Revels Office had generated the devices for other royal shows.[44]

We should also bear in mind the specific technical meanings of the terms 'plat' and 'plot' that Gascoigne, Sidney, and Puttenham had integrated into their discussions of poetic form when considering one of the earliest overt uses of the term to refer to dramatic composition, specifically: Francis Meres's famous epithet for Anthony Munday in *Palladis Tamia* (1598) as 'our best plotter'. Meres's epithet for Munday appears in a long list of 'the best Poets for Comedy' that includes Lily, Lodge, Gascoigne, Greene, Shakespeare, Nashe, Heywood, Chapman, and Chettle but not Jonson, who appears on Meres's list of 'Tragicke Poets' in spite of the fact that none of Jonson's tragedies from this period have survived.[45] None of the other names on the list are qualified by any similar distinction, a fact that

---

[42] Henslowe (1977, vol. ii, MS I, no. 100).

[43] 'Lent unto Bengemen Johnsone the [2, corrected to] 3 of desemb[er] 1597 upon a Bocke wch he was to writte for us befor crysmas next after the date herof wch he showed th[e] plotte unto the company I saye lent in Redy money unto hime the some of...xx s (Henslowe 1961: 73); 'lent unto Bengemen Johnson the 3 of desemb[er] 1597 upon a boocke wch he showed the plotte unto the company wch he promysed to dd unto the company at cryssmas next he some of...xx s' (same payment as above; Henslowe 1961: 85); 'Lent unto Robart shawe & Jewbey th[e] 23 of octob[er] 1598 to lend unto m^r Chapman[e] one his playe boocke & ij ectes of A traged[i]e of bengemens plott[e] th[e] some of...iij^{li} (Henslowe 1961: 100).

[44] Cf. Thomas Heywood's Prologue to the 1637 quarto of *If You Know Not Me, You Know No Bodie*, complaining that 'some by Stenography drew | The plot: put it in print: (scarce one word true)' (cited by Chartier 1999: 30). Still in 1656 Abraham Cowley could refer to an early play, published without his permission, as 'but *rough-drawn* only', a sketch or 'hasty *first-sitting* of a *Picture*' (Cowley 1656: 78. 11, 24).

[45] Meres (1598: 319–20); cf. the comments in Greg (1931: 1).

might well suggest not Munday's relative superiority as a dramatist but rather his skill in a specific *kind* of composition or a particular facility in one of the many aspects of dramatic production to draw on practical artisanal techniques.[46] A typically vivid comment by Thomas Nashe regarding his relationship to Robert Greene speaks of the plotting of plays in terms that are nearly identical to those of Puttenham when he described the use of the compass in generating a graphic structure, outline, or 'plat' for a poem:

. . . [Harvey] girds me *with imitating of* Greene, let him understand, I more scorne it than to have so foule a jakes for my groaning stoole as hys mouth; & none that ever had but one eye, with a pearle in it, but could discern the difference twixt him & me; while he liv'd (as some Stationers can witnes with me) hee subscribing to me in any thing *but plotting Plaies, wherein he was his crafts master.*[47]

It is impossible to know for certain whether Nashe had been reading Puttenham's treatise, but it is typical of Nashe to integrate distinctive words and phrases from other contemporary writers into his own associative style, and the similarity in phrasing here is striking. In the case of Jonson, however, the evidence is conclusive: his copy of Puttenham's book survives in the British Library with his annotations, and the pages pertaining to the use of the compass and to the poet's 'plat' bear the habitual marks of his reading.[48]

Before moving to consider how both Dekker and Jonson adapted geometrical and iconic modes of semiosis to the conventions of the platform stage, and by way of conclusion to the first part of this book, it will now be useful to consider what their unusual collaboration on *The Magnificent Entertainment* contributed, first, to both Jonson and Dekker's understanding of language as a tool of representation and, secondly, to how both men might use this understanding to position

---

[46] Herford and Simpson have demonstrated (Jonson 1925–52: i. 305–7) that the scene satirizing Munday as Anthony Balladino, 'Pageant Poet to the City of *Millaine*', in Jonson's early *The Case is Altered* (iii. 1. 2. 29–30) is a later addition to the play dating from after 1600. The passage was thus added after Jonson's early experiments in comical satire but *before* his selection in 1602 or 1603 as poet for the *Entertainment* celebrating James's coronation. Munday had clearly already acquired a reputation as a writer of pageants or Jonson would not have characterized him in this way, and it seems plausible that the jab was intended to diminish his stature as a potential competitor for the commission. Although Munday's first surviving Lord Mayor's pageant dates only from 1602, he may well have been the author of the pageants for 1597, 1598, 1600, and 1601 which no longer survive (Robertson and Gordon 1954, p. xxxv; Bergeron 1971: 137, 140–62); he went on to enjoy a long string of successful pageants over the next two decades, writing those of 1605, 1609, 1610, 1611, 1614, 1615, 1616, as well as the City's Water Show at the investiture of Henry as Prince of Wales in 1610. In 1617 Munday submitted a 'plot' for the Grocers' pageant, but Middleton was selected instead (Robertson and Gordon 1954, pp. xxxv–xxxvi); in 1621 he was paid for making pageants and shows along with Middleton and Garrett Christmas, and he again composed a Water Show in 1623 for the Drapers.

[47] Nashe (1904–8: iii. 132. 15–23; second emphasis mine); cited by Greg (1931: 1 n. 2), who does not note the echo to Puttenham.

[48] BL, 11548, with Jonson's autograph on title page; reproduced in Jonson (1925–52: i, between 264–5); no. 147 in McPherson (1974: 79–80); also A. W. Johnson (1994: 31–2); Jonson (1925–52: xi. 282–3).

themselves as writers—as *poets*—within the overlapping hierarchies of power and authority that made London such a complex field of literary production, with unusual risks and unique rewards. In the first place, both of their accounts are centrally concerned with articulating two distinct modes of iconicity that are in collision and that derive from two heterogeneous epistemological traditions, each of which was fundamental to the conceptual definition of 'literary' and 'scientific' fields of knowledge at the beginning of the seventeenth century. Jonson pursues an emblematic and 'symbolic' iconicity that has its roots in heraldry and the arts of discourse, particularly the topological and mnemonic traditions of dialectic and rhetoric. As such it may be termed a 'qualitative' form of semiosis; for Jonson, at least, it requires a disavowal of practical geometry as a separate mode of iconic representation that was becoming both more legitimate in its authority and more widely available as an epistemology. Dekker, in contrast, develops a quantitative form of representation that acknowledges the power of measurement and geometric representation as a mode of iconicity, incorporating it and giving it a broader extension, a greater range of objects, and an application to the social and political world as well as to nature. Both approaches pre-date the earliest seventeenth-century schemes for a universal language, and both reflect different aspects of how these projects would later develop, whether as a system of signs designed to communicate immediately relations among concepts and ideas (as in Descartes or Mersenne) or as one that would capture the full objectivity of things in their material, empirical reality (as in Bacon, Ward, Wilkins, or Comenius).[49]

Secondly, it is important to recognize that these 'experiments' in iconic representation, both of which anticipate several aspects of later developments in seventeenth-century epistemology, develop in the specific social, economic, and political context associated with London's urbanization at the turn of the seventeenth century and are elaborated by both Jonson and Dekker, in different ways, in order to solve problems of representation that are peculiarly urban. The specific nature of these problems is the subject of Chapter 6, but it may be stated briefly here: as a social process, urbanization is empirically invisible or inaccessible *except* through formal abstractions that are of an iconic nature, and this remains true of all analysis of social process in the modern social sciences. Algebraic equation, statistical modelling, photography, mapping: all are modern forms of iconic abstraction that may be set alongside typical early-modern forms of iconic representation such as the diagram, the scale, the design, the painting, the sketch, or the linear mark of the pencil that denotes the geometrical idea of 'line' itself (cf. Peirce 1931–58: ii. 304). All are classified as icons by Peirce not simply on the basis of their relationship of resemblance and analogy to their signified but also on the basis of their revelatory, demonstrative, or 'ostensive' aspect—like the *theatre*, which serves as one of the most important modes of iconic representation during the period. And it is the purpose of the pageant, after all, to 'theatricalize' or

---

[49] Cf. Elsky (1982, esp. 101); Reiss (1997: 128–9).

'perform' the city by transforming urban elements into icons: icons of themselves, as 'Fenchurch' and innumerable other locations become, simultaneously, physical places and symbolic representations of those locations, and icons of the larger conceptual entity that is London itself.

Jonson's technique is to seek a single iconic expression for the city: to compress the material world of the city, with its competing sources of authority and social stratification, into a single sign whose power is to sublate and idealize the living world by removing it from the historical present, in this way subordinating the city and its population to the eternal power of its new monarch. The full *event* of the *Entertainment*, in all its contingency, its multivocality, its living movement and articulation, has vanished beneath the floating surfaces of Jonson's ideograms, which rise up in a detached series before the reader through his busy enumeration of colours, allusions, emblematic components, and foreign words. Thus Jonson's conception of the composition is finally typographical: the city is not a picture but a word—LONDINIUM—that has been 'inscribed' 'in a great capitall letter' (lines 5–6), much like a modern hieroglyph (see Fig. 4.8); the arch at Temple Bar is no longer a 'scene' but a 'frontispice of a temple' (line 372), a structure to be opened like a printed book. This typographical conceit is fully in keeping with the way Jonson has deflected the actual historical performance onto the disposition of the page and his system of annotation, which cannot be 'read' in a conventional sense but must be decoded by correlating letters to one another as indices rather than as word components. The reader is invited to commemorate the founding moment of James's entry with an act of silent collation, in this way extending into the infinity of future readings that 'point of Time' which has the power to gather up all previous moments of conquest and bury them in the remote inaccessibility of history.

Rather than invent a single emblem for the city, Dekker seeks to generate a total system out of many individual iconic semantic elements, each of which can be coordinated into a mode of written representation that borrows the iconic power of measurement to generate an analytic portrait of the city and its constitutive parts, like a painting or—and we have seen the fundamental importance of this analogy to Dekker—like a map. In measurement it is suddenly possible to posit new forms of equivalence among objects, and thus to generate new forms of translation and representation; it is possible to write the city in a new register, using an entirely different system of elements and epistemological presumptions. The sudden and seemingly gratuitous eruption into Dekker's narrative discourse of these enumerative, mathematically descriptive passages can be seen as the irrepressible delight of a writer experimenting with the novelty of this mimetic convention, probing and experimenting with its representational possibilities and socio-political implications. It is not enough for the arches, or 'scenes', to mirror the commercial communities of the city in a form of symbolic expression, or even to model them in a quasi-realist way using principles of geometric projection and construction, as Harrison had done. These communities needed to recognize themselves *in the very*

FIG. 4.8. Stephen Harrison, *The Arches of Triumph* (1604)

code used to reproduce and commemorate the city as a living stage for James's accession, a code whose authority derived not from rhetoric and emblematics but from the entirely different epistemological field of mathematics and practical geometry that was flourishing in urban institutions such as Gresham College. As Dekker would later have Candido, the honest merchant, patient man, and very emblem of *homo economicus*, proclaim in *2 Honest Whore* (performed 1608, Q 1630):

> Of Geometricke figures the most rare,
> And perfect'st are the Circle and the square,
> The Citty and the Schoole much build upon
> These figures, for both love proportion.   (1. 3. 50–3)

This geometric code has been borrowed from the very communities who made up London's political, economic, and social tissue: it is the code of private property, commodification, and reification that formed the basis of their economic, political, and cultural power.

This code permits a very different apprehension of the object that it represents— London—than does Jonson's emblematic mode of writing. Where Jonson's typographic icon compresses an entire city into an ideogram that forecloses analytic thought—in its stasis and fullness, the promise of the emblem or the ideogram is that it leaves nothing unsaid, and in this sense it is the perfect ideological vehicle of absolute monarchy—Dekker's narration establishes the built 'scenes' of the city as an abstract field of representation in which the different constitutive members of the city and its topographic elements could be assembled and delineated, while the principles of their interrelationship (social, political, economic) could be studied in detail. His mathematical realism makes possible a structural representation of the *Entertainment* as a historical event with individual parts, sequence, actors of production and execution, each of whom is equivalent to one another; he uses the codes of spatial abstraction to strip away the emblematic programme necessary to absolute monarchy and in this way to sever the semiotic connection between emblem and metaphysical principle, clearing instead a new representational space in which an alternative social and economic community may emerge alongside the monarch as his political equal.

In this way the texts of both Dekker and Jonson—in their style and form as well as in their content—also imply the different audiences to whom each writer addresses himself and the competing authorities that these audiences wielded. For Jonson the *Entertainment* becomes the occasion to solicit royal patronage by demonstrating his skill in generating an ideology of absolutism. No less significantly, however, the *Entertainment* suggests the central place that the city would occupy in the plays Jonson would write for the public theatres and the uneasy relationship with the urban, paying playgoing audience that would plague him throughout his career. It also provided an early occasion in which Jonson encountered the methods and conventions of the practical spatial arts, which, as we shall see in subsequent chapters, constituted an important source for his evolving ideas about problems of dramatic form and structure, no matter how much he might try to disavow the 'mechanical intelligence' or attempt to subordinate it to the rhetorical and ethical traditions of neo-classical literary theory.

For Dekker, the *Entertainment* becomes a way of addressing a specifically urban and commercial London audience of citizens and craftsmen who fill the offices of the city's neighbourhoods, wards, and companies, from the very bottom to the apex of its political hierarchy. His purpose, too, is to solicit patronage by presenting himself as a 'maker' of images and forms, but as a writer who is able to draw directly on the new epistemological potential of the practical spatial arts and its mimetic conventions in order to generate forms in which the City can represent itself to itself and to others—especially to the King and court. These would take the form not of court masques but of the annual Lord Mayor's shows, of which Dekker would go on to write three—*Troia-Nova Triumphans* (1612), *Britannia's Honour* (1628), and *London's Tempe* (1629)—and in which he would adapt the emblematic principles of royal iconography to the Lord Mayor's office. But they would also take the form of a specific mode of comedy, written for the public theatres, in which the topography of the city and its everyday life became a central formal and ideological preoccupation, and it is to the role of the stage in this project and the semiotic conventions upon which it depended that I now turn.

PART II

STAGE, WALL, SCENE, PLOT

5

Theatre as a Spatial Art

Mais enfin le drame? S'il a, chez l'auteur, sa fulgurante origine, c'est à lui de capter cette foudre et d'organiser, à partir de l'illumination qui montre le vide, une architecture verbale—c'est-à-dire grammaticale et cérémoniale—indiquant sournoisement que de ce vide s'arrache une apparence qui montre le vide.

(But the drama? If it has its dazzling origin in the author, it is up to him to capture this thunder and to organize, out of the illumination that shows the void, a verbal architecture—one that is grammatical and ceremonial—indicating, craftily, that from this void is torn an appearance that shows the void.)

(Jean Genet, 'L'Étrange mot de . . .')

BRAYNE, BURBAGE, SHAKESPEARE

In a real sense the very possibility of Renaissance drama as we know it depended on the business acumen, the corporate status, and the practical skill of the men of the building trades, from the earliest foundations of the commercial theatres. In 1567 the London grocer John Brayne brought suit in the court of the Carpenters' Company against one William Sylvester, a member of the company with whom he had contracted for 'skaffoldes...at the house called the Red Lyon in the parishe of Stebinyhuthe [Stepney]' and which he found deficient. Ruling on the case, the Master and wardens determined 'that William Buttermore, John Lyffe, Willyam Snellinge & Richard Kyrbye, Carpenters, shall with expedicon goe & peruse suche defaultes as are & by them shalbe found of in & aboute suche skaffoldes... & the said Willyam Sillvester shall repaire & amend the same with their advize substancyallie, as they shall thinke good'. Brayne was to pay Sylvester what was owed but also to 'deliver to the said Willyam such bondes as are now in his custodie for the performaunce of the bargaine', as the court book stipulated, once the scaffold—either galleries for an audience or the stage itself—had been proved adequate to its function: 'after the playe, which is called the storye of Sampson, be once plaied at the place aforesaid'.[1] And among the four wardens presiding over the

---

[1] Chambers (1923: ii. 379–80).

case for the company was none other than 'Mr. Richard More', author of the popular *Carpenter's Rule* (1602), as we have seen in Chapters 2 and 4, a book dedicated to the Master, wardens, and assistants of the Carpenters' Company.

Unfortunately for the members of the company, Brayne was a litigious employer, and two years later he was back in court, this time suing John Reynolds, 'citizen and carpenter of London', for the payment of damages stemming from further construction at the Red Lion property during the same 1567 summer. The structure in dispute was again a 'skaffolde', a term that this time clearly describes a stage, as Janet Loengard has shown:

one Skaffole or stage for enterludes or playes of good new and well seasoned Tymber and boords whyche shall conteyne in height from the grounde five foote of assyse and shalbe in lengthe Northe and South fortye foote of assyse and bredthe East and West thyrty foot of assyse Well and sufficientlye stayed bounden and nailed with a certayne space or voyde parte of the same stage left unborded in such convenyent place of the same stage . . .[2]

Reynolds was to add to the structure a turret, mounted in the playing area. Reynolds contended that Brayne himself had impeded the work and had made it impossible to finish, and although the outcome and exact cause of the suit remain unknown, we may suspect a conflict of opinion over the stage design: the 'certayne space or voyde parte' described a trap door that was to be placed 'as the said *John Braynes* shall think convenyent', as the suit stipulated (my emphasis), and Reynolds may have grown annoyed at this incursion into his craft.

But this was only the beginning for John Brayne, the London Grocer, as we now know: for he had a brother-in-law, a joiner and former actor named James Burbage, who shared his entrepreneurial interest in the players and who had the ambition, the expertise, and the acquaintances—but not the capital—to undertake a grand project. Together they set out to build what most historians regard as the first permanent building in England designed expressly for the performance of plays to a paying public: the Theatre, to be located to the North outside the city wall.[3] Like Braynes's earlier efforts, the partnership with Burbage quickly proved contentious, sponsoring twenty years of lawsuits punctuated by insults, fist fights, public beatings, and arrests. In 1591 Brayne's widow, Margaret, was still wrangling with Burbage for her share of the takings, leaving Brayne's friend Robert Miles to inherit the cause after her death in 1593; by 1595 Miles had given up, but in 1600 he still retained the two bonds for £600 that Brayne had received from Burbage long ago in surety for his initial investment.[4]

---

[2] Loengard (1983: 309); Ingram (1988: 28–34; 1992: 102–13, and 109 n. 25 (on 'scaffolds'), with speculation as to Burbage's probable involvement, 104–5 and 111–12).

[3] On the Theatre, see Chambers (1923: ii. 383–400); Wallace (1913); the essays and documents collected in Berry (1979a, esp. Hosley); I. Smith (1964: 132–3); and the thoughtful re-evaluation of evidence and historiography by Ingram (1992, esp. 115–18 and 182–218, speculating that Robert Burbage, James's brother, was the carpenter who built the Theatre (190–2); also 95–102 (on Burbage's history)).   [4] Chambers (1923: ii. 388–9, 393 n. 2).

In February 1596, meanwhile, the ambitious Burbage acquired 'seven great upper rooms' in the Blackfriars precinct, located in a fashionable neighbourhood within the London wall, in the hopes of using the property as a permanent indoor theatre for adult play companies.[5] Despite the fact that the same property had been used since 1576 as a playhouse for a variety of boys' companies, several powerful neighbours, including Sir George Carey, Lord Hundson, the son of the recently deceased Lord Chamberlain, objected to the notion of an adult 'public' theatre and petitioned the Privy Council to halt the project, which they promptly did. When Burbage died in February 1597, the Blackfriars property passed to his son Richard, the actor and colleague of Shakespeare, who leased the property to several iterations of boys' companies until the King's Men took up their long-standing winter occupancy in the same space in 1609–10. The Theatre property, meanwhile, passed to Burbage's son Cuthbert, who found himself in renewed legal contention with Giles Allen, the owner of the property, over the terms of the original lease. And so in January 1599 Cuthbert availed himself of a provision in the original agreement that allowed him to dismantle the theatre building, hiring the carpenter Peter Street to transport the timbers across the river to Bankside, where he was to build the new Globe theatre out of the old timber frame, reassembling it piece by piece.

Andrew Gurr has described the Elizabethan playhouse as a 'patched-up, jerry-built contrivance' that resembled the classical theatres of antiquity in name more than in design, and Glynne Wickham has convincingly argued that Brayne and Burbage drew their original structural inspiration from the local gaming houses and bear-baiting amphitheatres that had long served the recreational needs of the London public.[6] Surviving building contracts for the public playhouses indicate that they were to be constructed according to practical methods identical to those I have discussed in Part I, including the generation of a schematic plot or ground plan of the total structure, a drawing that in later contracts would be explicitly modelled on previous designs, with appropriate modifications. In 1600, having just completed his erection of the Globe, Street contracted with the theatre manager Philip Henslowe and the actor Edward Allen to build the Fortune, who stipulated:

the erectinge, buildinge & settinge upp of a new howse and Stadge for a Plaiehouse in and uppon a certeine plott or parcell of grounde appoynted oute for that purpose.... with

---

[5] On the Blackfriars, see I. Smith (1964); Chambers (1923: ii, esp. 503–15).

[6] Gurr (1992, esp. 131), cautioning against neo-classical precedents; see also Gurr (1997; 2000, pointing out that the reuse of old timbers in the Globe's construction resulted in a 'necessary conservatism' (p. 262) of design first established by Burbage's Theatre); Wickham (1959–81, esp. ii/1. 153–205). For an account of theatre design that looks in part (although not exclusively) to classical architectural theory see Orrell (1988), whose arguments are most persuasive when they concern the obviously neo-classical designs of Jones; Cerasano succinctly refutes the lines of argument Orrell represents and, like Gurr, argues for the practical nature of theatre design during the period. See also Greenfield (1997a, b); I. Smith (1963: 34–46), who provides an accessible account of the joinery techniques used in the construction of the Globe; Adams (1961: 15–30). B. R. Smith (1999: 208–17) emphasizes the sonic qualities of the theatre space.

suchelike steares, conveyances & divisions withoute & within, as are made & contryved in and to the late erected Plaiehowse on the Banck in the saide parishe of Ste Saviours called the Globe; With a Stadge and Tyreinge howse to be made, erected & settupp within the saide fframe with a shadowe or cover over the saide Stadge, which Stadge shalbe placed & sett, as alsoe the stearecases of the saide fframe, in such sorte as is prefigured in a plott thereof drawen...And the said Stadge to be in all other proporcions contryved and fashioned like unto the Stadge of the saide Plaie howse called the Globe.[7]

On 20 August 1613 Henslowe contracted with another carpenter, this time one Gilbert Katherens, to build a playhouse with movable stage to be used for both plays and bear-baiting; again the contract stipulated that Katherens should 'builde the same of suche large compasse, fforme, widenes, and height as the Plaie house called the Swan' or again 'in such forme and fashion, as the saide plaie house called the Swan'.[8]

We can only speculate as to what Shakespeare may have made of all the contention, construction, and changes of venue. On 10 March 1613 he himself bought property within the Blackfriars precinct, a gatehouse probably intended for use as a London lodging and with it 'all that plot of ground on the west side of the same tenement...which said plot of ground was sometime parcel and taken out of a great piece of void ground lately used for a garden', the entire property lying only a hundred yards from the Blackfriars Theatre itself.[9] Three years later he was dead. But his plays give some indication of the momentous changes taking place around him: when, in 1595, Quince the carpenter, Bottom the weaver, Flute the bellows-mender, Snout the tinker, Snug the joiner, and Starveling the tailor entered the playing space—almost certainly the stage of Burbage's Theatre— to open *A Midsummer Night's Dream* by declaring 'this green plot shall be our stage' (3. 1. 3) their entrance not only recalled the boisterous entrance of the guild players onto the *platea* of the mystery plays but collapsed into a single usage all the transformation in early-modern ideas about space, property, and performance consequent upon the dissemination of practical geometry through English culture. For all their humour, the scenes offer Shakespeare's nodding and perhaps uncomfortable acknowledgement of the continued proximity between the man of the theatre and the practitioners of the spatial arts.[10]

Like Peter Quince and his company (whatever their ineptitude), the play-wrights, actors, stage managers, and prompters working in the public theatres had at their disposal a variety of performative conventions that had endured from the medieval religious drama in the pageants, interludes, and occasional entertain-ments of the early Tudor and Elizabethan periods, and it is the purpose of the entire second part of this book to examine the nature of early-modern drama as a *performative form* in more detail. As Patrice Pavis, Erika Fischer-Lichte, and Kier Elam have demonstrated, theatrical performance presents an unusually complex

---

[7] Chambers (1923: ii. 436–7); cf. Cerasano (1989: 487–90), on the Fortune and Rose.
[8] Chambers (1923: ii. 466–7).   [9] I. Smith (1964: 251).
[10] Cf. Weimann (2000: 80–8); Parker (1996: 43–8); Harris (2002*b*: 37–41).

and polyvalent semiotic medium, since the co-presence of voice, body, object, and stage architecture as distinct signifying elements results either in an unusual level of semiotic redundancy—if we assume that each element reinforces the signified of the others—or in a remarkable potential for semiotic conflict and divergence.[11] The 'rude mechanicals' of *A Midsummer Night's Dream*—with their lantern-for-moonshine, their rhetorical 'disfigurement', and their emblematic and personified 'wall'—are perhaps the most spectacular example of the semiotic redoubling that is typical of stage performance: by accentuating signification to the point of representational confusion and mimetic rupture, the play disarticulates the individual elements through which the process of cultural coding occurs, defamiliarizing these codes and inviting an audience to hesitate between the world of representation and the semiotic and theatrical processes through which this world comes into being.

It will not be my purpose in the chapters that follow to examine all of these semiotic elements and their possible codes in detail: they include *linguistic* signs in their semantic and acoustic or rhetorical modes of expression (the meaning of words, as well as the tone of voice, speed, and emphasis in which they are delivered); *paralinguistic* signs such as music, sound effects, props, lighting, and scenic decoration; and, finally, as a subset of paralinguistic signs, *kinesic* signs, or signs that depend on bodily movement: facial expression (mimic signs), gesture (gestural signs), and physical motion across the space of the stage, or *proxemic* signs. Each type of theatrical sign may be reduced to two primary iconic forms, which will be my primary focus in what follows: iconic signs originating from or pertaining to the *actor and his body*, and iconic signs originating from and pertaining to the *stage as an architectonic or spatial element*. For the working dramatist, the 'emplotment' of a dramatic action on stage during performance fundamentally depended on the dynamic and always changing relationships that might be established between these two basic signifying units: between the actor as a voice and body that projected characters and actions in time, and the space of the stage as the primary mimetic medium in which this fictional projection would occur.

My first step towards recovering this history of the theatre as a spatial art will be pursued through a discussion of Shakespeare's *King Lear*, performed in 1605 at the Globe: I will argue that no play more self-consciously engages the power of the early-modern platform stage to take up and transform, in the process of its fiction and for the duration of that fiction only, the spatial medium in which a dramatic action took place. Explicit verbal reference to the stage's mimetic capacity is largely absent from the play—with one important exception, as we shall see—and yet the sheer scope of its action, with its wanderings, displacements, and geopolitical sub-plot, ensures that the stage's potential as a 'device' in which to examine the theatre as a spatial art, specifically, remains fully felt throughout. In some scenes,

[11] I draw especially on Elam (2002: 1–87, esp. 4–27, 50–70, 105–13); Fischer-Lichte (1992, esp. 13–17, 18–63, 93–114); Pavis (1996; 1982*b*, esp. 13–21, 25–35); Carlson (1990); B. R. Smith (1999: 206–45, esp. 242–5, on the acoustic signifiers of the stage).

moreover, the space of the stage would appear to move beyond tacit convention to become the subject of direct theoretical and formal inquiry, and this not always in an overtly rhetorical manner. Indeed, one of the central questions the play forces us to confront is finally this: how might the platform stage allow the exploration of a series of spatial concepts in a way that is beyond print or words, even beyond the language of poetry?

Writing in 1904, A. C. Bradley has already articulated in another vocabulary and sensibility the problem that I will be discussing here, writing of *King Lear* that the 'very vagueness in the sense of locality...give[s] the feeling of vastness, the feeling not of a scene or particular place, but of a world; or, to speak more accurately, of a particular place which is also a world'.[12] If Bradley prefers this immediate re-formulation of his own statement, it is because the phrase not only describes with greater precision a sense of space that he perceives almost intuitively in the play, a space that seems to exceed the stage, filling it with a looming and unrepresentable significance, but because it does so by fixing the 'overwhelming' (p. 244) space of the stage into a convenient and predictable dialectical relation. Bradley's comments formulate a long-standing set of critical objections to the play, and the categories and oppositions he introduces are central to the analysis that I will be proposing:

The stage is the test of strictly dramatic quality, and *King Lear* is too huge for the stage. Of course I am not denying that it is a great stage-play. It has scenes immensely effective in the theater...But...that which makes the *peculiar* greatness of *King Lear*—the immense scope of the work; the mass and variety of intense experience which it contains; the interpenetration of sublime imagination, piercing pathos; the vastness of the convulsion both of nature and of human passion; the vagueness of the scene where the action takes place, and of the movements of the figures which cross this scene; the strange atmosphere, cold and dark, which strikes on us as we enter this scene, enfolding these figures and magnifying their dim outlines like a winter mist; the half-realized suggestions of vast universal working in the world of individual fates and passions—all this interferes with dramatic clearness even when the play is read, and in the theater not only refuses to reveal itself fully through the senses but seems to be almost in contradiction with their reports.... *King Lear*, as a whole, is imperfectly dramatic, and there is something in its very essence which is at war with the senses, and demands a purely imaginative realisation. (pp. 247–8)

'A purely imaginative realisation': these are Bradley's terms for a *reader* who already seems to participate in the cruel world of the play and to 'enter this scene'. If we are to recover the true magnitude of the play, Bradley argues, it is only as readers that we will be able to do so. The power of poetry, even of language itself, is at stake:

The influence of all this on imagination as we read *King Lear* is very great; and it combines with other influences to convey to us, not in the form of distinct ideas but in the manner proper to poetry, the wider or universal significance of the spectacle presented to the inward eye. But the effect of theatrical representation is precisely the reverse. There the poetic atmosphere is dissipated; the meaning of the very words which create it passes

---

[12] Bradley (1960: 261).

half-realized; in obedience to the tyranny of the eye we conceive the characters as mere particular men and women; and all that mass of vague suggestion, if it enters the mind at all, appears in the shape of an allegory which we immediately reject. (p. 269)

The two passages suggest, somewhat paradoxically, that *King Lear*'s 'peculiar greatness' derives from its pre-eminent spatial qualities—its 'immense scope', 'huge' action, and 'vagueness of scene' (p. 261)—but that the platform stage, arguably the most fully spatialized mode of representation, can finally only obscure the play's total achievement. The stage 'overpowers' (p. 261) the viewer, disrupting the operation of linguistic meaning and even the effect essential to tragedy: that which strikes us as 'revolting or shocking' in performance 'is otherwise in reading', where 'imagination...can do its duty as a stimulus to pity' (p. 251) and make possible a recognition of the characters' terror and grief. The stage's insufficiency derives from its particularity, its rootedness in a precise time and place. The 'tyranny' (p. 269) of the sensory eye, riveted in the particular and the mundane, must give way to the 'spectacle of the inward eye' (p. 269) possessed by the reader who contemplates the 'vastness' (p. 256) of the drama from a 'wider point of view' (p. 253). Elements that appear inconsistent, implausible, superfluous, or excessively graphic on the stage are resolved on the page into the majesty of 'one of the world's greatest poems' (p. 277). Bradley's analysis transforms the lived space of the stage and body into the idealized and metaphorical space of perspective, 'intellect', and 'speculation' (p. 264); this space is in turn aligned with aesthetic judgement, and, through 'imagination', with consciousness itself.

By adopting a critical attitude that imagines 'a particular place which is also a world' (p. 261), Bradley thus gives spatial form to the larger allegorizing movement from particular to general—and from stage to page—that allows him to secure the play's ultimate moral and aesthetic relevance. But it is striking that even as Bradley turns to the page as a tool of hermeneutic authority, he finds that the conventions of the platform stage are too persistent to be overlooked and finally intrude to disrupt his gesture. *King Lear*, he observes, presents unusual difficulties by virtue of its very placelessness, a placelessness that is typical of the Elizabethan theatre. Although in *Hamlet*, *Macbeth*, and *Othello* 'the imagination is...untroubled' by lack of precise locations, in *Lear* 'the indications are so scanty that the reader's mind is left not seldom both vague and bewildered'.[13] This is the problem of the entire play, and he singles out several scenes in particular as exemplary instances of the confusing effects of early-modern stage practice and the necessity of overcoming them with the printed text:

A similar conflict between imagination and sense will be found if we consider the dramatic centre of the whole tragedy, the Storm scenes.... The Storm-scenes in *King Lear* gain nothing and their very essence is destroyed.... [it is] such poetry as cannot be transferred to the space behind the foot-lights, but has its being only in imagination. (pp. 269–70)

<hr />

13 Bradley (1960: 259).

Bradley's reluctance to locate these scenes is notable: even in imagination, they unfold in a 'place' that remains as undesignated as the scenes that unfold on the platform stage. His hesitation is perhaps all the more surprising in that for nearly 200 years Shakespeare's editors had proposed a location for these scenes that had come to seem self-evident: this place is the 'heath'.

The moment, however, is also a testament to Bradley's critical perceptiveness: the so-called 'heath', in fact, appears nowhere in either the 1608 Quarto or the 1623 Folio editions of Shakespeare's play. No single line in any of the early texts records any such place; only Lear's tirade and a brief direction—'storm still'—that appears silently but insistently six times in the Folio, and *not* in the Quarto, provide any indication of a specific placement for the scene.[14] Not until Rowe's 1709 edition of Shakespeare's works does a stage direction appear specifying 'A Heath', and no doubt the entire weight of a later tradition intrudes on this moment—that of the Restoration stage with its perspective scenery and careful attention to the unities of time, place, and action—filling with a simple, single word a textual moment that Rowe's retrospective eyes could perceive only as absence or error.[15] But to presume location at all points in the case of *Lear*, as Rowe and later eighteenth-century editors do, is to take as self-evident a set of logical, imaginative, and mimetic relationships that the play itself seeks to examine in all their complexity and to hold in tension, rather than to resolve—relationships that lay at the core of the spatial arts and their distinctive epistemology during the period.

I have examined Bradley's reading in such detail because, at bottom, his analysis is centrally concerned with this aspect of the play, even if his appeal to universal categories finally prevents a full elaboration of the representational problems involved and forecloses some of their more radical implications. The analytic categories that he favoured—stage and page, viewer and reader—remain fundamental to critical discussion of early-modern drama, but their relationship must be further elaborated and their separate spatial sensibilities specified in more detail. No doubt it is impossible to displace this binarism fully or even to circumvent it with other axes of inquiry, and I have not tried to do so; indeed, it is only by examining the historical formation of this binarism more closely, as William Worthen has argued, that we will be able to provide a more complex account of how critical ideas about early-modern drama have shifted over time between these two poles of analysis and of the very different notions of dramatic form that each

---

14 All citations follow the *Norton Shakespeare: Based on the Oxford Edition* because it makes facing-page Folio and Quarto versions of the play easily accessible. I have followed the Norton Folio (F) version as my copy-text, but provide separate citations for the Quarto (Q) where relevant. The direction in question appears first at 3. 1. 0. 1, then at 3. 2. 0. 1, 3. 4. 3. 1, 3. 4. 55. 4, 3. 4. 90. 1, and 3. 4. 145. 1. The direction 'Storm and tempest' has already appeared at 2. 2. 449. 1. I will return to the significance of this recurrence in more detail in the argument that follows.

15 Flahiff has also noted the absence of any place designations in the play, including the 'heath', and points out that Rowe's direction derives from Nahum Tate's 17th-century adaptation, where the location appears as 'A Desert Heath'. I have chosen to focus on Rowe's stage direction because of its foundational role in the formation of an editorial apparatus for the Shakespeare canon. See also H. S. Turner (1997) and Gillies (2001), a more recent discussion of the absence of the 'heath' in the play.

of these poles presume. To this end I have divided my analysis of the play into two sections. The first reads several key episodes in the context of early-modern performance practice and argues that they can be fully understood only when the specific epistemological protocols of the platform stage are taken into account. The second section then examines how the categories of 'place' and 'space' are modified when the play is translated into print and become essential components of an emerging notion of 'dramatic' structure: when printed according to certain techniques and in certain formats, the play on the page has a conceptual integrity that differs from the play in performance. Contained within the physical confines of a bound page that may be held, contemplated, analysed, and moved through at varying rates, the printed text prepares the way for our more modern notions of dramatic form, notions that themselves depend on the way modes of understanding and representing 'place' and 'space' changed in England during the sixteenth and seventeenth centuries as a result of the dissemination of practical geometry as a distinct epistemology for spatial thinking throughout early-modern English culture.

STAGE

Nearly fifty years ago Glynne Wickham proposed that, from the fifteenth to the early seventeenth century, English theatrical representation underwent a fundamental shift from an 'emblematic' to a 'realist' mode of mimesis and that this shift was most visible in the way that location, in particular, was represented during stage performance. Since Wickham's argument will provide the basis for much of my own analysis in the entire second part of this book, I will cite it at length:

My argument, stated in its simplest terms, is that a stage of mediaeval invention, employed for indoor and outdoor performances alike, religious and secular, was transmitted from the fifteenth century to the sixteenth and from the first of the Tudor sovereigns to the last. James Burbage's 'Theater' of 1576 and the other Public Playhouses imitated from it and were novel in giving permanency to both a stage and an auditorium which had previously been built as required and dismantled immediately after use, a stage and auditorium where place had been represented in terms of symbols or emblems. Neither before nor after this change-over from occasional to permanent structures was the representation of place on the stage governed by notions of verisimilitude or photographic reproductions of actual landscape. By contrast, the proscenium arched stage designed by Inigo Jones in 1605 for Jonson's *Mask of Blackness* clearly sought to express place in a landscape painter's terms of reference. . . . Viewed from this standpoint, Shakespeare's Globe and all other playhouses resembling it in architectural design are theatres which provide permanent homes for a stagecraft based on representation by formal symbols: the theater of the Stuart Court Mask and the Restoration public playhouse has rejected this form of representation and is groping its way, however fitfully, towards the naturalism of actuality. From the Globe one can look backwards over the centuries and, in the *sepulchrum* of the liturgical *quem quaeritis* and in the *sedes* of later ceremonies, trace the beginnings of its stage conventions; but one cannot look forward. Its stage conventions do not develop: they are superseded. From the theater of *The Mask of Blackness* one can look forward over the next three centuries to fully changeable scenery, to actuality for scenic background photographed by the ciné-camera, and nowadays transmitted instantaneously by the miracle of television; but one cannot look back. Its stage conventions do develop; but they have no English antecedents.[16]

Wickham's primary opposition, while heuristically valuable, requires some adjustment, since Inigo Jones's scenes for the masque obviously remained highly emblematic in their conventions, and the plays of Shakespeare, Jonson, and his contemporaries certainly become highly 'realistic' in many moments. More importantly, however, Wickham's notion of 'verisimilitude' or 'actuality' remains underdeveloped, although by reformulating it in the semiotic terms I have introduced in Chapter 4 we may grasp the enduring value of his insight. This is to describe a shift *from one code of iconic representation to another*, a shift that we have already seen taking place in Jonson and Dekker's competing accounts of *The Magnificent Entertainment* and that was occurring in different genres of plays and across many types of theatres at the same time, be it an outdoor amphitheatre like the Theatre, Globe, or Fortune, an indoor hall theatre like the Blackfriars, or the playing spaces at Paul's or at court. It would be more accurate to say that early-modern performance gradually moves away from an emblematic mode of iconicity, in which objects, gestures, and bodies represent allegorical ideas and moral abstractions, and towards a referential, empirical, or 'realist' mode of iconic representation that it shares with modern scientific inquiry. And it is this moment of transition *between* modes of iconic representation that several peculiar spatial 'cruxes' in *King Lear* make visible to us.

What is the nature of stage iconicity during performance? In the first place, it implies a hierarchy of functions for objects and bodies, one in which their primary sign-function is to represent a fictional version of themselves: a diegetic object that is identical in form, material, and use but which has become immanent in the physical prop, like a shadow or mirror reflection in which the mimetic fold has been reduced to a minimum of perceptibility. The fact that so many plays of the Renaissance period highlight the conventional aspects of this mimetic process should be enough to remind us that the early-modern theatre was never a fully realistic mode—*A Midsummer Night's Dream* again provides a famous example. Nevertheless, we may distinguish different modes of signification across genres or within individual plays, such that at one moment an object will simply signify its own presence relatively neutrally, as one of several details in a scene, while in other moments the same object will assume a secondary layer of 'poetic' or 'symbolic' associations. In the first instance, the range of the object's connotative meaning is both reduced in scope and subordinated to its denotative aspect. Desdemona's handkerchief in *Othello* offers a familiar example: the primary purpose of the cloth brought on stage is to signify its own material properties; the conceptual transformation from the simple cloth of the theatrical prop to a fictional 'handkerchief'

---

[16] Wickham (1959–81: ii/2. 4–5).

requires a minimum of metonymic translation, but this primary mimetic realism must be distinguished from the secondary layer of connotative meanings that the fictional handkerchief then assumes as part of the larger thematic or ideological preoccupations of the play—domesticity, intimacy, betrayal, the distortion of jealousy, and the fantasy of 'empiricism' itself—and which would be impossible without this first, more fundamental translation into humble domestic object.[17]

Similar distinctions operate in the case of place-signifiers on stage, whether verbal or physical. Following the work of Wickham, Granville-Barker, Styan, Bentley, Bevington, Dessen, and Weimann, among others, it has become a commonplace to observe that the early-modern open stage was not illusionistic: that it did not strive to represent with perfect fidelity the realistic details of locations in the way of the nineteenth-century theatre but instead relied on language, props, and stage elements to signify locations in an emblematic way.[18] In this view, signifiers of place, when they appear, have primarily a symbolic rather than a realist function; for many critics, it is this symbolic content that organizes the scene, whether they examine this symbolic content in rhetorical, poetic, thematic, emotional, or ideological terms. A bed, for instance, never *merely* signifies location but signals intimacy, sexuality, desire, domesticity, betrayal, wealth, social position, violence, and so forth. This symbolic aspect obviously remains a fundamental attribute of the place-signifier in every instance. But it is important not to allow its persistence to occlude what I will call a *topographic* approach to theatrical representation: those moments in which the physical features of a location are designated as descriptively or flatly as possible and the connotative charge recedes relative to the signifier's denotative aspect. As we shall see, this mode is particularly common in genres that tend towards realism, such as comedy, satire, farce, domestic tragedy, and revenge tragedy, where the physical features of location are designated with a relatively neutral semiotic value and the scene becomes crowded with spatial detail.

In spite of warnings by recent editors and scholars as to the anachronism of using location directions in modern editions of Renaissance plays, I suspect that like Rowe and his successors many of us find it difficult *not* to map the action of a play onto an imaginary topography. The habit says a great deal about our own understanding of space and illuminates, somewhat surprisingly perhaps, how

---

[17] I draw on Fischer-Lichte (1992: 107–10); Barthes (1964, 1977*a*, *b*, 1986, 1988*a*); Baudrillard (1978). For a recent survey of how objects have figured in critical accounts of the drama, see Harris and Korda (2002) and, in the same collection, the excellent survey by Bruster (2002), with additional bibliography, and Yachnin (2002), on Desdemona's handkerchief.

[18] See, in addition to the work of Wickham (1959–81), Chambers (1923: iii. 50–102, esp. 60, 102); Bentley (1964, esp. 53–63); Beckerman (1962); Styan (1967); Weimann (1978; 2000, esp. 180–215); Hattaway (1982); Dessen (1977; 1984, noting that 'editors have imposed upon many, most, or all Elizabethan scenes a later sense of "place" or locale . . . Thanks to generations of editing and typography, modern readers have thereby been conditioned to expect placement of a given scene ("where" does it occur?), regardless of the fluidity or placelessness of the original context or the potential distortion in the question "where?" '; 84); Bevington (1984, esp. 99–134); Gurr (1992: 172–211); Haynes (1992, esp. 23–4 (opposing a 'symbolic' use of location to a more 'empirical' one typical of Jonson) and 31 (on William Haughton's *An Englishman for my Money*)).

dependent it is on the printed book. But the tendency is not always as illegitimate as it might seem. As Bradley himself observes, in any single play the places of the action may emerge more or less distinctly at different points, and in some respects his characterization of *Lear* is perhaps too categorical: we do, after all, glimpse the 'casement' of Edmund's 'closet' (1. 2. 58); the action seems at one point to be outside a 'hovel'; we overhear occasional references to France; and some characters travel to 'Dover', where the imaginative detail of a particular place is magnificently realized. Several scholars have commented on the episode at the cliffs of Dover, noting its obvious references to perspective painting and on the cleverness of its stage business.[19] The journey towards Dover, by both Gloucester and Edgar and by Lear and his party *simultaneously* (and I will return to the importance of this simultaneity below), already foregrounds the flexibility of the platform stage to represent distant locations, but the trip itself would in fact be unremarkable in spatial terms—simply one more instance of a freedom that Sidney had derided and that Jonson, as we shall see, would condemn in even stronger terms—without the vertiginous scene at Dover 'itself'.

The striking thing about the scene, however, is less its self-conscious *debt* to perspective painting than the way it strives to trump a two-dimensional technique. The sheer knowingness of the scene is so blatant that it nearly becomes a cruel joke, as witnessed by the way in which Edgar's sudden aside to the audience—'Why I do trifle thus with his despair | Is done to cure it' (4. 5. 33–4)—registers a niggling need to justify the entire conceit. As Edgar stands at the supposed edge of the cliff, his lines invoke the structure of monocular point of view only to undermine it, first by substituting a *verbal* description for the geometrical forms and mathematically derived proportions typical of perspective painting, and then, additionally, by turning this illusion into a second-party narration for a blind man who, after all, *cannot see anything*:

Come on sir, here's the place. Stand still. How fearful
And dizzy 'tis to cast one's eyes so low!
The crows and choughs that wing the midway air
Show scarce so gross as beetles. Halfway down
Hangs one that gathers samphire, the dreadful trade!
Methinks he seems no bigger than his head.
The fishermen that walk upon the beach
Appear like mice, and yon tall anchoring barque
Diminished to her cock, her cock a buoy
Almost too small for sight. The murmuring surge
That on th'unnumbered idle pebble chafes
Cannot be heard so high. I'll look no more,
Lest my brain turn and the deficient sight
Topple down headlong.   (4. 5. 11–24)

[19] On the scene, see Orgel (1984); Goldberg (1984); Armstrong (1995); Guillén (1971); Weimann (2000, esp. 182, 186–7); Adelman (1978, esp. 1–2); Levin (1959, esp. 96–9).

At the very moment that the ocular illusion should be at its most breathtaking and convincing, the audience is caught up short by the grotesque reality of Gloucester's gaping eye-sockets; it is as though Edgar finds himself carried away by his own verbal skill and is unable to resist luxuriating in the ecstasy of vision, even as he stands next to a man who will never see again.

In the second place, the scene departs from the usual horizontal view of two-dimensional perspectival exercises by unfolding along a precipitous *vertical* axis. Imogen's imagining of Posthumus' departure in *Cymbeline* or Aspatia's mournful stare in Beaumont and Fletcher's *The Maid's Tragedy* are more conventional in this respect; the clear association between looking, perspectival space, and subjectivity in these scenes is also striking.[20] In *Lear*, however, the scene's elaborate technique draws our attention as much to the devices used to represent the space as to the final effect of that space itself—so much so that Samuel Johnson is said by Boswell to have complained about Shakespeare's execution of the scene, remarking that 'the crows impede your fall'.[21] This is an important point, since it serves as a corrective to some readings of the scene which rely on Albertian perspective theory. As James Elkins has shown, the conventional notion that Renaissance painters, artisans, engineers, architects, natural scientists, and mathematicians deployed a single perspective 'theory' is a modern misconception, as the sheer variety of practitioners just listed might well indicate. So-called 'perspective' (Albertian or otherwise) in fact consisted more of a loosely related series of practices and methods than a formal, codified, and unified theory; as a consequence, Elkins argues, multiple perspectives were used to represent particular objects in paintings and not to achieve a homogenized, rationalized, or mathematically derived 'picture space', a space of extension that preceded those objects.[22]

Edgar's lines thus establish a direct relationship between the technique of perspective in this scene and techniques as practised in fifteenth- and sixteenth-century paintings, and they even make evident a paradox in how 'space' itself is conceived. The focus of Edgar's lines is not space but *smallness*: his use of multiple and shifting metaphors creates an illusion of diminution—crows mutate into beetles, the body of a beachcomber shrinks (or expands) to the size of his head, fishermen scramble like mice—of which 'space' could only be an after-effect. The persistent details of crows and samphire-gatherers make evident the fact that the

[20] 'I would have broke mine eye-strings, cracked them, but | To look upon him till the diminution | Of space had pointed him sharp as my needle; | Nay, followed him till he had melted from | The smallness of a gnat to air, and then | Have turned mine eye and wept' (*Cymbeline*, 1. 3. 17–22); 'Sit down, and let us | Upon that point fix all our eyes, that point there. | Make a dumb silence till you fell a sudden sadness | Give us new souls' (Beaumont and Fletcher, *The Maid's Tragedy*, 2. 2. 79–82).
[21] Cited in Levin (1959: 97).
[22] Elkins (1994, esp. 45–80, 14–15): 'the phrase "perspective space" is a Janus figure, half Renaissance and half modern. The Renaissance artists had no conceptual equivalent for our term *space*, and when they juxtaposed *prospettiva* and *spazio* (or *perspectiva* and *spatium*), they usually had something decidedly scholastic or humanistic in mind. The Renaissance painters made perspective pictures without the benefit of a concept of space.... artists and writers thought first of objects and second of what we call perspective space or fictive space.'

eye can never fully apprehend pure, expansive 'space' but only individual places and objects. As William Ivens has argued, the simplest experiment is enough to demonstrate that our view can perceive only objects in a spatial field and not the spatial field itself, unless that field is understood as the effect of particular objects grouped in a particular way and especially if those objects are grouped according to principles that emphasize interrelatedness—and proportion, in whatever guise, is first and foremost such a principle.[23] The closest analogy I can think of to a visual perception of pure 'space' might be the experience of looking out of an aeroplane window during flight, as the plane enters a cloud: in this moment we see 'nothing'. In the history of spatial concepts (which is not, after all, the same as artistic technique), single point perspective is significant less because it offers a method for representing space to the eye than because it marks the emergence of an analytical, abstract space of mathematical principles that is strictly 'invisible' (it is impossible to 'see' the space described by an equation) and which is itself conceptually distinct from the idea of the visual geometry of the picture plane or the 'window' illusion.

But Edgar's narration of space in this scene is, after all, much more than a reference to perspective technique: as Stephen Orgel, among others, has observed, it is paradigmatic for all treatment of space on the platform stage. In a theatre that used no perspective backdrops, a minimum of stage properties, and rudimentary sound and lighting effects, the primary illusionistic tool for designating location *was* spoken dialogue, and the final power of the scene depends on this awareness of stage convention. When Edgar and Gloucester re-enter the stage space after the exchange between Regan and Oswald, and Gloucester asks, 'When shall we come to th' top of that same hill?' (4. 5. 1), the audience is prepared to believe that they *are* in fact climbing a hill—after all, the characters' disappearance into the offstage space has readily been accommodated into the diegetic space of the 'journey'. It is only when Gloucester begins to question the topography ('Methinks the ground is even'; 4. 5. 3) that the illusion opens or bifurcates by introducing a disjuncture between the verbal signs that Edgar articulates and the proxemic signs that are visible through Gloucester's movement across a flat surface, and which *his* language weakly confirms. The originary diegetic space is now supplemented by the additional spatial conceit of the approach to the cliff, and the audience is faced with the tension of either identifying with Gloucester and entering this secondary layer of illusion or identifying with Edgar and recognizing the illusion as such—which immediately forces an awareness of the larger enabling illusion taking place on the stage before them. To recognize the well-intentioned nature of Edgar's deception, therefore, is to recognize the limitations of performative language and thus to question the very possibility of stage representation itself through other kinds of signifying conventions; and just when the audience has been led, like Gloucester, to this point of dizzying mimetic

[23] Ivens (1946: 5); Wittkower (1978: 127).

complexity, Gloucester jumps—and flops down onto the flat, bare playing space before them. The resounding impact caps the scene by asserting, once more, the representational potential of the platform stage, as Gloucester crawls about on the 'beach' and believes he has survived the fall.

The final irony, however, is that even as Gloucester's blindness makes it impossible for him to perceive the specific location of the 'cliff' (requiring Edgar's designation: 'here's the place'; 4. 5. 11), this same blindness is precisely what will allow him to perceive 'space' while Edgar cannot. A comment by Ivens makes clear that Gloucester's difficulty is simultaneously perceptual, representational, and logical:

Tactically, things exist in a series of *heres* in space, but where there are no things, space, even though 'empty,' continues to exist, because the exploring hand knows that it is in space even when it is in contact with nothing. The eye, contrariwise, can only see *things*, and where there are no things there is nothing, not even empty space, for that cannot be seen. There is no sense of contact in vision, but tactile awareness exists only as conscious contact. The hand, moving among the things it feels, is always literally 'here,' and while it has three dimensional coördinates it has no point of view and in consequence no vanishing point; the eye, having two dimensional coördinates, has a point of view and a vanishing point, and it sees 'there', where it is not. The result is that visually things are not located in an independently existing space, but that space, rather, is a quality or relationship of things and has no existence without them. (1946: 5)

Just as later the blind Gloucester will reply to the mad Lear, 'I see it feelingly' (4. 5. 141), at Dover Gloucester can only be said to 'see nothing', and in the proxemic signs of his tentative, groping progress towards the audience and the subsequent silence of his leap the stage offers a momentary apprehension of what neither perspective nor the linguistic signification of perspective could represent: a fissure in the fictional location through which we apprehend a larger dimension. It is a moment for which there is no easy conventional language, given the pervasiveness of the perspective metaphor that is already beginning to take hold in these 'scenes'—is it a 'representation' of space? An 'image'? A 'view'? It is both a 'scene' enacted *in* space and a 'scene' *of* space.

Consider now another episode, equally obvious in its citation of a specific early-modern spatial art: the infamous 'division scene'. In contrast to the mimetic ambiguities of Dover, Lear's peremptory 'Give me the map there' (F 1. 1. 35) at the opening of the play would seem to promise a precise and measured spatial sensibility for the action that follows.[24] Even more, the appearance of the map confirms the royal power to administrate and allocate space, not least because the map itself seems to function, initially, less as a *necessary* instrument of power than simply as a convenience, a way for Lear to illustrate and re-enact for those gathered before him the content of a royal act which has already been completed and which

[24] Several critics have addressed the topic of cartography in the play: in addition to Flahiff (1986), see Armstrong (1995); Sullivan (1998: 92–123); Avery (1998); Klein (2001: 95); and Gillies (2001). Gillies (1994: 45–7, 65–7; 1998: 27–41) discusses other Shakespearean references to map or maplike documents.

did not require the map to do so ('Know that we *have divided* | In three our kingdom'; 1. 2. 35–6; my emphasis). Of course the map is more than a simple prop, since it demonstrates in an unspoken (but for that no less blatant) way Lear's power not simply to distribute space but to control its very representation, and then to treat this representation as a casual attribute of power. In this way the map becomes a metonym, in spatial form, for the burden of power itself ('rule | Interest of territory, cares of state'; 1. 1. 47–8), and the ease with which Lear wields both device and the property it encompasses would seem, at first glance, to be beyond question.

Already, however, the Quarto's shorter and more ambivalent 'The map there' (Q, sc. 1, line 35) casts the relationship between authority and spatial representation in another light. Does Lear *command* the map? Or simply gesture weakly in its direction? And where is 'there', except already at a *distance* from the king and his authority? Lear's demonstrative pronoun hovers indistinctly over a referential point that refuses to materialize, and seems suddenly not to capture a location but to resist any correspondence; as readers we are, like the Quarto Lear, suddenly confronted by a representational surface that promises some kind of spatial order but also insists resolutely on its distance and inscrutability. The Quarto's 'shake all cares and business from our *state*' (sc. 1, line 37; my emphasis) would seem to underscore the link between political authority and spatial representation, but in this context 'shake' suggests not the infirmity and 'age' of the Folio (1. 1. 37) but a trembling fear of cartography and its ability to make Lear's decision irrevocable by permanently inscribing it. Does Lear shrink from the map, an instrument whose power he recognizes but which he does not fully understand? These are precisely the questions that the printed text, in its two distinct versions, forces upon us.

In the terms of Henri Lefebvre, the map is, moreover, both a 'representational space' and a 'representation of space':[25] on the one hand the map represents the 'territory', presumably England, and more specifically a land 'With shadowy forests and with champaigns riched, | With plenteous rivers and wide-skirted meads' (F 1. 1. 62–3). Even more specifically, however, this is the *Folio's* gift of place to Goneril; the Quarto gives her less. But on the other hand the map also represents what we might call a 'modern' idea of space as a quantifiable and measurable geometric abstraction—'all these bounds even from this line to this' (1. 1. 61)—and this initial abstraction becomes more and more salient in the subsequent exchanges between Regan and Lear and finally between Lear and Cordelia, as the 'spatial' qualities of the map assert themselves over the form of the bequest. Regan gets 'this ample third of our fair kingdom, | No less in space,

[25] I have discussed these categories in more detail in Turner (1997, 2007). Cf. Lefebvre's (1991) comments on the space of the theatre: 'To the question of whether such a space is a representation of space or a representational space, the answer must be neither—and both. Theatrical space certainly implies a *representation of space*—scenic space—corresponding to a particular *conception* of space (that of the classical drama, say—or the Elizabethan, or the Italian). The *representational space*, mediated yet directly experienced, which infuses the work and the moment, is established as such through the dramatic action itself' (p. 188).

validity and pleasure' (1. 1. 79): hers is exactly a space and not a place, a gift of equivalence more than content, and what content it does have ('validity and pleasure') is also abstract. The latent unfairness of Lear's division now emerges precisely in the precision with which he uses the quantitative language of space to describe the gifts, since they are equal *only* in the abstract; each daughter gets 'a third', but Cordelia's is already 'a third more opulent' (1. 1. 84). In preferring one daughter over the others, Lear has already opted for the particularity of place and property over the equalizing commensurability of geometrical and mathematical space that makes cartographic representation itself possible.

As we may begin to suspect, Lear's strategic use of spatial rhetoric is, in short, duplicitous, and it is not surprising to find the same language of insincerity in the mouths of Goneril and Regan. The first avows her love in the language of spatial abstraction ('Dearer than eyesight, space, and liberty'; 1. 1. 54); the second in arithmetic figure, commercial value, and geometric form ('prize me at her worth . . . which the most precious square of sense possesses'; 1. 1. 68–72). Lear's mistake is to uncouple the power of kingship from the instruments and attributes which made that power appear self-legitimizing. Since Goneril and Regan understand the power of the map to convert space into property—so well that they glibly speak in the cartographic register—they understand also that Lear's use of the map has rendered him powerless by assisting him in his distribution of his kingdom, and it is no wonder that they follow his action to its logical conclusion by forcing him to renounce his knights in the later scenes.

Cordelia, however, uses a different language: her 'nothing' obviously speaks volumes—or, to be more precise, it *enacts* its meaning. The elaborate rhetoric of both Goneril and Regan can only belie their gestures towards the inadequacy of speech; Cordelia, recognizing here the duplicity of language, actualizes her meaning by saying 'nothing' and thus reducing the conceptual and emotional content of her response to the absolute minimum of verbal expression. Lear's enraged retort—'Nothing will come of nothing. Speak again' (1. 1. 88)—focuses her response into a paradox: as Rosalie Colie, Paul Jorgensen, and Edward Grant have discussed, in very different contexts, the crucial epistemological dilemma turns on whether or not the concept of 'nothing' is in fact 'something'.[26] What would it mean for Cordelia—or Lear, for that matter—to 'possess nothing'?

The frequent recurrence of the term 'nothing' throughout the play has sponsored no small amount of critical commentary, but its connection to the notions of attribute, property (in both the material and the philosophical or scientific senses), and space requires further elaboration. The problem is formulated most

---

[26] See Colie (1966: 220–72, 461–81, esp. 470–5), who discusses the paradox of 'nothing' and 'something' in relation to debates over Creation and the existence of a vacuum, although with a theological and 17th-century emphasis that is only partially applicable to *King Lear*. Grant (1976, 1981) provides an accessible discussion of the philosophical context during the period; see also Jammer (1954). On Shakespeare's use of 'nothing' in particular see Tayler (1990); Jorgensen (1962); Kastan (1982: 117–19); Burckhardt (1966); Wilburn (1980).

concisely by France, when he reassures Cordelia that 'thou losest here, a better where to find' (1. 1. 259): is 'here' the location in which Cordelia suffers the act of losing (property)? Or is 'here' exactly what she loses, her proper portion of her father's realm (as the syntax of 'where' would suggest)? Both readings seem possible; as queen of France, after all, Cordelia could be said simply to lose one place only immediately to gain another. But Lear is in a more difficult position, since he now moves uneasily through the space that he once ruled; indeed, given the close association between 'space', property, and authority in the division scene, the term 'space' would seem inappropriate to describe the medium of his dispossessed state.

Which brings us to the 'storm scenes'. For when Lear wanders out into the storm he is wandering out into a place over which he once exercised dominion, but does no longer; indeed, that place and his dominion over it was recognizable to him only on the map and in the spatial terms it made available, in which this location was simply a smaller part within the larger whole that contained it—'a particular place which is also a world', to use Bradley's phrase. Once this representation of space has been removed, once 'space' itself, as a property of kingship, is no longer something Lear can in any way lay claim to, this 'containing' relationship is also removed, and Lear begins to move in a dimension that is probably best described in the terms that the play uses: 'nothing'. Certainly the play explores these problems at the linguistic level, especially in the repeated use of the term 'nothing' and the variations of the *ex nihilo* phrasing that recur in both plot and sub-plot and the many associations among 'place', property, and power scattered throughout the early scenes. But these resonances are simply the verbal expression of a theoretical problem that is enacted performatively and non-verbally during the storm. To understand this we must consider the space of the stage during performance in more detail.

A comment by Sir Walter Greg illustrates some of its paradoxical qualities. Greg has made a brief excursus into the use of stage directions in manuscript copy, and to illustrate the documents' 'bewildering...diversity' adduces the example of the term 'within':

> The use of 'within' for off the stage is sometimes cited as belonging to the theatre. Logically this is doubtless so, though in fact the use is common to nearly all writers. But there is no consistency even in the playhouse. A character leaving the stage goes 'within' from the point of view of the actors, and goes 'out' from that of the spectators....Any writer, whether actually writing for the stage or not, will use 'within'—it is the only word available.[27]

The passage leaves us with many points to consider, not the least of which is the phrase 'point of view', which Greg introduces as casually as Bradley does but to a somewhat different effect. When perspective, ostensibly the most rational mode

---

[27] Greg (1931: i. 208); cf. P. W. K. Stone (1980: 111): 'It is well known that in Elizabethan theatrical parlance the stage was "out" or "without" and the tiring-house "in" or "within," though a spectator would most naturally take the opposite view.' Weimann (2000: 209) makes a similar observation; cf. Chambers (1923: iii. 64).

of spatial representation, becomes Greg's paradigm for thinking about the space of the stage in practice, it marks the limits of bibliographic and literary analysis and only multiplies the potential confusion of theatrical performance.

I would like to focus on another aspect, however: the initial dualism that animates the term 'within' conceals an additional set of interrelated meanings that are central to understanding the practical use of stage space. It is evident from Greg's comment that the terms 'within' and 'out' signify a direction, or a vector of movement. The stage 'plotts' and 'platts' studied by Greg and David Bradley in such detail provide a glimpse of how this fundamental boundary between offstage and onstage space might appear in its most abstract and schematic form: posted backstage in the public theatres of the 1590s, these remarkable documents subdivided the intrigue of the play into discrete performative units by distributing the entrances and the exits of the actors into ruled columns and boxes (see Fig. 5.1).[28] The stage platt represents the fundamental boundary between offstage and onstage space from the 'offstage' point of view, as it were, although it obscures a view of that backstage area itself, which always remains invisible. The platt provides only a technical abstraction of a purely formal limit to theatrical performance; indeed, it accomplishes this 'view' through a double translation, first by representing it as the effect of the actor's proxemic signs—his physical movement from one area of the stage to another, which demarcates an invisible line—and then by translating these movements into an iconic, graphic diagram that distributes all the entrances and exits of the play into a series of ruled columns and boxes. By spatializing and abstracting these movements, the platt provides a *structural* translation of the actor's movement through space, since each box designates a discrete episode in the mimetic action: these are 'scenes', or, most neutrally and descriptively, they are segments of action marked by entrances and exits. For this reason, historians of early-modern performance practice have designated the 'scene' as a momentarily cleared stage, onto which the subsequent entrance of the actor would open a new line of action or resume one that had previously been dropped in an earlier character grouping.

At the same time, however, the entrance might also designate a new *location* for the action, and although locations are not indicated in the backstage 'plotts' or 'platts' and although early-modern play texts make it clear that designating location was often unnecessary, Greg elsewhere takes it as axiomatic that scenes and locations may be correlated in this way.[29] The entrance of the actor onstage across the threshold had the performative power to create, instantaneously and in its movement, the very location that would give that entrance a fictional significance.

[28] Greg (1931: i. 1–11, 70–171); Bradley (1992, esp. 23–39 and 75–94, emphasizing the practical quality of the platt and of the origins of the term; 89).

[29] Cf. Greg (1955: 142): 'According to the custom of the Elizabethan stage division into scenes is structural and follows directly from the action: a new scene begins whenever the stage is clear and the action is not continuous; *whenever, that is, a change of locality is possible*' my emphasis); Bradley (1992, *passim*, esp. 29–34); Chambers (1923: iii. 50 n. 2), emphasizing 'a continuous section of action in an unchanged locality' rather than 'a momentary clearance of the stage'.

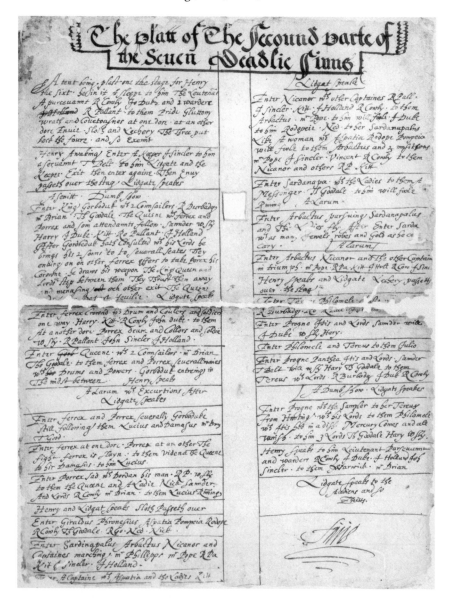

FIG. 5.1. Theatrical 'platt': *The Second Part of The Seven Deadly Sins* (c.1590–1)

In doing so, his movement tended to link the 'scene' as a coherent unit of the total action based on character grouping to a notion of fictional location, the setting in which the action being represented before the audience was imagined to take place. In Greg's analysis of the 'platts', the term 'within', of course, designates a kind of location, a place that the actor goes 'to', even if this place remains elusive: perhaps it is 'offstage', and thus in the theatre; perhaps it is 'elsewhere', and thus in the fiction. The terms are difficult to situate outside of a purely reciprocal relation to one another, in which the backstage wall acts as a pivot point or formal differentiating principle *out of which place emerges*; Greg attempts to resolve the potential ambiguity by invoking a larger conceptual abstraction (the 'theatre', the 'fiction') as well as a point of view (the actor, the spectator) to surround and thus to provide a measure of precision and definition to the places that the terms would seem to designate.

If the 'platt' has provided a glimpse of this performative mimetic process from the backstage point of view, the Prologue's evocation of the 'Wooden "O" ' in *Henry V* neatly captures this process from the onstage point of view and particularly that of the audience: the phrase describes a static, transparent spatial medium contained by the theatre building, the 'air' through which the actor moves and 'in' which a series of scenes will be represented.[30] But whether we consider the problem from the onstage or the offstage perspective, the genuinely *spatial* capacity of the platform stage is apprehensible only momentarily—at the instant the performance begins or ends, or in the slight break between scenes, if at all—since these fleeting appearances are simultaneously moments of dissolution and disappearance, as the 'space' of the stage is instantaneously converted into the specific 'places' of the fiction that the performance brings to life. Even in the Chorus's passages—in which the empty space of the stage would seem to appear most clearly—the audience is urged to fill this space with a dazzling sequence of fictional *places*: 'the vasty fields of France' (Prologue, 13), 'the perilous narrow ocean' (Prologue, 22), from London to Southampton to France and then back again to 'Dover pier' (3. 0. 4). Wardrobes, pastures, ship-boys climbing in the tackle—the stage is not a blank platform but a tableau of almost cinematic proportions, in which 'space' is obscured by all the bustling detail. If space 'itself' is to emerge onto the stage, it must be in a different mode, and more indirectly.

However: if an actor were to enter the stage as a character recognizable from the play and fail to designate a new location; as a character, moreover, who has been excluded first from one fictional place and then from another; if this actor were to occupy the stage and gesticulate wildly, gratuitously, even to run about the playing area, as other characters entered to him from the world of the play and urged him to depart with them to other places in that world; and if, despite their entreaties, this actor were to remain stubbornly on stage and refuse to recognize the presence of these characters or the locations they spoke of: 'where' exactly would this actor be? And how would a superstitious world describe such a character, except as mad?

---

[30] Cf. Pavis (1996: 13), who describes two possible 'spatial experiences' on the part of the audience: 'an empty space which must be filled just like a container or an environment' (which he associates with Artaud) and 'space...considered as invisible, limitless and as an extension of the user, starting from the latter's place, movement and trajectory'; also his entire discussion of 'gestural space' (pp. 14–15).

In such a moment the places of the theatre and of the fiction would coincide with equal vividness—and if this 'moment' was one of any duration, it might even qualify as a 'scene'. The resolute *negation* of place by one character, surrounded by the equally persistent affirmations of place by others, would result in a glimpse of the stage's potential to produce these places, and thus of its *space*.

The storm marks such a moment. All the peculiar qualities of the platform stage, usually subordinate to the fiction unfolding upon it, begin to crowd through a rift in this fiction and suddenly become visible with unusual vividness. The text records only attributes or qualities, but no location: the 'storm and tempest' marked by the Folio at 2. 2. 449. 1, 'the night', 'high winds' (2. 2. 464), the 'wild night' (2. 2. 472), and a deranged old man, whose hair 'the impetuous blasts make nothing of' (Q, sc. 8, line 8). Like Gloucester at Dover, Lear has been 'blinded' by his madness, floundering in the 'eyeless rage' of the storm (Q, sc. 8, line 7); like the madman Poor Tom, Lear will 'embrace' the 'unsubstantial air' (4. 1. 7), allow the storm to 'Invade us to the skin' (3. 4. 7), and, if he is to speak at all, will adopt the language of the storm: 'I will say nothing' (3. 2. 37).

Intriguingly, this is Lear's response to Kent, who enters in disguise as Caius (and like an actor) and who struggles repeatedly, in the face of Lear's 'madness', to *relocalize* the scene and to draw it back firmly either into the world of the fiction or onto the space of the stage: 'Alas, sir, are you here?' (3. 2. 41); 'hard by here is a hovel' (3. 2. 60); 'Here is the place, my lord. Good my lord, enter. | The tyranny of the open night's too rough' (3. 4. 1–2); 'Good my lord, enter here' (3. 4. 4); 'Good my lord, enter' (3. 4. 5); 'Good my lord, enter here' (3. 4. 22). The phrase becomes incantatory, frustrated and desperate in its attempts to manage the spatial disorder that surrounds the feeble party, but the technical language of the actor goes unrecognized and the cue ignored. When Lear suddenly decides to enter ('but I'll go in'; 3. 4. 25), the 'scene' would presumably snap into focus, except that he never actually *does* enter and the inconsistent exit markings in both Quarto and Folio make it unclear whether the episode takes place inside or outside the 'hovel' (which seems to be offstage). The silent stage direction 'storm still' offers no indication of location but only of turbulence and dim outlines.

Greg has maintained that 'within' is the 'only word available' to describe the relation between onstage and offstage space, but he has already provided another, and I will combine them to form a third term that describes this spatial 'crux': this term is 'without'. Lear refuses to leave the stage, declines to move either 'within' or 'out' and instead wanders 'without' into a breach in fictional space to flail in the *potentia* that surrounds him, a point somewhere *between* a coherent location and the platform stage: he is not in one, nor is he entirely in the other. He has, in these moments, become the full impersonation of the Fool's earlier witticism 'Now thou art an O without a figure' (1. 4. 158). The phrase concisely articulates, in arithmetic terms, the paradox of 'nothing' that is also 'something', designating the 'placeholder' that carves out a space for an imagined content (the figure) even as it simultaneously negates that content by occupying the space reserved for it. It is a sudden emblem not only for the spatial capacity of the empty platform stage but for Lear's own displaced position during the storm, in which his mere presence on stage simultaneously invites the audience to imagine a fictional location and then prevents that location from becoming fully realized.

An analogy from another discursive field may help make this 'space' more read-ily comprehensible: if the scene at Dover, through its invocation of perspective, gestures towards the mathematical and spatial concept of infinity, the 'nothing' of the storm could be said to perform the quasi-scientific space of the 'vacuum' or 'void', concepts debated in both natural philosophy and in the newer Stoicism and Neoplatonism of Campanella, Bruno, Francesco Patrizi, and many others. The 'nothing' of the platform stage would thus seem to frame in a different discur-sive context—and above all in a different mode of *practical* representation—a moment of transition in spatial thinking that we can also see operating at the most rarified levels of Renaissance academic argument, between a neo-Aristotelian scholastic philosophy that could conceive only of container or 'place' and the emergence of a distinct notion of 'space' understood as a homogeneous, extended medium that precedes and receives all bodies and their movements.[31] And lest we find these conceptual distinctions somewhat remote from the Elizabethan playhouse, Lear's peculiar epithet for Poor Tom as he insists on remaining 'without'—'let me talk with this philosopher' (3. 4. 137, 155, 158); 'this same learned Theban' (3. 4. 140); this 'good Athenian' (3. 4. 162)—suggests, however ironically, a philosophical context for the scene. As Edward Grant has demon-strated, scholastic arguments over vacuum and void space during the sixteenth and seventeenth centuries were in fact regularly posed as problems of 'nothing' (*nullam, nihil*); even more significantly, these debates took place through recourse to a concept of 'imaginary space' (*spatium imaginarium*): that quality of space which the mind is able to conceive of and project beyond itself, whether as fiction or even as 'nothing' at all.[32] And the Greek term *skēnē*, after all, designated a 'hut' or 'house' to the side of the ancient platform stage, where the actors could change costume 'offstage'—much like the 'hovel' that Lear refuses to enter *to*, preferring to remain 'without'.

PAGE

To reimagine the 'nothing' of the stage as the expanse of 'space' itself, and thus to translate 'performative form' into 'dramatic form'; to transform the mysterious 'hovel' offstage into the neo-classical 'scene', and thereby to contain the power of the storm in a familiar location: if these are tasks well suited to the philosophers and critics of the seventeenth century, it will be accomplished in another register

---

[31] See Grant (1981: 5–8 and *passim*); Jammer (1954).
[32] Grant (1981, esp. 11–13, 117–21, 182–255); on the Greek *skēnē*, see Carlson (1989: 130–1).

by the readers of the centuries that follow. In his preference for the printed page, Bradley is, after all, only elaborating a judgement made nearly a century earlier by Charles Lamb, who objected even more strongly to the pretensions of performance and declared Lear 'essentially impossible to be represented on a stage', because 'on the stage we see nothing but corporal infirmities and weakness, the impotence of rage: while we read it, we see not Lear, but we are Lear' (Lamb 1811: i. 107). In order to chart the differences between the 'nothing' of the platform stage and the mental space of the modern reader, it will now be useful to consider briefly how the relationship between 'place' and 'space' is reconfigured by the translation of a play into print and how a location direction comes to be regarded as indispensable to the editorial and critical apparatus.

Both the Quarto and the Folio *Lear*s have been variously linked to the conditions of the early-modern playhouse and to performance.[33] The predominant interest in bibliographical discussion of performance has been, understandably, to establish the status of *copy* and by extension the authority of the text on which it is based. In what follows, however, I would like to direct critical attention away from debates over copy and to focus instead on the effects of performance practice on print *format*, or the space of the page, and through this on the reader. In this respect, also, the Folio and Quarto *Lear*s differ remarkably from one another, and two aspects in particular contribute significantly to the sense of space and dramatic structure that each offers: the markings of act and scene divisions and the use of stage directions.

The question of act and scene division in early-modern drama is a difficult one, and if the evidence for actual practice were not already confusing and elusive enough, discussion is often made even more complicated by a failure to distinguish four separate aspects of the problem: acts and scenes in composition, in literary theory, in performance, and in the printing house. The first two aspects are often treated as being virtually identical to one another, but they are not necessarily so; acts in performance are properly speaking act-*intervals* and not units of action. The difficulty resulted precisely from the long-standing difference between stage and page, 'theatre' and 'drama': as early as Donatus' fourth-century commentaries on Terence, critics had struggled to reconcile structural principles derived from stage performance with those generated by the retrospective and

---

[33] Q2, printed in the shop of William Jaggard in 1619 (one of the so-called 'Pavier Quartos' and perhaps part of an early attempt at a volume of collected works) essentially reproduces Q1 and for this reason I have omitted it from my discussion. For the text of Q1 scholars have proposed memorial reconstruction, either by two actors (typically those playing Goneril and Regan) or by the entire group on provincial tour; shorthand transmissions by a member of the audience; surreptitious glances at a prompt-book; and, more recently, autograph foul papers. F, traced through copies of either Q1 or, as is now thought, Q2 annotated with any number of prompt-books or other manuscript copies, departs from Q1 in ways that have been taken to suggest either deliberate theatrical or authorial revision or a combination of both. Halio provides a concise discussion of the major points in *Shakespeare* (*c.*1605, esp. pp. 58–81 and 265–89); see also the essays surveying the debates on this subject, along with a bibliography of its major statements, collected in Taylor and Warren (1983).

theoretical analysis of a written text.[34] 'Acts' were regarded both as episodes of *diegetic action* and as the trace of the Chorus in mimetic *performance*, a structural component that had ceased to exist in Roman comedy and which remained only as the momentary cleared stage. Both definitions persisted simultaneously in Donatus' analysis, as T. W. Baldwin has demonstrated, and were difficult to reconcile with one another: the first conceived of the act as a quantitative unit of composition that extended for a given number of scenes and pages, while the second understood it as a purely negative principle of division, a cut or break that was itself without content but which could be used to identify stages in the development of the intrigue. Since Terence and other authors often sought deliberately to suppress this break in favour of continuity of action, Donatus admitted, identifying acts in this way could be difficult; Terence himself, meanwhile, had left no definitive statements on the question.[35]

Aside from a few entries in Henslowe's diary, most of which concern a single author, there is scant evidence to suggest that early-modern plays intended for performance in the so-called public theatres were composed according to a five-act structure before the second decade of the seventeenth century. The evidence of the stage 'plotts' indicates that English writers composed plays in a series of scenes that were meant to be played continuously in the theatre, and not in five acts; even Jonson's plays, for all their self-conscious classicism, reflect this fundamentally scenic structure, as we shall see in Chapter 7.[36] Henry Snuggs makes the remarkable observation (1960: 49–50) that Thomas Heywood, whose *Apology for Actors* clearly shows familiarity with the major statements of dramatic theory as early as 1607 (and perhaps before), does not seem in practice to have composed his plays according to these principles until after 1610.

Even here, however, the evidence concerns primarily the *printed* text, which immediately introduces conventions and habits which should be kept distinct from the use of divisions in composition, literary theory, or performance, even if finally all four categories tend to converge. We might assume that act and scene divisions in a printed text often indicate copy that has been modified in some way

[34] The distinction is clear as early as Donatus' 4th-century comments on Terence's *Hecyra*: 'Varro teaches that neither in this play nor in the others is it to be wondered at that the acts may be unequal in number of scenes and *pages*, since this distribution is determined by the proper division of the intrigue, not by the number of verses, not only with the Latins, but even with the Greeks themselves' (Donatus 1962: ii. 192; my emphasis), cited by Baldwin (1947: 8, 28).

[35] See Baldwin (1947: 1–52). In *Hecyra* Terence uses the term *actus* (*primo actu placeo*; line 39) to mean a section of the play but never indicates five acts or the total number of divisions in his plays or of their action. He alludes only to an unspecified kind of division between the opening and the beginning of the action but does not say where this takes place or how to identify it. The major divisions of the plays into five parts was supplied by Donatus, who derived the system from fragments of Varro's commentaries on Terence and Plautus and from Horace's comments in the *Ars Poetica* that plays should have five acts.

[36] See, in addition to Baldwin (1947, 1965), the discussion in Greg (1955: 143–5; 1931: i. 79–81, 206–7, 210–13); Chambers (1930: i. 118, 123–4, 199–201); Snuggs (1960, esp. 35–51); Jewkes (1958); and D. Bradley (1992, *passim*, esp. 4–6, 29–34); McKenzie (1977: 112–16); and G. Taylor (1993*a*), the most recent and by far the most comprehensive discussion of surviving evidence.

for use in the theatre; Greg, Snuggs, and Chambers all agree that divisions in manuscript documents prior to *c.*1610 are very likely to be the product of a later hand and that authors seem to have added divisions to their playscripts gradually in deference to stage practice.[37] But these later divisions, as well as those in printed play texts, may equally be the classicizing gestures of a professional scribe and thus similar to other scribal conventions (such as the massed entrances attributed to Ralph Crane) that sought to emulate the printing—or page—conventions of Roman comedy; in both cases, furthermore, the divisions are often arbitrary, and it is hard to say how much 'literary' or 'structural' role they actually play.[38]

To argue in this way is again, however, to resort to the categories of author and copy, but it is important to remember that 'structural' theories of act and scene divisions are in some respects possible only from the position of the reader, who has the capacity to arrest the flow of the action temporarily, to pause over scenes, flip through pages, carefully weigh one moment with another, and gradually distinguish the architecture of the composition. On the page, act and scene divisions do not simply reproduce a break in performance: they contribute a conceptual unity to the play by subdividing its action into discrete parts, and these parts are then presumed by the reader to fit together into a coherent structural whole. Redistributed across the page in deliberately segmented units of action, the newly unified 'work' makes possible a completely different sense of space from that which predominates on the stage: it allows the reader to project across the play in its entirety a homogeneous, unbroken, 'containing' space that is imagined to link or underlie the various 'places' of the fiction, whether these be onstage or off, 'within' or 'without'. The Folio *Lear*, with its full use of act and scene divisions, obscures the specific performative tension between 'space' and 'place' that is the basis of emplotment in the theatre—the dynamic whereby space, as potential, 'solidifies', as it were, into a specific location, which in turn redissolves into 'emptiness' and another potential location—and moves gradually towards a notion more similar to 'setting' which inserts the action into a pre-existing spatial dimension. A stage direction such as 'Storm still' (in F but *not* in Q) is significant not least because it implies a concern for spatial continuity in the fiction best characterized as a space of simultaneity, in which separate subjects and their actions are understood as taking place at the same time and are thus linked to one another within a homogeneous, extended space: the imagined 'world' of the play that contains both Gloucester's castle and Dover, both England and France.

But for the critics of the eighteenth century the act and scene divisions did more than provide a sense of structural unity: the divisions definitively sutured this 'literary' structure to a concept of 'place' which rendered the play's action comprehensible and made possible a final aesthetic judgement. We can see this

---

[37] Inter-act music was a convention of the hall theatres as early as 1604 (as evidenced by Marston's *Malcontent*), and after the occupancy of the Blackfriars theatre by the King's Men in 1609 the practice seems to have spread to the Globe and the other amphitheatres. See Chambers (1930: i. 200); Snuggs (1960: 37–45); G. Taylor (1993*a*).   [38] Cf. G. Taylor (1993*b*, esp. 239–41).

subsequent development quite vividly as early as Pope's edition of the plays. In keeping with the Continental critics, Pope correlates scene division with the 'removal of place' in the name of consistency and clarity:

The Scenes are mark'd so distinctly that every removal of place is specified; which is more necessary in this Author than in any other, since he shifts them more frequently: and sometimes without attending to this particular, the reader would have met with obscurities. (Shakespeare 1725, p. xxii)

Moreover, the entire work is conceptualized in a striking architectural metaphor such that all the action is given a continuous spatial structure and coherence:

I will conclude by saying of *Shakespear*, that with all his faults, and with all the irregularity of his *Drama*, one may look upon his works, in comparison of those that are more finish'd and regular, as upon an ancient majestick piece of *Gothick* Architecture, compar'd with a neat Modern building: The latter is more elegant and glaring, but the former is more strong and more solemn. It must be allow'd that in one of these there are materials enough to make many of the other. It has much the greater variety, and much the nobler apartments; tho' we are often conducted to them by dark, odd, and uncouth passages. (Shakespeare 1725, pp. xxiii–xxiv)

Fifteen years later Lewis Theobald picks up the image but dilates it to encapsulate the architectural within the perspectival, and both within a much more expansive world or city:

The attempt to write upon SHAKESPEARE is like going into a large, a spacious, and a splendid Dome thro' the Conveyance of a narrow and obscure Entry. A Glare of Light suddenly breaks upon you, beyond what the Avenue at first promis'd: and a thousand Beauties of Genius and Character, like so many gaudy Apartments pouring at once upon the Eye, diffuse and throw themselves out to the Mind. The Prospect is too wide to come within the Compass of a single View: 'tis a gay Confusion of pleasing Objects, too various to be enjoyed but in a general Admiration; and they must be separated, and ey'd distinctly, in order to give the proper Entertainment.[39]

The passage marks the emergence of a 'metaphorics' of perspective as pluralism and cultured selection, a refinement that depends on distance and separation. By the time of Edward Capell's 1767 edition, the space of the Shakespearean text has been thoroughly redistributed: noting that he has derived a principle of scene division (the removal of location) from those plays in the Folio which have already been divided 'as of the Author's own settling', Capell proceeds to locate the action with stage directions that further subdivide an interior space: virtually all the scenes are assigned to '*A State-room in King* Lear's *Palace*'; '*A Hall in the Earl of* Gloster's *Castle*'; '*A Room in the Duke of* Albany's *Palace*'; '*An outer Hall in the same*', such that Pope's metaphor of linked apartments has been literalized into a world of intimacy and domestic realism.[40]

---

[39] Theobald, Preface, in I. Smith (1963: 59).
[40] Shakespeare (1767–8: i. 25; stage directions from ix. 3, 14, 19, 20); cf. McKenzie (1977: 110–11).

If we now return to compare the format of the Folio *Lear* to that of the first Quarto, we notice that the earlier text lacks all act and scene divisions and unfolds in a space that we might characterize as linear or sequential. Here the Quarto format preserves, to some degree, a sense of stage and performance space that is 'Elizabethan', typical of public theatres, and disappearing from historical view: stage directions are few, exits and entrances are omitted, and the organizational 'unit' (to import spatial and structural terms that are better suited to the page) is more closely linked to character groupings and their movements—but these movements are *not* correlated with any sense of 'place', and the relation between onstage and offstage space remains as elusive as ever. Here any dramatic pause between scenes would lack by definition the conceptual substance of a break between acts: true neo-classical 'Acts' and 'Scenes' are meaningful only in the context of the conceptual integrity that the larger 'work' provides, and vice versa; this dependency derives from the more general dialectic between any part and its whole. In any case, distinctions of this sort inevitably beg the textual question, since the action of *Lear* as it is printed in the Quarto advances with no clear division whatsoever and consequently does not offer the same spatial or structural skeleton to the reader.

It has often been remarked that the Folio was a text printed specifically for a reading market and for readers of some affluence. Many aspects of the collection suggest this, among them the size and quality of the book and its elaborate prefatory materials, not the least of which are the dedicatory poem 'To the Reader' by 'B.I.' and Heminge and Condell's own direct address 'To the great Variety of Readers'. I have thus aligned the format of each version of *Lear* with one of the distinct spatial sensibilities I have been discussing: the Folio with what I will call a 'readerly' space of abstraction and the Quarto with a 'performative' space of movement that produces more of itself. But early-modern printing-house practice offers a technical distinction that also serves as a convenient metaphor for the spatial modes materialized on their pages. This is the difference between composing and printing by casting off, and composing and printing seriatim. The former technique, whereby a compositor estimated the total number of printed pages required for a given portion of the control text at hand (whether print or manuscript), and only then set his type into formes accordingly, necessitated a *spatial grasp of an entire segment of text*—either a page, a forme, a sheet, or the complete work—that was subsequently 'translated' by the compositor into the blank expanse of the page. Composing seriatim, in contrast, meant that the compositor set his type sequentially, in a linear spatial fashion and with no necessary regard for the total dimensions of the text before him, and worked from the beginning of the copy through to the end. As historical coincidence would have it, Nicholas Okes set the Quarto *Lear* seriatim, while the compositors in Isaac Jaggard's print shop set the Folio according to the more conventional process of casting off.[41]

---

[41] See Blayney (1982, esp. 89–150) and Hinman (1963: i. 47–51). Both of the spatial sensibilities I am describing obviously operated simultaneously during the period of 1608 to 1623, even if the

Perhaps it will be impossible for us to grasp fully the peculiar spatial properties of this 'nothing' that, paradoxically, manages to fill the platform stage, especially when, as modern readers, the idea of imagination itself so quickly assumes a spatial dimension and when the very conventions of literary analysis—citation by act and scene, for instance—make it difficult to separate a modern idea of dramatic form and structure from ideas of space and location that depend on the printed book. Moments such as these appear nonsensical to a critical tradition that has become accustomed to the conventions of the text, accustomed both to the presence of a particular location 'in' the world of that text and to the presence of a particular character 'in' that particular location—a character, moreover, who has become emblematic of subjectivity in its most acute, most essential aspect.[42] This is a critical tradition that derives its analytical categories from the text rather than from the theatre, its heuristic authority from the concept of the author rather than from the stage and its practical performative techniques. These moments, peculiar to the platform stage, appear in the early texts only through a silent absence; by designating them with terms such as 'without' that recall stage *practice* rather than readerly imagination or editorial convention, we may mark the moment when *King Lear* turns on itself and begins to explore its own conditions of possibility as a spatial art.

It will now be useful to consider by way of a conclusion several points that have emerged in the preceding discussion and which are pertinent to any study of the stage as an apparatus that uses space as a medium of representation, as well as to the history of spatial thinking more generally. We may begin by stating a now familiar lesson: that to speak of the 'drama' it is necessary to consider both stage and page simultaneously and to admit all the potential difficulties, both theoretical and practical, that this implies for the scholar and editor.[43] As much as scholars

---

overall historical movement during the 17th century and beyond is towards the 'readerly' space of the Folio. Several features of both texts suggest that the period was one of transition in spatial thinking, among them the Folio's very inconsistency in dividing plays into acts and scenes (nineteen plays fully divided, including *Lear* (three imperfectly); eleven into acts alone (two imperfectly); and six not at all (they indicate *Actus primus Scena* (or *Scœna*) *prima* only)). Although Okes actually *printed* the Quarto using seriatim methods, an analysis of type and watermarks by Blayney (1982: 96–100) indicates that Okes knew in advance exactly how much paper the entire job would require. Considered from the bibliographic unit of the sheet or page, therefore, Q reflects a seriatim spatial practice, but when considered as a total book it reflects a spatial understanding more typical of casting off.

[42] Cf. Knights (1959: 92): '*Lear*... is a universal allegory.... In the scenes on the heath, for example... we are caught up in a great and almost impersonal poem in which we hear certain voices which echo and counterpoint each other; all that they say is part of the tormented consciousness of Lear; and the consciousness of Lear is part of the consciousness of human kind.'

[43] Dessen (1984: 22–7) has pointed out that the needs of theatrical historians and conventional editors are the inverse of one another: for the study of performance, texts that bear evidence of staging—the more revisions the better—are of primary importance, while texts with no direct connection to the stage are of no particular interest. When the critical goal is not composition but the conditions of play production, the entire range of texts produced in this process—so-called 'foul papers', scribal copy, plot summaries, prompt-books, and all printed Quartos, 'bad' or otherwise, in addition to the Folio—serve as potentially authoritative sources; see also Kastan (1999: 78).

may be committed to recognizing the enduring qualities of the play *text*, in another words, they must be concerned with the limitations of this text, with what it can only gesture at but never reveal. If the transfer from stage to print ultimately makes possible a more familiar and more modern sense of space, location, and dramatic structure—of 'emplotment', in a single word—moments in the early-modern play text such as that of the storm also produce spatial confusion, rupture, tensions, fault lines: seams in the spatial fabric that are accentuated because the conventional stage solutions are no longer present. Editorial attempts to defuse the undecidability of these moments—whether through the use of location directions (which hypostatize the space of fiction) or a reconstructed *refusal* to use them (which hypostatize the space of the stage)—inevitably foreclose the capacity of these scenes to show us (at least) three critical aspects.

In the first place and most obviously, the scenes reveal the full historicity and contingency of performative theatrical representation and, with it, the emergence of an idealized notion of 'dramatic form' that depends on the suppression of this very contingency and historicity. Here the question of 'form' re-emerges as one that is indispensable to a literary, theoretical, or historical analysis of theatre as a spatial art, as I have argued in the Introduction, above. In a materialist sense, the form of a play is not the ideal 'dramatic' object of New Criticism but the physical shape of the play when printed and extended across the page, with its title bars, rules, margins, and binding. The 'form' of performance is more difficult to describe verbally, and this is, after all, one of the play's central insights: it is a series of forces and movements, of semiological overdetermination that coalesces into a recognizable 'scene' and then into sequences of scenes. In this process, as we shall see, the function of the stage wall as a concrete instantiation of a purely abstract formal limit to stage representation is of particular importance to a theatre based on narrative, since it provides a way of separating and isolating different events, allowing some episodes to be shown and others to be inferred. But the boundary between onstage and offstage space is equally fundamental to any ideological analysis of the relationship between theatrical representation and early-modern social life, since it provided a conceptual structure in which some aspects of early-modern culture could emerge while others remained occluded or structurally invisible.

Secondly, these peculiar 'scenes' demonstrate how complex the iconic and performative conventions of the early-modern theatre as a spatial art had become by the first decade of the seventeenth century and how fully they could be exploited by playwrights who understood them. At a purely formal level, *King Lear* may be regarded as a play experimenting with differing modes and degrees of iconicity, with the way in which iconicity functions as a mode of theatrical semiosis, and with the kind of knowledge that iconicity makes possible. Painting, map, diagram, body, platform: all can be classified as iconic signs, and the ostensive qualities of this mode of signification, as well as the fact that the icon always tends to take a spatial form, is one of the play's central preoccupations. But this is already to anticipate the third and final insight furnished by these crucial 'scenes', and the full significance of this insight is the subject of the chapters that follow: they demonstrate not simply the historicity and specificity of 'performative form' or its representational protocols but the way in which performance itself functioned *as a practical mode of knowledge through representation* in ways that were continuous with the practical measuring manuals or Sidney's approach to the poetic image. How did the particular exigencies and material conditions of a theatre performance differ from a play book, and what analytic insights did they make possible to early-modern people as they sought to examine their historical moment through different narratives, characters, actions, and locations?

As a king and father excluded from the castles of his daughters who has been deprived of all authority, property, and title, Lear is in a distinctly liminal situation in the diegetic world of the play. And he lacks a proper position on the stage as well: he is 'without' the fictional place that is itself barely visible and defined only negatively or by attributes. Assimilating the 'nothing' of these scenes to a later, post-Newtonian 'absolute space' or Kantian a priori is at the very least anachronistic; perhaps the term 'space' itself even becomes insufficient in these cases, in that it inevitably implies these subsequent ideas. But to reimagine the scenes according to these later notions is also to foreclose the radical potential of their 'nothing' and to appropriate it for more conventional ideological uses, reconceiving it as 'emptiness' that can be owned or bequeathed (space as property), invaded (the space of the nation and the threat of France), or filled with subjective content (the space of humanism and literary history as it has traditionally been understood). It is significant that the heterogeneous, unfamiliar 'space' that appears in the storm scenes is also the point of articulation for a radical critique of power, justice, kingship, normative sexual systems, and other early-modern conventions necessary to a specific mode of production.[44] Whether we find in these moments, after Robert Weimann, an assertion of the festive and radical multivocality of the *platea* over the more univocal *locus*, with its 'worthy' matter; an older, fully embodied, and 'presentational' mode of performance disrupting an act of composition aligned with the humanist arts of language and Renaissance poetic theory; or a contest between player and dramatist, 'author's pen' and 'actor's voice', in each case it is the unspeakable elements of early-modern culture—literally the 'ob-scene'—that press upon the spectator or erupt suddenly into view. By managing the boundary between onstage and offstage, early-modern dramatists not only defined the 'scene' as a unit of composition and began to experiment with location as a way of organizing dramatic narrative in a topographic fashion: they 'translated' into symbolic expression much broader changes and tensions in early-modern culture that were unthinkable in any other way except through the symbolic forms and limits that the theatre made available to them, and it is this analytic function of the stage icon that we must now examine in more detail.

---

[44] Cf. Halpern's (1991) reading of the play in terms of property and an economics of *dépense*, and De Grazia (1996).

6

The Topographic Stage

My intent is not here to prosecute at large the Plotting of Grounds, being a
thing handled by others, treating of Surveying, but.... I shall crave leave to
digresse a little to shew this use of it, as briefly as I may... make a Booke in a
long Octavo, and... having taken and set down your notes in the Field on the
left sides or Pages of your Booke... set down in the first Columnes on the right
side, how many Degrees the Lines upon which you have traversed are distant
from the North or South part of the Meridian towards the East or West, and in
the second Columes, the quantity of the same Lines... Which done I take the
Table, and find there the Northing and Southing, Easting or Westing answerable to these Degrees and Distances, and set them down accordingly... And
being thus returned to my first station, I sum up severally these foure columnes,
of North, South, East, and West; and finding that the summe of the North
colume is equall to the South, and the summe of the East is equall to that of the
West, I conclude the whole worke to be truely performed . . .

(Richard Norwood, *The Seaman's Practice*, 1637)

THEATRE, DIAGRAM, AND MAP

If the history of the Renaissance stage as we know it depended on the initiative and
skill of the men of the building trades, it would have been impossible, too, without
the many changes attendant upon London's urbanization during the late sixteenth
and early seventeenth centuries. The land that Burbage leased for twenty-one years
from Christopher and Giles Allen on 13 April 1576 had belonged to a Benedictine
priory and had long since been broken up among several owners, but the property
still retained its status as a Liberty and thus constituted a legal space at least partially
outside City jurisdiction.[1] A site that had once been silent, sacred and enclosed,
infused with divine presence and remote from the business of daily life, had with
the Dissolution been secularized and inventoried, quantified into plot and
property that could be alienated at will; within this parcel the structure of the

---

[1] Chambers (1923: ii. 383–400); I. Smith (1964: 132–3); on the legal status of the liberties and
the place of the theatres in them, see Mullaney (1988, esp. 1–25, 47–59); Bruster (1992, esp. 1–28),
revising Mullaney's arguments; Sullivan, Jr. (1998), a further qualification of Mullaney's thesis; Gurr
(2000, esp. 256–61).

Theatre itself was built on so-called 'void ground', or land without prior existing buildings or specific use. The terms of the lease stipulated that Burbage could 'take down such building as should...be erected on the sayd voyde growndes for a theatre or playinge place' and also that he improve the surrounding grounds and barn, which he eventually converted into tenements.[2] Later Allen would complain in court that the tenements had become a nuisance to the neighbourhood because their residents had been reduced to begging for their rents: these were precisely the problems that gave the suburbs their reputation as a place of disease, poverty, and social instability and which prompted both City and Crown to begin passing a series of Acts restricting new buildings and the subdivision of property.[3]

My purpose in this chapter will be to consider how the iconic techniques of the platform stage made possible an analytic knowledge about the historical experience of London's urbanization, in so far as the process of urbanization itself presented a series of specific epistemological and representational difficulties.[4] Foremost among these is the simple fact that urbanization was for many different reasons unthinkable and unrepresentable *as a total social process* to early-modern writers: the many effects of London's sudden and often chaotic growth, while obvious to moralists, historians, and state authorities, eluded a systematic, structural explanation in a culture that lacked the analytical tools of modern social science. Most obviously, London was physically larger than any other English town or urban conglomeration: it could not be seen in its entirety by the naked eye alone, unlike individual buildings, streets, fields, or meadows. The process of coming to knowledge about the consequences of urbanization thus depended on generating artificial models and projections: forms and images in which 'the city' as a conceptual entity could be rendered as an object of knowledge, its often conflicting self-definitions examined, reconciled, or subordinated to one another.[5]

---

[2] Chambers (1923: ii. 387).   [3] Chambers (1923: ii. 399).

[4] For the social and economic history of London's urbanization during the period see Rappaport (1989), emphasizing stability maintained by urban institutions; Archer (1991), emphasizing change and potential for unrest; Boulton (1987), on Southwark; Griffiths and Jenner (2000); Fisher (1948); Thirsk (2000); Beier and Finlay (1986). For the history of London's political and mercantile culture and its relationship to the Civil War, see Pearl (1961); Ward (1997), a recent revision of Pearl's work; and Brenner (1993), a major study of London's merchant communities. Keene (2000) and Sacks (2000, esp. 20–6; 2002) provide helpful overviews and additional bibliography. Brett-James (1935) provides an excellent descriptive history of London's physical development and topography; see also Pearl (1961: 9–29); Ward (1997, esp. 7–26, 27–44); Schofield (1987, 1994, 2000); L. Stone (1980); Power (1972, 1978); and Shaw (1996), on 14th-century London. Accounts of London's demographic change during the period have been the subject of debate; see esp. Harding (1990); Finlay and Shearer (1986); Sacks (2000: 22–6). The representational problems associated with the process of London's urbanization has been of particular interest to literary scholars, although none discuss the performative, iconic conventions of the theatre and its relationship to geometric modes of representation and emplotment. See, in addition to the works cited in the Introduction and below, Barton (1978); Levin (1986); Paster (1986); Wells (1981); Manley (1995); Haynes (1992); Howard (2000, 2001, 2002, 2007); McNeill (1997); Newman (1991, 2000, 2002); B. R. Smith's (1999) analysis of urban 'soundscapes' (pp. 52–71); Dillon (2000); Fumerton (2000); and R. West (2001); M. Smith *et al.* (1995); Orlin (2000*a*).

[5] Marin (1988: 169–2; 2001: 202–18); De Certeau (1984, esp. 92–3).

In so far as London's identity was so closely associated with its mercantile activity, it was particularly important for contemporaries to find a mode of representation for the different forms of wealth that were typical of an urban environment, specifically the relationship between production, trade, capital investment, and land (the traditional form of wealth), the way that private property was defined and understood, and the means by which markets were regulated. In the city, property was more fungible and money more kinetic than in the country: as the centre of the land market, London was the place where the quantification and abstraction of space effected by the surveying manuals became necessary; it was the place where the countryside could become an imagined space projected outward and idealized, abstracted into a thing that could be occupied, used up, or converted into a commodified form. In Chapter 2 and elsewhere (Turner 2002*b*) I have described this process in more detail. But a similar development was taking place in the heart of London itself, partly through a thriving trade in new buildings and partly through the subdivision of larger structures, many of them former monastic properties, to form individual tenements. We may compare Aaron Rathborne's technical illustrations for surveying a private manor (Figs. 6.1 and 6.2) with the 'plotts' drawn by Ralph Treswell, a member of the Painter–Stainers' Guild commissioned to make a series of surveys of rental property in the city for Christ's Hospital (*c*.1612–1613) and the Clothworkers' Company (*c*.1612; Figs. 6.3, 6.4, and 6.5).[6] Rural surveys such as Rathborne's required the reduction of a vast, irregular figure into a series of regular geometric forms, often through a process of triangulation. The urban survey also might subdivide a larger figure into smaller component figures, but it required, too, the generation of regular figures within already existing, fixed boundaries. In both cases, the geometry handbooks furnished the techniques necessary to the cognitive operation: Recorde's sixteenth and seventeenth conclusions in *The Pathway to Knowledge* ask the reader to generate quadrilateral figures (rectangles and parallelograms) that will match a given angle, and then to position these figures in relation to another fixed line and angle which have been supplied (Div^v–Eii^v). Theorems 36–44 prove the equality of square figures that have been generated from lines subdivided arbitrarily (Figs. 6.6 and 6.7). Aaron Rathborne's *The Surveyor* (1616) sets similar problems for his reader, who is asked to generate a variety of figures given certain lengths and proportions, to reduce one figure into another of different proportions but identical area, or to subtract one square figure from another and to use the remainder to generate a third square (Figs. 6.8 and 6.9).

Directly associated with these basic economic questions for early-modern contemporaries were the categories of urban social hierarchy they produced, particularly those of class and status, the relationship between class and status to administrative categories such as office or guild membership, and the relationship

---

[6] See Schofield (1987; 1994; 2000, esp. 309–14); Orlin (2000*b*).

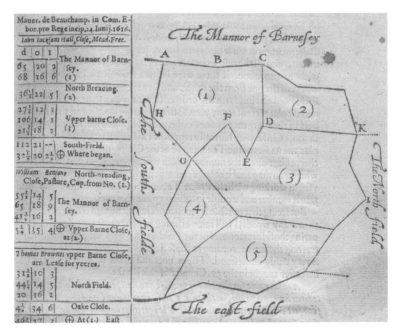

Fig. 6.1. Manorial survey, Aaron Rathborne, *The Surveyor in Four Books* (1616)

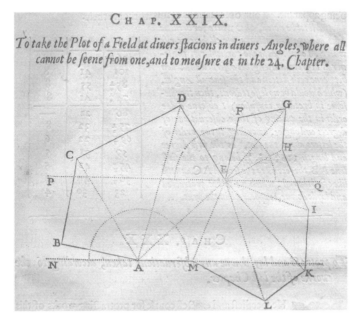

Fig. 6.2. Rural triangulation, Aaron Rathborne, *The Surveyor in Four Books* (1616)

FIG. 6.3. Survey of shops, yards, rooms, and kitchens at 9–10 Basing Lane by Ralph Treswell (*c.*1612); cf. Schofield (1987, nos. 5, 8)

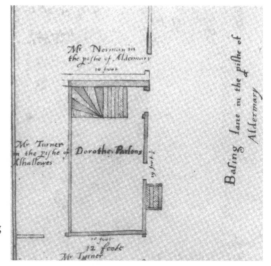

FIG. 6.4. Survey of shops, yards, rooms, and kitchens at 20 Basing Lane by Ralph Treswell (*c.*1612); cf. Schofield (1987, nos. 6, 9)

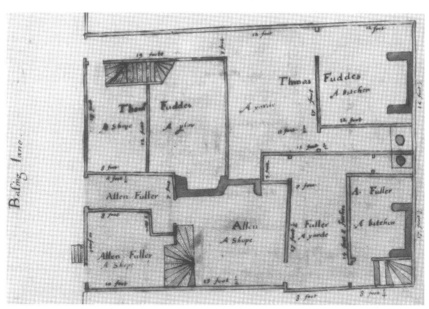

among all three public categories to private ones such as the family.[7] As both capital and port, London was a site of unusual social and cultural heterogeneity; its position as an international trading market meant that it was home to many goods and 'strangers' from other countries: merchants and diplomats but also

---

[7] I take the distinction between 'class' and 'status' groups from Weber (1978), for whom 'classes' are groups defined by their access to the market and their power and flexibility over market processes, while 'status' describes those groups defined through the possession of social honour and a 'style of life'.

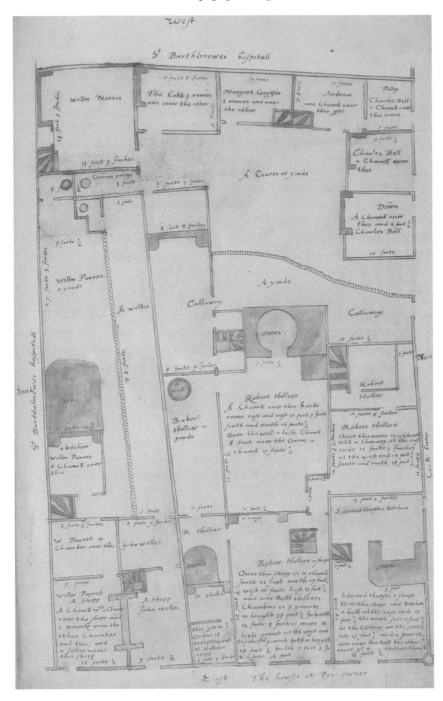

FIG. 6.5. Survey of 'The howses at Pye Corner' by Ralph Treswell (*c.*1611); cf. Schofield (1987, nos. 25, 29, and pl. 7)

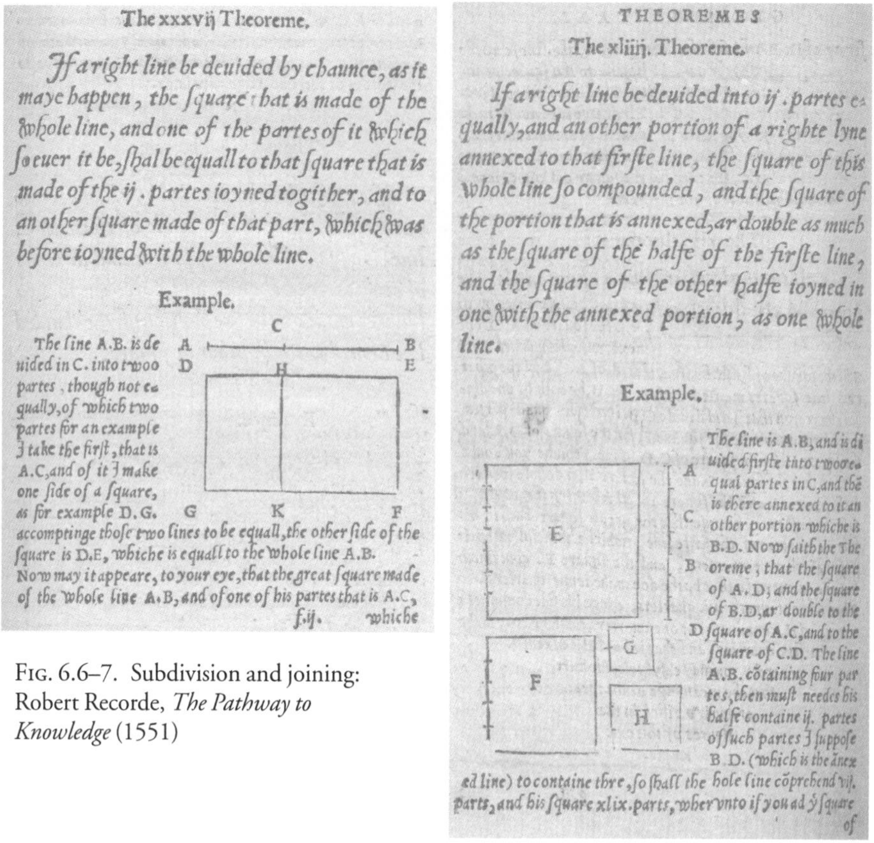

The xxxvij Theoreme.

If a right line be deuided by chaunce, as it maye happen, the square that is made of the whole line, and one of the partes of it which soeuer it be, shal be equall to that square that is made of the ij. partes ioyned togither, and to an other square made of that part, which was before ioyned with the whole line.

Example.

The line A.B. is de-uided in C. into twoo partes, though not e-qually, of which two partes for an example I take the first, that is A.C, and of it I make one side of a square, as for example D.G, accomptinge those two lines to be equall, the other side of the square is D.E, whiche is equall to the whole line A.B. Now may it appeare, to your eye, that the great square made of the whole line A.B, and of one of his partes that is A.C,
f.ij. whiche

THEOREMES
The xliiij. Theoreme.

If a right line be deuided into ij. partes e-qually, and an other portion of a righte lyne annexed to that firste line, the square of this whole line so compounded, and the square of the portion that is annexed, ar double as much as the square of the halfe of the firste line, and the square of the other halfe ioyned in one with the annexed portion, as one whole line.

Example.

The line is A.B, and is di-uided firste into twoo e-qual partes in C, and the is there annexed to it an other portion whiche is B.D. Now faith the The oreme; that the square of A.D; and the square of B.D, ar double to the square of A.C, and to the square of C.D. The line A.B. cotaining foure par tes, then must needes his halfe containe ij. partes of such partes I suppose B.D. (whiche is the annex ed line) to containe thre, so shall the hole line cōprehend vij. partes, and his square xlix. partes, wherunto if you ad y square of

FIG. 6.6–7. Subdivision and joining: Robert Recorde, *The Pathway to Knowledge* (1551)

religious refugees from the Continent whose presence brought a fear of religious unrest, of political spies, and of secret Catholic communities.[8] As a thriving commercial capital, London also attracted 'foreigns' of all types: English people originating outside the city and its legal, commercial, and political structures who threatened, in the eyes of contemporaries, to bring poverty, thievery, prostitution, and illegitimacy, especially in the suburbs that lay outside the city wall. Rendering these effects of urbanization even more threatening to contemporaries was the fact that they so often seemed to be opaque: the process of urbanization was in many ways a process of interiorization, as the subjects of the city withdrew indoors into private rooms, to be glimpsed partially through windows and doorways or over a garden wall. Finally, London's spatial relationships were articulated through a basic syntax of proximity, which might become garbled and alarming: the

---

[8] On the presence of 'strangers' and international goods in the city, as in England more broadly, see esp. Howard (2000); Thirsk (1978, 2000); Bartolovich (2000); Mukerji (1983); Dietz (1986).

significant variable in its topographic structure was one of relative distance between elements, its relevant 'functions', as in a spatial equation, those which either collapsed these distances or accentuated them through unfamiliar juxtapositions.

Both the Privy Council and London authorities believed they could contain the pernicious effects of urbanization by controlling the material topography of the city, and the representational methods of practical geometry and the professional bodies associated with it provided some of the first ways that social changes might be conceptualized and regulated—literally 'given form' so that they could be

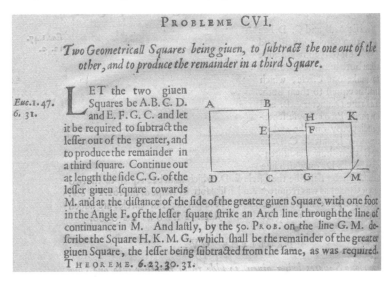

PROBLEME CVI.

Two Geometricall Squares being giuen, to subtract the one out of the other, and to produce the remainder in a third Square.

Euc.1.47.
6. 31.

LET the two giuen Squares be A. B. C. D. and E. F. G. C. and let it be required to subtract the lesser out of the greater, and to produce the remainder in a third square. Continue out at length the side C. G. of the lesser giuen square towards M. and at the distance of the side of the greater giuen Square, with one foot in the Angle F. of the lesser square strike an Arch line through the line of continuance in M. And lastly, by the 50. Prob. on the line G. M. describe the Square H. K. M. G. which shall be the remainder of the greater giuen Square, the lesser being subtracted from the same, as was required. Theoreme. 6.23.30.31.

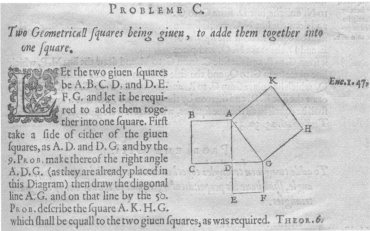

PROBLEME C.

Two Geometricall squares being giuen, to adde them together into one square.

Et the two giuen squares be A. B. C. D. and D. E. F. G. and let it be required to adde them together into one square. First take a side of either of the giuen squares, as A. D. and D. G. and by the 9. Prob. make thereof the right angle A. D. G. (as they are already placed in this Diagram) then draw the diagonal line A. G. and on that line by the 50. Prob. describe the square A. K. H. G. which shall be equall to the two giuen squares, as was required. Theor. 6.

Euc.1.47.

Fig. 6.8–9. Subdivision and remainder: Aaron Rathborne, *The Surveyor in Four Books* (1616)

studied and submitted to the intervention of the state. We may take as an example the City Viewers, high-ranking members of the Carpenters' and Masons' companies who were sworn into the office by the Court of Aldermen and whose duty was to visit building sites or domestic residences in order to gather evidence in matters of public and private nuisance: encroachments of property, legal boundaries, party walls, decaying structures, water drainage, sanitation, or unlicensed building.[9] A similar role might be played by private commissions, or, when royal property was at issue, by the Surveyor of the King's Works, and Inigo Jones served in this capacity on several occasions. At the instigation of the Lord Mayor, Elizabeth had begun issuing in 1580 a series of Royal Proclamations (continued under James and Charles) that prohibited new urban building and the subdivision of property, all with the avowed purpose of imposing order on the City and the surrounding suburbs, which had long been associated with the worst aspects of contemporary urban life.[10] A document concerning the 'prejudices' of excessive building in the suburbs cites among them the burden on parish charges by the in-migration of the poor, the criminal, and the destitute; the regular violation of laws of apprenticeship; the proliferation of individuals without trade who take up a living without Company sanction, who are forced 'to doe other servile workes', or who open alehouses; the perversion of youths 'who by Ill companie arre drawun to Lewdnes, and after doe lyve in Alehowses and such like place[s]'; the production of 'comodyties all Counterfeyt wherby the Comon wealthe is greatlie preiudyced'; and finally: 'the devideing of howses tollerating of Inmate[s], and garden houses to be made dwelling houses Causethe the most daungerous papists in the Realme to Resort hither because here theye maye hyde themselves and plott theyre conspyracies without being espyed'.[11] As one of four similar documents composed in approximately 1610, the anonymous brief offers a litany of complaints calculated to arouse the worst fears of any self-respecting alderman or Privy Counsellor, pleading finally for penalties on those landlords who permit the subdivision of property and for the regular formation of Carpenters' and Masons' companies in the suburbs.

At the same moment that the City Viewers were giving spatial form to the complex social relationships of an urban community and subordinating them to the legal claims of private property or to the apparatus of civic and royal control, playwrights such as Thomas Dekker, Ben Jonson, Thomas Middleton, and many others were adapting the iconic conventions of the early-modern stage to create 'inventions' in which the many social and cultural concerns that spoke most directly to an urban audience could be modelled and understood. The 'city' plays produced by these playwrights provided its spectators with a reproduction in

---

[9] On the history of the office and the nature of surviving evidence from the 16th and 17th centuries, see Loengard (1983, pp. xi–lxii); Orlin (2000*b*), who uses the records to shed additional light on Treswell's surveys; and Schofield (1994: 59); cf. Shaw (1996), on the medieval Assize of Nuisance, space, and notions of privacy.

[10] See Pearl (1961: 9–29); Brett-James (1935, esp. 15–267); Ward (1997, esp. 7–26, 27–44).

[11] BL, Lan. MS 169, fo. 131; see Ward's discussion of these documents (1997: 18–21).

miniature of specific, identifiable elements in the streets around them, in this way functioning as an objective screen for the processes of identification through which viewers recognized themselves as part of the collective civic entity, correlating a concept of citizenship not simply with a sense of legal and institutional belonging but with physical placement in a realistic urban topography. Like other texts of the same period that tend towards iconic abstraction—*The Magnificent Entertainment*, or the several maps of London and other European cities by John Norden, Braun and Hogenberg, and the anonymous 'Copperplate' map-engraver—the theatre provided a representational space in which different urban subjectivities and communities could project themselves, as in a cartographic mirror. Workshops, alehouses, prisons, and private residences: all emerge as structuring principles for representational action in English comedy because these were the very sites in which the conflicts and fantasies of everyday urban life were taking place.

We have seen in the Introduction, above, how Dekker recognized the mimetic capacity shared between stage and practical geometry, prefacing his *Old Fortunatus* by drawing a direct comparison between the representational space of the platform stage and that of the map projection. For Dekker, the stage compresses all the mimetic functions of the diagram, or 'groundplat', into its own performative conventions, and these conventions are employed 'Not when the lawes of Poesy doe call | But as the storie needes' (Dekker 1953–61: i, Prologue, lines 22–3): they are practical solutions to the problem of dramatic emplotment that Dekker explicitly opposes to theoretical principle—the operative logic is generated only by the need to convert 'storie' *into* plot through effective scenic representation. Several of Dekker's plays, notably *Match Me in London* (licensed by George Buc on 1623 as 'An Old Playe' and printed in 1630–1) and *1* and *2 The Honest Whore* (1604, 1608; the first part written with Middleton), may be usefully examined for their 'cartographic' logic; the uncanny mirror effect of setting famous English institutions such as Bethlem Hospital, and Bridewell in Milan (as in *1* and *2 Honest Whore*) or of setting all of *Match Me in London* not in England but in *Spain*—in Madrid, Córdoba, and Seville—is simply the consequence of merging the Ciceronian truism that comedy is *imitatio vitae, speculum consuetudinis, imago veritatis* with the comparative, international view that Hopton's *Speculum Topographicum* or an atlas such as Braun and Hogenberg's *Civitatis Orbis Terrarum* now made possible.

In order to demonstrate how the early-modern theatre might function as a mode of topographesis that drew on the conventions of the spatial arts—in order to take seriously Dekker's own analogy—I turn now to three collaboratively written plays, all produced within twelve months of one another, that take their fundamental structuring principle from cartography and other modes of geometric projection: Dekker and Webster's *Westward Hoe* (Q 1607), performed late in 1604 by the boys at St Paul's; George Chapman, Ben Jonson, and John Marston's *Eastward Hoe* (Q 1605), performed before May 1605 at the Blackfriars; and Dekker and Webster's *Northward Hoe* (Q 1607), performed late in 1605 at Paul's in direct response to Chapman, Jonson, and Marston's earlier play. The particularly intense competitive atmosphere surrounding these three plays allows us to discern with unusual clarity how the specific genre of comedy they represent was generated not simply through changes in ideas, kinds of language, or the satiric observation of character types but through the imaginative mapping of an entire topography that was meant to correspond with the most intimate details of everyday urban life.[12]

The primary purpose of my discussion will be to continue my arguments about the use of location and the scene that I began in Chapter 5 by demonstrating how important the backstage wall was to the practical solutions that playwrights developed in order to manage the problem of emplotment in its structural, mimetic, and ideological aspects. As an architectonic element of the theatre building, the backstage wall formed the boundary that served as the most basic structuring principle of drama as a 'performative form', as we have seen: the opposition between onstage and offstage space.[13] Mimetically, however, the backstage wall, along with the doors, windows, balconies, and discovery spaces that constituted its primary features, also came to represent fictional 'walls' of various paradigmatic types: interior, exterior, private, public, commercial, and administrative walls; walls of houses, streets, shops, closets, warehouses, taverns, brothels, prisons—a diverse, but not infinite, series of topographic units. Out of these topographic units, playwrights began to generate regular scenic sequences, joining them to produce a conventional structure of formal emplotment that articulated, at the same time, competing spatial grammars of the city: categorical differentiations, oppositions, and hierarchies; syntagmatic combinations; privileged itineraries that organized the lived experience of the city's different inhabitants. In what follows I have devoted more attention to the structure of Dekker and Webster's *Westward Hoe*, both because it opens what is an explicitly imitative sequence of three plays and because it offers a particularly dense topographic 'statement' concerning the nature of early-modern urbanization. Rather than failures of

[12] Both *Westward* and *Northward Hoe* are only partially 'city comedies' in the way that Gibbons (1980) has defined them: plays in which a clear satiric theme and moral argument function as central organizing principles, in which character and setting are meant to assume larger emblematic significance, and in which observation and description is subordinated to symbolism, 'metaphoric richness', and a critical representation of 'deeper sources of conflict and change' (p. 4). Neither *Westward* nor *Northward Hoe* reflects an overtly emblematic structure, as Jonson's work continues to; nor do they depend on the organizing principles that Doran (1954: 293–340) has identified as typical of the drama more broadly, and particularly of Shakespeare: problems of psychology and character development, the examination of action and its moral consequences, the elaboration of images and poetic language, or the integration and revision of historical source material. Each mode of organization leads Doran occasionally to extend the notion of 'plot' beyond its conventional meaning of action and events such that it becomes, in moments, a broader principle of thematic, emotional, or 'poetic' organization. Much the same can be said of R. Levin's (1971) analysis of the multiple plot; in Levin's terms, Dekker's plays reflect a 'material' ('least artistic of the four modes'; p. 8) and 'efficient' (also a secondary mode) principle of cause; cf. Hunter (1986), comparing Dekker to Shakespeare.

[13] See especially the comments by Bradley (1992) on the implacable structuring effect of the stage doors (pp. 4–5, 24–5, 29–31), and his analysis of stage entrances, (pp. 23–39, esp. 23); also Gibbons (1996); Chambers (1923: iii. 73–5, 98–101).

critical realism and moral satire, Dekker's plays reveal how a notion of plot as an interconnected sequence of action and events *was emerging out of and remaining inseparable from* modes of topographic representation conjoined with performative theatrical techniques.[14]

'FREE IN THIS INTRICATE LABORINTH OF A HUSBAND': *WESTWARD HOE* AND *NORTHWARD HOE*

By placing the very opening of *Westward Hoe* on a threshold between a London street and the door to Mistress and Master Justiniano's house, Dekker and Webster structure the initial scene of the play such that the basic opposition between onstage and offstage space immediately leaps into relief by assuming a semantic as well as a structural importance. Birdlime's entrance at one door, her movement across the stage, and her approach towards the backstage wall opens a performative unit with several simultaneous discursive purposes: to establish the significance of the wall as an iconic architectonic element within the fictional action by designating it in dialogue ('Stay Taylor, This is the House', 1. 1. 1), and thus to project into the unseen backstage a space of private domesticity that is categorically opposed to the public space of the street; to establish the transgressive eroticism of this public space with a series of bawdy double entendres, in this way initiating a much larger dialectic between implicit and explicit sexual transgression that will constitute one of the primary elements in the topographic syntax of the entire play; to establish a status hierarchy of feminine positions within this sexualized public space, in which the 'Cittizen's wife' instructs the 'Lady or Justice-a-peace Madam' in the objects and subterfuges of consumption as a means of securing autonomy and authority over her husband; and, finally, to mark the essential foreignness of the Italian merchant Justiniano within this urban topography and the perverse hierarchy of desire it has established.[15]

---

[14] Both Knights (1951) and Gibbons (1980) regard Dekker as a 'hack-dramatist', a 'conventional' playwright whose work never achieves the aesthetic, stylistic, or intellectual level of his contemporaries; see Knights (1951: 228–43, esp. 228); also Gibbons (1980, esp. 1–13). The very characteristics that Gibbons (1980) regards as derivative in Dekker and the sign of second-rate artistry—scenes that lack 'satiric point' (p. 103), 'a simple causal plot and articulation derived largely from the journeying of the characters from one street to another' (p. 106), a 'sensational' or purely enumerative use of place names (pp. 107–8)—are simply the characteristics of a drama that takes a topographic method of emplotment as its central organizing principle: a mode that depends on the use of place to manage the order in which an action is represented in scenic units. See also R. Cohen (1973), a detailed discussion of the structural role of setting in the play that extends Perkinson's (1936) earlier notion of 'topographical comedy' by adding neo-classical structural principles; also Champion (1982), comparing the structure of *Westward* and *Northward Hoe*, with a survey of the largely negative critical opinions on the plays.

[15] On the role of Justiniano's Italianness in the play, see Howard (2000). Morgan-Russell (1999) provides an excellent discussion of the sexual topography of the play and the place of 'Brainford' (Brentford) in early 17th-century plays of sexual transgression more generally; on the sexual politics of the play, see also Dowd (2003).

Simply by entering from within the house to finger the velvet gowns and cosmetics sent by the Earl, Mistress Justiniano has made the first move in what will constitute not simply one of the play's two primary trajectories of action but what could also be described as its paranoid structure of imagined sexual transgression, which it will be the purpose of the play's double emplotment to resolve. Her very appearance at the threshold of the door signals a perforation in the domestic fabric, a seam, gap, or fissure in the primary (hetero)erotic relation that organizes the citizen household and makes possible the entire action that follows; her compromised position in this relation is expressed through a kind of theatrical double articulation, first by her mixed characterological status (an Englishwoman unhappily married to a foreign merchant) and then by her liminal architectonic position at the edge of the stage, poised between two worlds. No sooner has she entered than any possibility of balance in the private domestic world disappears irrevocably, not simply into an always inaccessible backstage space but into a perpetual past tense of events that precede the scene unfolding before the spectator's eye: with her entrance the lure of a consumer market and its motive force—desire—floods the stage, immediately reconfiguring the categorical oppositions that have opened the play. Now we find a domestic space always *already* compromised by Justiniano's essential foreignness and jealousy, by his profligacy and bankruptcy, by the Earl's long wooing ('the old suit'; 1. 1. 61), and by a whiff of premarital impropriety, for which Mistress Justiano is perhaps in Birdlime's debt ('I have heard he loved you before you were married intyrely, what of that?'; 1. 1. 86–7).

This is the logic of a theatrical 'scene' that unfolds before the spectator in a perpetual present tense: a seamless citizen domesticity has now *never* existed; it remains offstage and unrepresented throughout the duration of the performance, an implied ideal but a practical impossibility, or so the play's total emplotment would seem to argue. The very habits that define the citizen dweller—'Your prodigality, your diceing, your riding abroad, your consorting your selfe with Noble men, your building a summer house hath undone us, hath undoone us[!]' (1. 1. 188–90)—are the same habits that erode his foundation and provoke his ruin, initiating a primary rupture in the household and making possible the action that follows. This action will take the form of a spatial movement, as Mistress Justiniano and her husband begin their separate trajectories through the moral shoals of city life, the former an emblem of wandering misfortune ('Even whether my misfortune leades me'; 1. 1. 201), the latter an emblem of nothing less than the process of dramatic emplotment itself:

JUST. . . . Have amongst you citty dames? You that are indeede the fittest, and most proper persons for a Comedy, nor let the world lay any imputation upon my disguises, for Court, Citty, and Countrey, are merely as maskes one to the other, envied of some, laught at of others, and so to my comicall businesse. (1. 1. 225–9)

Justiniano has in fact only transferred his estate temporarily to his friends so that he may conduct what is now revealed to be an invention calculated to reveal the true fidelity of his wife and to purge his own jealous obsessions, and one that requires a primary topographic fiction in order to begin: 'Farewel my care, I have told my wife I am going for Stoad' (1. 1. 218–19). Each of the subsequent lines of action depends, in different ways, on the action that Justiniano has set in motion, and each takes the form of a movement from one location to another—the play will be resolved simply when all the characters find themselves in the same place.

The primary topographic syntagm of the initial scene—household–threshold–street—thus gives form to several discursive syntagma that will be fundamental to the 'argument' of the play as a whole and which the emplotment of that argument will develop. It establishes two primary spheres of action in urban life—private–domestic and public–commercial—while disrupting any simple opposition by marking out a point of transfer between the two and designating two characters, Birdlime and Justiniano, whose expertise in each sphere controls the movement of other characters between them. It identifies two different modes of consumption, masculine and feminine, assigning to each different objects of desire—cosmetics, fabric, money, status, the female body—as well as different instruments and the knowledge necessary to attain those objects. Female beauty requires glister pipes, 'choiyce dyet, excellent Physicke', and a secret, practical intelligence in which Birdlime is expert ('no German Clock nor Mathematicall Ingin whatsoever requires so much reparation as a womans face'; 1. 1. 77–80). At the same time, the commercial instruments and institutions that organize the public, corporate life of the City are used by Justiniano to fabricate his own bankruptcy so that he may gain access to the world of feminine desire, and by Tenterhook, Honysuckle, and Wafer to cover their withdrawal into the recesses of Birdlime's house. In this way the scene also establishes a primary conceptual correlation between 'debt' and 'adultery', two forms of excess or negativity that are logical necessities and practical realities of the citizen household but whose constitutive role must always be refused or suppressed. The purposes of subsequent scenes will be to specify how these two negative principles together constitute citizen values and identity, shape attitudes towards gender, sexuality, and economic processes, and even determine the material landscape of urban life; as hard as Justiniano will work to push these principles 'backstage' and out of view or convert them into a positive moral principle, the process will only render them more explicit and demonstrate their underlying persistence.

The entrance of Master Tenterhook, his wife, Clare, the young gentleman Monopoly, and a Scrivener in the next scene, for instance, inverts the topographic disposition of the first by bringing a domestic space from the backstage into the foreground, and with it a new permutation in the larger equations the first scene has established. Monopoly signs a bond for gold from Tenterhook, to be repaid 'the tenth of August' (1. 2. 13–14); Tenterhook informs Clare that Justiniano, 'a friend of yours and mine[,] hath broke' and immediately prepares to leave, but without indicating his true destination, which will be revealed later only by accident; the implied course is to the Exchange, where he will provide insurance for Justiniano's property. Tenterhook's exit, followed quickly by the servant, whom Clare dismisses on an errand, leaves Monopoly alone with Clare so that they may reveal their romantic intrigue, which can be sustained only so long as the bond between Monopoly and Tenterhook remains unpaid, as Clare points out—the contract of debt thus makes possible their proximity and attachment, and Clare will later exploit the contract to her advantage in later scenes by arranging for Monopoly's arrest and then securing his release with her diamonds. Monopoly's departure coincides with the arrival of the two remaining citizen wives, Mistress Honysuckle and Mistress Wafer, who inform Mistress Tenterhook of their 'excellent secret': they are learning to write, instructed by a 'wryting Mechanicall Pedant' (2. 1. 21. 2) named Parenthesis, who is none other than Justiniano in disguise.

As the third scene shifts to the home of Master Honysuckle, newly returned from Rochelle in France, Justiniano now enters as Parenthesis; they discuss the decay of London landmarks—emblematic, perhaps, of the city's moral ruin—and then Mistress Honysuckle's progress at forming letters. After several exchanges of bawdy innuendo, Mistress Honysuckle herself enters and Master Honysuckle, like Tenterhook before him, immediately leaves the house to begin a public itinerary, which he describes vaguely—'To the Custome-house: to the Change, to my Ware-house, to divers places' (2. 1. 124–5)—and which will finally expose his own philandering hypocrisy. The scene of 'instruction' that then follows between Justiniano–Parenthesis and Mistress Honysuckle provides a remarkable lesson in the realities of civic jurisdiction and commercial regulation that contrasts sharply with the professional topography implied in Honeysuckle and Tenterhook's movements:

JUST. Is he departed? Is old *Nestor* marcht into *Troy*?

MIST. HONY. Yes you mad Greeke: the Gentlemans gone.

JUST. Clap up coppy-bookes: downe with pens, hang up inckhornes...were I the proprest, sweetest, plumpest, Cherry-cheekt, Corrall-lipt woman in a kindome, I would not daunce after one mans pipe.

MIST. HONY. And why?

JUST. Especially after an old mans.

MIST. HONY. And why, pray!

JUST. Especially after an old Cittizens.

MIST. HONY. Still, and why.

JUST. Marry because the Suburbes, and those without the bars, have more priviledge then they within the freedome: what need one woman doate upon one Man? Or one man to be mad like Orlando for one woman?...Why should I long to eate of Bakers bread onely, when theres so much Sifting, and bolting, and grynding in every corner of the Citty....Why theres no Minute, no thought of time passes, but some villany or other is a brewing: why, even now, at holding up of this finger, and before the turning downe of this, some are murdring, some lying with their maides, some picking of pockets, some cutting purses, some cheating, some weying out bribes. In this Citty some wives are Cuckolding some Husbands....therefore sweete Scholler, sugred Mistris Honisuckle, take Summer before you, and lay hold of it? why, even now must you and I hatch an egge of iniquity. (2. 1. 138–94)

The passage inverts the utopic communal view that Dekker had offered in *The Magnificent Entertainment* and replaces it with a dystopic vision of a city that everywhere exceeds its legal, institutional, and physical limits and whose economic impetus is desire itself. The 'literacy' that Justiniano as Parenthesis offers the wives is an expertise in the codes of a public urban space that has, until now, been reserved for their husbands, as Justiniano the *merchant* well knows: it is critical knowledge about 'the policy of husbands to keepe their wives in' (1. 2. 116–17), as Mistress Honysuckle argues, or the knowledge necessary to become 'free in this intricate laborinth of a husband' (3. 1. 34–5), as Mistress Tenterhook will put it later in the play. The process of coming to this new, more critical knowledge about citizen domesticity requires the wives to learn a lesson that their husbands already understand: they must use their conventional routes through the space of the city as a pretence, in order to make their way to the rendezvous that Justiniano has arranged 'at the Rhenish-wine-house ith Stillyard' (2. 1. 209–10): 'Fewh! excuses: You must to the pawne to buy Lawne: to Saint Martin's for Lace; to the Garden: to the Glasse-house; to your Gossips: to the Powlters: else take out an old ruffe, and to your Sempsters: excuses?' (2. 1. 213–17). To arrive there the wives will follow another, very different route through the symbolic centre of public life: 'through Paules: every wench take a piller, there clap on your Maskes: your men will bee behind you . . . and man you out at severall doores' (2. 1. 220–3).

Despite the obviously 'staged' quality of Justiniano's lines, however, the audience never actually sees the scene but only rejoins the wives as they enter the wine house in the Steelyard, masked and in the company of the three gallants, in two complementary groups of three. The actual staging invites the audience to complete the new topographic sequence imaginatively by projecting the route of the wives backstage, in this way forming a new, continuous unit; the backstage wall performs a conjunctive function by joining Paul's walk with the interior of the wine house at the Steelyard and the different forms of consumption that it makes available to the wives for the first time. This new theatrical syntagm— hyphenated, as it were, by the double semiotic value of the wall's two sides—is both topographic and scenic, both discursive and structural: the wall completes the ellipses formed by the interposing scene at Birdlime's between the Earl and Mistress Justiniano (2. 2), in this way joining 2. 1 and 2. 3 to form one continuous line of dramatic action. At the same time, the wall establishes a larger imaginative, spatial, and temporal continuity between all three scenes: both lines of action *together*—Birdlime and the Earl; the journey of the three wives—constitute the emplotment of the play as a whole, and their structural juxtaposition through the backstage wall is meant to facilitate the construction of a broader dramatic statement about the nature of gender and consumption, debt and desire in contemporary London life.

The scene at the wine house in the Steelyard (2. 3) forms a crucial pivot point in the development of this topographic statement, precisely because it offers very little 'action' aside from marking out the different fictional spaces that the wives will occupy and consume. The backstage wall separates the wives and gallants (Sir Gozlin, Lystocke, and Whirlepoole) from the other rooms of the wine house, which are designated by the entrance of the server Hans 'with cloth and Buns', by the unexpected arrival of Justiniano as Parenthesis, by the cries of the gallants and wives, by peering offstage to see if the husbands have in fact arrived, as Justiniano claims in order to gauge the wives' response:

JUST. Which roome? where are they? wo ho ho, ho, so ho boies.
GOZ. Sfoot whose that? lock our roome.
JUST. Not till I am in: and then lock out the divell tho he come in the shape of a puritan.
ALL 3 [WIVES]. Scholemaister, welcome? well-come in troth?

  .   .   .   .

JUST. Whose there? Peepers: Intelligencers: Evesdroppers.
OMN. Uds foot, throw a pot ats head?
JUST. Oh Lord? O Gentlemen, Knight, Ladies, that may bee, Cittizens wives that are, shift for your selves, for a paire of your husbands heads are knocking together with *Hans* his, and inquiring for you.
OMN. Keep the doore lockt.
MIST. HONY. Oh I, do, do: and let sir *Gozlin* (because he has bin in the low Countries) swear gotz Sacrament, and drive 'em away with broken Dutch.
JUST. Heres a wench has simple Sparkes in her: shees my pupile Gallants: Good-god? I see a man is not sure that his wife is in the Chamber, tho his owne fingers hung on the Padlocke: Trap-doores, false Drabs, and Spring-lockes, may cozen a Covy of Constables.... Come: drinke up *Rhene*, *Thames* and *Mæander* dry, Theres Nobody... I did but make a false fire, to try your vallor... (2. 3. 25–61)

The repeated references to minute mechanical devices are inserted by the dialogue into the scene to generate a virtual volume of secret enclosure, to which only the practical intelligence of the devious—'Peepers: Intelligencers: Evesdroppers'— allows access; Justiniano is able to enter the room because he has employed this form of intelligence—what Puttenham had specifically compared to the *poetic* intelligence, as we have seen in Chapter 4—to arrange the entire action of the scene and the larger 'comicall business' of which it forms a part. Now the gallants name a series of places from which the wives are asked to choose, as though from a map ('Ham', 'Black-wall', 'Lime-house', and finally 'Brainford'); they agree to meet 'At some Taverne neare the water-side, thats private', concluding upon 'The Grey-Hound, the Greyhound in Black-fryers, an excellent *Randevous*', where they will 'take a Boate at Bridewell Dock most privately' (2. 3. 103–8). The repeated insistence on 'privacy' throughout the scene cloaks the intrigue and shields it from public view; the play will not stage the journey to Brainford but instead withdraws it backstage, using the dialogue of the current scene to delineate a 'realistic' topography that is necessary to the way that intrigue will subsequently develop.

   This temporary pooling of action around one particular location (the tavern at the Steelyard) forms a necessary moment in the larger dialectical process of emplotment that gives the play its structure, a moment that in fact consists of two simultaneous movements, one 'theatrical' or performative and one 'dramatic' or structural, which are impossible to separate from one another and for which there can be no strict priority of sequence. One movement, the performative rotation, oscillation, or alternation around the backstage wall that I have just described, defines the scenic unit as a pause or 'rest' in the intrigue; we watch for several minutes as the wives talk, flirt, drink, order more wine, and express alarm at the thought of discovery by their husbands. This scenic unit in turn, however, facilitates the projection of the total dramatic intrigue forward and outward towards the suburbs, an imaginary space that really only lies just offstage on the other side of the backstage wall and which may emerge 'theatrically' at any moment to form a later scene. Each movement, furthermore, produces two different *scales* of spatial detail, each of which corresponds to the play's two distinct trajectories, one directed inwards towards ever-shrinking and receding interior spaces—alehouses, banqueting rooms, bedchambers, and closets—the other directed outwards, beyond the walls of London and towards the outlying suburbs. The larger trajectory serves as an organizing principle for the play as a whole and thus also provides a template for the subsequent plays that respond to it, which literally map a similar axis of movement according to the logic of the cardinal compass points. The smaller movements are confined to individual scenes, and these function *within* each play, or even between different plays, as structural models for other scenes of similar spatial disposition. As in a conventional cartographic or diagrammatic scale the relation between these units is a reversible one that may be read in either direction simultaneously, since it is possible to see embedded 'in' the individual scene of the Steelyard the outlines of a much larger action, of which this individual scene forms only a smaller part.

At one level, therefore, the scenic unit is perfectly coincident with the representational space of the private room, and the precise delineation of walls and doors in dialogue establishes a ground plan for the action *in* the scene that is the theatrical equivalent of the surveyor's drawings produced by Ralph Treswell—Dekker and Webster are literally building the scene out of the material that the backstage wall provides. In this sense, the iconic quality of the wall gives it a realist function very similar to a schematic diagram of a real or imagined object drawn at a scale of one-to-one proportion: the wall corresponds at several points to its object and yet it remains at the same time utterly distinct from it, a 'token' or 'image' of the thing with which it has merged during performance, in this way generating out of a single architectonic element a series of scenes and rooms whose structure is fundamentally analogous. This process of scenographic modelling, as I will call it, is particularly evident if we compare the scene at the wine house with the series of scenes at Brainford (5. 1, 5. 2, 5. 3) or with the scene at Birdlime's house (4. 1): the first repeats the scale and disposition of the room at the wine house while extending it continuously over three scenes, as the wall becomes again a marker between several different chambers; the wives arrive at the inn to sequester themselves away from the gallants, feigning illness and locking the doors to their private room:

MIST. HONY. O for love, let none of em enter our roome, fie. (5. 1. 24)
MIST. HONY. Get two roomes off at least if you love us.
MIST. WAF. Three, three, maister *Lynstocke* three. (5. 1. 138–9)
LYN. why youle let me call to em but at the key-hole.
MONO. Puh, good maister *Lynstocke*, Ile not stand by whilst you give Fire at your Key-holes[!]
  Ile hold no Trencher till an other feedes: no stirrup till another gets up: be no doore-keeper.
  I ha not beene so often at Court, but I know what the back-side of the Hangings are made
  of. Ile trust none under a peece of Tapistry, *viz.* A Coverlet. (5. 1. 243–9)

Again the spatial disposition of the scene is essential not simply to the resolution of the action but to the moral lesson that it has been calculated to reveal, as the wives prove to everyone—gallants, husbands, friends, audience, themselves—their basic fidelity and good judgement. The husbands arrive only to find the door locked; as Justiniano speaks for the husbands outside the door, the wives, positioned offstage, mistake him for Monopoly and proudly refuse him entrance in the name of their anxious husbands waiting at home; peeking out, they see the husbands preparing a ruse to enter and then step on stage boldly to confront them. When Tenterhook demands the diamonds that he knows neither Monopoly, Ambush, nor Clare have in their possession, hoping to make explicit the romantic intrigue that he had begun to suspect, Clare is in fact able to produce them; Tenterhook's surprise is matched only by that of the audience, who now finds that *Birdlime* has somehow entered the locked chamber of the wives, unseen, through an undesignated sequence of backstage actions—only a vague reference by Mistress Wafer earlier in the scene has given any indication of her presence.[16]

Like Justiniano, Birdlime's function is to join several different lines of action by facilitating access to spaces that normally remain secret or removed, by juxtaposing places in scandalous combinations, or by revealing a movement between places that usually goes unacknowledged by other characters. Like Justiniano she traffics in secretive and only partially legitimate forms of knowledge, cosmetics, and midwifery, which she uses to disguise her role as bawd (2. 3. 118–20, 128); like him she instigates lines of action by luring Mistress Justiniano off the threshold of her home and even directs her to the rendezvous with the Earl through the 'middle Ile in Pawles' (2. 2. 44). Like Justiniano, too, she mysteriously seems to know the location of the wives at every point, passing easily into the locked room at the Steelyard to furnish Mistress Tenterhook with crucial information concerning Monopoly or now entering the wives' room at Brainford to supply them with the diamonds that will prove Mistress Tenterhook's innocence and reveal the husbands' infidelity.

---

[16] '*Mist. Waf.* [*responding to Wafer's knocking and peeking outside*] You cannot enter indeed la, gods my pittikin our three husbands somon a parlee: let that long old woman either creepe under the bed or else stand upright behind the painted cloth' (5. 4. 149–52); Sir Gozlin's mocking reference to Birdlime as 'Long-*Meg* of Westminster' in 5. 3 establishes the reference, as does Monopoly's speech cited in the note above.

Birdlime's house, like the wine house, forms a central gathering point for the different trajectories of the play and depends on a similar series of stage movements, although at a reduced scale: in 4. 1 the scene is divided internally into a series of smaller spaces, as first Master Honysuckle, then Tenterhook, and then Wafer all arrive in sequence to visit Luce, the prostitute; Luce remains 'above' in her 'Chamber' or 'dining Chamber' (4. 1. 18, 45–6); and Honysuckle is thrust into a 'closet' (4. 1. 44) upon the arrival of Tenterhook, who exits to go 'up'. The simultaneous splitting of the scene that follows enables Wafer to arrive downstairs even as Tenterhook is frustrated in his interview upstairs alone with Luce—who, eyes covered playfully, proceeds to name nearly every male figure in the play and several others, all to Tenterhook's obvious dismay:

LUCE. Faith I can name many that I do not know, and suppose I did know them what then? I will suffer one to keepe me in diet, another in apparrel; another in Phisick; another to pay my house rent. I am just of the Nature of *Alcumy*; I wil suffer every plodding foole to spend monie upon me, marrie none but some worthie friend to injoy my more retir'd and use-full faithfulnes.
[*Above, to Tenterhook*] . . . In troth I love thee: You promist me seven Elles of Cambrick . . . (4. 1. 70–87)

BIRD [*Below, to Wafer*]. . . . In good faith shees very poore, all her gowns are at pawne: she owes me five pound for her dyet, besides forty shillings I lent her to redeem two halfe silke Kirtles from the Brokers, And do you thinke she needed be in debt thus, if shee thought not of Some-body[?]

WAF. Good honest Wench.

BIRD. Nay in troth, shees now entering into bond for five poundes more, the Scrivener is but new gon up to take her bond.

WAF. Come, let her not enter into bond, Ile lend her five pound, ile pay the rest of her debts, Call downe the Scrivener?

BIRD. I pray you when he comes downe, stand mufled, and Ile tell him you are her brother. (4. 1. 113–24)

The doubled structure of the scene across two different levels of the playing area opens a representational space in which an entire alternative urban economy can suddenly be glimpsed, one conducted through debt, loan, pawn, gifts, and promise of sexual favours—the underside of the fully capitalized market and its constitutive forms of value, from which London's merchant community derived its status, political power, and moral authority. Upon his descent, Tenterhook, now posing as the 'Scrivener', recognizes Wafer's voice as Honysuckle steps out of the closet; all three husbands confront one another, just as Justiniano enters to reveal his disguise and disclose the voyage of the three wives to Brainford in the company of the gallants, which he has set in motion.

Justiniano's 'comicall business' is most obviously a kind of 'humours' intrigue instigated to test the fidelity of his wife and to purge his own paranoid fantasies of jealousy and sexual betrayal by submitting other husbands to the same ordeal. His vision of urban space is one in which every man is a cuckold, skulking through narrow streets beneath the shadows of looming buildings (1. 1. 151–63); where French whores crowd into England from the Isle of Wight, where farmers flock to squander their meagre wealth on lechery, where sexual appetite never rests and all men—'Captains, Schollers, Servingmen, Jurors, clarks, Townesmen, and the Blacke-guarde' (3. 3. 20–1)—visit the same dubious establishments, spreading lice and scabs throughout the town (3. 3. 9–25). He torments his wife by projecting onto her dreams his own fascinated obsessions:

O the villany of this age, how ful of secresie and silence (contrary to the opinion of the world) have I ever found most women. I have sat a whole afternoone many times by my wife, and lookt upon her eies, and felt if her pulses have beat, when I have nam'd a suspected love, yet all this while have not drawne from her the least scruple of confession. I have laine awake a thousand nights, thinking she wold have reuealed somewhat in her dreames, and when she has begunne to speake any thing in her sleepe, I have jog'd her, and cried I sweete heart. But when wil your love come, or what did hee say to thee over the stall? Or what did he do to thee in the Garden-chamber? (3. 3. 46–51)

This is the secret world of Birdlime, who is such a complementary figure to Justiniano that she might as well be his own projection: throughout the play she provides a glimpse into receding interiors where the threat of *actual* sexual transgression can be implied but held just offstage and outside representation: where Mistress Justiniano will meet the Earl, emerging from 'the greene velvet Chamber' (2. 2. 53); where Monopoly will make vague plans to meet later at the 'Lyon in Shoreditch' in the company of 'some delicate face, that I ha not seene' (2. 2. 234–7); where the three husbands will eventually intersect while seeking the favours of Luce, only to listen indignantly as she enumerates her many previous visitors.

The purpose of Justiniano's entire 'invention' is to recuperate the essential negativity of the two principles that erode the citizen household—debt and adultery—and recast them into the positive form of a moralizing lesson, but to do so he must dispel the many threats to citizen domesticity that the play has illustrated by displacing them onto the figure of Birdlime. The final resolution of the plot requires Justiniano to castigate her as a 'mother of Iniquity' who must be banished beyond the legal and physical boundaries of the city 'to the place of sixe-penny Sinfulnesse the suburbes' (5. 4. 247–50). At the same time he renarrates the preceding action as *mere* performance and frivolity:

Let that ruine of intemperance bee rakt up in dust and ashes . . . for you see your Wives are chast, these Gentlemen civill, all is but a merriment, all but a May-game; she has her Diamonds, you shall have your money, the child is recovered, the false Collier discovered, they came to *Brainford* to be merry, you were caught in Bird-lime; and therefore set the Hares-head against the Goose-giblets, put all instruments in tune, and let every husband play musicke upon the lips of his Wife whilst I begin first. (5. 4. 275–84)

The speech forms a would-be *argumentum* for the preceding action by reiterating it in a tidy sequence of paratactic clauses, in this way cheerfully glossing over the question of the husband's habitual infidelity, omitting the entire process of emplotment itself, and thereby foreclosing the dystopic urban view that this process has provided. By circulating out through the public spaces of the city and only flirting with the possibility of sexual transgression offered by its interiors, the play encourages the wives to come to a new knowledge of urban space and the modes of acculturation it offers but at the same time to remain *only* at the point of knowledge without converting it into regular, habitual action. Justiniano as Parenthesis, the 'wryting Mecanicall Pedant', provides access to some modes of acculturation while holding others at a distance; the wives will learn to read and write, to manipulate the financial instruments of their husbands, to apprehend the commercial and legal hierarchies that structure civic space, and even to acquire the codes of a more leisured consumer, but in doing so they are meant to replace the kinds of knowledge that Birdlime offers and that threaten to turn Mistress Justiniano into a cautionary figure.

By drawing together and juxtaposing these two primary lines of action in the play—the three wives, and the three husbands, on the one hand; Mistress Justiniano and the Earl, on the other—the role of Justiniano and Birdlime is both structural and discursive, since they focalize two competing and equally extreme visions of urban space that all four women must negotiate by finding a middle path between them—both lines of action, after all, have been plotted through 'the middle Ile in Pawles', which becomes a pivot point in the wives' ethical civics lesson as well as of the intrigue. However, within the *formal* theatrical parameters set by the backstage wall, the two distinct lines of action also suggest two very different *generic* solutions to the problem of 'domesticating' women that is the play's primary ideological preoccupation. The realism, topographic detail, satiric comment, and colloquial prose exchanges of the 'comic' citizen plot all contrast with the long moralizing and rhetorically intricate soliloquies of Mistress Justiniano and the Earl, which are broken only by the sudden entrance of Birdlime or Monopoly, the Earl's nephew, speaking the vernacular of another social landscape and another type of play. These latter scenes force a resolution to the seduction plot through supernatural devices more typical of domestic tragedy or revenge tragedy: the Earl 'drawes... strange Characters' (4. 3. 7–8) and delivers a long excursus in defence of 'delicious pleasure' (4. 2. 18) as he prepares to conjure the spirit of Mistress Justiniano and bend her to his will. An elaborate dumbshow follows, in which Justiniano enters masked and dressed as his own wife; upon removing the mask, the Earl recoils when he finds what he believes to be a demon and then listens in astonishment as Justiniano reveals himself and draws a curtain to discover his wife's dead body, whom he claims to have poisoned. Her sudden revival provokes the Earl's sudden conversion:

EARL. Mirror of dames, I looke upon thee now,
   As men long blind, (having recovered sight)
   AMAZD: scarce able are to endure the light:
   Mine owne shame strikes me dumb: henceforth the book
   Ile read shall be thy mind, and not thy looke.   (4. 2. 162–6)

He departs the play with a neat rhyming couplet that encapsulates the lesson of his several scenes—'Lust in old age like burnt straw, does even choake | The kindlers, and consumes, in stincking Smoake' (4. 2. 172–3)—and Justiniano and his wife, now joined by the three husbands, immediately depart for Brainford and the comic resolution that the final scenes effect through their topographic arrangement.

We shall see in Chapter 7 how a similarly detailed and spatialized mode of emplotment might indeed be adopted by playwrights working in dramatic genres other than comedy, such as the history play and domestic tragedy. But before considering Jonson, Chapman, and Marston's somewhat different use of these methods in *Eastward Hoe*, the second play to appear in this three-part sequence of topographic comedies, I would like to consider briefly Dekker and Webster's *Northward Hoe* in order to demonstrate how similar patterns and techniques of scenographic modelling operate across Dekker's work as a whole. The term 'plot' appears frequently in Dekker's work in a self-consciously 'dramatic' sense, although it remains closely associated with the practical, mechanical, and projective forms of intelligence that were typical of late sixteenth-century English thought, as we shall see in more detail in Chapter 7. In *Northward Hoe* the meta-dramatic element is even more explicit than it had been in *Westward Hoe*, the imitative relationship between Dekker's different plays and their structures even more obvious. The citizen Mayberry sketches a series of amusing rural episodes, any of which he 'could make an excellent discription of...in a Comedy' (1. 1. 39–55); Bellamont leaves off writing the tragedy that he hopes will be performed at the French court and instead turns his attention to assisting Mayberry, as he 'plots' a suitable revenge upon Featherstone and Greenshield:

MAY. A Commedy, a Canterbury tale smells not halfe so sweet as the Commedy I have for thee old Poet: thou shalt write upon't Poet.
BELL. Nay I will write upon't ift bee a Commedie, for I have beene at a most villanous female Tragedie: come, the plot, the plot.
MAY. Let your man give you the bootes presently, the plot lies in *Ware* my white Poet: Wife thou and I this night, will have madd sport in *Ware*, marke me well Wife, in *Ware*. . . .
BELL. Very good: to the plot. (4. 1. 208–21)

As the final act moves out to a series of inns in the suburbs and surrounding region, the burst of reversals, disguises, and intrigues is again accompanied by a proliferation of place names as imagined sites of sexual transgression, again as though Dekker were consulting a map as he composed this portion of the play: Ware, Puckridge, Wades-mill, Roistone—and, inevitably, 'Brainford', site of the inn where the action of *Westward Hoe* also concludes. Both Greenshield and Mayberry invoke 'Brainford' (5. 1. 42, 247) as the spot where each will find his wife in flagrante delicto, but the town has already appeared at the beginning of the play in an ironic comment by the apprentice, who has been ordered by Mayberry to search for his missing wife 'by land, and by water' (1. 3. 16–17): 'Well Sir, the land Ile ferret, and after that Ile search her by water, for it may be shees gone to *Brainford*' (1. 3. 18–17). The entire web of exchanges indicates a remarkable level of generic awareness and self-referentiality, as the characters begin to model their own strategic action in the play upon the total trajectory of the play in which they are themselves acting, a play that is itself modelled on Dekker and Webster's earlier work.

A similar moment occurs when Doll the courtesan, accompanied by her serving men Leverpoole and Chartley, decides upon a course of action that derives from her strategic knowledge of city topography and the possibilities offered by the contemporary practice of subdividing property:

> so soone as ever the terme begins, Ile change my lodging, it stands out a the way; Ile lye about Charing-crosse, for if there be any stirrings, there we shall have 'em . . .
>
> LEVER. If thou't have a lodging West-ward *Doll*, Ile fitte thee . . .
>
> DOLL. Stay: I have had a plot a breeding in my braines—Are all the Quest-houses broken vp?
>
> LEVER. Yes, long since: what then?
>
> DOLL. What then? mary then is the wind come about, and for those poore wenches that before Christmasse fled West-ward with bag and baggage, come now sailing alongst the lee shore with a Northerly winde, and we that had warrants to lie without the liberties, come now dropping into the freedome by Owle-light sneakingly.
>
> CHART. But Doll, whats the plot thou spakst off?
>
> DOLL. Mary this: Gentlemen, and Tobacco-stinkers, and such like, are still buzzing where sweete meates are (like Flyes) but they make any flesh stinke that they blow upon. . . . I will therefore take a faire house in the Citty: no matter tho it be a Taverne that has blowne up his Maister: it shall be in trade still, for I know diverse Tavernes ith Towne, that have but a Wall betweene them and a hotte-house . . . (1. 2. 56–88)

Here the complex legal circumstances surrounding the City's repeated attempts to regulate the unincorporated suburbs and to forestall the subdivision of property within the walls are represented as an echo of the dramatic figures and generic movements provided by Dekker and Webster's own earlier play ('a lodging West-ward;' 'those poor wenches that before Christmasse fled Westward'), which now provides Doll herself with a 'plot' that involves an inverse movement *inward*, from suburbs to city and from street to Tavern, to private chamber. In this way Doll dramatizes the very scenographic techniques that Dekker himself was using to compose many of his comedies, including the current play of which her action forms a part—the correlation of dramatic plot with city locations and the use of the wall to subdivide interior scenes—and this moment of meta-dramatic awareness itself provides a glimpse of the way that early-modern dramatists more generally gave form and structure to larger historical processes and made them available to their audience for subsequent identification.

'NOW, LONDON, LOOK ABOUT': CHAPMAN, JONSON, AND MARSTON'S *EASTWARD HOE*

Sometime during the spring of 1605 Jonson began to work with George Chapman and John Marston on the only collaborative play of his that still survives, the elaborately structured *Eastward Hoe* (1605), in which a traditional prodigal son narrative was grafted onto a comedy of honest tradesmen, unruly apprentices, usurers, and fortune-hunting knights. Dekker and Webster's *Westward Hoe* had been performed some six months earlier, and there is every reason to think that the commercial success of their play was precisely what prompted Chapman, Jonson, and Marston to write their own, even though the verse prologue to the play explicitly disavows it:

> Not out of Envy, for ther's no effect
> Where there's no cause; nor out of Imitation,
> For we have evermore bin Imitated
> Nor out of our contention to doe better
> Then that which is opposed to ours in Title,
> For that was good; and better cannot be . . .

> (Jonson 1925–52: iv. 524. 1–6)

In contrast to *Westward* and *Northward Hoe*, Jonson, Chapman, and Marston's play is much more overtly emblematic in form, but it is finally no less subtle in its use of a topographic structure. The entire action of the play follows a broad trajectory from Touchstone's goldsmith's shop in the opening scene to the Counter of the final act, but the function of both workshop and prison is primarily to provide a clear symbolic *locus* for the series of moral oppositions that the play asserts through the arc of its prodigal narrative.[17] The title of the play itself appears repeatedly as an emblematic tag-line, as at 1. 1. 109, 120, and 124, where it indicates Quicksilver's intention to 'turne gallant' (1. 1. 124) and leave his apprenticeship: to go 'East' is to adopt the course of the prodigal, of the vain and aspirant Gertrude, and the speculative and deceitful Sir Petronel Flash; it is to chase the promise of 'castles in the air' (2. 2. 227–35) and speculative investment in overseas plantations rather than to rely on the tactile, massy industry of the working tradesman; it is to purchase titles and prestige on credit rather than to pursue a career within the hierarchies of livery companies and City government.

---

[17] See Gibbons (1980: 8–11); Leggatt (1973: 47–53).

The basic morality structure of the play is visible also in the characters of Syndefie and Security, who announces himself with all the portentousness of a traditional vice-figure ('I am Securitie it selfe, my name is *Securitie*, the famous Usurer'; 2. 2. 9–10), as well as in the adages and *sententia* that pepper the dialogue or conclude a scene:

Where ambition of place goes before fitnesse of birth, contempt and disgrace follow. (1. 2. 34–5)

> This match shal on, for I intend to proove
> Which thrives the best, the meane or loftie love.
> Whether fit Wedlock vowd twixt like and like,
> Or prouder hopes, which daringly orestrike
> Their place and meanes . . .   (1. 2. 171–5)
>   . . . Tradesmen (well tis knowne)
> Get with more ease, then Gentrie keepes his owne.   (2. 1. 174–5)

. . . he that rises hardly, standes firmely: but hee that rises with ease, alas, falles as easily. (2. 2. 88–90)

> Now London, looke about,
> And in this morall, see thy Glasse runne out:
> Behold the carefull Father, thrifty Sonne,
> The solemne deedes, which each of us have done;
> The Usurer punisht, and from Fall so steepe
> The Prodigall child reclaimd, and the lost Sheepe.   (5. 5. 205–10)

And so forth. The pat, clichéd phrasing suggests a certain irony on the part of Chapman, Jonson, and Marston towards the prodigal theme, as both Gibbons and Leggatt have argued; the prodigal framework may have been the simplest way to provide a minimum of structure so that the business of writing individual scenes and lines could be parcelled out. Its primary virtue must have been the cyclical spatial and moral trajectory it implied: a first movement out from a symbolic location (house, home, family), a period of circulation away, concluded by a final return to the original location and submission to a figure of authority. In *Eastward Hoe* this minimal story-pattern has been plotted onto the key institutions that constituted London as a legal and social entity, in particular onto the physical *sites* where the power of those institutions was most clearly instantiated, and in this respect the play follows directly the precedent that Dekker had produced six months earlier.

Eastward Hoe is, however, 'talkier' than either of Dekker and Webster's plays, and given its pronounced emblematic design it is not surprising to find that the scene functions as a compositional unit much as it does in Jonson's *Every Man Out of His Humour* or in other satiric comedies of the period, as we shall see in Chapter 7, opening a discursive space for the observation of character and overt social commentary rather than a space of narrative action. Those scenes that reflect a careful spatial disposition do so primarily to frame the basic rhetorical positions articulated in the play, as when Touchstone decides to 'eavesdrop' (2. 1. 51) on Golding and Mildred as they discuss the relative merits of marriage to a knight or to an apprentice, or when he again eavesdrops at the conclusion of the play on the imprisoned Quicksilver, who reformulates the preceding action into penitent, moralizing doggerel. As in *Every Man Out of His Humour*, however, the scene shifts occasionally to a more realistic topographic mode, as when Sir Petronel Flash plans to meet his fellow adventurers 'at the Blew Anchor Taverne by Billinsgate' (3. 1. 51, 3. 2. 204), where they will sup triumphantly before their departure for Virginia and at the same time cuckold Security by tricking him into pandering his own wife in disguise ('a rare device'; 3. 2. 293). The entire 'Virginia' plot involving the sale of Gertrude's lands to Security by Quicksilver and Flash is in fact developed using the technical language of the practical spatial arts: when Security asks after Gertrude's land, Quicksilver responds in the terms of the surveyor, whose knowledge of geometry is here represented as reducing a precious inheritance into liquid revenue:

SECU. You know his wives Land?

QUICK. Even to a foote Sir, I have been often there: a pretie fine Seate, good Land, all intire within it selfe.

SECU. Well wooded?

QUICK. Two hundered pounds woorth of wood readye to fell. And a fine sweete house that stands just in the midst an't, like a Pricke in the midst of a Circle ... (2. 2. 140–8)

At one level, therefore, the central action of the play turns on the several meanings of the term 'plot' that were beginning to emerge during the period, pursuit of land generating a strategic 'action' (2. 2. 177) on the part of Quicksilver and Flash that will be pursued 'with the more engines' (2. 2. 178), in this case the introduction of Syndefie as Gertrude's servant. The same set of associations returns again at the conclusion of the play, as Touchstone designates Security as the real 'plotter of all this: he is your Inginer, I heare' (4. 2. 316–17), aligning the illegitimacy of usury with the threat of mathematics and mechanical knowledge and in this way displacing onto Security all the disruptive forces of speculative investment that have threatened to undo the city's traditional commercial, social, and juridical hierarchies.

Surprisingly little action in the play takes place beyond the city walls: despite the sprinkling of references to going 'Eastward', the only actual *movement* east-ward takes place in a single scene (4. 1), as Flash, Quicksilver, and Security are flushed down the river towards 'Cuckold's Haven'. Floundering in the rushing Thames, each is carried forward by the movement of a line of action that he has set in motion but can no longer control, and as such each is a figure also for Jonson and his collaborators, who suddenly found themselves faced with the formal diffi-culty of representing a scene of scope and movement that far exceeded the stage's capacity but a scene that was nevertheless demanded by the logic of the action they had themselves begun. The solution is a masterstroke of performative emplotment, as Slitgut, the butcher's apprentice, climbs a 'tree' and *narrates* the entire action that is putatively unfolding offstage behind the wall, and then watches silently as each character washes up on 'shore' *onstage* in sequence to resume his part. When Flash and Seagull stumble forward and mistakenly imagine that they have arrived in France, they reveal themselves to be ignorant not simply of geography but of the latest currents in dramatic theory—on Jonson's stage, at least, a displacement of such scope would be unthinkable. Slitgut has no further role beyond this scene: he is at once character and Chorus, actor and author, playwright and surveyor, a figure brought onstage to contain a plot threatening to overspill its bounds by re-creating a unity of place through the power of his word and view.

The entire sequence has become unavoidable because the larger prodigal design of the play requires it: the scene marks the moment that Flash, Quicksilver, and Security begin their reverse trajectory back towards the city and its institutions of authority. Within this total design Touchstone plays a role throughout the play not unlike that played by Slitgut in the single river scene, in that he focalizes the thematic qualities of the action through his eavesdropping, his commentary, and his brief narrations of events that have taken place offstage and remain unseen. Foremost among these is Golding's parallel and somewhat mysterious rise within the hierarchy of city governance. We hear only that he 'was sent for to the Guildhall' (4. 2. 30), and the play thus partially withholds from view the very process of civic advancement that, at one level, it is explicitly meant to celebrate. This structure of partial visibility itself, however, only heightens the overall feeling of institutional power that pervades the play: Golding is suddenly and arbitrarily promoted to deputy by the Alderman of his ward ('an Accident somewhat strange'; 4. 2. 35), 'intelligence' is gathered discretely from a 'false Brother' (4. 2. 87–8), and officers have already been dispatched to wait at the port where Flash, Quicksilver, and Security are delivered up by the previous scene with an almost providential expedience—'A miracle! the Justice of Heaven!', as Touchstone exclaims upon hearing the news (4. 2. 91).

At this level, the process of emplotment itself—the formal decision to represent some events onstage while withholding others from view, and the related decision to use specific urban sites as the visible, material form in which these events and themes can be shown or apprehended—implies an ideological orientation more latent but no less emphatic than the explicit moralism that the play expresses rhetorically. Even as the workshop and the prison are brought forth to contain, literally, the disruptive actions of the unruly apprentice and the bankrupt knight— they form two alternative, exclusive, and equally appropriate 'interiors' for a young man in London—other civic institutions that are even more powerful (Guildhall) remain parenthetically in the background. The real power that Golding wields is that of appointed office, which is finally impossible to locate except in abstraction or as always originating elsewhere, 'offstage'; for this reason, when Quicksilver and Flash are arrested, Golding may simply command that they be 'brought *here* before me' (4. 2. 97; my emphasis)—there is no need for the play to designate with any more precision a power that accompanies him everywhere.

The very convenience of events and the neatness of the play's formal organization—the obvious opposition between Golding and Quicksilver, the fortuitous rising of the storm, as the prodigals set off for Virginia, the suddenness and thoroughness of their repentance—suggest how much Chapman, Jonson, and Marston recognized that the commercial attractiveness of the prodigal plot derived above all from its power as a pattern of citizen wish-fulfilment. Golding's appointment as deputy only renders him a more effective instrument of Touchstone, his father-in-law and former master ('How to my wish it falls out, that thou hast the place of a Justicer upon 'hem'; (4. 2. 100–1), who proceeds to arrest ships (4. 2. 99), bring charges, pay bonds, and finally forgive all debts and all transgressions. The canned pieties of Golding and the bombastic, self-aggrandizing gestures of Touchstone render them distinctly less appealing than Quicksilver, and the play finally seems to address two audiences simultaneously: on the one hand the 'Citty' tradesmen, apprentices, and officers to whom it is overtly dedicated (Prologue, 14) and whose simple commercial moralism it reflects in its mottoes and providential design, and on the other a sophisticated urban playgoer more similar to Chapman, Jonson, and Marston themselves, one whose critical distance allows him to recognize the conventions of the form, to appreciate the clever gestures of scenic composition and emplotment it has required, and to savour the parody of Quicksilver's mimicking phrases.

Eastward Hoe was Jonson's first play immediately following *The Magnificent Entertainment*, and if the collaborative circumstances of the play's production and its union of topography and emblem were not enough to suggest an essential similarity between a city comedy, a royal pageant, and an annual Lord Mayor's show, its final epilogue clearly indicates that the authors explicitly imagined there to be one:

QUICK. Stay Sir, I perceive the multitude are gatherd together, to view our comming out at the *Counter*. See, if the streets and the Fronts of the Houses, be not stucke with People, and the Windowes fild with Ladies, as on the solemne day of the *Pageant*!

O may you find in this our *Pageant*, here,
The same contentment, which you came to seeke;
And as that *Shew* but drawes you once a yeare,
May this attract you, hether, once a week.　　　(1–9)

It now remains to examine in more detail how Jonson attempted to reconcile the practical techniques of dramatic composition and performance that he encountered while working on *The Magnificent Entertainment* and in the public theatres with his dogmatic attachment to a principle of 'authorship' and self-conscious design. As we shall see in the two chapters that conclude this book, Jonson represents the most complex example of the way in which a playwright might self-consciously attempt to change the definition of his field of activity and in this way to provide the terms by which his own expertise in that field might be secured. He is a pivotal figure in the way that English drama, as a distinct domain of intellectual pursuits, social relationships, status, modes of writing, and economic positioning within the larger literary field, began to distance itself from the mechanical arts by subordinating them to an explicitly theoretical and neo-classical discourse of structure, form, and moral authority.

7

Dramatic Form and the Projective Intelligence

O no, these are too nice observations . . . we should enjoy the same licence, or free power, to illustrate and heighten our invention as [the Ancients] did; and not bee tyed to those strict and regular formes, which the niceness of a few (who are nothing but forme) would thrust upon us.

(Ben Jonson, *Every Man Out of His Humour*)

No playwright did more than Ben Jonson to extend the ethical project of poetics as it had been formulated by Elizabethan critics such as Sidney into the domain of the public drama, despite his own evident ambivalence towards the conditions of the theatre and his aspirations to become a court poet who enjoyed royal patronage rather than commercial success. No doubt these aspirations were partly responsible for prompting Jonson towards the outlines of a comprehensive theory of dramatic poesy, one that combined a belief in drama's power to critique and reform society with a close analysis of its structural organization and a canon of formal requirements. The impulse is most visible in his *Timber; or, Discoveries*, a commonplace book of statements on matters of style and form compiled over an indeterminate period and not published until the posthumous Folio of 1640. As an attempt at theorization, however, *Discoveries* remains unsystematic and derivative, a series of loosely connected passages translated out of other writers, and many of Jonson's most precise critical statements are instead to be found in his plays, in the mouths of individual characters or in the prologues and inter-act framing devices that he seems to have found irresistible. These sequences invariably display a clever awareness of stage conventions as well as of received critical doctrines, and they demonstrate how Jonson's theoretical positions developed out of contemporary playhouse practice as much as from the classical and Continental sources he so assiduously consulted. Moreover, the structures of his plays do not always conform to the principles articulated by their critical personas, and this inconsistency indicates the enduring gap between theatrical practice and a critical theory of 'drama' that was beginning to circulate during the period, as well as how important the *idea* of theory was to Jonson in his attempt to fashion a distinct professional identity for himself.[1]

My purpose in the chapter that follows is to revisit the intellectual background for Jonson's scattered theoretical statements and to examine how he responded to the practical requirements that he faced as a working playwright. Having traced the terms 'plat', 'plot', and their cognates back to the domain of the spatial arts and shown how they became assimilated to discussions of poetics more generally, it is now necessary to demonstrate how they became integrated into contemporary theories of 'dramatic poesy', specifically: neo-classical arguments that recognized the peculiarities of mimetic representation on stage but that were beginning to generalize about stage representation, codify it, and gradually redefine the object of the dramatic poet as a critical and textual object rather than as a performative and theatrical one. As is well known, these arguments derived from two principal sources: commentaries on Horace's *Ars Poetica*, along with the new translations of and commentaries on Aristotle's *Poetics* by Castelvetro, Scaliger, and others; and the work of classical playwrights themselves, notably Seneca, Plautus, and Terence, and, in the case of the latter in particular, the elaborate tradition of commentary that had become associated with the plays in school textbooks. Jonson draws on classical critical principles more self-consciously than any of his contemporaries, although he adapts them to suit his evolving notions about the purpose of comedy and occasionally questions classical authority: the ancients are to be 'Guides, not Commanders', as he wrote in *Discoveries* (Jonson 1925–52: viii. 567. 138–9).

Precisely because Jonson was so acutely self-conscious of his classicism, however, it is all the more significant that we can trace throughout his work an active awareness of practical thinking and especially of spatial arts such as geometry, surveying, architecture, and military engineering, no matter how much he attempted to *obscure* these habits of thought in his work or to distance himself from them by invoking alternative classical genealogies. In Chapter 8 we shall see how Jonson's collaboration with Inigo Jones and his book-ownership and reading habits informed his attitude towards the mechanical arts in general; we shall also examine how he employed techniques of representation that derived from the spatial arts in the composition of *The Alchemist* (1610), one his most famous plays. The current chapter turns to another aspect of practical knowledge that I have examined in Chapters 2 and 3 but that now requires further discussion: a cunning, deliberative, and strategic mode of intelligence that was typical of surveying and military engineering and that derived in part from the influence of Aristotle's and Machiavelli's writings on English readers, Gabriel Harvey and Philip Sidney among them. I will call it a 'projective intelligence': a way of 'thinking forward' about human action through models and artificial inventions; a mode of practical thinking that assimilates particular instances to general

---

[1] On Jonson's attitude to the stage, see esp. Barish (1973; 1981: 132–54); Burt (1993 esp. 33–4); Loewenstein (1985, 2002a), and the works cited in Ch. 8 n. 1, below.

principles in order to formulate a future plan of intervention or decision, a plan whose parameters have been already determined in part by the circumstances at hand but which, in execution, will adjust or reshape the very parameters that have made it possible. Both Juan Huarte and George Puttenham compare this type of practical thinking directly to the poetic imagination, as we have seen in Chapters 3 and 4; it lies at the core of one of the most influential texts of the entire sixteenth century, Cicero's *De Officiis*; and it is a fundamental source for English approaches to the problem of emplotment in the public theatres that has not received the attention it deserves.[2]

The primary argument of the chapter that follows is that the vocabulary and methods of reasoning associated with the projective intelligence allowed Jonson to generate self-consciously 'dramatic' insights out of the larger patterns of action that gave plays their form as theatrical events. As a distinct mode of practical knowledge, the projective intelligence has a determining influence on many playwrights writing at the turn of the seventeenth century, in different playing spaces and across other genres, and in the second half of my discussion I consider several examples in order to demonstrate its pervasiveness. My central focus, however, will be on Jonson's *Every Man Out of His Humour* (Q 1600), the first play he published and perhaps the first play ever to be performed at the new Globe theatre in 1599. The play demonstrates with unusual clarity the tension between practical modes of theatrical representation and a self-consciously theoretical and 'literary' notion of dramatic form that will continue to animate Jonson's work throughout his career: it provides a singular example of how Jonson habitually turned to Roman sources in an attempt to formulate a model of humours comedy and 'comical satire' when confronted by theatrical conventions that resisted any simple reduction to theoretical principles. To do so, he creates a fictional 'Grex', or Chorus, of two characters who watch the play and comment upon its action, arriving at their critical, theoretical principles about 'drama' partly by comparing the precedents of Roman literary theory with the actual performance that unfolds before them and partly by inducing these principles out of that very performance as it occurs. As a consequence, the ingenuity of *Every Man Out of His Humour* lies in the way that Jonson's theoretical speculation about 'drama' is itself presented *as a function* of theatrical performance: 'drama' results from a sublation of the theatre into the all-seeing, analytical eye of the critic, who, like the mathematical practitioner we have considered in Chapter 2, comes to discern within the performed action the very principles that would appear to have been determining the play all along but which are in fact only ever visible retrospectively, once the performance that generates them has been completed.

---

[2] Hutson's insights into the relationship between modes of prudential thinking, military strategy, and an emerging sense of narrative order are especially relevant to what follows (1993, esp. 88–92; 1994: 91–114, esp. 105–11); cf. W. West (2002, esp. 151), who compares Jonson's 'plotting' to ballistics; and Vérin's (1993) discussion of pragmatic thinking in French military manuals (Ch. 2, above).

'SPEAKE YOUR OPINIONS, UPON EVERY SCENE': *EVERY MAN OUT OF HIS HUMOUR*

With the production of *Every Man Out of His Humour*, performed in 1599, Jonson launched the first *essai* in what would prove to be a career-long project to revise English theatrical practice according to the theoretical prescriptions of Roman literary authorities, and to do so in the service of social commentary and moral reform as well as in the interests of professional self-advancement. In the first Grex, or Chorus, that opens the play, as a kind of Induction, Asper, the author of the play-within-the-play that is about to begin, and thus a figure for Jonson himself, enters in the company of his two companions, Cordatus and Mitis, who will observe the play, anticipate any possible objections, and provide critical commentary on its action. With a comparison to painting drawn from both Horace and Plutarch but expressed in a less moderate tone, Asper proclaims that his

>   language
> was never ground into such oyly coulours,
> To flatter vice and daube inquitie.   (lines 13–15)

and begins to rant against the

> fooles, so sicke in taste,
> That they contemne all phisicke of the mind.   (lines 131–2)

>   I will scourge those apes;
> And to these courteous eyes oppose a mirrour,
> As large as is the stage, whereon we act:
> Where they shall see the times deformitie
> Anatomiz'd in every nerve, and sinnew,
> With constant courage, and contempt of feare.   (lines 117–22)

Asper establishes the quasi-medicinal purpose of the performance immediately: its function is revelatory and diagnostic, an instrumental device whose effect is to purify individuals and society alike. The play will be something like Old Comedy, Cordatus informs Mitis, and thus a pointed, biting, and sometimes personal satire of contemporary mores: a bitter tonic, 'pills to purge' (line 175), much like the ones Jonson–Horace will administer to Marston–Crispinus in *Poetaster* only a few years later, prompting him to vomit up his inkhorn terms. In response to Mitis's objection in 3. 6 that Asper might have written a traditional romantic comedy more similar to Shakespeare's *Twelfth Night*—'a duke to be in love with a countesse, and that countesse to bee in love with the dukes sonne, and the sonne to love the ladies waiting maid: some such crosse wooing, with a clowne to their servingman' (3. 6. 196–9)—Cordatus again invokes the definition of comedy traditionally ascribed to Cicero: '*Imitatio vitæ, Speculum consuetudinis, Imago veritatis*; a thing throughout most pleasant, and ridiculous, and accommodated to the correction of manners' (3. 6. 206–9). In typical rhetorico-Horatian fashion

Asper's goal is to please only those

> attentive auditors,
> Such as will joyne their profit with their pleasure,
> And come to feed their understanding parts, (Induction, 201–3)

and similar passages may be found throughout all of Jonson's later plays.[3]

'To feed their understanding parts': what, precisely, did this imply? In place of the stage devices that both Dekker and Shakespeare, among others, were exploiting to great effect, Jonson proposes instead a critical apparatus that gains its legitimacy from its strict adherence to classical 'rules' or 'laws'. Such were the terms of the Prologue that would open *Volpone* (Q 1607), prefaced by a letter addressed to 'the Two Famous Universities', in which Jonson developed his position with an antiquarian rigour that is not yet as firm in the early plays. The existing practical tradition in the theatre is not simply critically naive but morally suspect, even deplorable, he maintains. Soon he would sharpen his attack in the Prologue to the 1616 Folio revision of *Every Man In His Humour*, by which point he had written at least ten comedies and two tragedies and felt secure enough to articulate a more inflexible critical programme.[4] The arguments are famous, the nod to Shakespearean practice is direct, and Jonson's dismissal could hardly be more explicit:

> Though neede make many *Poets*, and some such
> As art, and nature have not better'd much;
> Yet ours, for want, hath not so lov'd the stage,
> As he dare serve th'ill customes of the age:
> Or purchase your delight at such a rate,
> As, for it, he himselfe must justly hate.
> To make a child, now swadled, to proceede
> Man, and then shoote up, in one beard, and weede,
> Past threescore yeers: or, with three rustie swords,
> And helpe of some few foot-and-halfe-foote words,
> Fight over *Yorke*, and *Lancasters* long jarres:
> And in the tyring-house bring wounds, to scarres.
> He rather prayes, you will be pleas'd to see
> One such, to day, as other playes should be.
> Where neither *Chorus* wafts you ore the seas;
> Nor creaking throne comes downe, the boys to please;
> Nor nimble squibbe is seene, to make afear'd
> The gentlewomen; nor roul'd bullet heard
> To say, it thunders; nor tempestuous drumme

---

[3] Cf. *Volpone* (F 1616), Prologue, 82–4, 121–3; *Epicoene* (F 1616), Second Prologue, 1–2; *The Alchemist* (F 1616), Prologue, 11–18; *The Staple of News* (1631), Epilogue, 1–2, 36–41. On English dramatic satire, see Kernan (1959, esp. 137–9, and 156–62, on *Every Man Out of His Humour*, hereafter EMOH).

[4] Herford and Simpson (Jonson 1925–52: i. 333) attribute the Prologue to *c*.1612; cf. Haynes (1992: 34–43).

Rumbles, to tell you when the storme doth come;
But deedes, and language, such as men doe use:
And persons, such as *Comœdie* would chuse,
When she would shew an Image of the times,
And sport with humane follies, not with crimes.

(*Every Man In His Humour*, Prologue, 1–24)

These were opinions calculated to give voice to a new authoritative persona for their author, whose Folio they inaugurated: *Every Man In His Humour* was positioned auspiciously at the opening of the volume, newly revised to reflect more than a decade of work in the public theatres, its early Italian characters and clichéd settings updated in a colloquial English vernacular, spoken by English types recognizable from the many city plays that Jonson himself and his contemporaries had worked to define as sub-genre, in local neighbourhoods that lay just outside the theatre walls.

It is often noted that Jonson's objections in the 1616 Prologue to *Every Man In His Humour* imply an awareness of at least two of the three neo-classical unities, time and place; he does not note that of action, the only unity that Aristotle himself had directly recognized and the one that in practice Jonson himself was less inclined to respect. The Ciceronian and Horatian derivation is more explicit, but the even stronger influence is Sidney's brief discussion of the 'laws of Poesy' and good tragedy in the *Defence*: the passage reiterates nearly verbatim the charges that both he and Stephen Gosson had levelled against the Elizabethan theatre.[5] Even in Gosson's case these objections had been as formal as they were moral, and if we look again at Jonson's lines we see that they reflect this same formal emphasis: the 'ill customes of the age' are not declinations from an *ethical* norm guiding individual and social behaviour, as we might expect in satire, but are, more surprisingly, excesses in theatrical technique, an unrestrained use of the mimetic freedom that the platform stage allowed. Like Sidney before him, Jonson objects less to violations of neo-classical prescriptions for unity than to the *semiotic* presumptions that motivated all aspects of Elizabethan performance, of which freedom in time and place were only two of many possible effects. Sidney's sarcasm in the *Defence* make it clear that, to his mind at least, the devices used to represent location were particularly objectionable:

where you shal have *Asia* of the one side, and *Affrick* of the other, and so many other under-kingdoms, that the Player, when he commeth in, must ever begin with telling where he is, or els the tale wil not be conceived. Now ye shal have three Ladies walke to gather flowers, and then we must beleeve the stage to be a Garden. By and by, we heere newes of shipwracke in the same place, and then wee are to blame if we accept it not for a Rock. Upon the backe of that, comes out a hidious Monster, with fire and smoke, and then the

---

[5] Cf. Atkins (1951: 226–7).

miserable beholders are bounde to take it for a Cave. While in the meantime two Armies flye in, represented with foure swords and bucklers, and then what harde heart will not receive it for a pitched fielde? (197. 13–27)

Both Sidney and Jonson are pained by the naivety and obvious implausibility of earlier emblematic stage techniques. But whereas Sidney's objections are those of a knowing spectator informed by recent Italian criticism, Jonson's comments in *Every Man In His Humour* are those of a working playwright who is familiar with the practical backstage devices of playhouse performance: the 'creaking' machinery and the sonic effects of drums and rattling cannon balls that emanated from the 'tyring-house' in order to amaze the paying public.[6]

However necessary Jonson may have found the emblematic conventions of Elizabethan stage performance to be when writing his pageants or masques at court, he viewed them with more suspicion when it came to writing for the public stage, where they conflicted with Cicero's prescription that comedy provide a *realistic* imitation of contemporary life. In 1599 he was still trying to coordinate several impulses: a theoretical interest in classical definitions of genre and discussions of imitative art; a desire, driven partly by literary ambition and partly by commercial necessity, to update models of Roman intrigue comedy so that they might speak to contemporary audiences. As Madeleine Doran has argued, the fundamental problem facing all playwrights during the period was the need to give an articulated form to a proposition, idea, or pre-existing body of narrative material so as to produce a play that had structural integrity and, particularly in Jonson's case, a play that could be regarded as a critical as well as a commercial success. Doran has pointed out how the very mimetic flexibility of the platform stage tended to work against, rather than in favour of, structural coherence; *Every Man Out of His Humour* presented additional structural difficulties, furthermore, since it had never been organized around a *single* action: its title promised *every* man out of his humour, after all, which meant that Jonson would be required first to elaborate each of his characters individually and then to invent a device to put them 'out' during the course of the play.

In order to do so, Jonson adopted two distinct approaches to the 'scene' as a fundamental unit of structure that it will now be necessary to examine more closely: as a *stage* unit, or a discrete portion of performance time; and as a *narrative* unit, or an episode in the fiction of the play.[7] Both modes of scenic composition

---

    [6] Cf. B. R. Smith (1999: 217–22).
    [7] For my discussion of the 'scene' in what follows I draw on Granville-Barker (1946–7, esp. i. 381–90); Bevington (1962); Bradbrook (1935, 1955); Jones (1971); Rose (1972); Dessen (1971), on Jonson's use of the morality tradition; Daly (1998 (on emblematic traditions), esp. 59–60, 144–5, 162–7). Cf. Haynes's comments on the 'scene' in plays preceding Jonson's (1992: 13–33, 43–51); for additional commentary on the structure of *EMOH*, see Jonson (1925–52: i. 378–9, 384–5); Barish (1967: 79, 100); Gibbons (1980: 56–8, 62; also 48, 51); Maus (1984: 30, 34–5); Danson (1984: 184–6); W. West (2002, esp. 148–55, 170–4). Ostovich (1999) provides an excellent discussion of the significance of Paul's walk to the play; for this reason I have not undertaken an extended analysis of Paul's in what follows, but her comments (esp. pp. 89–90) may usefully be read in conjunction with my discussion and of the structural place of Paul's walk in Dekker's work in Ch. 6, above.

are visible in *Every Man Out of His Humour* and are a frequent object of dispute among Cordatus and Mitis. If the gradual correlation of the 'scene' with 'place' constitutes one of the most significant developments in English Renaissance drama, as I have been arguing in previous chapters, then it will be important to examine how Jonson attempts to give theoretical expression to a process that we have already seen operating at a practical level in *King Lear* or in the city plays of Dekker and others: to demonstrate how a transition in *mode* or *means* of representing location on stage that Wickham has identified also accompanies a development in methods of *structural* organization, in which location becomes a fundamental principle in the selection, composition, and representation of events in scenic form.

Early in the play, Jonson adapts methods of emblematic staging that derived from earlier Elizabethan performance traditions in order to express his 'conceit', 'subject', or 'argument': he employs the scene as a relatively independent unit that is combined in simple linear succession. Although the scene defines a minimal fictional sequence, it is above all a unit of stage time, as Mitis indicates during an exchange after 2. 3 when he complains that:

> Me thinkes, CORDATUS, he dwelt somewhat too long on this *Scene*; it hung i' the hand.
> COR. I see not where he could have insisted lesse, and t'have made the humours perspicuous enough.
> MIT. True, as his subiect lies: but hee might have altered the shape of his argument, and explicated 'hem better in single *Scenes*.
> COR. That had been single indeed: why? be they not the same persons in this, as they would have been in those? and is it not an object of more state, to behold the *Scene* full, and reliev'd with varietie of speakers to the end, then to see a vast emptie stage, and the actors come in (one by one) as if they were dropt downe with a feather, into the eye of the spectators? (2. 3. 288–301)

As Cordatus' response indicates, Mitis is proposing a formal organization similar to a pageant or masque, a progression of individual types in which the ordering principle—the 'shape of the argument', as Mitis calls it—is one of isolated juxtaposition rather than interaction and development. Cordatus' alternative is not as different as it might appear, however, since here the same structure of juxtaposition has simply been consolidated into a single scene, in which different characters enter to reveal their fundamental qualities at the same time rather than individually in sequence.

After Wickham, I will call this mode of scenic composition 'emblematic' in its approach; it conforms to what Kenneth Burke has called 'qualitative form',[8] it is

---

[8] See Burke (1931, esp. 158); Loewenstein's (1984) comments on the structure of *Cynthia's Revels*, pp. 78–92, esp. 78–9, citing Lyly's 'paratactic dramaturgy' as a formal influence on Jonson; Barton (1984, esp. 58–73); and Kernan: 'If we take plot to mean, as it ordinarily does, "what happens," or to put it in a more useful way, a series of events which constitute a change, then the most striking quality of satire is the absence of plot' (1959: 30).

fundamental to humours comedy as Asper defines it in the first Induction,[9] and it produces what Jonas Barish has described as 'verbal satire': the mimicry of specialized or arcane formulations in the service of a critique of character as it is revealed in language.[10] The emblematic scene is primarily rhetorical in its effect: it opens a discursive field rather than a space for 'action', providing a frame for the linguistic exploration of an idea, intellectual problem, tone, or emotional development. It produces meaning in an associative way, since it depends on a perceived similarity between some qualities of character or aspects of ideas that are explicitly represented and others that are not. In these cases, the scene operates like a 'speaking picture' or portrait with very little action, and in the exchange that follows 1. 3, Mitis and Cordatus defend two different approaches:

MIT. . . . MACILENTE went hence too soone, hee might have beene made to stay, and speake somewhat in reproofe of SORDIDO's wretchednesse, now at the last.
COR. O, no, that had beene extremely improper, besides, he had continued the *Scene* too long with him, as't was, being no more in action.
MIT. You may enforce the length, as a necessary reason; but for propriety, the *Scene* would very well have borne it, in my judgement.
COR. O, worst of both: why, you mistake his Humour utterly then. (1. 3. 149–60)

Here the so-called 'action' of Macilente is simply the way in which he demonstrates the overall conceit of the play by revealing the qualities of his dominant humour, and the purpose of both scene and commentary is to make this qualitative principle of design as explicit as possible. In these moments the Grex has a descriptive and explanatory function similar to the relationship between *subscriptio* and *pictura* that was typical of the emblem:

MIT. What may this fellow be, CORDATUS?
COR. Faith, if the time wil suffer his description, Ile give it you. He is one, the Author calls him CARLO BUFFONE, an impudent common jester, a violent rayler, and an incomprehensible *Epicure*; one, whose company is desir'd of all men, but belov'd of none; hee will sooner lose his soule then a jest, and prophane even the most holy things, to excite laughter: no honorable or reverend personage whatsoever, can come within the reach of his eye, but is turn'd into all manner of varietie, by his adult'rate *simile's*.
MIT. You paint forth a monster. (Induction, 354–65)

Within the discursive space of the scene, the commentary of the Grex opens a secondary discursive inset to graft moral observations onto its critical dicta: here it suggests that Carlo's 'adult'rate' use of simile mixes sameness and difference indiscriminately, resulting in an 'incomprehensibility' that extends beyond language to include all aspects of heterodox conduct, appetite, and even belief.

---

[9] Induction, 89–114, esp. 105–9: 'As when some one peculiar quality | Doth so possesse a man, that it doth draw | All his affects, his spirits, and his powers, | In their confluctions, all to runne one way, | This may be truly said to be a Humour.'
[10] See esp. Barish (1967: 104–13, 276–7).

With the use of the term 'argument', Mitis indicates the Roman origin of his (and Jonson's) theory of formal organization as it pertained to humours comedy. *Argumentum* was the term Terence, Donatus, Evanthius, and others had used to denote the 'subject', 'topic', or 'story' of a play; along with *fabula* and *historia*, the term was used by Quintilian and others to describe the different kinds of narrations in oratory.[11] Donatus and Diomedes had followed Terence in reserving the term *fabula* for plays in general and in using *argumentum* or *ficta argumenta* in reference to their fictional content; by the early sixteenth century *fabula* was commonly used to refer specifically to an idea of 'arranged action', with the Italian *favola* and the French *fable* providing the obvious cognates in the vernacular treatises.[12] Other terms had long been basic to both the writing and critical analysis of artful discourse: these included general words such as *imitatio* or *fictio* but also more technical terms such as *narratio* (the initial statement of facts or position in forensic oratory), *dispositio*, *collocatio*, or *compositio* (the structuring or arranging of parts in an oration), *ordo* (a general sense of order, either natural or artificial), and finally *oeconomia*, the broadest term for 'internal proper arrangement', one that Aristotle had used (1453ª10) and one that Quintilian had deemed to be of pre-eminent importance in the study of literary texts (*Inst. Orat.* 1. 8. 17).[13]

It is tempting to see a modern idea of plot prefigured in the classical *argumentum*, but in fact the *argumentum* provided a reader only with a statement of pure, formless content and no sense of coordination or subordination of parts into an organized whole. Early-modern editions of classical drama sometimes prefaced each individual play with a brief prose summary of its action, a convention that Jonson observed when he published both *Sejanus* (Q 1605) and *The New Inn* (O 1631). An example from a 1581 edition and translation of Seneca's *Hercules Furens* is typical (Fig. 7.1): here the *argumentum* is in fact not a plot but a plot *summary*, an appendage that is meant to remind the reader of a content he or she is already supposed to know so that it may be disregarded in favour of more specific questions: problems of etymology, difficult grammatical uses, analogues to rhetorical structure (noting, say, a transition from *exordium* to *narratio*), *decorum* of character and speech, or notable *sententia* for a commonplace book.[14] In this sense, the *argumentum* is most similar to the story, *fabula*, or *histoire* of modern narratology: it provides a minimal delineation of the 'who' and the 'what' of the play but leaves undeveloped any sense of 'how' those elements have been selected or arranged.

---

[11] Cf. Quintilian, *Inst. Orat.* 2. 4. 2–3; also *Ad Herr.* 1. 8. 13; Cicero, *De Inv.* 1. 19. 27, which provides identical definitions and cites Terence's *Andria* as an example of *argumentum*.

[12] Donatus distinguished *argumentum* and *ficta argumenta* from both the *uerae narrationis* of history and the 'mere narration of the argument', to which he preferred the physical acting out of the scene; he was followed in this usage by Jocodus Badius Ascensius (1462–1535), author of commentaries on both Terence and Horace that were used in England as late as 1627; see Baldwin (1947: 333–46, esp. 337). For vernacular usages in French and Italian, see Lawton (1972) and Weinberg (1950, 1963); Herrick (1950) provides a detailed and concise survey of Latin terminology; see also Herrick (1946: 36, 69–73).

[13] See Herrick (1950: 6–35, 90–106); Joseph (1962); Vickers (1968, esp. 30–59, 96–115).

[14] Cf. Chartier (1999: 56–8).

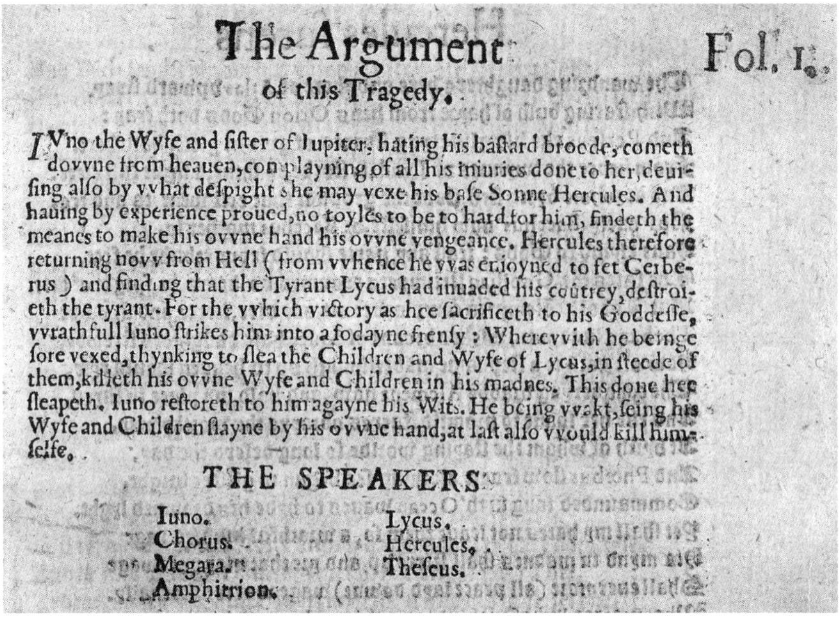

The Argument of this Tragedy. Fol. 1.

*I*Vno the Wyfe and fifter of Iupiter, hating his baftard broode, cometh dovvne from heauen, conplayning of all his iniuries done to her, deuifing alfo by vvhat defpight fhe may vexe his bafe Sonne Hercules. And hauing by experience prooued, no toyles to be to hard for him, findeth the meanes to make his ovvne hand his ovvne vengeance. Hercules therefore returning novv from Hell (from vvhence he vvas enioyned to fet Cerberus) and finding that the Tyrant Lycus had inuaded his coûtrey, deftroieth the tyrant. For the vvhich victory as hee facrificeth to his Goddeffe, vvrathfull Iuno ftrikes him into a fodayne frenfy : Wherevvith he beinge fore vexed, thynking to flea the Children and Wyfe of Lycus, in fteede of them, killeth his ovvne Wyfe and Children in his madnes. This done hee fleapeth. Iuno reftoreth to him agayne his Wits. He being vvakt, feing his Wyfe and Children flayne by his ovvne hand, at laft alfo vvould kill himfelfe.

THE SPEAKERS

Iuno.   Lycus.
Chorus.   Hercules.
Megara.   Thefeus.
Amphitrion.

Fig. 7.1. 'Argumentum': *Hercules Furens*, Seneca, *Ten Tragedies* (1581)

In the sixteenth-century commentaries, a notion of structural 'emplotment' was addressed through the three-part structure that Evanthius and Donatus had disseminated: the *protasis*, *epitasis*, and *catastrophe*, to which Julius Caesar Scaliger had added a fourth part, the *catastasis*, and which critics worked ingeniously to reconcile with the traditional belief that plays should always have five acts. Late in his career Jonson would invoke Terentian categories elaborately in *The Staple of News, The New Inn*, and *The Magnetick Lady*, but he alludes to them only once and in passing in *Every Man Out of His Humour*, when Cordatus advises that 'now the *Epitasis*, or busie part of our subject, is in act' (3. 8. 101–2). In the Induction to the play Mitis invokes division into acts and scenes as a principle of structure, when he asks whether Asper will 'observe all the lawes of Comedie' in his play— 'the equall division of it into *Acts*, and *Scenes*, according to the *Terentian* manner, his true number of Actors; the furnishing of the *Scene* with GREX, or CHORUS, and that the whole Argument fall within compasse of a dayes businesse' (Induction, 237–41)—but as we have seen in Chapter 5, even in the classical period the method of dividing acts and scenes was not as straightforward as he makes it out to be. Cordatus' response to Mitis recognizes this difficulty and indicates that the play to follow will not exactly conform to classical principles: 'O no, these are too nice observations . . . we should enjoy the same licence, or free power, to illustrate and heighten our invention as [the Ancients] did; and not bee tyed to those strict and regular formes, which the niceness of a few (who are nothing but forme) would thrust upon us.'[15] The 'act' is indeed structurally irrelevant to *Every Man Out of His Humour*, as Asper implicitly indicates when he asks Cordatus and Mitis to 'Speake your opinions, upon every *Scene*, | As it shall pass the view of these spectators' (Induction, 155–6).[16]

In the second mode of scenic composition, in contrast to the first emblematic mode I have been describing, the scene is clearly identifiable as a narrative episode and takes its significance from the structural role it plays in the motivation of the total dramatic action, whether by opening lines of development, complicating them, or closing them (often all at once). Characters do not simply speak to elaborate themselves qualitatively in a static frame but act in concrete circumstances towards a specifically defined goal. This compositional use of scene bears some resemblance to the intrigue of classical Roman comedy, in that 'action' is often developed through the exercise of verbal skill, the weaving of intricate narratives and counter-narratives that manage to shape a character's perception of events by creating a linguistic context in which the most unexpected and outlandish circumstances may be given a plausible explanation. The use of the scene by Jonson and his contemporaries is somewhat different, however, in that a strategic use of language is always also tied to a strategic use of place and the physical environment, much as in Dekker's work and in *Eastward Hoe*. For this reason I will call it a 'topographic' scene: it is highly denotative, rather than connotative, in its use of detail, and it represents a physical action or movement among characters that always takes place in a particular location. The topographic scene exhibits a semiotic approach that may be described as typical of iconic realism, as I have described it in Chapter 5: details signify themselves and do not gesture beyond themselves to a hidden, 'higher', or symbolic meaning.

This is not to say that the emblematic scene completely eschews the use of location entirely, but in this case invocations of location are always subordinated to the larger conceit that organizes the scene as a whole. In the early scenes of *Every Man Out of His Humour*, for instance, the use of location always elaborates the qualities of specific humours; when Sogliardo boasts of his farms, houses, and lordships in 1. 2 (18–19, 34–5), they are details in Jonson's portrait of a country fool who aspires to be a gentleman and who will soon need to convert 'foure or five hundred acres of your best land into two or three trucks of apparel' (41–2) so that he may move from manor to court. Similarly, when Cordatus reminds Mitis that 'The scene is the country still' (1. 3. 198), he locates the moralism of the

---

[15] Induction, 242–70; cf. *Discoveries*, 2555–65.

[16] See Donovan (1999, esp. 62–3), on how the classicizing gestures of the Folio revision of *EMOH* (massed entries, act and scene divisions) conflict with 'theatrical' details that persist in the format of the Quarto, which occupies a transitional place, he argues, in the way that Jonson's attitudes towards the stage were reified in his treatment of his printed plays; also Ostovich's discussion of the different approaches to the 'scene' in Q and F, 76–7; and Loewenstein's (2002*a*) careful arguments on Jonson's anti-theatrical attitudes, observing that the 1600 Quarto of *EMOH* expresses less an 'anti-theatrical' position than an 'idealizing' of theatrical performance.

surrounding scenes in a typology of the country, where greedy farmers withhold grain in times of dearth and then ruin themselves by relying on the spurious authority of almanacks. As the scene shifts to Deliro's house in the city in 2. 4, so also the ethical index shifts to admit of excesses in 'citizen' character; the detailed inventory of interior spaces serves to elaborate Fallice's basic capriciousness and vanity—

> Shee (late) hath found much fault with every roome
> Within my house; one was too big (shee said)
> Another was not furnisht to her mind   (2. 4. 83–5)

—and Deliro's slavish devotion. When Fallace withdraws to her 'private chamber' behind a locked door at the end of the scene, the spatial arrangement still remains primarily connotative, indicating her fundamental self-involvement and obsession with Fastidious Briske: the withdrawal adds no complexity to the action of the scene and opens no new line of intrigue.

If we compare the representation of interior space in these early scenes with the tavern scenes of 5. 4–5. 7 and 5. 9, we realize that Jonson is now using location to a very different effect. Interiors are realized in a denotative fashion, occasionally with stage directions that simply describe movement and position: 'He puts forth the drawers, and shuts the dore' (5. 4. 36–9). More importantly, interior space serves as a fundamental structuring principle, a node or gathering point for the various strands of action that Malicente has set in motion: some characters arrive in one place while others are removed elsewhere; these figures no longer appear framed by a minimally delineated place that is meant to elaborate them as an emblematic backdrop but move *through* and interact with specific places as they encounter other figures. The 'action' of the scene is now supplied by this process of movement and intersection rather than by the revelation of specific qualities. It may be described as quantitative rather than as qualitative in form: the difference between the two modes can be measured by summarizing 1. 2—Sogliardo, Carlo, and Macilente discuss the 'rare qualities, humours, and complements of a gentleman' (1. 2. 22–3) in punning, associative language—and comparing it with a summary of 5. 7: the constables and drawer burst into the room; Puntarvolo, Carlo, Macilente, Sogliardo disperse, while Fastidious Briske is left behind; Fungoso hides under the table; Briske is taken to the Counter; Macilente returns; Fungoso is discovered and berated by the drawer; Cordatus warns Mitis 'Lose not your selfe now signior' (5. 7. 76). In the latter, topographic scene, a series of individual actions *accumulate* or accrue in a linear, numerical sequence, directly provoking one another. This is not to say that the emblematic, qualitative use of location has entirely disappeared from the play at this late point—it persists in the portrait of 5. 4, for instance, when Carlo pledges his own health and reveals himself to be a ridiculous parody of a carousing gallant—but the fulfilment of the total humours design requires Jonson to use the final scenes in a topographic way, isolating characters from one another spatially and positioning them in a larger cause-and-effect sequence.

EXPERIMENTS IN PROJECTIVE EMPLOTMENT: JONSON, MARLOWE, MIDDLETON, SHAKESPEARE, ANONYMOUS

Within the action of the play, this topographic mode of organizing action among characters is most fully exploited by the character Macilente, and Jonson describes the operation of his particular 'humour' in a surprisingly consistent language drawn from military engineering—a language that includes the term 'plot' in a specialized sense typical of the operation of a mechanical, projective intelligence. In this meaning it is very similar to the term 'design', which Jonson would refer to in 'An Expostulation with Inigo Jones' (1631) as 'that specious Fyne terme | of architects'.[17] Both words carried intellectual and mechanical connotations simultaneously: in 1598 John Florio translated the Italian *disegno* as 'a purpose, an intent, a desseigne, a draught, a modle, a plot, a picture, or pourtrait', while Randle Cotgrave (1611) rendered the French *desseign* as 'A designe, plot, project, purpose, determination, resolution'.[18] Derived from the French *complot*, this definition of *plot* as intrigue, design, or a strategy of action, particularly one of devious or harmful intent, was proximate to the less pejorative Latin *ingenium* or the English 'device'; its meaning is close to our modern sense of dramatic action but remains, in the sixteenth century, distinct from it.[19] At the conclusion of 4. 8, for instance, when Mitis notes a sudden change in Macilente's character, Cordatus responds in terms drawn from river-works or harbour fortification:

Now do's hee (in this calme of his humour) plot, and store up a world of malicious thoughts in his braine, till hee is so full with 'hem, that you shall see the very torrent of his envie breake forth like a land-floud: and, against the course of all their affections oppose it selfe so violently, that you will almost have to wonder to thinke, how 'tis possible the current of their dispositions shall receive so quick, and strong an alteration. (4. 8. 152–9)

As his schemes increase in complexity, Macilente invokes the imagery of the mechanical arts of munitions, urging Carlo to 'spare no sulphurous jest that may come out of that sweatie forge of thine: but ply 'hem with all manner of shot, minion, saker, culverine, or any thing what thou wilt' (5. 5. 28–31); when he

---

[17] Jonson (1925–52: viii. 404. 55–6); cf. D. J. Gordon (1975, esp. 94–6).

[18] Baxandall (1990: 206). Similar uses appear throughout many of Jonson's plays, but particularly *A Case is Altered*, *A Tale of a Tub*, and *The Devil is an Ass*, where 'plot' is used within some thirty lines to describe both a scheme of erotic deception (2. 3. 2) and a project for economic profit and social advancement (2. 3. 34; also 4. 2. 45). The play is centrally concerned with satirizing mechanical knowledge as it pertained to the many economic projects of the period: Ingine, Fitzdottrel's broker and go-between, conspires with Meercraft, 'the great Projector', to swindle Fitzdottrel with elaborate parodies of industrial investment: making dog skins into leather, making ale, making wine of raisins, and finally the recovery of drowned land ('I have computed all, and made my survay | Unto an acre' (2. 1. 52–3); 'All *Crowland* | Is ours, wife; and the fens, from us, in *Norfolke*, | To the utmost bound of *Lincoln-shire*! we have view'd it, | And measur'd it within all; by the scale!'; 2. 3. 49–52).

[19] Baxandall (1971); Vérin (1993: 19–42); Lewis (1960: 86–110).

reports that, unexpectedly, 'three of our ordinance are burst' (5. 5. 4), Carlo responds by asking 'which of the munition is miscarried?' (5. 5. 10). Other characters adopt a similar mechanical language: Carlo is suspicious of Macilente's volatile nature, confiding to Sogliardo that 'his spirit's like powder, quick, violent: hee'le blow a man up with a jest: I feare him worse then a rotten wall do's the cannon, shake an houre after, at the report' (1. 2. 215–18). Later he muses that Macilente must be 'plotting some mischievous device' (5. 4. 25–6), while at court Puntervolo prepares to expose the courtier Saviolina according to Macilente's plan, urging his comrades to 'let not other matters carrie us from our *project*: but (if we can) single her forth to some *place*... And bee not too suddaine, but let the device induce it selfe with good circumstance' (5. 1. 33–7; my emphasis). In the wings, meanwhile, Mitis expects 'the issue of the other device' (5. 1. 91–2) and wonders 'what *engine* hee will use to bring the rest out of their humours' (3. 8. 95–6; my emphasis).

Jonson's use of the term 'plot' and related language from the mechanical arts in these scenes registers a new convergence in the meanings of the term that was only gradually becoming assimilated to a specifically literary discourse. The machinations of Macilente should be understood as an expression, in a performative and theatrical context, of a mode of deliberation about human action that was typical of early-modern military strategy and other forms of practical thinking, one that derived from the probabilistic reasoning of classical prudence but which had been divorced from metaphysical moral principles by Valla, Machiavelli, Harvey, and other humanist thinkers, on the one hand, and which had been increasingly spatialized by the practical geometrical manuals and the habits of thought that they were disseminating through English culture, on the other.[20] This 'projective' intelligence provides a way of imagining an action that unfolds forward in time, through the process of its own acting and doing, according to principles that become explicit only through their enactment or through retrospective analysis. But it also supplied a mode of *situated* reasoning: of thinking about action in concrete spatial circumstances, action that was forced to respond to specific environments, physical obstacles, and counter-actions even as it reshaped the circumstances in which it took place.

The classical origins of this projective and situated reasoning are nowhere more clearly illustrated than in Cicero's discussion of *modestia* near the end of the first book of his *De Officiis*, arguably the most influential analysis of virtue and prudence after Aristotle's *Nicomachean Ethics* and a fundamental authority for Sidney, among many others.[21] *Modestia* consisted of the ability to perceive the proper

[20] Cf. Ch. 3 n. 21, above; cf. Kahn (1994) and Pocock (1975, esp. 83–5, 156–218), with reference to Machiavelli; Jardine (1986: 45) and Grafton and Jardine (1990: 61, 55), with reference to Harvey, and the notes that follow below. W. West (2002, esp. 155–6), also places the play in the context of prudential thinking during the period, linking it to the 'encyclopedic' aspects of European humanism.

[21] For the central place of Cicero's *De Officiis* in 16th-century England, see Wood (1990), who notes that Burghley was said to carry a copy of the work in his pocket at all times; it is among the first works Sidney recommends to Edward Denny; see Ch. 3, above.

course of action appropriate to any particular situation. This aspect of *decorum*, Cicero explained, consisted in the act of 'collocation' (*collocare, collocatio*), literally 'ordering', 'disposing', and 'proper placing', a synthesis of spatial and temporal judgement that defined the singular event and then 'composed' things, action, and speech so that they would be suitable to the occasion. *Modestia*, Cicero writes, was defined by the Stoics as the

'science of disposing aright everything that is done or said' (*scientia rerum earum, quae agentur aut dicentur, loco suo collocandarum*). So the essence of orderliness (*ordinis*) and of right-placing (*collocationis*), it seems, will be the same; for orderliness they define also as 'the arrangement of things in their suitable and appropriate places' (*compositionem rerum aptis et accommodates locis*). By 'place of action,' moreover, they mean seasonableness of circumstance (*locum autem actionis opportunitatem temporis esse dicunt*); and the seasonable circumstance for an action is called in Greek ευκαιρια, in Latin *occasio* (occasion). (I. 40. 142)

'Moderation', Cicero concludes, 'is the science of doing the right thing at the right time. A similar definition can be given for prudence,' because

we have confidence in those who we think have more understanding than ourselves, who, we believe, have better insight into the future (*prospicere futura*), and who, when an emergency arises and a crisis comes, can clear away the difficulties and reach a safe decision according to the exigencies of the occasion; for that kind of wisdom (*prudentiam*) the world accounts genuine and practical (*utilem*). (1. 40. 142–3; cf. 2. 9. 33)

This form of intelligence is finally the distinguishing mark of the human itself, since animals are condemned to live in a perpetual present, Cicero maintains, but man alone 'comprehends the chain of consequences, perceives the causes of things, understands the relation of cause to effect and of effect to cause, draws analogies, and connects and associates the present and the future' (1. 4. 11).

The distinctively spatial aspect to the prudential and projective intelligence only became more pronounced during the sixteenth century, as the sites, occasions, and instruments of its deployment proliferated. We may again turn to Juan Huarte's account of the kinds of imagination suitable to the physician, the poet, and the military captain, which we have already considered in Chapter 3. For Huarte, as for Aristotle, the imagination mediates between the particulars of sense perception and the universal principles grasped by higher reason or 'understanding' and in this way allows for the formulation of judgements (1594: 178; cf. 180, 135). For this reason, the imagination is critical to the deliberation about future action, as Huarte argues:

the prudence and readiness of the mind which Galen speaketh of, apperteineth to the imagination, whereby we know that which is to come, whence Cicero sayd, Memorie is of things passed, and Prudence of those to come. The readinesse of the mind is that, which commonly they call a sharpenesse in imagining, and by other names, craftines, subtiltie, cavelling, wilinesse: wherefore Cicero sayd, Prudence is a subtiltie which with a certaine reason, can make choise of good things and of evill [*De Off.* 1. 43. 153]. This sort of

Prudence and readinesse, men of great understanding do want, because they lack imagination. (pp. 85–6)

This ability to study conditions in the present and to find within them the contingencies and unrealized potential for future action is particularly necessary in the art of war, Huarte argues: 'This propertie to attain sodainly the means is *solertia* (quickness) and appertaineth to the imagination,' he writes, citing Cicero and calling it a type of 'wisdom of the imagination' that should be used only with enemies and not with friends: 'with our enimies we must practise wisdome, and with our friends plainnesse and simplicitie' (p. 203). It is secretive, like magic and fortune telling, or like the kind that makes 'clocks, pictures, poppets, & other ribaldries which are impertinent for mans service' (p. 183), much the way Puttenham would compare the poetic mode of intelligence to those who made locks and other mechanical devices. So also those who excel at game-playing are endowed with this imaginative skill, since games such as chess allow the prudent man to model larger decisions in miniature: 'For at every moment, there are offered occasions in this play, by which a man shall discover, what hee would do in matters of great importance, if oportunitie served' (p. 112).

The military captain in particular, argues Huarte, must possess this special 'wisdom of the imagination' so that he may 'plot down' (p. 201) his actions, 'frameth many plots' (p. 209), and seize 'convenient occasion' (p. 203); his imagination must be of the type that is 'forecastfull, warie, and which can skill to discern the wiles which come vailed with anie couverture' (pp. 204–5), just like those men who use imagination to make war instruments. This is precisely why Gabriel Harvey, in his marginalia, admires Caesar so much: he is 'the cunningest in huge artificial works', is 'allwaies invincible' in the 'finest designes, that could be plotted bie himself in the profunditie of his surprising conceit'.[22] In *The Governor*, Sir Thomas Elyot, too, emphasized the importance of drawing, because 'by the feate of portraiture or payntyng, a capitaine may . . . also perceyve the placis of advauntage, the forme of embataylynge of his enemies: the situation of his campe, for his mooste suertie: the strength or weakenes of the towne or fortresse whiche he intendeth to assaulte' (1531: i. 44–5). Skill in drawing is valuable to princes in their childhood because:

it served them afterwarde for devysynge of engines for the warre: or for making them better that be all redy devysed. For, as Vitruvius (which writeth of buyldynge to the emperour Augustus) sayth, All turmentes of warre, which we cal ordinance, were first invented by kinges or governours of hostes, or they were devised by other, they were by them made moche better. (i. 44)

Richard Moryson's English translation of Sextus Julius Frontinus' *Strategemata* (*c.* AD 84–96), *The Strategemes, sleyghtes, and policies of warre* (1539), a work that we know Harvey was reading in both 1578 and 1580, collects the ruses, tricks,

---

[22] Cited by Grafton and Jardine (1990: 55).

and deceptions deployed by ancient captains in their successful military campaigns but also emphasizes the importance of mechanical knowledge when it is applied to military fortification and armament.[23] 'It hath ben somtyme moved', Moryson writes in his prefatory dedication to Henry VIII:

whether in warre, Polycy of mynde, or Strength of body, shulde do more. [B]ut longe experience, hath put his thyng so out of question, that in all battayles, the specialle prayse or disprase remayneth to the Capitayne. Yea some men are not affrayde to affirme, that it is moche better to have an armie, where the Capitayn is a lyon, and all the hoste fearefull dere, than to have a dere the capitayne, and al the host lyons. Ajax was stronge, Ulysses wise: Homere gyveth moche more praise to the laste, than to the fyrste. Ajax was hardye and valyant in fyght: but Ulisses knew the time & place, where hardinesse might prevayle. Strength stryketh, but Policie provydeth, that the stronge be not overmatched, and that they bestowe strokes in a ryghte place, and at tyme convenient. Many mo fieldes have ben lost for lacke of polycie, than for wante of strength. [M]any townes wonne by sleightes, whyche a longe season easilye were kepte ageynst greatest myght, strength, and force. (Aiiii^{r-v})

Henry is himself the model for all such captains in his attention not only to modes of strategic thinking but in working 'with your own handes, continually manegynge tooles, continually inventyng newe sortes of weapons, newe kindes of shyppes, of gunnes, of armure' (aiiii^r). To Moryson, Henry's activity as a 'captain' is simply the martial equivalent to his legislative duty as monarch:

Moste hygh excellente, and myghtye Prynce, mooste dere and dradde soverayne lorde, if the love, whyche your hyghnesse beareth unto this your noble empyre, stylle enforceth your graces harte, not onely to bestowe the better parte of all dayes, but of all nyghtes alsoo, in devysynge in tyme of peace mooste godly lawes, statutes, and proclamations, for the tranquillitie and quietnesse of your subjectes sowles, in tyme of warre, plattes, blocke howses, bulwarkes, walles, casteles, with other munitions, ingins, and fortresses, for the safetie and surenes of their bodies . . . Can I without my great shame, not be styred to worke somewhat for my parte? (aii^{r-v})

Moryson's portrait of Henry is identical to Harvey's comments about Caesar and about himself, as we have seen in Chapter 3: both are ideal models for the strategic,

---

[23] The very year he entered the household of the Earl of Leicester and thus two or three years after the reading of Livy with Sidney but at the time of the composition of the *Defence*; see Chapter 3, above; Grafton and Jardine (1990: 49–50); Stern (1979: 138 n. 4, 140; also 161–4, on Harvey's purchase in 1580 of Whitehorne's English translation of Machiavelli's *Arte of Warre* (1573) and his extensive knowledge of practical military authors, both English and Continental). In a letter to a 'Mr. Wood' written *c*.1580, Harvey testifies to the contemporary interest among some Bachelors at Cambridge in practically oriented subjects such as history or political philosophy—they are 'active rather than contemplative philosophers'—and reporting that Aristotle's *Politics* and *Economics* were gaining favour over his books of logic and that authors such as Bodin, Machiavelli, and Moryson's translation of Frontinus were becoming increasingly popular; cited by Curtis (1959: 128 and n. 7; also 126–48 on the extra-statutory, 'utilitarian' studies of Harvey and others at Cambridge during the late 16th and early 17th centuries); and Scott (1984: 151), citing Harvey's third letter to Spenser ('sum good fellowes amongst us begin nowe to be pretty well acquainted with a certayne parlous booke called . . . Il Principe'). See also Raab (1964); for additional discussion of practical geometry in a military and dramatic context, see De Somogyi (1996, esp. 97–8); Cahill (2004).

pragmatic agent who draws on his experience in the mechanical arts to develop a systematic 'art' of successful action, both military and civil.

Jonson's accomplishment in *Every Man Out of His Humour* is to adapt the sixteenth-century interest in projective thinking that we find in Cicero, Huarte, Elyot, Moryson, Harvey, and Sidney into a new theoretical discourse for examining problems of action during theatrical performance, especially as they arose in comedy and its sub-genres. Since, as I have argued in Chapter 2, the ratiocinative methods associated with prudence and rhetoric provided a discursive framework in which the practical modes of intelligence associated with the mechanical arts could be addressed in a self-conscious theoretical way and used to solve technical problems posed by the spatial arts, these methods of reasoning were also ideally suited to the problems that confronted a working playwright such as Jonson, who sought to reconcile classical ideas about language and human action with the many practical techniques that were necessary to theatrical representation. But Jonson represents only a particularly self-conscious example of this derivation, which is visible much more widely in many plays of the period, across different genres and types of playing spaces. In what follows I am concerned merely to suggest how widely practical and projective modes of intelligence may be traced through Renaissance plays; my readings are not meant to be exhaustive, and no doubt many examples could be found in plays beyond those I have considered here.

Macilente's strategic and deliberative humour is typical, first, of the English 'Machiavel' more generally, from Barabas to Iago to Richard III: each character demonstrates with particular clarity the way in which the crafty, deceptive, and manipulative mode of imagination that has long been associated with the stage Machiavel is also inseparable from his associations with military strategy, practical geometry, and the projective mode of deliberation about action that was of interest to sixteenth-century humanists such as Harvey and Sidney.[24] In the *Jew of Malta*, performed in 1589, probably at the Theatre, again in 1592–3 at the Rose, and revived again in *c.*1632 at the Cockpit, Marlowe has, of course, explicitly invited a comparison between Barabas's machinations and Machiavellian political principles, both in the play's Prologue (spoken by Machiavel himself) and in the concern for 'policy' (5. 2. 121 and elsewhere) that is so conspicuous. But Barabas has also served as an 'engineer . . . in the wars twixt France and Germany', one who 'Slew friend and enemy with my stratagems' (2. 3. 186–90, 5. 2. 99, 5. 5. 83) and who now draws on his technical expertise first to invite the Turks into Malta through the sewers and hollow rocks of the city (5. 1. 87–94) and then to overcome them by immuring them in a monastery beyond the city walls. As the

---

[24] On the possible influence of Machiavellian ideas on English drama and especially on characterization, see Meyer (1897), citing the chorus between Acts 2 and 3 of *EMOH* (pp. 93–4) and noting that Jonson's *Discoveries* demonstrates that he had read *Il Principe* closely (pp. 100–1); Praz (1928), building on Meyer's work; Scott (1984), a reassessment of Meyer's argument with additional bibliography; Lupton (1987); Boughner (1968), esp. 152–8, on *EMOH* (without, surprisingly, noting its Machiavellian aspects)); W. A. Armstrong (1948), esp. 25–35); Watson (1976); Bawcutt (1971); Bushnell (1990).

play draws towards its conclusion, the elaborate constructions that Barabas erects with the help of carpenters become physical, mechanical actualizations of his earlier mental 'plot' and 'device' (4. 1. 116; 5. 2. 117):

> How stand the cords? How hang these hinges? Fast?
> Are all the cranes and pulleys sure?   (5.5.1–2)
>
> And, governor, now partake of my policy:
> First, for his army, they are sent before,
> Enter'd the monastery, and underneath
> In several places are fieldpieces pitch'd,
> Bombards, whole barrels full of gunpowder,
> That on the sudden shall dissever it,
> And batter all the stones about their ears,
> Whence none can possibly escape alive.
> Now as for Calymath and his consorts,
> Here I have made a dainty gallery,
> The floor whereof, this cable being cut,
> Doth fall asunder, so that it doth sink
> Into a deep pit past recovery . . .   (5. 5. 24–36)

The entire project is a 'plot . . . As never Jew nor Christian knew the like' (4. 1. 116–17), as Barabas promises in an earlier passage, and thus a form of projective intelligence that is fundamental to the play's development at the level of action and event but that remains alien from *both* of the two competing systems of value ('Jew', 'Christian') that give the play its rhetorical or discursive structure. When Ferenze betrays Barabas by plunging him to his death, even as he profits from the scheme to massacre the Turkish army and take Calymath prisoner, the play's resolution produces a basic alignment between several different forms of heterodoxy that shadow the edges of the English world-view: the ethical indeterminacy of Machiavellian political philosophy, encroaching communities of non-Christian believers, and the quasi-occult power of practical mathematics.

In *Every Man Out of His Humour*, Jonson, too, links mathematics and mechanical knowledge to black magic and astrology in ways that were commonplace during the period.[25] Puntervolo is ludicrous as the kind of knight who cultivates geometrical knowledge as a mode of 'gentle' fashion, and in 2. 3 Jonson singles out for ridicule his tendency to use geometrical terms as a kind of private courtly language. He is a man who 'makes congies [farewell bows] to his wife in geometricall proportions', explains Cordatus to an incredulous Mitis (2. 3. 39–40); Jonson describes him in his brief character sketch as a 'Jacobs staffe of complement' (Jonson 1925–52: iii. 423. 16–17), a man whose partial knowledge of mathematical

---

[25] Cf. Johnston (1991: 320); E. G. R. Taylor (1947: 130–1); Cosgrove (1988: 257); Shapin (1994: 49, 58, 76).

instruments is put to ridiculous use.[26] The superstitious Puntervolo seeks to protect himself against supernatural intervention as he draws up his insurance contract before travelling to Turkey: 'That (after the receit of his monie) he shall neyther in his own person, nor any other, eyther by direct or indirect meanes, as magicke, witchcraft, or other such exoticke artes, attempt, practise, or complot anie thing, to the prejudice of mee, my dogge, or my cat' (4. 3. 27–31); the term 'practice' itself appears in several of Jonson's plays in reference to this kind of secret, immoral, or simply unpredictable course of action, a meaning that was commonplace during the period. In 4. 3, meanwhile, Jonson uses the illegitimate associations of practical geometry to sketch a portrait of illicit sexuality, as Carlo narrates that Sogliardo and Whiffe have retreated to the tavern to smoke tobacco in 'a chamber, and all private to practise in' (4. 3. 88–9):

I brought some dozen, or twentie gallants this morning to view 'hem (as you'ld doe a piece of *Perspective*) in at a key-hole: and there wee might see SOGLIARDO sit in a chaire, holding his snowt up like a sow under an apple-tree, while th'other open'd his nostrils with a poking-sticke, to give the smoke a more free deliverie. (4. 3. 91–6)

Like an anamorphic projection that requires a displaced, off-centre viewing position, the perspective 'peep-show', as Herford and Simpson gloss the line, seems to offer the gallants two simultaneous but very different views of Sogliardo and the man Carlo refers to as 'his villanous GANIMEDE' (4. 3. 83), inviting the audience to perceive the outlines of a perverse sexual encounter that nevertheless remains unspecified, 'offstage', and outside the representational space of the play.

In Thomas Middleton's *A Mad World, My Masters*—a boys' company play, performed in 1605–6 at Paul's and revived in 1640 at the Salisbury Court theatre, each somewhat different playing spaces than either the Theatre or the Globe—a similar emphasis on projective thinking enables a satire of urban consumer culture in which homoerotic double entendres compete with equally knowing meta-theatrical references. Follywit is the 'captain' (1. 1. 1, 3. 3. 67, 5. 2. 72, and throughout) of a group of urban gallants whose stature is secured by his ingenious ability to grasp the possibilities of any occasion and to 'forecast' (1. 1. 4) his actions by thinking ahead of others—to 'cast your plots into form', as he boasts to his companions at the opening of the play (1. 1. 4–5). This 'plot' will include dressing up in various disguises so that Follywit may be entertained at the house of his rich uncle, Sir Bounteous Progress, but also rob him at the same time; having done so—'Was't not well manag'd, you necessary mischiefs? Did the plot want either life or art?' (3. 3. 1–2)—Follywit mixes a lady's frock or 'gentlewoman's lower part' (3. 3. 81–2) with a male doublet and poses as a rival courtesan in order

---

[26] 'To the perfection of complement (which is the Diall of the thought, and guided by the Sunne of your beauties) are requir'd these three specials: the *gnomon*, the *puntilio's*, and the *superficies*: the *superficies*, is that we call, place; the *puntilio's*, circumstance; and the *gnomon*, ceremony: in either of which, for a stranger to erre, 'tis easie and facile, and such am I' (2. 2. 19–25). See also 3. 4. 13–40, where Jonson makes fun of the academic language affected by Clove and Orange.

to discredit Sir Bounteous's prostitute mistress and rob him a second time. The 'invention' (3. 3. 65) depends on what Follywit terms 'probability' (3. 3. 109): the ability to grasp probable modes of reasoning as necessary to action in contingent circumstances, as well as to a convincing theatrical performance ('Why, carry yourselves but probably, and carry away enough with yourselves'; 1. 1. 78–9). Follywit's ability to turn even the most inauspicious occasion to his own advantage is neatly demonstrated at the play's conclusion, when he and his companions arrive at the house of Sir Bounteous disguised as players and 'desire to interlude' (5. 1. 25) before his guests; when a constable arrives unexpectedly to arrest them in mid-scene, Follywit's new 'invention' (5. 2. 47) is to improvise his lines so that the entering constable is thought by the audience to be a member of the company and the performance. Gagging him and binding him to a chair, the players escape offstage to the delighted laughter of Sir Bounteous, who confuses performance for reality and then promptly realizes that they have stolen his watch and chain; as Follywit enters through another door, now dressed as himself, the watch rings in his pocket and exposes him as the actor in the scene-within-the-scene that has just concluded. The 'lady' whom Follywit has married earlier in the play now steps forward to declare herself a courtesan, and the full contingency of events suddenly undoes him—revealing Middleton as the true 'captain' of the play we have just witnessed.

The case becomes even more interesting when we consider a series of plays that would seem at first glance to owe very little to the influence of the spatial arts but much to the practical and projective thinking typical of military strategy: the Shakespearean history plays. Scholars have conventionally explained the structure of Shakespeare's plays, whether at the level of individual scenes or at that of the management of the total action, as the effect of specific problems of character development, philosophical inquiry, or patterns in logical imagery and rhetorical devices. In the history plays, these micro-structural techniques coincide with the macro-framework provided by the chronicles and tend to be tightly focused around the conflicts between personal ambition and dynastic lineage. For this reason it seems natural to describe their structure in chronological rather than spatial terms. Since all plays occur in time, the genre of the history play, indeed, offers an unusually strong correlation between content and form: the intrigue surrounding individual historical events provides both the narrative substance of the genre and the object of its intellectual or 'thematic' attention, even as the temporal progression of these events provide the structural logic for the play as a series of mimetic actions unfolding during the time of performance.

Already in 1591, however, we find that the spatial and projective senses of the term 'plot' have become closely related in Shakespeare's mind, much as in the work of Harvey, Sidney, Huarte, Puttenham, and Jonson, and that these two meanings are beginning to generate a third, distinctly dramatic and literary usage. In the history plays, we may suspect that this new meaning results from the very coincidence of content and form that is typical of the genre and that, in

Shakespeare's hands, often results in a pronounced meta-dramatic sensibility, as in
2 Henry VI:

> I know their complot is to have my life,
> And if my death might make this island happy
> And prove the period of their tyranny,
> I would expend it with all willingness.
> But mine is made the prologue to their play,
> For thousands more that yet suspect no peril
> Will not conclude their plotted tragedy.   (3. 1. 147–53)

Gloucester's lines neatly capture the multi-layered senses of the term, even as they
bespeak Shakespeare's own emerging method as a playwright: *complot* or
Machiavellian intrigue is selected from the chronicles and isolated into discrete
speeches and scenic episodes, which are then combined to produce both a new
form (the 'play', or theatre) and a new generic set within that form (tragedy in
history, and vice versa). By the end of the passage, the term 'plot' has described a
circle: shifting out of its strategic, devious meaning, it moves through the
'prologue' of performance and concludes in a specifically dramatic register that
nevertheless remains closely associated with the first pragmatic usage.

As in the case of both Dekker's and Jonson's work, so also in Shakespeare's
history plays the term retains its spatial associations, as in *2 Henry VI* (performed
*c.*1592, probably at the Theatre), when York describes Buckingham's use of priests
and magicians to ensnare the Duchess of Gloucester as 'A pretty plot, well chosen
to build upon' (1. 4. 54), or when Salisbury and Warwick fatefully pledge their
allegiance to York:

> And in this private plot be we the first
> That shall salute our rightful sovereign
> With honour of his birthright to the crown. (2. 3. 60)

Here actions and events that will determine the structural shape not merely of the
play that follows but of two entire tetralogies of plays are literally rooted in a single
topographic scene. This same spatial sensibility inflects *1 Henry VI* (performed in
1592–3, perhaps at the Rose), as evidenced in the French Gunner's assassination
of Salisbury and Sir Thomas Gargrave in 1. 5 and 1. 6, where the play specifies the
Gunner's technical preparations and the ensuing position of Salisbury and Talbot
with conspicuous precision (especially 1. 5. 6–15 and 1. 6) or in Talbot's many
skirmishes with the French army, as Joan La Pucelle, conceding a battle to the
superior strategy of the English, calmly argues that they must simply 'lay new
platformes to endammage them' (2. 1. 78).

Indeed, the history plays only become increasingly spatial, rather than chronological, in their imagery, as Shakespeare moves from the first to the second tetralogy.
Richard III (*c.*1592, perhaps at the Theatre) excels in strategic deception and
proudly declares his devious, practical intelligence to the audience in his opening

soliloquy ('Plots have I laid, inductions dangerous'; 1. 1. 32). Later, Richmond's preparations for battle with Richard include drawing 'the form and model of our battle' with 'ink and paper' (5. 4. 21–2). Hotspur, Glendower, Mortimer, and Worcester employ precisely this type of projective and spatial intelligence as they attempt to divert rivers and redraw the political map of *1 Henry IV* (1596, perhaps at the Theatre): to 'plot' treachery against the state requires a graphic literacy and technical know-how, and the plot is 'ruminated, plotted, and set down' like a surveyor's plan (1. 3. 268; cf. 2. 4. 14–16). The anonymous letter that Hotspur receives in 2. 4 uses the term in an image derived from statics ('your whole plot [is] too light, for the counterpoise of so great an opposition'; 2. 4. 10–12), an engineering analogy that is developed elaborately in *2 Henry IV* (1597–8, perhaps at the Theatre), when Mowbray, Hastings, Bardolph, and the Archbishop discuss their impending treachery in terms that recall York's in *2 Henry VI*:

> . . . When we mean to build,
> We first survey the plot, then draw the model;
> And when we see the figure of the house,
> Then must we rate the cost of the erection,
> Which if we find outweighs ability,
> What do we then but draw anew the model
> In fewer offices, or, at least, desist
> To build at all? Much more in this great work—
> Which is almost to pluck a kingdom down
> And set another up—should we survey
> The plot of situation and the model,
> Consent upon a sure foundation,
> Question surveyors, know our own estate,
> How able such a work to undergo,
> To weigh against his opposite; or else
> We fortify in paper and in figures,
> Using the names of men instead of men,
> Like one that draws the model of an house
> Beyond his power to build it, who, half-through,
> Gives o'er, and leaves his part-created cost
> A naked subject to the weeping clouds,
> And waste for churlish winter's tyranny.[27]

The passage is remarkable for the way in which it figures treachery, political intrigue, and state-building in terms that might have been drawn directly from the surveying and building manuals that were circulating throughout English culture, clearly grasping how numbers, models, and diagrams provided an entire signifying system to rival that of language ('the names of men instead of men') and one that had become a crucial tool in the overlapping domains of cartography, navigation,

---

[27] 1. 3. 41–62; compare the very similar passage in Elyot (1531: i. 45); cf. Eriksen's thoughtful reading of the passage and its biblical and medieval analogues (2000: 1–9).

engineering, and geopolitics. As we have seen in both the Introduction and Chapter 5, above, Shakespeare also viewed geometrical and mathematical projection as fundamental to theatrical representation; in both *1* and *2 Henry IV* he conjoins many different lines of action through an interlocking series of scaled topographic units, from bench to wine cellar to inn yard to post road to battlefield to nation, using the scene to frame character, anchor types of language, and shape events. By the time of *Henry V* (1599, at the Curtain and/or the Globe), this scale has widened to include much of France as well as England, and Shakespeare's meta-dramatic interest has become preoccupied by the uniquely spatial dimension to stage mimesis—the most explicitly chronological dramatic genre finally furnishes the period's most famous defence of theatre as a spatial art.

Identical projective language and topographic scene types also organize a domestic tragedy such as the anonymous *Arden of Faversham* (performed *c.*1592 at the Rose), in which modes of practical deliberation and techniques of representation derived from the spatial arts provide the motivations for the different individual scenic actions that constitute the play's total intrigue. Alice and Mosby, 'a mean artificer' (sc. 8, lines 77 and 135), employ the assistance of the painter Clarke, the servant Michael, and the former soldiers Black Will and Shakebag in order to kill Alice's husband, Arden, the new possessor by 'letters patents from his majesty' of 'All the lands of the Abbey of Faversham' (sc. 1, lines 4–5), even as his neighbour Greene also attempts to kill him in revenge for his dispossession of those same lands. The various 'devices' of Alice (sc. 13, lines 68, 125; sc. 14, line 131, in response to sc. 14, line 122) and the botched attempts on Arden's life by Black Will and Shakebag lend the play a comic atmosphere that jars with the grim determination of Alice and the vengefulness of Greene; in each case, the machinations are articulated using a technical geometrical vocabulary and as a problem of situated action and practical thinking in space. Greene offers to 'lay the platform' (sc. 2, line 100) of Arden's death that Black Will refuses ('Plat me no platforms!'; sc. 2, line 101), and this perhaps explains why Black Will continually fails in execution: he has no *design* for future action, despite that fact that Greene continually points out opportune circumstances—particular times and locations—during which they will be best able to execute their intent:

SHAKEBAG. Where is he?
GREENE. He is now at London, at Aldersgate Street. (sc. 2, lines 104–5)

SHAKEBAG. But, give me place and opportunity . . .
GREENE. And now sirs, seeing this accident
　　Of meeting him in Paul's has no success,
　　Let us bethink us on some other place . . . (sc. 3, lines 110–18)

MICHAEL. Where you may front him well on Rainham Down,
　　A place well fitting such a strategem. (sc. 8, lines 18–20)

Indeed, it is not until Black Will finally agrees with Mosby that he will 'Perform the complot that I [Mosby] have laid' (sc. 14, line 97) that the murder succeeds.

Earlier, when confronted by Black Will outside Arden's London house, Michael maps out an itinerary through the front door, up the stairs, and into Arden's bedroom such that, for a moment, the performative space of the stage and its architectonic elements coincide iconically with the imagined domestic space where Arden is presumed to lie offstage or above, much as in Dekker and Webster's scenes:

> This night come to his house at Aldersgate.
> The doors I'll leave unlock'd against you come.
> No sooner shall ye enter through the latch,
> Over the threshold to the inner court,
> But on your left hand shall you see the stairs
> That leads directly to my master's chamber.
> There take him and dispose him as you please.
> Now it were good we parted company.
> What I have promised I will perform.   (sc. 3, lines 180–8)

Black Will has already threatened Michael by informing him that he has 'devised a complot under hand' (sc. 3, line 157) to expose him if he betrays the scheme, and his warning conclusively links the pragmatic mode of intelligence each of these characters employs to the larger poetic project of dramatic representation itself:

> Thy office is but to appoint the place,
> And train thy master to his tragedy;
> Mine to perform it when occasion serves.
> Then be not nice, but here devise with us
> How and what way we may conclude his death.   (sc. 3.165–9)

As Garrett Sullivan, Jr., has argued, the entire play offers a remarkably clear demonstration of the social conflicts that accompanied the Dissolution and the transformation in property relations that resulted from the dissemination of practical measuring techniques throughout the English countryside.[28] Of equal importance is the way that the interest in practical and projective methods of reasoning typical of sixteenth-century humanists such as Harvey and Sidney—the habits of thinking that helped make this transformation in spatial representation and quantitative conceptions of private property possible in the first place—came to constitute a source of English ideas about action on stage that is at least as significant as Roman literary theory or the classical examples of Terence and Plautus and certainly more immediately influential than the principles of Aristotelian poetics.

In his *Examination of Men's Wits*, Juan Huarte explicitly compares the imaginative faculty necessary to the practical intelligence to 'Music and stage' and argues that it is especially typical, too, of 'craftsmen of Bacchus or stage-plaiers . . . playing on the stage and ordering of feasts springeth from the . . . imagination, which inviteth a man to this maner of life'. Those who possess too much of this type of

---

[28] See Sullivan (1994, 1998), whose analysis of the play has inspired my own reading.

imagination are 'cholericke, subtle, malignant, and cavillers, and alwaies enclined to evill, which they can compasse with much readinesse and craft' (1594: 141). The passage perfectly characterizes Macilente in *Every Man Out of His Humour*. But Sir Philip Sidney, too, Elizabethan England's most famous soldier, was reputedly prone to melancholy throughout his life, and his mentor Hubert Languet worried that his study of geometry might aggravate this condition:

I know not whether it is wise to apply your mind to geometry, though it is a noble study and well worthy of a fine understanding... Besides, you are not over cheerful by nature, and it is a study which will make you still more grave, and as it requires the strongest application of the mind, it is likely to wear out the powers of the intellect, and very much to impair the health; and the greater the ability, the more intense is the interest excited, and therefore the more injurious; and you know you have no health to spare.[29]

Languet's warning is liable to seem peculiar to us, since it attributes to the study of geometry a compulsive or destructive effect that we would hardly associate with mathematical study today. For Languet, a full understanding of geometry seems impossible to achieve: the more deeply we pursue it, the more it degrades our reasonable faculties, and this self-consuming tendency is unfortunately most evident in those who are most apt to pursue higher mathematical studies—as Sidney allegedly was. For Harvey, meanwhile, melancholy threatened to disable everything that his pragmatic philosophy sought to achieve: 'Sharp, & fine Witt: pure Sanguin, or brave Choller: Melancholy an Asse in Witt, & Memory: Saturne A Beast in Behaviour, & Action—no baser, or viler wretch, then Melancholy'.[30] Macilente's particular humour, too, is a kind of melancholia, and in this sense he is an inverted image, in all senses of the term, of the 'pragmatic' that both Sidney and Harvey sought to become—the connection in Jonson's mind between practical thinking and perceived sexual deviance is persistent, as we shall see in Chapter 8. His tendency is to 'plot', provoke, and produce situations that can disrupt the vain illusions of contemporary social types; in Jonson's play, his actions betray an excessive humour that must be purged of its mechanical and melancholic associations by exercising and working through itself in a practical fashion, until it can be replaced by self-conscious, theoretical reflection: the voice of a Grex projected back retrospectively to punctuate each scene.

But we should remember that Macilente is being played by the author–character Asper, who introduces the fictional Grex before the play-within-the play begins, and so the play invites us to recognize the homology between Macilente's technical intelligence in resolving the 'humours' design within the play and Jonson's own commercial project in writing comical satire for the public theatre. This correlation is made explicit in the opening character sketch of Cordatus as 'The Authors

---

[29] Pears (1845: 25); see also Osborn (1972: 136–7, 142–3).
[30] From Harvey's annotations in his copy of Οικονομια, *seu Dispositio Regularum vtrivsque Iuris in Locos Communes breui interpretatione subiecta* (1570), with two date inscriptions, 1574 and 1580; Harvey (1913: 155–6).

friend; A man inly acquainted with the scope and drift his Plot' (Jonson 1925–52: iii. 427. 111–12), where the term appears to designate the design and intent of both Asper–Macilente *and* Jonson: the moment marks an early translation of meaning out of the practical, commercial milieu of the playhouse into a critical idea of form and dramatic structure that Cordatus articulates throughout the entire performance:

> the *Scene* is the country still, remember. (1. 3. 198)

> transferre your thoughts to the city, with the *Scene*; where, suppose they speake. (2. 3. 314–15)

MIT. What be these two, signior?
COR. Mary, a couple sir, that are meere strangers to the whole scope of our play; only come to walke a turne or two, i' this *Scene* of *Paules*, by chance. (3. 1. 16–19)

> Let your mind keepe companie with the *Scene* still, which now removes it selfe from the countrey, to the court. (3. 8. 98–100)

> you understand where the *Scene* is? (3. 9. 154)

> let your imagination be swifter then a paire of oares: and by this, suppose PUNTARVOLO, BRISKE, FUNGOSO, and the dogge arriv'd at the court gate, and going up to the great chamber. MACILENTE, and SOGLIARDO, wee'le leave them on the water, till possibilitie and naturall meanes may land 'hem. Here come the gallants, now prepare your expectation. (4. 8. 175–82)

The so-called classical rigour of Jonson's play resides *only* at this level of critical commentary, in a theoretical voice that insists on correlating sequences of action with discrete locations in respect of 'possibilitie and naturall meanes' but which is superimposed upon the actual performative and theatrical conventions of the play, which shifts its locations suddenly, sometimes without designation (as at 3. 7–8, when it returns to the country) and over considerable distances. In these moments Cordatus is concerned with preserving continuity of action in a realistic way in order to resolve any possible mimetic ambiguities that the conventions of Elizabethan staging might introduce, any question as to 'where' the action on stage takes place and 'where' characters who do not appear on stage might be located. At the same time that he constitutes a coherent action for Mitis, Cordatus also displays for the audience the fact that this very coherence derives from the operation of a critical and theoretical intelligence: that it is a principle of design through which some units of action are dramatized as scenic episodes and not others. Like Macilente, Mitis is taught to induce his critical principles out of the performative process, in this way purging himself of *his* particular humour, which is to judge and criticize: the plot of the play has been designed above all to bring him to a new, self-conscious knowledge of the problem of 'plot' itself.

8

Ben Jonson's Scenography

... the writers of these dayes are other things ... not only their manners, but their natures are inverted; and nothing remayning with them of the dignitie of Poet, but the abused name, which every Scribe usurps: that now, especially in *dramatick*, or (as they terme it) stage-*poetrie*, nothing but ribaldry, profanation, blasphemy, all licence of offence to god, and man, is practis'd.

(Ben Jonson, *Volpone*)

As the first work of Jonson's to appear in print, the 1600 Quarto of *Every Man Out of His Humour* marks a significant shift in early-modern attitudes towards theatrical representation that Jonson himself did much to advance. The Grex is less concerned with defending the theatre as an institution in early-modern social life than it is with imposing over the practical conventions of theatrical performance a system of principles that derived from the analysis of the play *text* and in this way to produce a self-conscious theory of 'drama' borrowed from the commentaries of the Roman grammarians. The purpose of the Grex is to circulate a new technical vocabulary for evaluating the individual composition, which is now to be judged according to its adherence to the purely formal categories that Jonson has gathered and begun to synthesize. Certainly the final ethical purpose of drama remains of fundamental importance to Jonson, but the success of this project is secured for him by these categories of form: the more systematic, de-materialized, and abstract the work is in its structural organization, the more effective it will be in reforming society. This is one reason why Jonson is so self-conscious of his theory and so persistent in his attempts to communicate it to his public, since the educated consumer of stage plays will be better equipped to receive their instruction in virtuous conduct and more inclined to recognize the excellence of Jonson's compositions.

The public was notoriously fickle, however, and Jonson often found himself on the defensive about his artistic principles when his plays proved unpopular; the commercial organization of the play companies themselves, meanwhile, who bought their plays and expected to retain authority over their subsequent production, inevitably circumscribed whatever authority Jonson himself might like to exercise. And this is finally why commercial publication would prove to be so important to him. For the larger purpose of *Every Man Out of His Humour* is to shift the terms of authority over dramatic production away from the audience, the play company, or the stage manager and towards a figure who was relatively new to the early-modern literary field: not simply to the 'author' or 'poet', as has been much discussed, but to the *critic*, poised somewhere between the circulation of the printed book and the public space of the theatre. Jonson's attempts to redefine his own field of activity by changing the basic categories through which poetics might be defined are inseparable from his efforts to change the professional position of the playwright from a 'practitioner' of the theatre, still closely associated with the mechanical and spatial arts, to the 'critic' who would become the dominant authorizing position in the field of seventeenth-century poetic discourse. It was in the name of the critic, and not that of the author, that the full *value* of the drama was to be determined: its quality, currency, and desirability, as measured by its commercial popularity and takings at the theatre door, but also the moral authority that the critic was now to guarantee. In this sense, Jonson's appeal to classical principles in the 1600 Quarto of *Every Man Out of His Humour* marks an early strategic thrust within the much larger process of 'autonomization' by which the field of literary production generated its own terms of definition and 'agencies of consecration', to adopt Bourdieu's terminology, although in Jonson's case the gesture was calculated at least in part to secure royal patronage and thus also reaffirms a long-standing and more conservative model of literary legitimization.[1]

We have seen in Chapter 4 how Jonson's collaboration with Dekker and the joiner Stephen Harrison provoked him to articulate a sharp distinction between the 'poetic' understanding of the learned viewer and the stupefied gaze of the 'mechanical' intelligence typical of the average citizen, eschewing various practical techniques of composition that were commonplace in the production of masques and pageants in favour of a deliberately classicizing, rhetorical, and overtly polemic vocabulary of form and structure. This polemic attitude would only become more pronounced during Jonson's twenty-five years of collaboration with the architect and stage designer Inigo Jones over the court masque, and in many ways the infamous quarrel between poet and architect can be explained as a confrontation over whether the structure of masque would be derived from rhetorical or geometrical principles, a bifurcation that a work such as Puttenham's *Arte of English Poesie* (1589), which Jonson himself owned and annotated, materialized in its very format. In this sense, the struggle was fuelled by the different ways in which both Jonson and Jones were attempting to reconceptualize their

---

[1] Bourdieu (1993: 112). On Jonson's use of print, see Murray (1987, esp. 30–93); Loewenstein (1985, 1991, 2002a); Boehrer (1993, esp. 296–7); Evans (1995: 32–5); Brady and Herendeen (1991), esp. van den Berg (1991); Helgerson (1983: 101–84, esp. 131–40); J. S. Peters (2000: 124–5). Jonson's role as critic has been addressed in detail by Dutton (1996); Burt (1993, esp. 13, 18–21, 26–77); Murray (1987, esp. 94–104); Barish (1981: 136–9); and Loewenstein (1985, esp. 109), who discusses the implications of Jonson's attempt to occupy a position between book and playhouse.

respective domains of activity by distancing their professions from the mechanical arts.[2] The enduring contradiction of Jonson's professional development, however, lies in the fact that he continued to occupy the position of both 'practitioner' and 'critic' simultaneously and uneasily throughout his career, and it will now be necessary to consider several sources for his formal vocabulary that retained a direct connection to practical geometrical fields and the techniques of spatial representation they made available, some of them taken from Jones's own profession.

The chapter that follows considers several of these sources, among them Vitruvius' *De Architectura*, in order to demonstrate how the practical epistemology that was typical of the spatial arts informed Jonson's work as a commercial dramatist, including the composition of his plays and, like his contemporaries, his use of scenic representation in the theatre as a method of objectifying and analysing the larger processes of London's urbanization that were transforming the social topography around him. The *De Architectura* was centrally concerned with practice and theory as distinct categories of knowledge, and for this reason it was ideally suited to Jonson's own larger project of transforming 'dramatic poesy' from a practical epistemology rooted in the theatre to a fully theoretical mode of knowledge that was distinct from it. Like Sidney before him, Jonson would eventually turn to Aristotelian literary criticism in order to define 'poesy' as a liberal art under the protection of the judicious critic. But while Sidney could look to alchemy, astrology, or technology as models for the way that poetic 'invention' might produce analytical knowledge of the natural and social world, for Jonson the proximity of poesy, and especially of dramatic poesy, to the practical epistemologies of his period was precisely what he finally needed to disavow.

JONSON'S VITRUVIUS

From *The Masque of Blackness* in 1605 until their rupture over *Love's Triumph through Callipolis* in 1631, both Jonson and Jones were concerned with finding new ways to unify a form that had remained more or less unchanged throughout the fifteenth and sixteenth centuries, and the primary limitation of the masque as a *poetic* form for Jonson lay in the fact that the specific elaboration of his 'invention' was often imposed externally upon him by the requirements of Jones's designs, which were liable to threaten what little integrity he had been able to establish. As the anti-masque became an increasingly prominent feature, so also the transition from anti-masque to masque proper became a more difficult structural problem for Jonson to negotiate. 'Upon this *hinge* the whole Invention moov'd', Jonson wrote in *Chloridia* (1631): even he admitted that the rhetorical

---

[2] For events leading to the quarrel and its documentation, see D. J. Gordon (1975); Jonson (1925–52: x. 689–92, xii. 151–2); Reyher (1909: 192–200); Loewenstein (2002*a*: 176–80); Yachnin (1997, esp. 45–64).

structure of the masque had come to depend on the mechanical movements of Jones's scenes.[3]

Jones himself, moreover, felt free to invoke a classical tradition of artisanship and 'making' in ways that began to encroach on what Jonson viewed as his exclusive province. *The Haddington Masque* (1608), for instance, which Jones invented independently of Jonson, featured Vulcan, lame artisan to the gods, whom Jonson describes in a typically showy note as the pre-eminent 'artificer' of the 'ancient Poets', as he tries to wrest authority for the conceit away from Jones by invoking a swarm of classical literary references, while describing his own verses—an Epithalamion to be sung between the dances—as '*made to be read an intire Poeme*'.[4] The next year, a note to *The Masque of Queens* (1609) defines the poet as 'yt kind of artificer, to whose worke is requir'd so much exactnesse, as indifferencey is not tolerable', and the preface that Jonson added to 1608 Quarto of *The Haddington Masque* defends his artistic judgement in similar terms by comparing 'Truth' to a 'rule' that cannot be bent.[5] The later anti-masque to *Neptune's Triumph* (1623/4), meanwhile, indicates the delicate way in which Jonson himself continued to borrow from the mechanical arts in order to describe his poetic efforts, even as he began to submit them to gentle satire. Here Jonson describes a common lineage between cookery, engineering, and poetry: 'the *Poet*', he writes, is 'a kind of Christmas Ingine; one, that is used, at least once a yeare, for a trifling instrument, or wit, or so' (682. 34–683. 36). To him the Cook replies:

Seduced *Poet*, I doe say to thee,—
A Boyler, Range, and Dresser were the fountaines
Of all the knowledge, in the *Universe*,
And that's the Kitchen . . .
A *Master-Cooke*! why, he is the man of men,
For a Professor! He designes, he drawes,
He paints, he carves, he builds, he fortifies,
Makes *Citadels* of curious foule, and fish,
Some he dry-ditches, some motes round with broths;
Mounts marrow-bones; cuts fifty-angled custards;
Reares bulwarke pies; and, for his outer workes,
He raiseth ramparts of immortall curst;
And teacheth all the *tacticks* at one dinner:
What rankes, what files, to put his dishes in;

---

[3] All citations to the masques are from Jonson (1925–52: vii) and will be by page and line number; the passage from *Chloridia* is at 750. 14 (my emphasis). Cf. *The Masque of Queens* 305. 454–6: 'She [Fame] after the Musique had done, wch wayted on the turning of the *Machine*, call'd from thence to *Vertue*, and spake this . . .'; see also J. S. Peters (2000: 198–9).

[4] 260. 342; for the description of Vulcan, see p. 257 n. a at line 249.

[5] *The Masque of Queens*, 288 n. p at line 132; *The Haddington Masque*, 249. 13–20. Cf. Boehrer's analysis of the problem of 'labour' in Jonson's attempts at self-fashioning, with additional references to metaphors from the handicrafts in Jonson's work (1993: 295, 303, 311 n. 49); Maus (1984: 12–14).

The whole *Art Militarie!* . . .
He is an *Architect*, an *Inginer*,
A *Souldier*, a *Physitian*, a *Philosopher*,
A generall *Mathematician*!   (684. 80–685. 105)

Acknowledging him as a 'Brother' in art, the poet goes on to share his 'argument' with him (and with the audience) (685. 115–17, 126), while the Cook proceeds to organize an anti-masque out of the kitchen staff. The speech has a whiff of Jonson's growing contempt for Jones, but this is not overt.

By 1631, however, Jones's constructions had become the specific object of Jonson's angry irony in 'An Expostulation with Inigo Jones', one of several public verse salvos as the relationship between the two men deteriorated:

> . . . O showes! Showes! Mighty Showes!
> The Eloquence of Masques! What need of prose
> Or Verse, or Sense t'express Immortall you?
> You are ye Spectacles of State! Tis true
> Court Hieroglyphicks! & all Artes affoord
> In ye mere perspective of an Inch board!
> You aske noe more then certeyne politique eyes,
> Eyes yt can pierce into ye Misteryes
> Of many Coulors! read them! & reveale
> Mythology there painted on slit deale!
> Oh, to make Boardes to speake! There is a taske
> Painting & Carpentry are the Soule of Masque . . .
>
> (Jonson 1925–52: viii. 403. 39–404. 50)

Jones's constructions threatened to communicate more effectively than Jonson's poetry ever could the values that a monarch like James expected to see emblematized in iconic form before him. Not to be outdone, and drawing on the semiotic precedents he himself had set in the earlier *Magnificent Entertainment*, Jonson had begun to employ geometrical and mathematical imagery throughout his masques as emblematic figurations of James's absolute power: the figures of Perfectio and Harmonia in *The Masque of Beauty* (1608), the former described as 'In her hand a *Compasse* of golde, drawing a *circle*', the latter wearing a 'robe painted full of *Figures*' (188. 221–7); the figures of Reason and Order in *Hymenæi* (1606), the former in '*garments* . . . *fill'd with* Arithmeticall *figures*' (214. 132–3), the latter dressed in 'Arithmeticall, *and* Geometricall *Figures* . . . *and in his hand a* Geometricall Staffe' (219. 275–7); or the 'bright *Faies*, and *Elves*' of *Oberon* (1611), ordered to dance towards James as their symbolic vanishing point:

> . . . tune your layes
> Unto his name: Then let your nimble feet
> Tread subtle circles, that may always meet

In point to him; and figures, to expresse
The grace of him, and his great empresse.[6]

As he had done in his collaboration with Dekker and Harrison, Jonson also turned to a domain in which he had an indisputable advantage over Jones: commercial publication. Print lent the masque a permanence and authority that it lacked in performance and allowed Jonson to assert control over the critical terms of its definition and reception. In short, he began to think 'volumetrically', to adapt a phrase of Michel Butor, using layout and typographical conventions to control the physical space of the page and to overwhelm the descriptions of Jones's scenes with a commentary that was every bit as virtuoso in its display, in this way making it seem as if Jones's scenes derived from his own erudition.[7] Against the stupefying effects of Jones's mechanical devices, Jonson substituted a superfluity of language in all its forms: passages of 'narration', or descriptive, denotative statements; verses in all metrical schemes and rhyme patterns; short songs; long exhortations and defences; detailed notes in Latin and Greek that filled the margins with geometrical regularity and buttressed the text with scholarly abbreviations and reference symbols. 'By this time, imagine the *Masquers* descended,' Jonson wrote in *Queens* (314. 710): as in the earlier *Magnificent Entertainment*, for Jonson the genuine mimetic act was occurring not on stage but before the mind's eye of the reader.

Jones, too, however, had begun to enjoy considerable success in his efforts to refashion his own professional field of activity, and with it his public identity: as early as 1606, contemporaries had begun to refer to him as the only genuine 'architect' in England, although the title testifies as much to the growing fashion for Italian theory among English readers as it does to any actual experience on Jones's part.[8] When, in 1610/11, Jones was named Surveyor of the Prince's Works and then in 1616 Surveyor of the King's Works, he had never attended university and had never built an actual building—a remarkable transformation for the son of a provincial clothworker, whose only previous professional employment was as

---

[6] 353. 360–4. Cf. *Blackness* (1605: 176. 236–7); *Hymenæi* (1606: 235. 747–50); *Love's Welcome at Bolsover* (1634: 813. 144–7).

[7] Butor (1964: 107, 116–17); cf. Genette (1969, 1982); Loewenstein (1991: 180–1; 2002*a*: 167–9, 176–81); Newton (1997, esp. 31–2); Murray (1987, esp. 64–93); McKenzie (1997).

[8] For the title 'architect', see the dedication to Jones by Edmund Bolton in 1606 cited by both Gotch (1928: 44) and Summerson (1966: 28–9), and discussed in Peacock (1995: 7–13); cf. the additional references cited by Gotch (1928: 53, 62, 68). In England the term had been applied to foreign builders or to men like John Shute, who had some knowledge of Italian works; see Summerson (1991: 52–7) and n. 33 below. On Jones's Palladianism, see Summerson (1966: 103–33); Orgel and Strong (1973: 29–47); E. Harris (1990); Tavernor (1991: 115–45); Wittkower (1974*b*); Peacock (1995); Cast (1993); and Gotch (1928). Wittkower (1971, 1974*a*) emphasizes the practical orientation of English architectural writing; cf. also Summerson (1991: 29–31, 34–6, 50–7); Girouard (1983); Salzman (1952: 1–29, esp. 1–11); Yates (1969); D. J. Gordon (1975: 90–6); Blunt (1940, esp. 48–57); Cerasano (1989), with specific reference to theatre design.

a court 'picture-maker', masque-maker, and occasional consultant in stage design.[9] A handful of wealthy, powerful, and high-status members of the building trades had long benefited from the professional freedoms that Jones now enjoyed.[10] But the primary difference between Jones and these professional builders was that the latter exercised no public claim to a *kind* of knowledge that was increasingly viewed as desirable by the 'building classes' of aristocracy and gentlemen. James Cleland's *The Institution of a Young Nobleman* (1608), for instance, would recommend to his readers only the

principles of Architecture: which I thinke necessarie also for a Gentleman to be knowne; not to work as a Maister Mason, but that he may be able in looking upon any building, both naturallie in respect of it self, and in respect of the eie, to tell what is *Frontispiece, Tympane, Cornishes, pedestals, Frizes*, what is the *Tuscane, Dorik, Ionik, Corinthian*, and *composed order* . . .[11]

'Not to work as a Maister Mason': words like these could only resonate harshly in the ears of Jonson, whose stepfather had been a bricklayer and who himself had apprenticed in the bricklayer's trade before departing on a career as an actor, playwright, and poet, only to return to the trade during 1598–9 as a full member of the Tylers' and Bricklayers' Company.[12] Jonson took as his personal emblem the 'broken compass', and contemporary tributes refer to his knowledge of masonry, geometry, and architecture, often drawing parallels between his early life as a bricklayer and his art in poetic composition, as A. W. Johnson has shown.[13] Several comments in *Discoveries* indicate Jonson's active interest in practical

---

[9] Jones may have apprenticed to a joiner in the 1580s and 1590s; he is named as 'picture maker' in 1603 by the Ambassador to Denmark, where he had been living at the request of Christian IV; see Summerson (1966: 15); Gotch (1928: 10, 26–7). By 1605 he may have made his first trip to Italy, since in the summer of that year he is referred to as 'one Mr. Jones, a great traveller' who consulted with the King's master carpenters and Comptroller of the Works on the building of a Serlian-style stage in Oxford for James's visit. Both the performance and the stage design were disliked, and the contemporary account of the occasion says that Jones 'performed very little to that which was expected' in spite of the fact that he had received a generous payment (Gotch 1928: 38). This was seven months after *Blackness*, his first masque at court. His earliest architectural drawings are from 1608, but Summerson calls them 'unrealizable in building terms' (1966: 27). He did not begin building until 1615–16; see Summerson (1966: 40; also 19, 25–9); Gotch (1928: 49). Wickham (1959–81; ii/2. 183–4) speculates that Jones worked in the tiring house of the public theatres in 1597.

[10] See Summerson (1991: 142–57), who suggests the term 'Artisan Mannerism' to describe the well-executed but generally derivative style characteristic of English building from 1615 until the mid-1670s; Alford and Barker (1968: 19, 27–9, 40–3); Girouard (1983); Salzman (1952: 30–67).

[11] Cited by Cast (1993: 181 n. 8) emphasis on 'principles' mine; cf. George Buck's description of London institutions appended to the 1615 edition of Stow's *Annals*, where the long-standing bias against the mechanical arts remains evident; ch. 45, p. 986), cited by Girouard (1983: 19).

[12] Riggs (1989: 9–10, 17, 20, 53–5, and 362 n. 5).

[13] See Riggs (1989: 205–6); for comparisons between bricklaying and poetry, see the anonymous lines cited in A. W. Johnson (1994: 1): 'Good lines, and brick and verse do well agree, | Jonson did famous grow for all the three'; and the elegy by John Taylor, the Water Poet, which calls the story of Jonson's upbringing 'A lying rumour' and casts his apprenticeship in the building trade as an enforced sabbatical from university, which Jonson never in fact attended; Jonson (1925–52: xi. 425. 153–426. 168), cited in A. W. Johnson (1994: 1).

modes of reasoning that were typical of the Roman rhetorical manuals as well as of the spatial arts in general, as we have seen in Chapters 2 and 3. 'I would bring my Precepts into practise,' Jonson writes at one point, directly echoing Quintilian. 'For rules are ever of lesse force, and valew, then experiments'.[14] Other passages treat of rhetorical style by comparing them to the practical arts of building or joinery:

The congruent, and harmonious fitting of parts in a sentence, hath almost the fastning, and force of knitting, and connexion: As in stones well squar'd, which will rise strong a great way without mortar. (623. 1976–80)

The next thing to the stature, is the figure and feature in Language: that is, whether it be round, and streight, which consists of short and succinct *Periods*, numerous, and polish'd; or square and firme, which is to have equall and strong parts, every where answerable, and weighed. The third is the skinne, and coat, which rests in the well-joyning, cementing, and coagmentation of words; when as it is smooth, gentle, and sweet; like a Table, upon which you may runne your finger without rubs, and your nayle cannot find a joynt. (626. 2061–70)

Identical analogies appear in several of the sixteenth-century humanists' favourite rhetorical authors. Dionysius of Halicarnassus, for instance—a contemporary of Vitruvius and for this reason a writer who may have been of particular interest to Jonson, as we shall see—compares the process of literary composition to the arts of building in an extensive passage that bears directly also on the problem of dramatic emplotment:

My view is that the science of composition has three functions. The first is that of observing the combinations which are naturally adapted to produce a beautiful and agreeable united effect; the second is that of perceiving how to improve the harmonious appearance of the whole by fashioning properly the several parts which we intend to fit together; the third is that of perceiving what is required in the way of modification of the material—I mean abridgment, expansion and transformation—and of carrying out such changes in a manner appropriate to the end in view. The effect of each of these processes I will explain more clearly by means of illustrations drawn from industrial arts familiar to all—house-building, ship-building, and the like. When a builder has provided himself with the material from which he intends to construct a house—stones, timbers, tiling, and all the rest—he then puts together the structure from these, studying the following three things: what stone, timber and brick can be united with what other stone, timber and brick; next, how each piece of the material that is being so united should be set, and on which of its faces; thirdly, if anything fits badly, how that particular thing can be chipped and trimmed and made to fit exactly. And the shipwright proceeds in just the same way. A like course should, I affirm, be followed by those who are to succeed in literary composition. (chapter 6)

The passage, as well as similar ones in Cicero and Quintilian, is a likely source for Puttenham's comparison between the arrangement of poetic verses by the poet

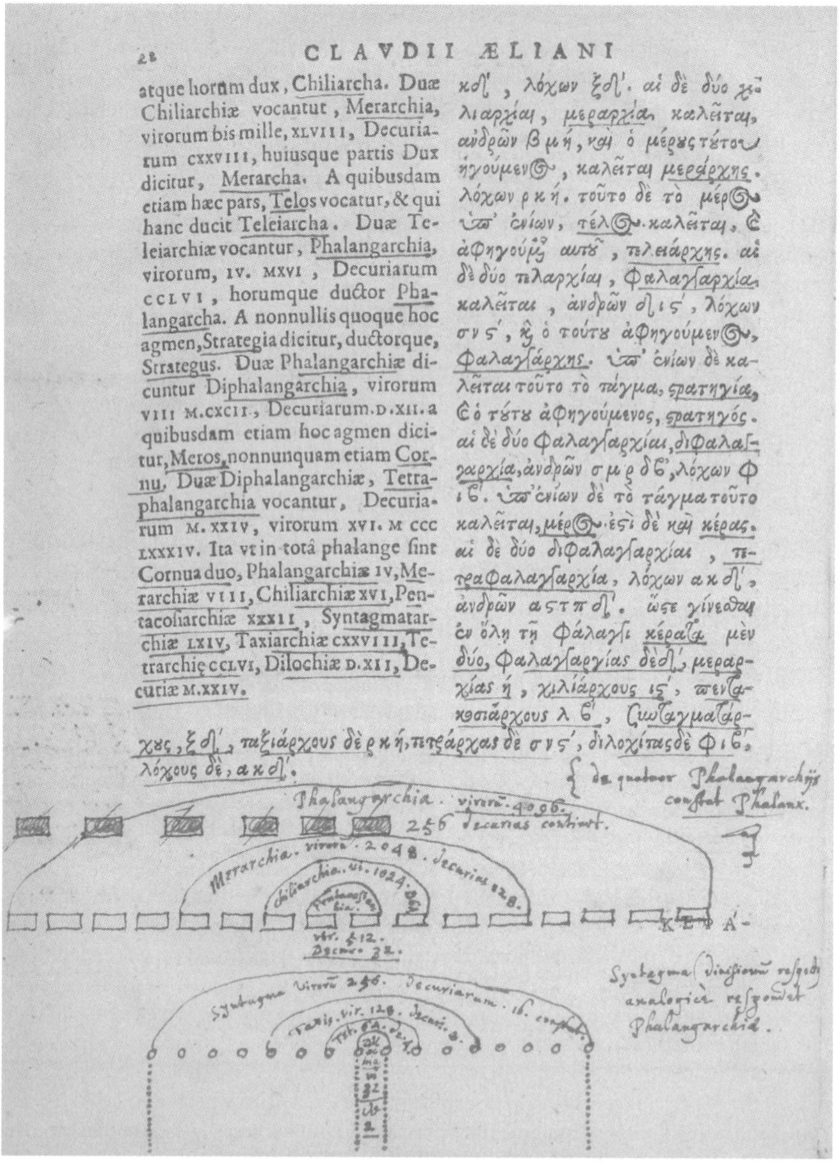

CLAVDII ÆLIANI

atque horum dux, Chiliarcha. Duæ Chiliarchiæ vocantut, Merarchia, virorum bis mille, XLVIII, Decuriarum CXXVIII, huiusque partis Dux dicitur, Merarcha. A quibusdam etiam hæc pars, Telos vocatur, & qui hanc ducit Teleiarcha. Duæ Teleiarchiæ vocantur, Phalangarchia, virorum, IV. MXVI, Decuriarum CCLVI, horumque ductor Phalangarcha. A nonnullis quoque hoc agmen, Strategia dicitur, ductorque, Strategus. Duæ Phalangarchiæ dicuntur Diphalangarchia, virorum VIII M.CXCII, Decuriarum D.XII. a quibusdam etiam hoc agmen dicitur, Meros, nonnunquam etiam Cornu, Duæ Diphalangarchiæ, Tetraphalangarchia vocantur, Decuriarum M. XXIV, virorum XVI. M CCC LXXXIV. Ita vt in tota phalange sint Cornua duo, Phalangarchiæ IV, Merarchiæ VIII, Chiliarchiæ XVI, Pentacosiarchiæ XXXII, Syntagmatarchiæ LXIV, Taxiarchiæ CXXVIII, Tetrarchiæ CCLVI, Dilochiæ D.XII, Decuriæ M.XXIV.

FIG. 8.1. Jonson's glosses and sketches: Aelianus, *Tactica* (1613)

and the use of 'bands' by the mason to erect a wall, which Jonson owned and seems to echo in his own comments.[15]

Jonson's own intellectual interests ranged beyond grammar, rhetoric, or philosophy to include books of practical geometry, and in this constellation he is much like Gabriel Harvey before him: he owned Leonard Digges's *A Geometrical Practical Treatize named Pantometria* (1591) and Edmund Gunter's *The Description and Use of his Majesties Dials in White-Hall Garden* (1624), both of which had been given to him by their authors, as well as Billingsley's translation of Euclid's *Elements*, with Dee's famous 'Mathematicall Preface' (1570).[16] Jonson would later live at Gresham College for a brief period in 1623, during Gunter's tenure, where he certainly would have become familiar with the programme of mathematical instruction that was undertaken there by mathematical practitioners such as Thomas Hood, William Gilbert, and others.[17] He even annotated Digges's work with cross-references to Jean Errard's *Les Neuf Premiers Livres des* Elemens *D'Euclide* (Paris, 1605), a practice he followed also in his edition of Aelianus' *Tactica* (Leiden, 1613), cross-referencing it independently to his edition of Euclid while adding comments on proportion and detailed sketches of the units of military formations arranged in a symmetrical, spatial form (Fig. 8.1).[18]

And yet to judge by Jonson's sharp attacks on Jones in 'An Expostulation' and elsewhere, he did not hold the mechanical arts in high opinion: they were mere 'shop-philosophy' fit only for 'Whirling his Whymseys' and a 'puppet-play'.[19] Contemporary criticism of Jonson even made explicit the connection between his background as a bricklayer and his technique as a playwright, as in Alexander Gill's 'Uppon Ben Jonsons Magnettick Ladye', a late play that the public had not liked:

> Butt to advise thee, Ben, in this strict Age
> A Brickehill's fitter for the[e] then A stage;

---

[15] Cf. *De Orat.* II. 79. 320, II. 80. 325; *Inst. Orat.* VII, proem 1. On Jonson's style in general, see Trimpi (1962) and Barish (1967); also Reiss (1997: 114, 118), on similar analogies in Sebillet's *Art Poétique François* (1573).

[16] McPherson (1974: 39–40, 43, 48–9), where Jonson's copy of Billingsley's Euclid appears as no. 59, his copy of Digges as no. 49, and his copy of Gunter as no. 73.

[17] He is recorded as '*Benjamin Johnson* of Gresham Colledge in London gent. aged 50 yeares & upwarde' in a sworn deposition of 20 October 1623 pertaining to a lawsuit between the widow of Sir Walter Ralegh and a prominent London jeweller; it seems unlikely, however, that he lectured at the college, as Herford and Simpson suggest; Jonson (1925–52: xi. 582–5).

[18] McPherson (1974, p. 23, no. 1; p. 13 (plate I)); on p. 40 McPherson corrects the comments by Herford and Simpson in Jonson (1925–52: xi. 597) regarding the annotations to Digges; see also A. W. Johnson (1994: 9–10); Evans (1995).

[19] Jonson (1925–52: viii. 405. 73–6). In addition to 'An Expostulation', Jonson's attitude towards the mechanical arts is most clearly presented in the other figures satirizing Jones: In-and-In Medlay in *A Tale of A Tub* (1633), Colonel Iniquo Vitruvius in *Love's Welcome at Bolsover* (1634), and Lantern Leatherhead in *Bartholomew Fair* (performed 1614, printed 1631). D. J. Gordon (1975) questions whether the last is an attack on Jones, but see the arguments by Herford and Simpson in Jonson (1925–52: i. 146–8). A similar sentiment is discernible in *The Fortunate Isles* (716. 268–78); cf. also an additional passage in *Discoveries*, where Jonson uses the term 'Ingineer' to describe spying and lying (Jonson 1925–52: viii. 604. 1341).

Thou better knowes a groundsell how to Laye
Then lay the plott or groundeworke of A playe,
And better canst erecte to Capp a Chimney
Then to Converse wth Clio, or Polihimny.
Fall then to worke, In thy old Age agen
Take upp thy Trugg and Trowell, gentle *Ben.*[20]

Gill's taunts suggest that the existing English vocabulary for problems of poetic form and structure may have been too closely rooted in the practical arts for Jonson's immediate purpose, since what he required in the quarrel with Jones was not simply to solve technical problems of structural composition but to defend poetry in polemical and philosophical terms, and to do so above all by *distinguishing* it from the mechanical arts, which he sought to portray as Jones's province.

Jonson was both scrupulous and competitive enough with Jones, however, to ensure that when he did include descriptions of Jones's scenes they would be as detailed and accurate as possible, and in keeping with his penchant for erudite display we may suspect that he used these occasions to parade his own mastery of classical design vocabulary as much as to give credit to Jones's ingenuity. A. W. Johnson has demonstrated that Jonson owned two sixteenth-century editions of Vitruvius' *De Architectura*—Daniele Barbaro's 1567 edition and commentary, as well as the 1586 edition and commentary by Guillaume Philander— both of which he read closely for their technical terms and annotated heavily with their English equivalents (Fig. 8.2).[21] Johnson has demonstrated how influential Vitruvius' work was to be on Jonson's masques for the court. I would now like to suggest how Jonson's reading of Vitruvius was also of particular significance to his development as a playwright working in the public theatres, since the text suggested to Jonson how mimetic techniques derived from building, surveying, and engineering could be used in the service of dramatic composition, even as it provided him with a model for how these practical techniques could be enfolded within an impeccable classical account of spatial structure, and one derived, more-over, from a literary tradition with which he was intimately acquainted: classical rhetoric.

---

[20] Jonson (1925–52: xi. 348. 51–8; also 347. 15–18); also the second part of *The Returne from Parnassus* (1606), under the heading '*Benjamin Johnson*': '*Iudicio.* The wittiest fellow of a Bricklayer in England. | *Ingenioso.* A meere Empyrick, one that getts what he hath by observation, and makes onely nature privy to what he endites, so slow an Inventor, that he were better betake himselfe to his old trade of Bricklaying, a bould whorson, as confident now in making of a booke, as he was in times past in laying of a brick' (Jonson 1925–52: xi. 364. 1–6), cited in A. W. Johnson (1994: 2 n. 2) and Newton (1997: 23, 27).

[21] A. W. Johnson (1994: 10–17) has reproduced all the pages with Jonson's annotations as plates 1–7. My argument in his chapter owes a significant debt to the evidence gathered by Johnson; see also Newton (1997), a study of geometrical ideas in Jonson's ideas of dramatic structure; Paster (1974), a discussion of Jonson's attitude towards architecture and his interest in its ethical claims; J. S. Peters (2000: 185–200), on the way architectural and scenic design influenced conceptions of theatrical space during the period, with much additional evidence.

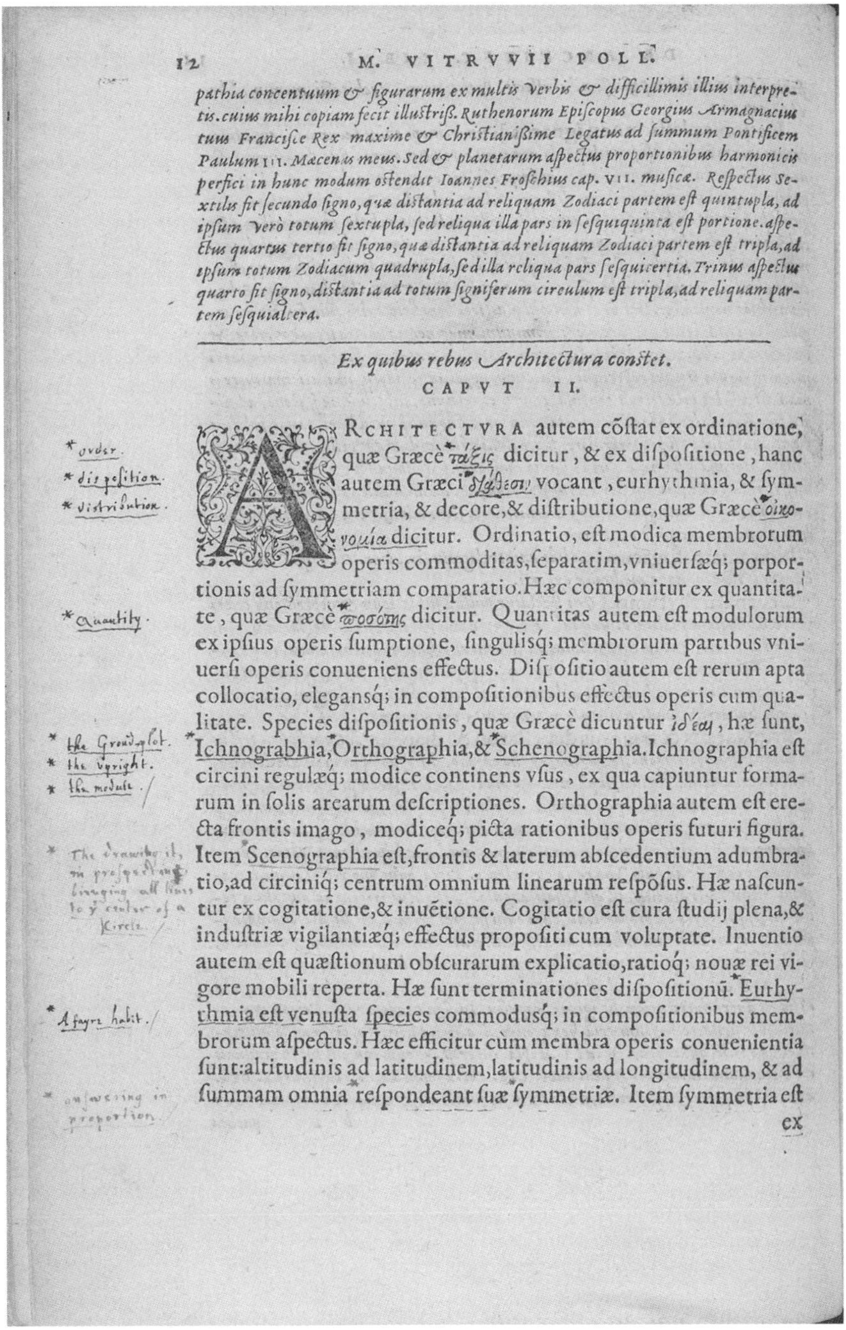

12 M. VITRVVII POLL.

pathia concentuum & figurarum ex multis Verbis & difficillimis illius interpre-
tis. cuius mihi copiam fecit illustriß. Ruthenorum Episcopus Georgius Armagniacus
tuus Francisce Rex maxime & Christianißime Legatus ad summum Pontificem
Paulum III. Mæcenas meus. Sed & planetarum aspectus proportionibus harmonicis
perfici in hunc modum ostendit Ioannes Froschius cap. VII. musica. Respectus Se-
xtilis fit secundo signo, quæ distantia ad reliquam Zodiaci partem est quintupla, ad
ipsum verò totum sextupla, sed reliqua illa pars in sesquiquinta est portione. aspe-
ctus quartus tertio fit signo, quæ distantia ad reliquam Zodiaci partem est tripla, ad
ipsum totum Zodiacum quadrupla, sed illa reliqua pars sesquitertia. Trinus aspectus
quarto fit signo, distantia ad totum signiferum circulum est tripla, ad reliquam par-
tem sesquialtera.

Ex quibus rebus Architectura constet.
CAPVT II.

ARCHITECTVRA autem côstat ex ordinatione, quæ Græcè τάξις dicitur, & ex dispositione, hanc autem Græci διάθεσιν vocant, eurhythmia, & symmetria, & decore,& distributione,quæ Græcè οικονομία dicitur. Ordinatio, est modica membrorum operis commoditas,separatim,vniuersæq; porportionis ad symmetriam comparatio.Hæc componitur ex quantitate, quæ Græcè ποσότης dicitur. Quantitas autem est modulorum ex ipsius operis sumptione, singulisq; membrorum partibus vniuersi operis conueniens effectus. Dispositio autem est rerum apta collocatio, elegansq; in compositionibus effectus operis cum qualitate. Species dispositionis, quæ Græcè dicuntur ιδέαι, hæ sunt, Ichnographia, Orthographia,& Schenographia.Ichnographia est circini regulæq; modice continens vsus, ex qua capiuntur formarum in solis arearum descriptiones. Orthographia autem est erecta frontis imago, modiceq; picta rationibus operis futuri figura. Item Scenographia est,frontis & laterum abscedentium adumbratio,ad circiniq; centrum omnium linearum respôsus. Hæ nascuntur ex cogitatione,& inuêtione. Cogitatio est cura studij plena,& industriæ vigilantiæq; effectus propositi cum voluptate. Inuentio autem est quæstionum obscurarum explicatio,ratioq; nouæ rei vigore mobili reperta. Hæ sunt terminationes dispositionû. Eurhythmia est venusta species commodusq; in compositionibus membrorum aspectus.Hæc efficitur cùm membra operis conuenientia sunt:altitudinis ad latitudinem,latitudinis ad longitudinem, & ad summam omnia respondeant suæ symmetriæ. Item symmetria est
ex

[marginal glosses in Jonson's hand:]
* order.
* disposition.
* distribution.
* Quantity.
* the Groundplot.
* the vpright.
* the module.
* The drawing it, in prospect, of bringing all lines to y center of a Circle.
* A fayre habit.
* answering in proportion.

FIG. 8.2. Jonson's glosses: Vitruvius, *De Architectura*, ed. Philander (1586)

The *De Architectura* opens with a preliminary discussion of the kinds of knowledge needed by the architect, and from the evidence of his annotations these are the passages that Jonson read most closely:

The architect's expertise is enhanced by many disciplines and various sorts of specialized knowledge; all the works executed using these other skills are evaluated by his seasoned judgment. This expertise is born both of practice (*fabrica*) and of reasoning (*ratiocinatione*). Practice is the constant, repeated exercise of the hands by which the work is brought to completion in whatever medium is required for the proposed design. Reasoning, however, demonstrates and explains the proportions of completed works skillfully and systematically (*sollertiae ac rationis*). (1. 1. 1)[22]

Fabrica, or the practice of building, might also describe the process of making typical of the workshop or trade;[23] *ratiocinatio* for Vitruvius is less a 'theory' or 'technology' (as Granger translates it) than a retrospective demonstration, or what we might call an 'enacted knowing': the ability to show or unfold the general principles behind a specific problem to someone else, and to do so with skill or cleverness, even deviousness.[24] This 'demonstration', or theory enacted and put to work, is furthermore defined by Vitruvius as a kind of semiotics; I have underlined the phrases that Jonson himself did:

In all things, but especially in architecture, there are two inherent categories: <u>the signified and the signifier</u> (*quod significatur & quod significat*). The signified is the proposed subject of discussion. That which signifies, however, is the demonstration set forth in systems of precepts (*demonstratio rationibus doctrinarum explicata*). <u>Thus we see that whoever puts himself forward as an architect should be practiced in both</u>. (1. 1. 3)[25]

Like Quintilian, Vitruvius also provided a model for a practical epistemology that sought its methods in many different fields, precisely the kind of lateral

[22] I cite from Jonson's copy of Philander's edition now in the D. M. S. Watson Library at the University of London, no. 200 in McPherson (1974: 97–8), unless otherwise noted; I have used the English translation of Vitruvius by Rowland, supplemented by that of Granger and occasional modifications of my own; passages are indicated by book, chapter, and paragraph.

[23] Cf. Fleury's commentary in Vitruvius (1990: 67), citing as a parallel usage Quintilian, *Inst. Orat.* II. 17. 10; cf. also Cicero, *De Natura Deorum* II. 13. 35 (comparing workmanship in painting and architecture [*fabrica*] to the work of nature); III. 22. 55 (*fabrica* as smithy); II. 60. 150 (the hand as tool); II. 47. 121 (where *fabrica* is equivalent to 'the structure of the limbs' of a body); also *De Divinatione* I. 51. 116 (where *fabrica* is equivalent to building materials). For Vitruvius' background, see Fleury's introduction to book 1, pp. ix–xvi, which dates the *De Architectura* to between 35 and 25 BCE (pp. xvi–xxiv). His comments on Vitruvius' professional position and the nature and audience of the work (pp. xxx–xxxvii) provide a good survey of recent scholarly opinion, following in general the thesis proposed by Gros (1994); cf. also Rowland and Howe in Vitruvius (1999: 2–3, 13–18).

[24] Cf. Vitruvius (1990: 66–9), where Fleury notes that *sollertia* could be quite distinct from *ratio* and more similar to *ingenium*; also Cicero, *De Natura Deorum* II. 48. 123 ('craft or cunning') and I. 33. 92 ('so that no art can imitate the cunning of nature'), and *De Officiis* I. 10. 33 ('sharp practice' or 'subtlety').

[25] Vitruvius (1990: 69–70), where Fleury translates *quod significatur* as 'the project about which we speak', i.e. the building, and *quod significat* as 'a presentation developed according to scientific methods', or 'the written explication that accompanies the work'.

intellectual movement that I have been arguing was typical of poetics, rhetoric, prudence, and geometry in the later sixteenth-century more generally:

To be educated (*litteratus*) he [the architect] must be an experienced draftsman (*peritus graphidos*), well versed in geometry, familiar with history (*historias*), a diligent student of philosophy, know music, have some acquaintance with medicine, understand the rulings of legal experts, and have a clear grasp of astronomy and the ways of the heavens . . . An architect should understand letters (*litteras*) so that he may strengthen his own memory by reading what has been written in the field. Next, he should have knowledge of draftsmanship (*graphidis*) so that he can more easily use illustrated examples at will to represent the appearance of the work he proposes. Geometry in turn offers many aids to architecture, and first among them, it hands down the technique of compass and rule (*euthygrammi & circini tradit usum*) which enables the on-site layout of the drawings of buildings as well as the placement of set-squares, levels, and lines (*normarumque et librationum et linearum*). Likewise, through knowledge of optics (*opticen*) light may be drawn directly from certain areas of the sky. Through arithmetic the expenses of building are totaled up and the principles of measurements are explained; difficult problems of symmetry may be solved through geometric principles and methods. (1. 1. 4)

Jonson has also carefully annotated the entire passage in the margin, translating '*opticen*' as 'perspective', writing 'in drawing' beside *peritus graphidos* and further down 'the rule and compass', 'straight lines, & levels', 'proportions mensurable', and other comments.[26] 'Architects who strove to obtain practical manual skills but lacked an education have never been able to achieve an influence equal to the quality of their exertions,' Vitruvius comments in 1. 1. 2, remarking later in the chapter that the error of the architect Pythias is that 'he fails to note that each individual art consists of two elements: the work itself and the reasoning behind the work; one of these is the particular property of those who are trained in an individual skill, namely, the execution of the work itself. The other (i.e. reasoning) is shared in common with every learned person.' And it is easy to see why Jonson went so far as to star the passage in his margin: Vitruvius here gave him the very ammunition Jonson needed to distance himself from builders like Harrison and Jones, with the further advantage that his arguments derived from an indisputable architectural authority.[27]

The opening paragraphs of book 1, ch. 2 in *De Architectura* are among the most theoretical in the treatise and present in a notoriously opaque and somewhat rapid fashion the fundamental principles of structural organization as Vitruvius

---

[26] Cf. Johnson (1994: 10–19). 1. 1. 17 is also heavily annotated, as are the passages pertaining to war-machines ('Slings. emissary engines for arrows. crossbows'), harmonic proportions used in the design of ancient theaters ('A fourth, A fifth, An Eight'), the mention of 'water-motions or musiques', the passages advising a knowledge of property law (writing 'draughts' (drains), 'water pipes' and 'Dropping of the eaves', 'Land-Lord & Tenant'), 'clocks, and dialls'.

[27] See also 1. 1. 12 (where Jonson underlines '*ad summum templum Architecturae*') and 13 (underlining '*agrammatus*', '*graphidos nonimperitus*', '*plastice non ignarus*' among other phrases); Johnson (1994: 18) draws a similar conclusion.

understood them. The chapters include one of the most extensively discussed passages in all sixteenth-century treatments of painting and theatre design, the definition of the three types of architectural drawings: *ichnographia, orthographia,* and *scenographia*. As we might expect, Jonson has read the passage carefully and has marked each term with a star in the text, to which he adds its English gloss in the margin. The entire passage runs as follows, in a modern translation; I have substituted Jonson's own marginal, English glosses in quotation marks and placed significant Latin terms in parentheses (Fig. 8.2):

Architecture consists of 'order' (*ordinatione*) which is called <u>*taxis*</u> in Greek, and of 'disposition' (*dispositione*)—the Greeks call this <u>*diathesis*</u>—and shapeliness (*eurhythmia*) and symmetry (*symmetria*) and correctness (*decor*) and 'distribution' (*distributione*) which is called <u>*oikonomia*</u> in Greek. 'Order' is the proportion to scale of the work's individual components taken separately, as well as their correspondence to an overall proportional scheme of symmetry. It is achieved through 'quantity' (*quantitate*), which in Greek is called <u>*posotēs*</u>. 'Quantity', in turn, is the establishment of modules (*modulorum*) taken from the elements of the work itself and the agreeable execution of the work as a whole on the basis of the elements' individual parts. Next 'disposition' (*dispositio*) is the apt placement of things (*rerum apta collocatio*), and the elegant effect obtained by their arrangement (*compositio*) according to the nature of the work. The species of 'disposition', which are called <u>*ideai*</u> in Greek, are these: 'groundplot' (*ichnographia*), 'upright' (*orthographia*), and 'module' (*scenographia*). 'Groundplot' is the skillful use, to scale, of compass and rule, by the means of which the on-site layout of the design is achieved. Next, 'upright' is a frontal image, one drawn to scale, rendered according to the layout for the future work. As for 'module', it is the shaded rendering of the front and 'the drawing it, in prospective, bringing all lines to the center of a circle'. These three arise from analysis and invention. Analysis (*cogitatio*) is devoted concern and vigilant attention to the pleasing execution of a design. Next, invention (*inuentio*) is the unraveling of obscure problems, arriving, through energetic flexibility, at a new set of principles. These are the terms for 'disposition' (*Hae sunt terminationes dispositionum*).[28]

I have interpolated Jonson's terminology above because it shows, first, how both Jonson and Vitruvius tended to think of built structure and *geometrical* systems of ordering in terms that were also used to describe syntactical and *verbal* structure in classical rhetoric. Louis Callebat has demonstrated how rhetoric provided Vitruvius not only with a model for the kind of treatise he sought to write—an educated synthesis and orderly presentation of technical questions—but also with basic vocabulary and conceptual categories. Rhetorical authors also sought to define the precise relationship between practical experience and rational precepts; 'like Vitruvian *ratiocinatio*,' Louis Callebat observes, 'rhetoric is an a posteriori theorization based on a reflection on words in action' (1994: 36). Both Vitruvius and Quintilian describe the relation between practice and demonstration in terms of signifier and signified; in defining rhetoric as an 'art', moreover, Quintilian

---

[28] Cf. Howe in Vitruvius (1999: 143–51); Fleury in Vitruvius (1990: 104–12).

compares it to other productive activities such as weaving, making clay vessels, and building (*fabrica*).²⁹ As we have seen in Chapter 7, *ordinatio, dispositio, distributio*, and *oeconomia* all pertained to the organization of written discourse, as did *compositio*, which Vitruvius uses elsewhere in his treatise to refer to architectural construction and which Alberti would extend to describe the arrangement of story elements (*historia*) within the picture plane.³⁰

But Jonson not only found a technical vocabulary in Vitruvius for ideas of structure and form that he would have recognized from a rhetorical tradition: he also translated these terms into English, and his glosses raise intriguing questions about how he understood the principles of architectural structure and how he might have extended them to his public drama. The translation of *ichnographia* as 'groundplot' was conventional; John Shute had used the same term in his *First and Chief Groundes of Architecture* (1563) and Jonson is possibly following his example directly, or that of Philander—whatever the immediate source, it is this technical term, ubiquitous throughout both the poetic and spatial arts, that is on the tip of Jonson's pen.³¹ 'Upright', too, is an unsurprising translation for *orthographia*. Somewhat more unusual, at least at first glance, is Jonson's gloss of *scenographia* as 'module', thereby linking it to the related discussion of quantity earlier in the same passage, 'the taking of modules (*modulorum*) from the parts of the work'. In Vitruvius the term *scenographia* clearly designates a kind of painting in perspective used as a backdrop (1.2. 2; 5. 6; 7, pref. 11), and as Vitruvius elaborates on the same page so Jonson adds a notation on 'prospective'. Through Barbaro's commentary *scenographia* had become closely related to the separate term *scena*, as Philander notes, which Vitruvius himself had used to designate not simply the wall behind the stage but the *entire* playing space in the ancient theatres, and which the commentaries came to restrict simply to the backstage wall, its various painted effects, and its mechanical devices.³² But Jonson is also using 'module' in the more conventional sense of a 'model', and here he certainly follows

²⁹ *Inst. Orat.* III. 5. 1; cited by Callebat (1994: 35); also II. 17. 3, 10, and II. 21. 14–23, and Ch. 2, above.

³⁰ Cf. Callebat (1994: 36–9); Baxandall (1971, esp. 130–5). Compare Vitruvius' use of *dispositio* and *ordo* to the pseudo-Ciceronian *Ad Herrenium*, for instance, written approximately seventy years before his work: '*Dispositio est ordo et distributio rerum, quae demonstrat quid quibus locis sit conlocandum*' ('Arrangement is the ordering and distribution of the matter, making clear the place to which each thing belongs'; I. 2. 3); cf. also *De Inventione* I. 7. 9; *De Oratore* II. 42. 181, II. 76. 307.

³¹ Shute's study was limited to the five orders and was expressly written as a practical, popularizing manual; it was the only work of architectural theory written by an Englishman to appear during the entire 16th century; see Summerson (1991: 53–4); Harris (1990: 418–22); Wittkower (1974a: 100); and n. 8, above. Philander's commentary also provides the usage: '*Ichnographia: Vestigium operas, quam platam formam, quasi planam formam dicas, mei Galli . . .*' (Vitruvius 1552: 13–14); here I cite from this edition of Philander's commentary, reprinted in the 1586 edition owned by Jonson.

³² See Wickham (1959–81, vol. i, p. xxxii (on 'scene' and 'scenery') and ii/1. 246–75); Campbell (1923); Klein and Zerner (1964); Kernodle (1994); Lemerle's introduction to Vitruvius (1552); Wiebenson, who observes that Philander's commentary was known by both Shute and Henry Wotton (1988: 70).

Philander, who observes that *scenographia* denotes neither elevation nor area but rather a 'model', 'the wooden form of the work that is about to be constructed' (*ligno formam futuri operis (modellum appellant) strueret*). This was done, Philander writes—in terms that are very similar to Shakespeare's *2 Henry IV*, as we have seen in Chapter 7—'so that errors may be detected and corrected in advance at the least expense and without any inconvenience' (*ita enim futura deprehenduntur errata, & minimo impendia, nulloq[ue] incommodo priusquam fiant, castigantur*); he compares it to the sculptor's making of a wax 'prototype' (*protypum*) and to the potter's clay model (*plastes creta proplasmata fingit*).[33]

Left the task of describing Jones's perspective backdrops and mechanisms at court, therefore, Jonson found in Vitruvius not only a vocabulary of classical orders and details but also several concepts and working methods that would be of first importance to his own work in the public theatre:

1. A classically derived distinction between theory and practice as two separate methods of coming to knowledge about problems of spatial structure; even more significantly, the distinction that was formulated as a problem of semiotics, or representation in language.

2. A lateral-moving, comparative approach to design that required knowledge of several fields, including language, drawing, theatre, narrative or *historia*, and geometry. On the authority of Vitruvius, geometry offered a particularly effective means of invention, or finding solutions to difficult problems in a clever or ingenious way, much the way Quintilian had argued, and much the way surveyors and other practitioners were encouraged to do in the sixteenth-century geometrical manuals, as we have seen in Chapter 2.

3. A definition of the 'scene' as a physical location in the theatre used for mimetic representation: the *scena* as playing space for the actor.

4. A definition of the 'scene' as a painted backdrop behind the stage, often in an iconic, geometrically derived, perspectival rendering: the *scena* as a particular *location* in the fiction of the play that might be used 'topographically' to structure the progression of the entire performance.

5. An approach to structure that allowed Jonson to imagine the *scena* as a quantitative *unit*—a 'module'—and to emphasize the formal relationship between those units, as well as between part and whole. In Vitruvius this concept of structure was presented by means of rhetorical and geometrical categories simultaneously: as a relationship of syntax or linear argumentative progression *and* as one of ratio and spatial proportion.

---

[33] Vitruvius (1552: 14–15). Thomas Blount's *Glossographia* (1656) defines *scenographia* as 'the model or draught of any work presented with its shadowes, according as the work itself shews, with its dimensions, according to the Rules of prospective' (cited by Wickham 1959–81, vol. i, p. xxxii); Cooper defines it as 'an adumbration or light description of the front and sides of an house, where the lines do answere to the compasse and center of every part'.

6. Projective techniques to be used in the process of composing an artfully arranged object: a method of representation—a 'scenography'—that isolated individual units, analysed their internal structure, and used them as 'models' for the entire work yet to come, so that structural problems could be anticipated and solutions devised. Wittkower has demonstrated in detail how Jones used a similar procedure in his drawings for royal building commissions;[34] so also the 'ground-platts' drawn by John Webb for Jones and Davenant's *Salmacida Spolia* (1640) provide a structural view of the masque scene by modelling its internal parts and the workings of its mechanics: the drawings make possible both analysis and diagnosis, as well explication or demonstration, i.e. they can be used for future revision or for adapting the mechanism to another occasion, as well as for indicating to others involved in the project, such as workmen or poets, how the scene is to be built or how it functions.[35]

It is impossible to know precisely *when* Jonson was reading Vitruvius, whose work can only have become more important to him as his collaboration with Jones on the masque became more involved. A. W. Johnson has convincingly argued that he did so sometime shortly after his work on *The Magnificent Entertainment* in 1604, which was already provoking him to think systematically about his art.[36] And the *De Architectura* was perfectly suited to address the conceptual problems Jonson faced: it crystallized a set of practical working methods by giving them an explicit vocabulary and associating them with a specific classical tradition, in this way redirecting them towards the more complex structures of his middle comedies even as his collaboration with Jones was becoming increasingly tense and constrained.

[34] Wittkower (1974*b*); a 1617 drawing for a new Star Chamber (never built) is called a 'modell or platforme' and labeled 'Modell' in Jones's hand on the reverse; cited by Gotch (1928: 94); cf. Thorpe (*c*.1600, esp. 53–4 and plate 17).

[35] Plates II and III in Reyher (1909, between 364–5, 370–1; discussed 359–60, 369–71); reproduced also in Orgel and Strong (1973: ii. 738–9, 740–1, with discussion on 736–7); Campbell (1923: 180–2, 189).

[36] Johnson (1994: 10–17), pointing out that the 1604 Quarto of Jonson's *Entertainment* describes the built structure of the arch as a 'pegme', an unusual usage that he traces to Francesco Colonna's *Hypnerotomachia Poliphili*, which had used hieroglyphics and triumphal arches in a similar way. The 1616 Folio substitutes the more self-consciously classical term 'scene' for the same arch, and Johnson takes this to indicate an encounter with Vitruvius sometime after 1604. Jonson could have known it as early as 1603, when he left London to live at the estate of Robert Cotton and enjoyed full access to his library (see Riggs 1989: 93); Palme (1959: 101–7) has suggested Vitruvius as the source for Jonson's structural vocabulary in the *Entertainment*. A self-consciously classical architectural vocabulary is evident throughout the scenic descriptions of many early masques, among them *Hymenaei* (performed January 1606, Q 1606), the *Masque of Blackness* (performed January 1605, Q 1608)—including a description of the '*Scene* . . . drawne, by the lines of *Prospective*' (171. 82–6)—and *The Masque of Beauty* (performed January 1608, Q 1608), which Jones did *not* design and in which Jonson included many elements derived from classical architecture. The term 'groundplat' appears in Jonson's description of the floating-island scene in the *Masque of Beauty*—'The ground-plat of the whole was a subtle indented *Maze*' (189. 241–2)—and this usage, too, provides circumstantial evidence that by 1608, at least, he was familiar with Vitruvius' text.

'OUR SCENE IS LONDON':
THE ALCHEMIST

The dedicatory letter to the Quarto edition of *Volpone*, dated 11 February 1607, furnishes the first clear indication that Jonson is considering the public stage from a restorative and purist standpoint typical of the antiquarian tendencies of Jones and his contemporaries. '*I have labour'd*', Jonson announces, '*to reduce, not onely the ancient formes, but manners of the* scene, *the easiness, the propriety, the innocence, and last the doctrine, which is the principall end of* poesie, *to informe men, in the best reason of living.*'[37] The stage poet must '*raise the despis'd head of* poetrie *againe, and stripping her out of those rotten and base rags, wherwith the Times have adulterated her form, restore her to her primitive habit, feature, and majesty*' (Jonson 1925–52: v. 21. 129–32); even more savagely, Jonson argues that '*the writers of these dayes are other things . . . not only their manners, but their natures are inverted; and nothing remayning with them of the dignitie of Poet, but the abused name, which every Scribe usurps: that now, especially in dramatick, or (as they terme it) stage-*poetrie, *nothing but ribaldry, profanation, blasphemy, all licence of offence to god, and man, is prac- tis'd*' (18. 32–8). As in *Every Man Out of His Humour*, Jonson associates a perceived erotic perversion not simply with other ideological heterodoxies but specifically with a mode of devious, practical intelligence that is particular to the *stage*: the anti-theatricalism of the passage has become more pronounced and more sexualized than in the earlier play and has become for Jonson a way of distancing his own compositions from the theatre and its practitioners. The emblematic satire of the early humours comedies, too, remains visible in the ani- mal conceit drawn from Horace, but in its intrigue the play is closer to Roman comedy than many of Jonson's other works, relying on rhetorical structures of argument, persuasion, verbal deceit, and even, in Act 4, an elaborate display of forensic oratory. The Prologue claims to observe the 'lawes of time, place, persons' (24. 31), and although Venice forms a generic background for the action, it remains structurally irrelevant to the actual development of individual scenes. Many of these are instead composed according to the much smaller-scale scenic modelling techniques that we have seen operating in Dekker's work; in each case, the scenic construction of the episode depends on a strategic use of the backstage wall and the apertures between the onstage and offstage space, and in each case the specific spatial disposition Jonson develops can be regarded as a working sketch or model for his later work.

In scenes 2. 2, 2. 3, and 2. 5, for instance, as Volpone and Mosca pose as mountebanks in the piazza, Jonson integrates the performance space of the stage into a mimetic episode that is *itself* an episode of performance, adaptation, and the

---

[37] Jonson (1925–52. v. 20. 104–9).

integration of existing spatial structures—here the placement of Celia's window on the wall above Volpone's makeshift stage—to suit Volpone's seduction plot. Over the course of the four scenes the window functions as a structural link to bridge 2. 4 (the retreat and further scheming of Volpone and Mosca) and join 2. 2, 2. 3, and 2. 5 to one another in a continuous plotted sequence. In 2. 5 the window then becomes the object of Celia's and Corvino's contrasting attempts to control its connotative significance, serving first as an index of Celia's somewhat naive innocence ('Alasse sir, be appeas'd! I could not thinke | My being at the windore should more, now | Move your impatience, then at other times'; 2. 5. 35–7) and then of Corvino's narrow, restrictive jealousy:

> First, I will have this bawdy light dam'd up;
> And, til't be done, some two, or three yards off,
> I'le chalke a line: o're which, if thou but chance
> To set thy desp'rate foot; more hell, more horror,
> More wilde, remorceless rage shall seize on thee,
> Then on a conjurer, that, had heedlesse left
> His circles safetie, ere his devill was laid.   (2. 5. 50–6)

As he multiplies the boundaries that would separate Celia from the world of public circulation, Corvino converts the space of the stage itself into a medium of confinement, a gesture completed by commanding her 'Away' (2. 5. 73) into the unrepresented space of the offstage area. In 1633 John Ford would adopt a similar structure in *The Broken Heart*, as the jealous Bassanes declares:

> I'll have that window next the street dammed up;
> It gives too full a prospect to temptation,
> And courts the gazer's eye, that sweats and travails,
> Plots, wakes, contrives, till the deformed bear-whelp
> Adultery be licked into the act,
> The very act. That light shall be dammed up;
> D'ee hear, sir?
> PHULAS. I do hear, my lord; a mason
> Shall be provided suddenly . . .
> BASSANES.   The city housewives, cunning in the traffic
> Of chamber-merchandise, set all at price
> By wholesale; yet they wipe their mouths and simper,
> Cull, kiss, and cry 'sweetheart,' and stroke the head
> Which they have branched; and all is well again.
> Dull clods of dirt, who dare not feel the rubs
> Stuck on their foreheads.   (2. 1. 129)

As with Corvino or Justiniano before him, Bassanes's glimpse of the city landscape produces a paranoid fantasy of sexual transgression in which he has always already been cuckolded; this fantasy in turn provokes his further withdrawal away from an inward-looking public gaze that is imagined to penetrate the interior of the house and drives him to avert his eye from the potential enticements of the window, which nevertheless continue to draw his look. This contradictory, twofold impulse can be resolved only by repressing his desire into a generalized jealousy and melancholia ('This house, methinks, stands somewhat too much inward; | It is too melancholy'; 2. 1. 103–4) and by sealing over the aperture, which becomes both psychic and generic: the possibility opened by the window is the possibility of other plots, of bawdy actions and cunning city wives, which Ford himself must foreclose in order to construct the tragic action of revenge and enforced marriage that is his play's subject.

Volpone also reflects Jonson's attempt to adapt the methods of scenographic composition to a five-act structure, such that the act assumes the same modelling function that an individual scene might also have. By using a linear method of staging to create five separate scenic episodes at the opening of the play, for instance, Jonson creates an 'act' in which first Volpone and Mosca, then Nano, Androgyno, and Castrone, and then Voltore, Corbaccio, and Corvino are brought onstage individually. The scenic breaks are marked performatively by the passage of each character out of the offstage space as they pass through the fictional 'door' to Volpone's inner chamber, and in this way the action of the episode assumes a built, *spatial* structure as well as the linear, temporal, and readerly structure implied by the use of the act division. Jonson is now working directly with scenographic methods very similar to those of Dekker and Webster's *Westward* and *Northward Hoe* or his own collaborative work on *Eastward Hoe*, and this is why his retrospective invocation of critical terms derived from the Roman tradition often seems forced and pedantic, if not inconsistent with the actual structure of his plays, as we have seen already in *Every Man Out of His Humour*. In the dedicatory letter to *Volpone*, indeed, Jonson finds it necessary to apologize for this very discrepancy:

And though my catastrophe *may, in the strict rigour of* comick *law, meet with censure, as turning back to my promise; I desire the learned, and charitable critick to have so much faith in me, to think it was done off* industrie. *For, with what ease I could have varied it, neerer his scale (but that I feare to boast my own faculty) I could here insert . . . I tooke the more liberty; though not without some lines of example, drawne even in the ancients themselves . . .* (Jonson 1925–52: v. 20. 109–18)

'Scale', 'lines of example drawn': even here the technical language of mapping and surveying intrudes to justify Jonson's actual compositional practice, and it suggests that when he examined classical drama as a model for dramatic *structure* rather than as a model for style or as a model for the didactic potential of comedy as a total genre, he tended to think of it as a graphic form, a schematic diagram in which a sequence of actions in time could be represented geometrically as a group of spatial relationships. And a remarkable woodcut from the 1496 Strasbourg edition of Terence's *Andria* indicates that this imaginative act of geometric projection was in fact a perfectly conventional way of representing Roman comedy in the period (see the frontispiece): the illustration positions characters in a receding landscape and links them with perfectly ruled, diagrammatic lines to delineate principles of interrelationship and the 'plot' of the play's total mimetic action.[38] Viewed in this light, as well as in light of Stephen Harrison's illustrations to *The Magnificent Entertainment*, as we have seen in Chapter 4, Jonson's use of the term 'scale' as a metaphor for critical judgement in the dedicatory letter to *Volpone* can hardly be *merely* metaphorical, since the relationship between act and scene as 'modules' (in both early-modern senses) is precisely one of scale and proportion: the basic structure of each opening scene and of the larger first act that contains them is identical, and the only difference consists in their size relative to one another.

By the time of *The Alchemist* of 1610, a similar scenographic technique has been used to give a performative structure to the *entire* action, which is now contained with the 'groundplat' of Lovewit's London house.[39] Because of its highly unified structure, *The Alchemist* is often regarded as the most neo-classical of Jonson's plays and is generally seen as fulfilling the promise of critical statements like those of *Volpone* or the Folio revision of *Every Man In His Humour*. But it is important to remember that these assessments are themselves the result of Jonson's efforts to redefine the categories by which the structure of the dramatic work might be discussed and evaluated, in part by subordinating representational techniques that derived from the practical arts to a neo-Aristotelian literary theory. In 1610, however, Jonson's turn to Aristotle had not yet taken place, and the complexity of *The Alchemist* lies in the way that Jonson undertakes an examination of several different practical epistemologies of his period—alchemy, astrology, early industrial 'projects', applied mathematics—and compares them directly to the arts of the theatre. In this sense, the play is nothing less than an examination *through* performance of the many operative and quasi-empirical modes of knowledge that flourished prior to the 'new science' of the seventeenth century: of their methods and aims; of their instrumentality, or their claims to transform self, nature, and society; of their seemingly miraculous productive and generative power; and of the different forms of wealth and status that they promised.

For Jonson, the theatre is not only continuous with these many practical epistemologies but serves as their most spectacular manifestation, since its mimetic conventions allowed him to examine their fundamental presuppositions and to expose their reliance on credulity and the suspension of disbelief, on

---

[38] Doran (1954) also includes the woodcut as the frontispiece to her book, discussing it on pp. 174–6; Peters (2000: 181–5, 192–3) discusses similar images in other editions of Terence.

[39] Herford and Simpson (Jonson 1925–52: ix. 223) locate the first performance at the Globe, but the play was almost certainly also performed at the Blackfriars (cf. Gurr 1992: 233); in September 1610 the King's Men took the play to Oxford; in 1612–13, in 1623, and in 1631 it was revived at court. On the structure of the play see especially Salinger (1986: 153–74); Smallwood (1981); Watson (1986); Crane (2002, esp. 179–84); Barton (1984: 136–53); Gibbons (1996: 34–5); and Donaldson (1977, esp. 66–88, 89–105), the only critic to link the unified setting of *The Alchemist* to Jonson's translations of Heinsius (as I discuss below) and his background as a bricklayer, although without noting Jonson's interest in the spatial arts more broadly. W. West (2002: 179–92) has argued that the play should be understood as a knowledge-*producing* performance in the tradition of European encyclopedic thinking, also emphasizing the practical and prudential aspects of Jonson's work.

'devices' and 'inventions', on gimmicks and disguise, and on persuasion, wit, and quick thinking. The play offers a parade of mirror reflections and hyperbolic distortions, the characters, sites, and modes of knowledge that gathered in the cracks and fissures of contemporary urban life as its negative image: bodies, objects, identities, social groups, and illegitimate modes of production that a triumphalist document such as *The Magnificent Entertainment* or the many maps and views of London were precisely designed to efface. By attempting to convert 'theatre' into *drama*—into a theoretically coherent tradition of genres and principles that may serve as an enduring repository for moral authority—Jonson is also attempting to convert, sublate, refine, or 'translate' the negativity of the images he creates into a source for critical judgement, self-differentiation, and self-cohesion. In *The Alchemist*, Jonson's subject matter is often matter as such—substantive thingness— or, to be more precise, the *limits* of matter: of what persists or remains of matter as it undergoes a process of physical transformation and sublimation—into gold, for instance, or into signifier.

Much of the spurious knowledge that Subtle professes depends on quasi-geo-metrical methods of reasoning, as when he promises Kastril '*Mathematicall* demonstrations | Touching the Art of quarrells' (2. 6. 67–8):

FAC.   Sir, for the *Duello*,
　　The Doctor, I assure you, shall inform you
　　To the least shadow of a hair; and shew you,
　　An instrument he has, of his owne making,
　　Where-with, no sooner shall you make report
　　Of any quarrell, but he will take the height on't
　　Most instantly; and tell in what degree,
　　Of saf'ty it lies in, or mortalityie.
　　And, how it may be borne, whether in a *right line*,
　　Or a *halfe-circle*; or may, else, be cast
　　Into an *angle blunt*, if not *acute:*
　　All this he will demonstrate. And then, rules,
　　To give, and take the lie, by.
KAS.   How? to take it?
FAC.   Yes, in *oblique*, hee'll shew you; or in *circle:*
　　But never in *diameter*. The whole towne
　　Studie his *theoremes*, and dispute them, ordinarily,
　　At the eating *Academies*.   (3. 4. 25–41)

The passage overtly satirizes institutions like Gresham College or Sir Humphrey Gilbert's 'Academy' for gentlemen, as well as independent 'mathematical lecturers' like Thomas Hood and practitioners like William Bedwell and Dee, an obvious figure for Subtle throughout the play. Jonson certainly has Dee in mind when Drugger arrives with 'the plot' for his new shop, to know

　　　　　　by art, sir, of your worship,
　Which way I should make my dore, by *necromancie*.

And, where my shelves. And, which should be for boxes.
And, which for pots (1. 3. 9–13)

or when he returns to seek a 'device' (2. 6. 14) for his shop sign:

He first shall have a bell, that's ABEL;
And, by it, standing one, whose name is DEE,
In a rugg gowne; there's *D.* and *Rug*, that's DRUG;
And, right anenst him, a Dog snarling *Er*;
There's DRUGGER, ABEL DRUGGER. That's his signe.
And here's now *mysterie*, and *hieroglyphick!*   (2. 6. 19–24)

The phrasing suggests an oblique dig at Jones and his 'shop-Philosophy', as well as a playful satire of Jonson's own emblems and the iconic semiotic conventions upon which they depended. Subtle also employs 'perspective' to create a viewing device for Kastril, in which the entire urban market for consumer goods will be grasped in an instant:

He'll shew a perspective, where on one side
You shall behold the faces, and the persons
Of all sufficient yong heires, in towne,
Whose bonds are currant for commoditie;
On th'other side, the marchants formes, and others,
That, without help of any second broker,
(Who would expect a share) will trust such parcels:
In the third square, the verie street, and signe
Where the commoditie dwels, and do's but wait
To be deliver'd, be it pepper, sope,
Hops, or tabacco, oat-meale, woad, or cheeses.
All which you may so handle, to enjoy,
To your owne use, and never stand oblig'd.   (3. 4. 87–99)

The device deploys the techniques of surveying to create a virtual inventory of all the commodities in London, representing not only individual objects but the devious schemes employed by unscrupulous merchants and moneylenders such as Middleton's Quomodo in *Michaelmas Term* to defraud young gentlemen of their inheritance, and in this way granting Kastril the power to intervene in the process at any point.

The passage is one of many in which Jonson examines the different modes of production and surplus extraction that flourished during his period, *before* a fully capitalized market had extended to saturate every corner and encompass every transaction.[40] In a similar way, the very first scene sets Subtle's alchemy, prostitution, and 'tricks | Of cosning with a hollow cole' (1. 1. 93–4) beside Lovewit's

---

[40] Cf. Knapp (2000: 585–94).

absence 'at his hop-yards' (1. 1. 184), a common proto-industrial project of the period that often required the surveying and draining of fenlands, as well as Doll's insistence on 'venter *tripartite*' (1. 1. 135) and 'commune worke' (1. 1. 156), and Face's attempts to skim an income out of household tasks:

> I know, yo'were one, could keepe,
> The buttry-hatch still lock'd, and save the chippings,
> Sell the dole-beere to *aqua-vitæ*-men,
> The which, together with your *christ-masse* vailes,
> At *post and paire*, your letting out of counters,
> Made you a pretty stock, some twentie markes,
> And gave you credit, to converse with cob-webs,
> Here, since your mistris death hath broke up house.   (1. 1. 51–8)

The passage is only one of several to fixate on leftovers and remainders: on a value-less particulate matter that Face nevertheless manages to *accumulate* and convert into a money form that he can then use to effectuate further purchases, exchanges, substitutions, and transformations, from object to coin and back to object again, much the way Face and Subtle have devised the entire fiction of 'projection' as a means of accumulating wealth for themselves.

Each field of knowledge that Jonson holds up to satire is a form of anti-*poiēsis* that promises to remake the world in the pursuit of 'profit and pleasure' that is more hedonist than Horatian. Flushed with the prospect of alchemical projection, Mammon dreams of 'a list of wives, and concubines | Equall with SOLOMAN' (2. 2. 35–6), of an 'oval roome'

> Fill'd with such pictures, as TIBERIUS tooke
> From ELEPHANTIS: and dull ARETINE
> But coldly imitated. Then, my glasses,
> Cut in more subtill angles, to disperse,
> And multiply the figures, as I walke
> Naked betweene my *succubæ*. My mists
> I'le have of perfume, vapor'd 'bout the roome,
> To loose our selves in; and my baths, like pits
> To fall into: from whence, we will come forth,
> And rowle us drie in gossamour, and roses.   (2. 2. 42–52)

For Mammon the process of projection is equivalent to the process of desire itself; it promises not simply a sublime moment of gratification but the power to multiply objects and desires '*ad infinitum*' (2. 1. 41), collapsing all taxonomies by gathering the most heterogeneous kinds of objects and reordering them through the solipsistic operation of his fantasy:

> My meat, shall all come in, in *Indian* shells,
> Dishes of agate, set in gold, and studded,
> With emeralds, saphyres, hiacynths, and rubies.
> The tongues of carpes, dormise, and camels heeles,

Boil'd i' the spirit of SOL, and dissolv'd pearle,
(APICIUS diet, 'gainst the *epilepsie*)
And I will eate these broaths, with spoones of amber,
Headed with diamant, and carbuncle.
My foot-boy shall eate phesants, calver'd salmons,
Knots, godwits, lamprey's: I my selfe will have
The beards of barbells, serv'd, in stead of sallades;
Oild mushromes; and the swelling unctuous paps
Of a fat pregnant sow, newly cut off,
Drest with an exquisite, and poynant sauce . . .   (2. 2. 72–85)

As Mammon revels in the sheer particularity and specificity of desire—in desire's simple power to invent and thus draw into consciousness an inexhaustible series of satisfactions, no matter how minute—we hear Jonson, too, revelling in the Midas-like capacity of dramatic language to nominate an infinitely detailed and absurdly differentiated reality.

Of course Mammon's desire remains unsatisfied, since the more particular he becomes, the more particular he must continue to become; his desire becomes a desire for particularity itself, which must be reiterated as a continued, performative assertion of the will through language and the act of naming: the conversion of things to nouns. A similar impulse is visible in the argument between Face and Subtle that opens the play:

Thou vermine, have I tane thee, out of dung,
So poore, so wretched, when no living thing
Would keepe thee companie, but a spider, or worse?
Rais'd thee from broomes, and dust, and watring pots?
Sublim'd thee, and *exalted* thee, and *fix'd* thee
I' the *third region*, called our *state of grace*?
Wrought thee to *spirit*, to *quintessence*, with paines
Would twise have won me the *philosophers worke*?
Put thee in words, and fashion? . . .
Slave, thou hadst had no name—   (1. 1. 64–81)

The quarrel between Face and Subtle articulates nothing less than Jonson's own statement on the methods of a dramatic mode that roots itself in a realism of locale, vernacular, and character—'Our scene is London', as the verse preface to the play announces—one that seeks to generate, out of the substance of this living world, a fictional world of surfaces and forms. The passage demonstrates a double attitude towards language as a signifying medium: with one gesture Jonson, like Bacon and later seventeenth-century language projectors, returns almost obsessively to the dream that language might actually be able to fully refer to matter: 'dung', 'broomes', 'dust', 'watring pots', 'cob-webs' (1. 1. 57), 'farts' (1. 1. 1), 'the heat of horse-dung' (1. 1. 84) Subtle's 'meale of steeme' eaten from 'cookes stalls at *pie-corner*' (1. 1. 25–6; cf. Fig. 6.5), the 'black, and melancholique wormes, | Like poulder-cornes, shot, at th'*artillerie yard*' (1. 1. 30–1) that pepper his complexion—each microscopic detail would seem to aim at a kind of degree-zero matter, 'fixing' it by designating it, naming it, and ushering it into representation. At the same time, however, the process produces not a mathematical realism of perfect reference but only metaphor—a catechrestic realism in which names can only refer silently to an insubstantiality that hovers behind the figure. This is not a vision of realism in a purely denotative mode but of realism as poetic alchemy: as a process by which matter is *converted into* language and an iconic sign that finally signifies nothing but its own insubstantiality and absence. This catechrestic realism, however improvised, temporary, and unstable, is finally Face and Subtle's finest invention: it is the 'art our writers | Us'd to obscure their art' (2. 3. 199–200), as Subtle argues to Ananias, a linguistic mode that *feigns* denotation and reference by directing our attention towards a mysterious process that eludes us by remaining perpetually offstage and out of view.

The quarrel between Face and Subtle that opens the play is only the first of its many meta-theatrical flourishes, establishing the place of action ('Your masters worships house, here, in the *friers*'; 1. 1. 17), a location that is also the location of the Blackfriars theatre, where the play was first performed; it narrates how Face brought Subtle out of the suburbs and gave him clothing and equipment, 'Advanc'd all your black arts; lent you, beside, | A house to practise in' (1. 1. 46–7). This spatial movement is presented as a change in shape, a physical transformation that creates an entirely new character: Subtle is a '*translated* suburb-Captayne' (1. 1. 19; my emphasis), a term that explicitly invokes the technical methods of the Revels Office but which also recalls the fears of contemporaries that the suburbs harboured nothing but 'Theeves, Cheaters, Cusoneres, Cutpurses, and such lyke', as warnings against the increase in new building advised:

here they are able to harbor themselves, without having their evil dealings espied, which they cannot do in any other part of the land . . . [and] there doth likewise resort hither certain people who beg about the City, and . . . go up and down as Egyptians, of which sort of people many do greivously abuse both themselves and their children in breaking their flesh and *changing the colors of their faces* to deceive the charitable minded givers.[41]

This 'changing the color' is precisely the 'translation' undergone by both Subtle and Face during the course of the play, particularly upon the return of Lovewit, master of the house, as Face prepares to enter 'into mine old shape againe, and meet him, | Of JEREMIE, the butler' (4. 7. 120–1), and we realize that it is impossible to determine whether he has been Jeremy acting as Face or Face acting as Jeremy all along.

The entire play asserts a basic homology between the process of alchemy and the process of dramatic poesy, since all the efforts of Face and Subtle finally produce only an endless stream of words and a wild variety of discourse: the slang of Surly the gamester and the curses of Kastril, the legal formulas of Dapper the

---

[41] BL, Lans. MS 169, fo. 131; my emphasis.

clerk, the astrological terms of Drugger the tobacconist and grocer, the alchemical language and pseudo-scholarship necessary to impress Sir Epicure Mammon, Surly, Ananias, and Tribulation Wholesome:

SUB. Can you *sublime*, and *dulcifie? calcine?*
　　Know you the *sapor pontick? sapor stiptick?*
　　Or, what is *homogene*, or *heterogene?*
ANA. I understand no *heathen* language, truely.
SUB. *Heathen*, you KNIPPER-DOLING? Is *Ars sacra*,
　　Or *Chrysopœia*, or *Spagirica*,
　　Or the *pamphysick*, or *panarchick* knowledge,
　　A *heathen* language?　　　　　　　　　　(2. 5. 9–16)

The process of 'projection' never occurs *except* as Subtle is able to describe it in language, of course, and since this language is finally always that of the playwright, Jonson is able to affirm poesy as the ultimate alchemical process whose 'projection' consists of nothing less than the production of further language, further imper-sonation, and further action, the desire for final sublimation being precisely what motivates the play and draws it forward.

But this homology between alchemy and dramatic poesy is also affirmed at the level of the play's form as a theatrical event, since 'projection' never involves *only* language but requires a constant hiding and withholding from view: it must be positioned offstage and can function only if other characters are tricked, partly through a referential linguistic mode and partly through a strategic use of the backstage wall during performance, to believe in its existence and potential. The purpose of Subtle and Face's many disguises is to create an entire physical environ-ment for each of the gulls who enter the house, a world peopled by the characters they impersonate and structured by the objects of desire they have promised. Subtle orders Face to 'Conduct [Dapper] forth, by the backe way' (1. 2. 163) as Drugger arrives, and is then tucked away into the 'privie' (3. 5. 78) to meet the Fairy Queen; Mammon is glimpsed through the window and is then addressed 'through the keyhole, the other knocking' (3. 5. 58), as the stage direction indicates; he is then ordered to remove Doll 'Into the laboratory. Some fitter place. | The garden, or great chamber above' (4. 1. 171–2). Each use of the backstage wall indicates the way Jonson has used techniques of scenic composition very similar to those that Dekker and Webster had employed, this time structuring the entire action, and not simply a single scene, around the distinction between onstage and offstage space. The scenes between Mammon and Doll make particularly evident the way the entire play depends upon a process of partial disclosure and withhold-ing, as a desired object is glimpsed momentarily but then removed into an imag-ined space of fulfilment that is projected backstage and outside of representation. Throughout the play, Face and Subtle exploit the desire of each character for access to the house's deepest interiors—Mammon's desire for Doll, Drugger's desire to see the Fairy Queen, the Brethren's desire to see projection, Surly's desire

to unmask Face and Subtle and to unveil the house's 'real' disposition—
and deflect that desire by suggesting a further interior that these characters can
never view.

With each change of scene the spectator's view has also been directed offstage to
the arrival of the next character: a glimpse through a window (1. 1. 180), 'through
the keyhole' (3. 5. 61), or through the door, designated in the play text by the
repeated stage directions for a knocking 'without' (1. 2. 162, 2. 4. 18, 3. 2. 159,
3. 3. 75). When Drugger arrives late in the play to meet the widow he hopes to
marry and Face sends him away to procure an appropriate disguise from the
'players', muttering that 'HIERONYMO'S old cloake, ruffe, and hat will serve'
(4. 7. 68–71), Drugger not only leaves the house but exits backstage into the tiring-
house of the theatre itself, where the disguise will be readily available. These
moments, along with the opening reference to the site of Lovewit's house 'here, in
the *friers*', demonstrate how Jonson has overlaid the imaginative world of the
play—its structure and physical location—on top of the actual stage and the
theatre building in which the performance is taking place; in this way, *the entire
play itself* becomes an icon, a diagrammatic representation of the historical neighbourhood in which the audience finds itself.

When the alchemical laboratory explodes 'offstage' without warning and the
action shifts suddenly to the surrounding neighbourhood, as each character
begins to converge upon the house unexpectedly, we realize that the structural
excellence of the play lies precisely in the way that Jonson has handled its offstage
space: in the way he has established a total coherence among every line of action
by leaving them to circulate *outside* the representational space of the first four acts,
only to bring them all together in a final confrontation. As Surly threatens to call
for 'officers, | And force the dore' (5. 3. 23–4) and Kastril vows to 'fetch the
scavenger, and the constable' (5. 3. 48), their convergence at the house reveals not
only the determinative impact of 'story' on 'plot' but also the importance of the
entire city and its history to theatrical form: the structures of neighbourhood hierarchy and order; of demographic influx (Lovewit is 'but newly come to town';
5. 5. 29); of patterns of property subdivision and of *rentier* culture ('let out my
house'; 5. 5. 33); of the requirements of plague regulations, and the potential
jurisdictional confusion caused by liberties such as Blackfriars in the systems of
City and Crown administration:

SUB.   You said he would not come,
   While there dyed one a weeke, within the liberties.
FAC.   No: 'twas within the walls.
SUB.   Was't so? Cry'you mercy:
   I thought the liberties . . .   (4. 7. 115–18)

Face is left with no recourse but to confess all and to encourage his master to join
the plot by stepping inside the house; no sooner has he done so than the frantic
action resumes, as Drugger cries out from within the privy and Face, Subtle, and

Doll scramble to inventory their takings, many of which have never appeared in the play at all and which seem to promise an infinity of devices and designs. In exchange for the disguise of the Spanish gentleman and the hand of the rich widow, Lovewit will open the door to the characters who clamber for entrance and resolve the plot by invoking his legal right to property ('Are you, sir, the owner?'; 5. 3. 13), using the authority it grants him to foreclose any rival account of the preceding action and thus any memory of emplotment as it has taken place.[42] Rather than offer his audience what every character, and particularly Mammon and Surly, have desired throughout the play—an explicit view behind the scenes—Jonson suddenly rotates the representational space so that what was once 'offstage' now simply fills in the onstage space and leaves a new, ob-scene remainder to be inferred behind the wall. As Mammon enters the house, he finds only the effect of the real and not the real itself, a litter of useless objects and the inscription of his desire scrawled for all to see:

LOV. The house is mine here, and the dores are open:
  If there be any such persons, as you seek for,
  Use your authoritie, search on o' god's name.
  I am but newly come to towne, and finding
  This tumult 'bout my door (to tell you true)
  It somewhat maz'd me; till my man, here, (fearing
  My more displeasure) told me [he] had done
  Somewhat an insolent part, let out my house
  (Belike, presuming on my knowne aversion
  From any aire o'the towne, while there was sicknesse)
  To a Doctor, and a Captaine: who, what they are,
  Or where they be, he knowes not.
MAM.   Are they gone?   They enter
LOV. You may goe in, and search, sir. Here, I find
  The emptie walls, worse then I left 'hem, smok'd,
  A few crack'd pots, and glasses, and a fornace,
  The seeling fill'd with *poesies* of the candle:
  And MADAME, with a *Dildo*, writ o' the walls.   (5. 5. 26–42)

Our final view of the house's interior is only a further gesture of emplotment that reveals nothing but the traces of 'projection' that the previous plot has left behind. The performative reversal demonstrates only how events may be retold and reconfigured in a thousand permutations and how the stuff of history may be 'translated' into a thousand forms, as Face helps Subtle and Doll 'over the wall, o' the back-side' (5. 4. 133) and they disappear offstage into the imaginary topography

---

[42] Cf. Watson (1986): 'Lovewit replaces the conspirators not because he is more socially ethical but because he is more theatrically self-conscious' (p. 362); Smallwood (1981); Ross (1988); Gurr (1999), on the Blackfriars neighbourhood and Lovewit's social type.

of the platform stage:

> . . . and all our goods aboord,
> East-ward for *Ratcliffe*, we will turne our course
> To *Brainford*, westward, if thou saist the word . . .   (5. 4. 75–7)

JONSON'S ARISTOTLE

Even as Jonson was working out an ideological stance towards dramatic language and theatrical performance in *The Alchemist* in 1610, his work at court was also prompting to search for a critical vocabulary that might rival the classical authority of Jones's 'design', that 'specious fyne Term of architects': a theoretical vocabulary that remained specific to poetic production, even exclusive to it, and one that could legitimize the idealizing attitude to poetics he was developing— what Joseph Loewenstein has described as a redefinition of 'the very ontology of the work of art'.[43] However popular Jones's 'Painting and Carpentry' might be, Jonson argued in 'An Expostulation' in 1631, they remained only glorified stage-props, mere attributes of the 'body' of the masque and distinct from its 'soul', or its informing, and properly poetic, fiction:

> Mr Surveyr, you yt first begann
> From thirty pound in pipkins, to ye Man
> you are; from them leapt forth an Architect,
> Able to talk of Euclide, and correct
> Both him & Archimede; damne Architas
> The noblest Ingenyre that ever was!
> Controll Ctesibius: overbearing us
> With mistooke Names out of Vitruvius!
> Drawne Aristotle on us! & thence showne
> How much Architectonice is your owne!
> Whether ye buylding of ye Stage or Scene!
> Or making of ye Propertyes it meane?
> Vizors or Anticks? or it comprehend
> Something your Surship doth not yet intend!
>
> .   .   .   .
>
> Whither? oh whither will this Tire-man growe?
> His name is Σκευοποιος we all knowe,
> The maker of ye Propertyes! in summe
> The Scene! the Engyne! but he now is come
> To be ye Musick Master! Fabler too!
> He is, or would be ye mayne Dominus doe
> All in ye Worke!
>
>   (Jonson 1925–52: viii. 402. 1–404. 65)

---

[43] Loewenstein (1985: 108; 2002*a*: 177).

Jones seems to have sought to elevate his own art by attributing to it the very ethical purpose—the *architectonikē*—that Sidney had already claimed for poetry, and to have done so on no less authority than that of Aristotle himself. To Jonson the claim must have seemed like a superlative arrogance, and he responded in kind, this time with a critique 'drawne' from the *Poetics*. There Aristotle had clearly stated that the work of the 'Tire-man,' or *skenopoion*—the visual aspects of the play, especially the costumes—were 'the least artistic element, the least integral to the art of poetry', and although he had granted the *skenopoion* authority over the poet as far as the spectacle itself was concerned (and here Jonson's allusion places him on shaky ground), nevertheless he clearly subordinated all the visual or material aspects of performance to the proper object of the poet: the imitation of the action. This was the *muthos, logos*, or *praxis*, the primary terms Aristotle had used to designate what he called 'the soul of tragedy' and the proper object of dramatic *poiēsis*.[44]

Like all of his contemporaries, Jonson's awareness of Aristotle is at second or even at third hand and takes the form of several long passages in *Discoveries* that he translated out of two seventeenth-century critics, Joannes Buchler's *Reformata Poeseos Institutio* (1633), a work that Jonson's editors describe as a 'poetical dictionary' or general reference work, and the Dutch humanist and critic Daniel Heinsius, whose *De Tragoediae Constitutione* (1611) offered not only a defence of tragedy but also a specific analysis of how a play might actually be composed.[45] On the basis of Jonson's exact wording, his marginal references to Heinsius' 1629 edition of Horace, and Heinsius' own revisions, Paul Sellin has firmly dated the *Discoveries* passages to some time after 1629, a date that fits exactly with the chronology of the Jones quarrel. Jonson has translated one long passage, which he begins by defining his terms:

Of the magnitude, and compase of any Fable, Epicke, or Dramatick.
To the resolving of this *Question*, wee must first agree in the definition of the Fable. The Fable is call'd the *Imitation* of one intire, and perfect Action; whose parts are so joyned, and knitt together, as nothing in the structure can be chang'd, or taken away, without impairing, or troubling the whole; of which there is a proportionable magnitude in the members. (645. 2680–7)

Now, that it should be one, and intire. One is considerable two waies: either, as it is only separate, and by it self: or as being compos'd of many parts, it beginnes to be one, as those parts grow, or are wrought together. That it should be one the first way alone, and by it self,

---

[44] See *Poetics* 1450[a]16–20, [b]20; Else (Aristotle 1957: 233–4 n. 44, 278).

[45] On Heinsius and Jonson, see Sellin (1968, esp. 147–63, with a checklist of his works); for a fuller discussion, also with bibliography, see Meter (1984, esp. 143–4, 23–33); also Becker-Cantarino (1978, esp. 143–53). In addition to editions of Horace's *Ars Poetica* (1610) and the *Poetics* (1611), Heinsius wrote two tragedies, edited Seneca (1611) and Terence (1618), and wrote commentaries on Horace's satires (1612). His 1611 edition of the *Poetics*, with *De Tragoedia Constitutione* appended, is available in facsimile; an English translation with introduction and notes has been edited by Sellin and McManmon.

no man that hath tasted letters ever would say, especially having required before a just Magnitude, and equall proportion of the parts in themselves. Neither of which can possibly bee, if the Action be single and separate, not compos'd of parts, which laid together in themselves, with an equall and fitting proportion, tend to the same end . . . (647. 2751–63)

For the whole, as it consisteth of parts; so without all the parts it is not the whole; and to make it absolute, is requir'd, not only the parts, but such parts as are true. For a part of the whole was true; which if you take away, you either change the whole, or it is not the whole. For, if it be such a part, as being present or absent, nothing concernes the whole, it cannot be call'd a part of the whole: and such are the *Episodes*, of which hereafter. (648. 2805–649. 2812)

The passages use purely abstract, quantitative categories derived from geometry and building to arrive at a structural understanding of the 'fable': to define it as a unitary thing, but, above all, to define it as a particular kind of unity, as a 'magnitude' or spatial unity that was distinct to geometry in the way that number formed the distinct unit of arithmetic. As in Vitruvius, this definition of unity and spatial structure is achieved by stating it as a dialectical relationship between part and whole, one in which the part is necessary to the whole and a single action considered whole in and of itself is dismissed as unthinkable. As a modular unit, the 'part' is itself understood both in temporal (an 'Episode') and spatial terms ('magnitude'), both in itself but above all in its combination with other partial units: the principle of combination that compares these units to one another and assembles them into a new, larger unity is the principle of proportion. Furthermore, the passage represents this principle of combination or assemblage a quasi-mechanical operation ('joyned', 'knitt', 'laid together'). Heinsius develops the mechanical aspect of his analogy in a passage that compares the planning of the dramatic action directly to the process of building:

As for example; if a man would build a house, he would first appoint a place to build it in, which he would define within certaine bounds: So in the Constitution of a *Poeme*, the Action is aym'd at by the *Poet*, which answers Place in a building; and that Action hath his largeness, compasse, and proportion. But, as a Court, or Kings Palace, requires other dimensions then a private house: So the *Epick* askes a magnitude, from other Poëms. Since, what is Place in the one, is Action in the other, the difference is in space. So that by this definition wee conclude the fable, to be the *imitation* of one perfect, and intire Action; as one perfect, and intire place is requir'd to a building. By perfect, wee understand that, to which nothing is wanting; as Place to the building, that is rais'd, and Action to the fable, that is form'd. It is perfect, perhaps, not for a Court, or Kings Palace, which requires a greater ground; but for the structure wee would raise. So the space of the Action, may not prove large enough for the *Epick Fable*, yet bee perfect for the *Dramatick*, and whole.

Whole, we call that, and perfect, which hath a *beginning*, a *mid'st*, and an *end*. So the place of any building may be whole, and intire, for that worke; though too little for a palace. As, to a *Tragedy* or a *Comedy*, the Action may be convenient, and perfect, that would not fit an *Epicke Poeme* in Magnitude. (645. 2686–646. 2711)

The analogy offers a loosely articulated theory of literary classification that depends on geometrical categories of size and dimension: epic poems are not just longer and differently structured than plays, but they are of greater magnitude— they literally extend further in space. The definition of different literary forms (epic, dramatic) as well as different literary genres (tragedy, comedy) depends on a principle of geometrical decorum: of accommodating the imagined spatial magnitude of the action properly to the formal mode in which it will be represented. The passage also recalls Serlio's distinction between the three generic theatrical scenes, the tragic, the comic, and the pastoral or satiric, which is in turn enfolded within a proto-theory of the unity of place, first asserted by Castelvetro in 1570 as a necessary corollary to the unity of time and action and advocated by both Sidney and Jonson on various occasions: place is not merely a 'site' or 'setting' for a build- ing but a fully informing structural principle that supersedes the category of time, like 'Action to the fable'. The final paragraph then converts a quintessentially Aristotelian definition of parts and linear progression in time—'a beginning, a mid'st, and an end'—into a geometrical, spatial dimension.

The most striking aspect of the passage, however, is its direct analogy between playwriting and surveying: just as the playwright must select, out of a series of possible events, meaningful units that are appropriate to the work at hand and then arrange or 'dispose' them to produce an action that has integrity and internal structure, so the surveyor must delimit a distinct area out of a larger spatial field and then dissect this area by drawing, in conformity to the limits he has described, a plan or 'groundplot' out of which he will generate the proportional units for the entire remaining edifice. Jonson has grasped the essential analogy of the passage and translated it into a specifically English term, for in the margin of the printed text, extending down the first six lines of Heinsius' definition of the fable, he has added: 'What the measure of a Fable is. The Fable, or Plott of a Poeme, defin'd' (645. 2680–5).

'The Fable, or Plott of a Poeme': Jonson's transcription gives us a glimpse of an emerging theory of playwriting: it is a theory of practice, in short, a way of gather- ing informal working procedures and formulating them into a tentative theoreti- cal statement. And there can be little doubt that Jonson finally turned to this particular passage in Heinsius because it provided irreproachable theoretical terms for what had become for him a coherent but largely unarticulated set of practical habits of composition, habits worked out during nearly thirty years of work on the pageants and masques and in the public theatres, as we have seen—the structure of *The Alchemist*, after all, conforms almost exactly to the spatial categories that Heinsius proposes, and yet the play was written at least a full year before the pub- lication of his treatise, and more than two decades before Jonson transcribed it.

But Heinsius himself, furthermore, has already modified Aristotelian doctrine with elaborate analogies taken from practical geometry, surveying, and building. The passage is simply reasserting, now through a partially digested Aristotelian critical theory, Hugh of St Victor's earlier link between the theatre and the spatial arts, as we have seen in the Introduction, above: it suggests that a fundamental shift towards the mechanical and mathematical systems of thought that would become one of the most significant epistemological developments in the seventeenth century—the enduring contribution of Galileo, Descartes, Kepler, and Newton—was also occurring in the field of early seventeenth-century literary discourse, and that this shift derived from the growing popularity and epistemological authority of the spatial arts in everyday early-modern life. Jonson's gloss indicates that the essential characteristic of the 'Fable' is a quantitative one, one that can be reduced to 'measure' and empty geometric form as much as to rhetorical, imaginative, inventive, or otherwise 'literary' qualities. The categories of mathematics are here asserted as equivalent to, even necessary to, the very idea of definition itself: to 'describe' or 'define' a thing will require the scientific categories of geometry and arithmetic, and this will be true even of an object as insubstantial and mercurial as an imaginary action.

References

PRIMARY (PLACE OF PUBLICATION IS LONDON UNLESS OTHERWISE NOTED.)

AGAS, RALPH (1596), *A Preparative to the Platting of Lands*.

ANON. (n.d.), British Library, Lansdowne MS 169, fos. 131–2, n.d., 'A briefe shewing the occasion of the increase of Buyldinge neere the Cytye of London'.

ANON. (*c.*1583), British Library, Harleian MS 3230, fos. 172–184ʳ, Commonplace book of arts curriculum subjects.

ANON. (*c.*1592), *Arden of Faversham*; repr. in Keith Sturgess (ed.), *Three Elizabethan Domestic Tragedies* (New York: Penguin Books, 1969), 55–148.

ANON. (1598–1601), *The Pilgrimage to Parnassus*; repr. in *The Three Parnassus Plays, 1598–1601*, ed. with introd. and comm. J. B. Leishman (London: Ivor Nicholson & Watson, 1949), 93–132.

ARISTOTLE (1926), *Nicomachean Ethics*, trans. H. Rackham, Loeb Classical Library (Cambridge, Mass.: Harvard University Press; rev. 1934; repr. 1994).

—— (1957), *Aristotle's Poetics: The Argument*, ed. and comm. Gerald F. Else (Cambridge, Mass.: Harvard University Press).

—— (1984), *The Complete Works of Aristotle*, ed. Jonathan Barnes, 2 vols. (Princeton: Princeton University Press).

ASCHAM, ROGER (1570), 'Imitatio', from *The Scholemaster*; repr. in Smith (ed.), *Elizabethan Critical Essays*, i. 1–45.

BACON, FRANCIS (1861), *The Works of Francis Bacon*, ed. James Spedding, Robert Leslie Ellis, and Douglas Denon Heath, 15 vols. (Boston: Brown & Taggard).

BEAUMONT, FRANCIS, AND JOHN FLETCHER (*c.*1608–*c.*1611), *The Maid's Tragedy*, ed. Howard B. Norland (Lincoln: University of Nebraska Press, 1968).

BEDWELL, WILLIAM (1635), *Via Regia ad Geometriam, The Way to Geometry . . . Written in Latine by Peter Ramus, and now Translated and much enlarged by the Learned Mr. William Bedwell*.

BILLINGSLEY, HENRY (trans.) (1570), *The Elements of geometrie of the most auncient philosopher Euclide of Megara*.

BLAGRAVE, JOHN (1585), *The Mathematical Jewel*.

BLUNDEVILLE, THOMAS (1589), *A brief description of universal mappes and cardes*.

—— (1594), *M. Blundeville His Exercises, containing six Treatises*.

—— (1599), *The Arte of Logicke*.

—— (1602), *The theoriques of the seven planets*.

BODLEIAN LIBRARY (1605), *The First Printed Catalogue of the Bodleian Library: A Facsimile* (Oxford: Clarendon Press, 1986).

BOURNE, WILLIAM (1578), *A Treasure for Traveilers*.

CASE, JOHN (1585), *Speculum Moralium Quaestionum* (Oxford).

—— (1596*a*), *Reflexus Speculi Moralis*, with *ABCedarium Moralis Philosophiae* (Oxford).

CASE, JOHN (1596*b*), *ABCedarium Moralis Philosophiae* (pub. with Case 1596*a*).

CICERO, MARCUS TULLIUS (1942), *De Oratore*, trans. E. W. Sutton, completed with introd. H. Rackham, Loeb Classical Library, 2 vols. (Cambridge, Mass.: Harvard University Press; repr. 1988).

—— (1947), *De Officiis*, trans. Walter Miller, Loeb Classical Library (Cambridge, Mass.: Harvard University Press; repr. 1956).

—— (1949), *De Inventione*, trans. H. M. Hubbell, Loeb Classical Library (Cambridge, Mass.: Harvard University Press).

COOPER, THOMAS (1578), *Thesaurus Linguae Romanae et Britannicae* (repr. Hildesheim: Georg Olms Verlag, 1975).

COTGRAVE, RANDLE (1611), *A Dictionarie of the French and English Tongues*.

COWLEY, ABRAHAM (1656), Preface to *Poems*; repr. in J. E. Spingarn (ed.), *Critical Essays of the Seventeenth Century*, ii. 77–90.

DEE, JOHN (1570), *The Mathematical Preface to the Elements of Euclid of Megara* (New York: History of Science Publications, 1975).

—— (1842), *The Private Diary of Dr. John Dee and the Catalogue of his Library of Manuscripts*, ed. James Orchard Halliwell, Camden Society, old ser., 19 (repr. New York: Johnson Reprint Corporation, 1968).

DEKKER, THOMAS (1953–61), *The Dramatic Works of Thomas Dekker*, ed. Fredson Bowers, 4 vols. (Cambridge: Cambridge University Press).

DESCARTES, RENÉ (1984–91), *The Philosophical Writings of Descartes*, trans. John Cottingham, Robert Stoothoff, and Dugald Murdoch, 3 vols. (Cambridge: Cambridge University Press).

DETHICK, HENRY [RAINOLDS, JOHN] (*c.*1572), *Oratio in Laudem Artis Poeticae*, ed. with introd. William Ringler (Princeton: Princeton University Press, 1940).

DIGGES, LEONARD (1554), *A Booke Named Tectonicon*.

—— (1555), *A Prognostication of right good effect*.

—— (1571), *A Geometrical Practise, named Pantometria*.

DIONYSIUS OF HALICARNASSUS (1910), *On Literary Composition*, ed. and trans. W. Rhys Roberts, with introd., notes, glossary, appendices (London: Macmillan; repr. New York: AMS Press, 1976).

DONATUS, AELIUS (1962), *Aeli Donati commentum Terentii*, 3 vols., ed. Paul Wessner (Stuttgart: Teubner).

ELYOT, SIR THOMAS (1531), *The Boke Named The Gouernour*, ed. Henry Herbert Stephen Croft, 2 vols. (London: 1883; repr. New York: Burt Franklin, 1967).

—— (1538), *The Dictionary of Syr Thomas Eliot, Knyght* (repr. Menston: Scolar Press, 1970).

FERRARIUS, JOANNES (1559), *A Woorke of Ioannes Ferrarius Montanus, touchynge the good orderynge of a common weale*, trans. William Bavande.

FEUILLERAT, ALBERT (ed.) (1908), *Documents Relating to the Office of the Revels in the Time of Queen Elizabeth*, with notes and indexes, in W. Bang (ed.), *Materialien Zur Kunde des älteren Englischen Dramas*, 22 (Louvain: A. Uystpruyst).

FORD, JOHN (1633), *The Broken Heart*, ed. Donald K. Anderson, Jr. (Lincoln: University of Nebraska Press, 1968).

FRAUNCE, ABRAHAM (1588), *The Lawiers Logike*.

FRONTINUS, SEXTUS JULIUS (1539), *The Strategemes, sleyghtes, and policies of warre*, trans. Richard Moryson.

GALILEO, GALILEI (1623), *The Assayer*, trans. Stillman Drake, in Drake (ed.), *The Controversy on the Comets of 1618* (Philadelphia: University of Pennsylvania Press, 1960).

GASCOIGNE, GEORGE (1575), *Certayne Notes of Instruction*; repr. in Smith (ed.), *Elizabethan Critical Essays*, i. 46–57.

GIBSON, STRICKLAND (ed.) (1931), *Statuta Antiqua Universitatis Oxoniensis* (Oxford: Clarendon Press).

GILBERT, HUMPHREY (1572), 'Queen Elizabethes Achademy', *Early English Text Society*, extra ser., 8 (1869), 1–12.

GREENE, ROBERT (1963), *Friar Bacon and Friar Bungay*, ed. Daniel Seltzer (Lincoln: University of Nebraska Press).

HARRISON, STEPHEN (1604), *The Arches of Triumph*.

HARVEY, GABRIEL (1579–80), 'Harvey–Spenser Correspondence'; repr. in Smith (ed.), *Elizabethan Critical Essays*, i. 87–122.

—— (1913), *Gabriel Harvey's Marginalia*, ed. G. C. Moore Smith (Stratford upon Avon: Shakespeare Head Press).

HEILAND, SAMUEL (1580), *Aristotelis Ethicorum ad Nicomachum libri decem*.

HEINSIUS, DANIEL (1611), *Aristoteles De Poetica liber . . . De Tragoedia constitutione* (Leiden; Facs. repr. Hildesheim: Georg Olms Verlag, 1976).

—— (1971), *On Plot in Tragedy*, trans. Paul R. Sellin and John J. McManmon, introd. and notes Paul R. Sellin (Northridge, Calif.: San Fernando Valley State College).

HENSLOWE, PHILIP (1961), *Diary*, ed. with suppl. material, introd., and notes R. A. Foakes and R. T. Rickert (Cambridge: Cambridge University Press).

—— (1977), *The Henslowe Papers*, 2 vols., ed. with introd. R. A. Foakes (London: Scolar Press).

HOBBES, THOMAS (1650), 'The Answer of Mr. Hobbes to Sr. Will. D'Avenant's Preface Before Gondibert'; repr. in J. E. Spingarn (ed.), *Critical Essays of the Seventeenth Century*, 3 vols. (Oxford: Oxford University Press, 1908), ii. 54–67.

—— (1651), *Leviathan*, ed. Edwin Curley (Indianapolis: Hackett, 1994).

HOOD, THOMAS (1590*a*), *A Copie of the Speache: Made by the Mathematicall Lecturer*; repr. in F. R. Johnson, 'Thomas Hood's Inaugural Address', 99–106.

—— (1590*b*), *The Use of the Celestial Globe in Plano, Set Foorth in Two Hemispheres*.

HOPTON, ARTHUR (1611), *Speculum Topographicum; or, The Topographicall Glasse*.

HORMAN, WILLIAM (1519), *Vulgaria*.

HOSKYNS, JOHN (*c.*1599), *Directions for Speech and Style*, ed. with introd. and notes Hoyt H. Hudson (Princeton: Princeton University Press, 1935).

HUARTE, JUAN (1594), *The Examination of Men's Wits*, trans. Richard Carew.

HUGH OF ST VICTOR (1961), *The Didascalicon of Hugh of St. Victor*, ed. and trans. Jerome Taylor (New York: Columbia University Press; repr. 1991).

JONSON, BEN (1925–52), *Works*, ed. C. H. Herford and Percy Simpson, 11 vols. (Oxford: Clarendon Press).

LAWTON, H. W. (1972), *Handbook of French Renaissance Dramatic Theory* (Westport, Conn.: Greenwood Press; first pub. Manchester: Manchester University Press, 1949).

LOENGARD, JANET SENDEROWITZ (1989), *London Viewers and their Certificates, 1508–1558*, London Record Society, 26 ([Bristol]: London Record Society).

MARLOWE, CHRISTOPHER (1587–8), *Tamburlaine the Great, Parts I and II*, ed. John D. Jump (Lincoln: University of Nebraska Press, 1967).

—— (c.1590), *The Jew of Malta*, ed. Richard W. Van Fossen (Lincoln: University of Nebraska Press, 1964).

MERES, FRANCIS (1598), *Palladis Tamia*; repr. in Smith (ed.), *Elizabethan Critical Essays*, ii. 308–24.

MIDDLETON, THOMAS (1604–6), *A Mad World, My Masters*, ed. Standish Henning (Lincoln: University of Nebraska Press, 1965).

MORE, RICHARD (1602), *The Carpenter's Rule*.

MOXON, JOSEPH (1683–4), *Mechanick Exercises on the Whole Art of Printing*, ed. Herbert Davis and Harry Carter (Oxford: Oxford University Press, 1958).

MULCASTER, RICHARD (1583), *Elementarie*.

NASHE, THOMAS (1904–8), *The Works of Thomas Nashe* (1956), ed. R. B. McKerrow, 5 vols. (London: A. H. Bullen).

NICHOLS, JOHN (1828), *The Progresses, Processions, and Magnificent Festivities, of King James the First*, 4 vols. (London: Society of Antiquaries).

NORDEN, JOHN (1618), *Surveiors Dialogue* (first pub. 1607).

NORMAN, ROBERT (1581), *The Newe Attractive*.

—— (1584), *The Safeguard of Sailors*.

NORWOOD, RICHARD (1631), *Trigonometrie; or, The Doctrine of Triangles*.

—— (1637), *The Sea-Man's Practice*.

PEACHAM, HENRY (1622), *The Compleat Gentleman*.

PEARS, STEUART A. (ed.) (1845), *The Correspondence of Sir Philip Sidney and Hubert Languet* (London: William Pickering).

PSEUDO-CICERO (1954), *Ad C. Herennium*, trans. Harry Caplan, Loeb Classical Library (Cambridge, Mass.: Harvard University Press; repr. 1989).

PUTTENHAM, GEORGE (1589), *The Arte of English Poesie*, ed. Edward Arber (n.p.: A. Constable, 1906; repr. [Kent, Ohio]: Kent State University Press, 1970).

—— (1904), *The Arte of English Poesie*; repr. in Smith (ed.), *Elizabethan Critical Essays*, ii. 1–193.

QUINTILIAN, MARCUS FABIUS (1921–2), *Institutio Oratoria*, trans. H. E. Butler, Loeb Classical Library, 4 vols. (Cambridge, Mass.: Harvard University Press, 1933–6).

RAINOLDS, JOHN (c.1570), *John Rainolds's Oxford Lectures on Aristotle's Rhetoric*, ed. and trans. with comm. Lawrence D. Green (Newark: University of Delaware Press; London: Associated University Presses, 1986).

RAMUS, PETER (1546), *Dialectici commentarii tres authore Audomaro Talon* (Paris).

—— (1574), *The Logike of the Most Excellent Philosopher*, trans. Roland MacIlmane.

—— (1636), *Via Regia ad Geometriam*.

RATHBORNE, AARON (1616), *The Surveyor in Four Books*.

RECORDE, ROBERT (1551), *The Pathway to Knowledge*.

—— (1556), *The Castle of Knowledge*.

ROBERTSON, JEAN, AND D. J. GORDON (eds.) (1954), *A Calendar of Dramatic Records in the Books of the Livery Companies of London, 1485–1640*, Malone Society Collections, iii (Oxford: for the Malone Society).

SERLIO, SEBASTIANO (1611), *The First Booke of Architecture, made by Sebastian Serly, entreating of Geometrie* (repr. New York: Dover Publications, 1982).

SETON, JOHN (1572), *Dialectica*, with comm. John Carter.

SHAKESPEARE, WILLIAM (1767–8), *Mr. William Shakespeare his Comedies, Histories and Tragedies*, ed. Edward Capell, 10 vols. (repr. New York: AMS, 1968).

—— (1997), *The Norton Shakespeare: Based on the Oxford Edition*, ed. Stephen Greenblatt, Walter Cohen, Jean E. Howard, and Katherine Eisaman Maus (New York: Norton).

SHUTE, JOHN (1563), *The First and Chief Groundes of Architecture.*

SIDNEY, SIR PHILIP (1904), *An Apologie for Poetrie*; repr. in Smith (ed.), *Elizabethan Critical Essays*, i. 148–207.

—— (1922–6), *The Complete Works of Sir Philip Sidney*, ed. Albert Feuillerat, 4 vols. (Cambridge: Cambridge University Press).

—— (1965), *An Apology for Poetry*, ed. Geoffrey Shepherd (London: Thomas Nelson & Sons).

—— (1973), *Miscellaneous Prose of Sir Philip Sidney*, ed. Katherine Duncan-Jones and Jan van Dorsten (Oxford: Clarendon Press).

SMITH, G. GREGORY (1904), *Elizabethan Critical Essays*, 2 vols. (Oxford: Oxford University Press).

SPENSER, EDMUND (1904), 'Spenser–Harvey Correspondence'; repr. in Smith (ed.), *Elizabethan Critical Essays*, i. 87–122.

SPRAT, THOMAS (1667), *History of the Royal Society*, facs. edn. with app. crit. Jackson I. Cope and Harold Whitmore Jones (St Louis: Washington University Studies, 1958).

TEMPLE, WILLIAM (1584), *P. Rami Dialecticae libri duo* (Cambridge).

TERENCE (2001), *Works*, ed. and trans. John Barsby, Loeb Classical Library, 2 vols. (Cambridge, Mass.: Harvard University Press).

THORPE, JOHN (*c*.1600), *The Book of Architecture of John Thorpe in Sir John Soane's Musuem*, ed. John Summerson (Glasgow: Robert Maclehose & Co. for the Walpole Society, 1966).

VITRUVIUS, MARCUS POLLIO (1552), *M. Vitruvii Pollionis De Architectura libri decem*, ed. Guillaume Philander (Lyons); repr. as facs. in *Les Annotations de Guillaume Philandrier Sur le* De Architectura *de Vitruve, Livres I à IV*, trans. with introd. and comm. Frédérique Lemerle (Paris: Picard, 2000).

—— (1586), *M. Vitruvii Pollionis De Architectura libri decem*, ed. Guillaume Philander (Lyons).

—— (1931), *On Architecture*, trans. Frank Granger, 2 vols. (Cambridge, Mass.: Harvard University Press; repr. 1955).

—— (1990), *De l'architecture*, trans. Philippe Fleury, with comm., i (Paris: Les Belles Lettres, 1990).

—— (1999), *Ten Books on Architecture*, trans. Ingrid D. Rowland, with comm. and illus. Thomas Noble Howe and additional comm. by Ingrid D. Rowland and Michel J. Dewar (Cambridge: Cambridge University Press).

WARD, JOHN (1740), *The Lives of the Professors of Gresham College*, annot. Ward, 2 vols., British Library, 611 m 16.

WILSON, F. P., AND R. F. HILL (1977), *Dramatic Records in the Declared Accounts of the Office of Works, 1560–1640*, Malone Society Collections, x, 1975 (Oxford: Oxford University Press for the Malone Society).

WILSON, THOMAS (1551), *The Rule of Reason.*

WRIGHT, EDWARD (1599), *Certaine Errors in Navigation.*

SECONDARY

ADAMS, H. J. (1967), *Catalogue of Books Printed on the Continent of Europe, 1501–1600 in Cambridge Libraries*, comp. H. M. Adams, 2 vols. (Cambridge: Cambridge University Press).

ADAMS, JOHN CRANFORD (1961), *The Globe Playhouse: Its Design and Equipment* (New York: Barnes & Noble).

ADELMAN, JANET (1978), Introduction to Janet Adelman (ed.), *Twentieth-Century Interpretations of* King Lear: *A Collection of Critical Essays* (Englewood Cliffs, NJ: Prentice-Hall), 1–21.

AGNEW, JEAN-CHRISTOPHE (1986), *Worlds Apart: The Market and the Theater in Anglo-American Thought, 1550–1750* (Cambridge: Cambridge University Press).

ALBANESE, DENISE (1996), *New Science, New World* (Durham, NC: Duke University Press).

—— (2002), 'Mathematics as a Social Formation: Mapping the Early Modern Universal', in Turner (ed.), *The Culture of Capital*, 255–73.

ALEXANDER, MICHAEL VAN CLEAVE (1990), *The Growth of English Education, 1348–1648* (University Park: Pennsylvania State University Press).

ALFORD, B. W. E., and T. C. BARKER (1968), *A History of the Carpenters Company* (London: George Allen & Unwin).

ALPERS, SVETLANA (1983), *The Art of Describing: Dutch Art in the Seventeenth Century* (Chicago: University of Chicago Press).

AMANN, K., and K. KNORR CETINA (1990), 'The Fixation of (Visual) Evidence', in Lynch and Woolgar (eds.), *Representation in Scientific Practice*, 85–121.

AMES-LEWIS, FRANCIS (ed.) (1999), *Sir Thomas Gresham and Gresham College: Studies in the Intellectual History of London in the Sixteenth and Seventeenth Centuries* (Aldershot: Ashgate).

ARBER, AGNES ([1946]), 'Analogy in the History of Science', in Montagu (ed.), *Studies and Essays*, 221–33.

ARCHER, IAN (1991), *The Pursuit of Stability: Social Relations in Elizabethan London* (Cambridge: Cambridge University Press).

ARMSTRONG, PHILIP (1995), 'Spheres of Influence: Cartography and the Gaze in Shakespearean Tragedy and History', *Shakespeare Studies*, 23: 39–70.

ARMSTRONG, W. A. (1948), 'The Influence of Seneca and Machiavelli on the Elizabethan Tyrant', *Review of English Studies*, 24: 19–35.

ASH, ERIC (2000), ' "A Perfect and an Absolute Work": Expertise, Authority, and the Rebuilding of Dover Harbor, 1579–1583', *Technology and Culture*, 41: 239–68.

ASHWORTH, WILLIAM B., JR. (1990), 'Natural History and the Emblematic World View', in Lindberg and Westman (eds.), *Reappraisals of the Scientific Revolution*, 303–32.

ATKINS, J. W. H. (1934), *Literary Criticism in Antiquity: A Sketch of its Development*, 2 vols. (Cambridge: Cambridge University Press).

—— (1951), *English Literary Criticism: The Renascence* (Cambridge: Cambridge University Press; first pub. 1949).

AVERY, BRUCE (1998), 'Gelded Continents and Plenteous Rivers: Cartography as Rhetoric in Shakespeare', in Gillies and Vaughan (eds.), *Playing the Globe*, 46–62.

BACHELARD, GASTON (1964), *The Poetics of Space*, trans. Maria Jolas, foreword Etienne Gilson (Boston: Beacon Press; first pub. 1958).

Baker, Keith Michael (1975), *Condorcet: From Natural Philosophy to Social Mathematics* (Chicago: University of Chicago Press).

Bal, Mieke (1997), *Narratology: Introduction to the Theory of Narrative*, 2nd edn. (Toronto: University of Toronto Press; first pub. 1985).

Baldwin, T. W. (1947), *Shakespere's Five-Act Structure* (Urbana: University of Illinois Press).

—— (1965), *On Act and Scene Division in the Shakspere First Folio* (Carbondale: Southern Illinois University Press).

Barish, Jonas A. (1967), *Ben Jonson and the Language of Prose Comedy* (Cambridge, Mass.: Harvard University Press).

—— (1973), 'Jonson and the Loathèd Stage', in William Blissett, Julian Patrick, and R. W. Van Fossen (eds.), *A Celebration of Ben Jonson* (Toronto: University of Toronto Press), 27–52.

—— (1981), *The Antitheatrical Prejudice* (Berkeley and Los Angeles: University of California Press).

Barker, Peter, and Roger Ariew (1991), Introduction to eid. (eds.), *Revolution and Continuity: Essays in the History and Philosophy of Early Modern Science* (Washington: Catholic University of America Press), 1–19.

Barthes, Roland (1964), *Elements of Semiology*, trans. Annette Lavers and Colin Smith (New York: Hill & Wang).

—— (1972), *Mythologies*, ed. and trans. Annette Lavers (New York: Hill & Wang).

—— (1977*a*), 'The Photographic Message', in id., *Image Music Text*, trans. Stephen Heath (Glasgow: William Collins; French edn. 1966), 15–31.

—— (1977*b*), 'The Rhetoric of the Image', in id., *Image Music Text*, 32–51.

—— (1977*c*), 'Introduction to the Structuralist Analysis of Narratives', in id., *Image Music Text*, 79–124.

—— (1986), 'The Reality Effect', in id., *The Rustle of Language*, trans. Richard Howard (Berkeley and Los Angeles: University of California Press; first pub. 1968), 141–8.

—— (1988*a*), 'Semantics of the Object', in id., *The Semiotic Challenge*, trans. Richard Howard (Berkeley: University of California Press), 179–90.

—— (1988*b*), 'Semiology and the Urban', in id., *The Semiotic Challenge*, 191–201.

Bartolovich, Crystal Lynn (1993), 'Boundary Disputes: Surveying, Agrarian Capital, and English Renaissance Texts', Ph.D. diss. (Emory University).

—— (1997), 'Putting *Tamburlaine* on a (Cognitive) Map', *Renaissance Drama*, NS 28: 29–72.

—— (2000), ' "Baseless Fabric": London as a "World City" ', in id., *The Tempest and its Travels* (Philadelphia: University of Pennsylvania Press), 13–26.

Barton, Anne (1978), 'London Comedy and the Ethos of the City', *London Journal*, 4: 158–80.

—— (1984), *Ben Jonson, Dramatist* (Cambridge: Cambridge University Press).

Baudrillard, Jean (1978), *Le Système des objets* (Paris: Gallimard).

Baxandall, Michael (1971), *Giotto and the Orators: Humanist Observers of Painting in Italy and the Discovery of Pictorial Composition, 1350–1450* (Oxford: Clarendon Press).

—— (1990), 'English *Disegno*', in Edward Chaney and Peter Mack (eds.), *England and the Continental Renaissance: Essays in Honor of J. B. Trapp* (Woodbridge: Boydell Press), 203–14.

BAWCUTT, N. W. (1971), ' "Policy," Machiavellianism, and the Earlier Tudor Drama', *English Literary Renaissance*, 1: 195–209.

BECKER-CANTARINO, BAERBEL (1978), *Daniel Heinsius*, Twayne's World Authors Series (Boston: G. K. Hall).

BECKERMAN, BERNARD (1962), *Shakespeare at the Globe, 1599–1609* (New York: Macmillan).

BEIER, A. L., and ROGER FINLAY (eds.) (1986), *London 1500–1700: The Making of the Metropolis* (London: Longman).

BENDALL, A. SARAH (1992), *Maps, Land and Society: A History, with a Carto-Bibliography of Cambridgeshire Estate Maps, c. 1600–1836* (Cambridge: Cambridge University Press).

BENNETT, J. A. (1986), 'The Mechanics' Philosophy and the Mechanical Philosophy', *History of Science*, 24: 1–28.

—— (1987), *The Divided Circle: A History of Instruments for Astronomy, Navigation and Surveying* (Oxford: Phaidon/Christie's).

—— (1991a), 'The Challenge of Practical Mathematics', in Pumphrey *et al.* (eds.), *Science, Culture, and Popular Belief*, 176–90.

—— (1991b), 'Geometry and Surveying in Early-Seventeenth-Century England', *Annals of Science*, 48: 345–54.

—— (2000), 'Instruments, Mathematics, and Natural Knowledge: Thomas Harriot's Place on the Map of Learning', in Fox (ed.), *Thomas Harriot*, 137–52.

BENTLEY, GERALD EADES (1964), *Shakespeare and his Theatre* (Lincoln: University of Nebraska Press).

—— (1971), *The Profession of the Dramatist in Shakespeare's Time* (Princeton: Princeton University Press).

BERGERON, DAVID M. (1971), *English Civic Pageantry, 1558–1642* (London: Edward Arnold).

BERRY, HERBERT (ed.) (1979a), *The First Public Playhouse: The Theatre in Shoreditch, 1576–1598* (Montreal: McGill-Queen's University Press).

—— (1979b), 'Aspects of the Design and Use of the First Public Playhouse', in id. (ed.), *The First Public Playhouse*, 29–45.

BEVINGTON, DAVID (1962), *From Mankind to Marlowe: Growth of Structure in the Popular Drama of Tudor England* (Cambridge, Mass.: Harvard University Press).

—— (1984), *Action is Eloquence: Shakespeare's Language of Gesture* (Cambridge, Mass.: Harvard University Press).

BIAGIOLI, MARIO (1989), 'The Social Status of Italian Mathematicians,' *History of Science*, 27: 41–95.

—— (1993), *Galileo, Courtier: The Practice of Science in the Culture of Absolutism* (Chicago: University of Chicago Press).

BINNS, JAMES W. (1975), 'Henry Dethick in Praise of Poetry', *The Library*, 30: 199–216.

BLAIR, ANN (1997), *The Theater of Nature: Jean Bodin and Renaissance Science* (Princeton: Princeton University Press).

—— (1999), 'Natural Philosophy and the "New Science" ' in Norton (ed.), *The Cambridge History of Literary Criticism*, iii. 449–57.

BLAYNEY, PETER W. M. (1982), *The Texts of* King Lear *and their Origins*, i (Cambridge: Cambridge University Press).

BLUNT, ANTHONY (1940), *Artistic Theory in Italy* (Oxford: Oxford University Press).

Boase, C. W., and Andrew Clark (eds.) (1885–9), *Register of the University of Oxford*, 2 vols. in 5 (Oxford: Clarendon Press for the Oxford Historical Society).

Boehrer, Bruce Thomas (1993), 'The Poet of Labor: Authorship and Property in the Work of Ben Jonson', *Philological Quarterly*, 72: 289–312.

Bono, James J. (1995), *The Word of God and the Languages of Man: Interpreting Nature in Early Modern Science and Medicine, i: Ficino to Descartes* (Madison: University of Wisconsin Press).

—— (2004a), 'Imagining Nature: Technologies of the Literal, the Scientific Revolution, and "Literature and Science" ', Paper delivered at the Renaissance Society of America 2004 Annual Meeting, New York, 3 Apr.

—— (2004b), 'Language, Inquiry, and Invention: The Metaphorics of Nature, Technologies of the Literal, and the Production of Natural Knowledge, Arts, and Objects', Paper delivered at the 'Inventive Intersections: Sites, Artifacts, and the Rise of Early Modern Science and Technology', Conference, Amsterdam, 22–4 Sept.

Boughner, Daniel C. (1968), *The Devil's Disciple: Ben Jonson's Debt to Machiavelli* (New York: Philosophical Library).

Boulton, Jeremy (1987), *Neighbourhood and Society: A London Suburb in the Seventeenth Century* (Cambridge: Cambridge University Press).

Bourdieu, Pierre (1977), *Outline of a Theory of Practice*, trans. Richard Nice (Cambridge: Cambridge University Press).

—— (1990), *The Logic of Practice*, trans. Richard Nice (Stanford, Calif.: Stanford University Press).

—— (1991), *Language and Symbolic Power*, ed. and introd. John B. Thompson, trans. Gino Raymond and Matthew Adamson (Cambridge, Mass.: Harvard University Press).

—— (1993), *The Field of Cultural Production: Essays on Art and Literature*, ed. and introd. Randal Johnson, trans. Richard Nice *et al.* (New York: Columbia University Press).

—— (1998), *Practical Reason: On the Theory of Action* (Stanford, Calif.: Stanford University Press).

Boutcher, Warren (1998), 'Pilgrimage to Parnassus: Local Intellectual Traditions, Humanist Education and the Cultural Geography of Sixteenth-Century England', in Yun Lee Too and Niall Livingstone (eds.), *Pedagogy and Power: Rhetorics of Classical Learning* (Cambridge: Cambridge University Press), 110–47.

Bradbrook, Muriel (1935), *Themes and Conventions of Elizabethan Tragedy* (Cambridge: Cambridge University Press; 2nd edn., 1980).

—— (1955), *The Growth and Structure of Elizabethan Comedy* (Baltimore: Penguin Books).

Bradley, A. C. (1960), *Shakespearean Tragedy* (New York: St Martin's).

Bradley, David (1992), *From Text to Performance in the Elizabethan Theatre: Preparing the Play for the Stage* (Cambridge: Cambridge University Press).

Brady, Jennifer, and W. H. Herendeen (eds.) (1991), *Ben Jonson's 1616 Folio* (Newark: University of Delaware Press).

Bredekamp, Horst (1995), *The Lure of Antiquity and the Cult of the Machine*, trans. Allison Brown (Princeton: Markus Wiener).

Brenner, Robert (1993), *Merchants and Revolution: Commercial Change, Political Conflict, and London's Overseas Traders, 1550–1653* (Princeton: Princeton University Press).

BRETT-JAMES, NORMAN G. (1935), *The Growth of Stuart London* (London: Allen & Unwin).

BROOKS, DOUGLAS (2000), *From Playhouse to Printing House: Drama and Authorship in Early Modern England* (Cambridge: Cambridge University Press).

BROOKS, PETER (1984), *Reading for the Plot: Design and Intention in Narrative* (Cambridge, Mass.: Harvard University Press).

BROTTON, JERRY (1998), *Trading Territories: Mapping the Early Modern World* (Ithaca, NY: Cornell University Press).

BRÜCKNER, MARTIN, and KRISTEN POOLE (2002), 'The Plot Thickens: Surveying Manuals, Drama, and the Materiality of Narrative Form in Early Modern England', *English Literary History*, 69: 617–48.

BRUSTER, DOUGLAS (1992), *Drama and the Market in the Age of Shakespeare* (Cambridge: Cambridge University Press).

—— (2002), 'The Dramatic Life of Objects in the Early Modern Theatre', in Harris and Korda (eds.), *Staged Properties*, 67–96.

BURCKHARDT, SIGURD (1966), *Shakespearean Meanings* (Princeton: Princeton University Press), 237–59.

BURKE, KENNETH (1931), *Counter-Statement* (New York: Harcourt, Brace).

BURROW, COLIN (1999), 'Combative Criticism: Jonson, Milton, and Classical Literary Criticism in England', in Norton (ed.), *The Cambridge History of Literary Criticism*, iii. 487–99.

BURT, RICHARD (1993), *Licensed by Authority: Ben Jonson and the Discourses of Censorship* (Ithaca, NY: Cornell University Press).

BUSH, DOUGLAS (1950), *Science and English Poetry: A Historical Sketch, 1590–1950* (New York: Oxford University Press).

BUSHNELL, REBECCA (1990), *Tragedies of Tyrants: Political Thought and Theater in the English Renaissance* (Ithaca, NY: Cornell University Press).

BUTOR, MICHEL (1964), 'Le Livre comme objet', *Répertoire II* (Paris: Minuit), 104–23.

BUTLER, MARTIN (ed.) (1999), *Re-presenting Ben Jonson: Text, History, Performance* (Houndmills: Macmillan).

BUXTON, JOHN (1954), *Sir Philip Sidney and the English Renaissance* (Houndmills: Macmillan; 3rd edn., 1987).

CAHILL, PATRICIA (2004), 'Killing by Computation: Military Mathematics, the Elizabethan Social Body, and Marlowe's *Tamburlaine*', in Glimp and Warren (eds.), *Arts of Calculation*, 165–86.

CALLEBAT, LOUIS (1994), 'Rhétorique et architecture dans le 'De Architectura' de Vitruve', in *Le Projet de Vitruve: Objet, destinataires et réception du* De Architectura (Rome: École française de Rome), 31–46.

CAMPBELL, LILY B. (1923), *Scenes and Machines on the English Stage during the Renaissance: A Classical Revival* (New York: Barnes & Noble).

CARLSON, MARVIN (1989), *Places of Performance: The Semiotics of Theatre Architecture* (Ithaca, NY: Cornell University Press).

—— (1990), *Theatre Semiotics: Signs of Life* (Bloomington: Indiana University Press).

CARRUTHERS, MARY J. (1990), *The Book of Memory* (Cambridge: Cambridge University Press).

—— (1993), 'The Poet as Master Builder: Composition and Locational Memory in the Middle Ages', *New Literary History*, 24: 881–904.

CAST, DAVID (1993), 'Speaking of Architecture: The Evolution of a Vocabulary in Vasari Jones and Sir John Vanbrugh', *Journal of the Society of Architectural Historians*, 52: 179–88.

CERASANO, SUSAN P. (1989), 'Raising a Playhouse from the Dust', *Shakespeare Quarterly*, 40: 483–90.

CHAMBERS, E. K. (1923), *The Elizabethan Stage*, 4 vols. (Oxford: Clarendon Press).

—— (1930), *William Shakespeare*, 2 vols. (Oxford: Clarendon Press).

CHAMPION, LARRY S. (1982), 'Westward–Northward: Structural Development in Dekker's *Ho* Plays', *Comparative Drama*, 16: 251–66.

CHARTIER, ROGER (1997), *On the Edge of the Cliff: History, Language, and Practices*, trans. Lydia G. Cochrane (Baltimore: Johns Hopkins University Press).

—— (1999), *Publishing Drama in Early Modern Europe*, The Panizzi Lectures, 1998 (London: British Library).

CHATMAN, SEYMOUR (1978), *Story and Discourse: Narrative Structure in Fiction and Film* (Ithaca, NY: Cornell University Press).

CLUCAS, STEPHEN (1999), ' "No Small Force": Natural Philosophy and Mathematics in Thomas Gresham's London', in Ames-Lewis (ed.), *Sir Thomas Gresham*, 146–73.

—— (2000), 'Thomas Harriot and the Field of Knowledge in the English Renaissance', in Fox (ed.), *Thomas Harriot*, 93–136.

CLULEE, NICHOLAS (1977), 'Astrology, Magic, and Optics: Facets of John Dee's Early Natural Philosophy', *Renaissance Quarterly*, 30: 632–80.

—— (1984), 'At the Crossroads of Magic and Science: John Dee's Archemastrie', in Brian Vickers (ed.), *Occult and Scientific Mentalities in the Renaissance* (Cambridge: Cambridge University Press), 57–71.

—— (1988), *John Dee's Natural Philosophy: Between Science and Religion* (New York: Routledge).

COHEN, H. FLORIS (1994), *The Scientific Revolution* (Chicago: University of Chicago Press).

COHEN, RALPH (1973), 'The Function of Setting in *Eastward Ho*', *Renaissance Papers*, 83–96.

COLIE, ROSALIE (1966), *Paradoxia Epidemica: The Renaissance Tradition of Paradox* (Princeton: Princeton University Press).

COLVIN, H. M. (gen. ed.) (1982), *The History of the King's Works*, iv: *1485–1660*, p. II (London: HMSO).

CONLEY, TOM (1992), *The Graphic Unconscious in Early Modern French Writing* (Cambridge: Cambridge University Press).

—— (1996), *The Self-Made Map: Cartographic Writing in Early Modern France* (Minneapolis: University of Minnesota Press).

—— (1998*a*), 'Putting French Studies on the Map', *Diacritics*, 28: 23–39.

—— (1998*b*), 'Mapping in the Folds: Deleuze *Cartographe*', *Discourse*, 20: 123–38.

COOGAN, ROBERT M. (1981), 'The Triumph of Reason: Sidney's *Defense* and Aristotle's *Rhetoric*', *Papers on Language and Literature*, 17: 255–70.

CORMACK, LESLEY (1997), *Charting an Empire: Geography at the English Universities, 1580–1620* (Chicago: University of Chicago Press).

COSGROVE, DENIS (1988), 'The Geometry of Landscape: Practical and Speculative Arts in Sixteenth-Century Venetian Land Territories', in Denis Cosgrove and Stephen Daniels (eds.), *The Iconography of Landscape* (Cambridge: Cambridge University Press), 254–76.

Cox, John D., and David Scott Kastan (eds.) (1997), *A New History of Early English Drama* (New York: Columbia University Press).

Crane, Mary Thomas (1993), *Framing Authority: Sayings, Self, and Society in Sixteenth-Century England* (Princeton: Princeton University Press).

—— (2001), *Shakespeare's Brain: Reading with Cognitive Theory* (Princeton: Princeton University Press).

—— (2002), 'What was Performance?', *Criticism*, 43: 169–87.

Cranz, F. Edward (1984), *A Bibliography of Aristotle Editions 1501–1600*, 2nd edn., with addenda, rev. Charles B. Schmitt (Baden-Baden: V. Koerner).

Crombie, A. C. (1952), *Augustine to Galileo: The History of Science A.D. 400–1650*, 2 vols. in 1 (Cambridge, Mass.: Harvard University Press; 2nd edn., 1961).

—— (1994), *Styles of Scientific Thinking in the European Tradition: The History of Argument and Explanation Especially in the Mathematical and Biomedical Sciences and Arts*, 3 vols. (London: Gerald Duckworth).

—— (1996a), 'Experimental Science and the Rational Artist in Early Modern Europe', in id., *Science, Art, and Nature in Medieval and Early Modern Thought* (London: Hambledon Press), 89–114.

—— (1996b), 'Expectation, Modelling and Assent in the History of Optics', in id., *Science, Art and Nature in Medieval and Early Modern Thought* (London: Hambledon Press), 301–55.

Culler, Jonathan (1975), *Structuralist Poetics: Structuralism, Linguistics and the Study of Literature* (Ithaca, NY: Cornell University Press).

Cunningham, Dolora (1955), 'The Jonsonian Masque as a Literary Form', *English Literary History*, 22: 108–24.

Curtis, Mark (1959), *Oxford and Cambridge in Transition* (Oxford: Oxford University Press).

Daly, Peter M. (1998), *Literature in the Light of the Emblem*, 2nd edn. (Toronto: University of Toronto Press).

Danson, Lawrence (1984), 'Jonsonian Comedy and the Discovery of the Social Self', *PMLA* 99: 179–93.

Daston, Lorraine (1991), 'Baconian Facts, Academic Civility, and the Prehistory of Objectivity', *Annals of Scholarship*, 8: 337–64.

—— and Peter Galison (1992), 'The Image of Objectivity', *Representations*, 40: 81–128.

Dear, Peter (1995), *Discipline and Experience: The Mathematical Way in the Scientific Revolution* (Chicago: University of Chicago Press).

—— (1997), Introduction to id. (ed.), *The Scientific Enterprise in Early Modern Europe: Readings from Isis* (Chicago: University of Chicago Press), 1–7.

De Certeau, Michel (1984), *The Practice of Everyday Life*, trans. Steven Rendall (Berkeley: University of California Press).

De Grazia, Margreta (1991), *Shakespeare Verbatim: The Reproduction of Authenticity and the 1790 Apparatus* (Oxford: Clarendon Press).

—— (1996), 'The Ideology of Superfluous Things: *King Lear* as Period Piece', in Margreta De Grazia, Maureen Quilligan, and Peter Stallybrass (eds.), *Subject and Object in Renaissance Culture* (Cambridge: Cambridge University Press), 17–42.

—— (1997), 'World Pictures, Modern Periods, and the Early Stage', in Cox and Kastan (eds.), *A New History of Early English Drama*, 1–21.

—— and PETER STALLYBRASS (1993), 'The Materiality of the Shakespearean Text', *Shakespeare Quarterly*, 44: 255–83.

DEHART, SCOTT M. (1995), 'The Convergence of Praxis and Theoria in Aristotle', *Journal of the History of Philosophy*, 33: 7–27.

DELEUZE, GILLES (1988), *Foucault*, trans. Seàn Hand (Minneapolis: University of Minnesota Press).

DE MAN, PAUL (1983), *Blindness and Insight: Essays in the Rhetoric of Contemporary Criticism*, introd. Wlad Godzich, 2nd edn., rev. (Minneapolis: University of Minnesota Press).

DE SOMOGYI, NICK (1996), 'Marlowe's Maps of War', in Darryll Grantley and Peter Roberts (eds.), *Christopher Marlowe and English Renaissance Culture* (Aldershot: Scolar Press; Brookfield, Vt.: Ashgate), 96–109.

DESSEN, ALAN C. (1971), *Jonson's Moral Comedy* (Evanston, Ill.: Northwestern University Press).

—— (1977), *Elizabethan Drama and the Viewer's Eye* (Chapel Hill: University of North Carolina Press).

—— (1984), *Elizabethan Stage Directions and Modern Interpreters* (Cambridge: Cambridge University Press).

DEVEREUX, DANIEL T. (1986), 'Particular and Universal in Aristotle's Conception of Practical Knowledge', *Review of Metaphysics*, 39: 483–504.

DIETZ, BRIAN (1986), 'Overseas Trade and Metropolitan Growth', in Beier and Finlay (eds.), *London 1500–1700*, 115–140.

DIJKSTERHUIS, E. J. (1986), *The Mechanization of the World Picture: Pythagoras to Newton*, trans. C. Dikshoorn (Princeton: Princeton University Press).

DILLON, JANETTE (2000), *Theatre, Court and City, 1595–1610: Drama and Social Space in London* (Cambridge: Cambridge University Press).

DOHERTY, M. J. (1991), *The Mistress-Knowledge: Sir Philip Sidney's* Defence of Poesie *and Literary Architectonics in the English Renaissance* (Nashville, Tenn.: Vanderbilt University Press).

DONALDSON, IAN (1997), *Jonson's Magic Houses: Essays in Interpretation* (Oxford: Clarendon Press).

DONOVAN, KEVIN (1999), 'Forms of Authority in *Every Man Out*', in Butler (ed.), *Re-presenting Ben Jonson*, 59–75.

DORAN, MADELEINE (1954), *Endeavors of Art: A Study of Form in Elizabethan Drama* (Madison: University of Wisconsin Press).

DOWD, MICHELLE (2003), 'Leaning Too Hard Upon the Pen: Suburb Wenches and City Wives in *Westward Ho*', *Medieval and Renaissance Drama in England*, 15: 224–42.

DUBROW, HEATHER (2000), 'Guess Who's Coming to Dinner? Reinterpreting Formalism and the Country House Poem', *Modern Literary Quarterly*, 61: 59–77.

DUNCAN-JONES, KATHERINE (1991), *Sir Philip Sidney: Courtier Poet* (New Haven: Yale University Press).

DUTTON, RICHARD (1996), *Ben Jonson: Authority, Criticism* (New York: St Martin's Press).

EAMON, WILLIAM (1994), *Science and the Secrets of Nature: Books of Nature in Medieval and Early Modern Culture* (Princeton: Princeton University Press).

ECO, UMBERTO (1976), *A Theory of Semiotics* (Bloomington: Indiana University Press).

—— (2000), *Kant and the Platypus: Essays on Language and Cognition*, trans. Alastair McEwan (New York: Harcourt Brace).

EDEN, KATHY (1986), *Poetic and Legal Fiction in the Aristotelian Tradition* (Princeton: Princeton University Press).

EDEN, PETER (1983), 'Three Elizabethan Estate Surveyors: Peter Kempe, Thomas Clerke and Thomas Langdon', in Tyacke (ed.), *English Map-Making*, 68–84.

EISENSTEIN, ELIZABETH L. (1979), *The Printing Press as an Agent of Change: Communications and Cultural Transformation in Early Modern Europe*, 2 vols. (Cambridge: Cambridge University Press).

ELAM, KEIR (2002), *The Semiotics of Theater and Drama*, 2nd edn. (London: Routledge).

ELKINS, JAMES (1994), *The Poetics of Perspective* (Ithaca, NY: Cornell University Press).

ELSKY, MARTIN (1982), 'Words, Things, and Names: Jonson's Poetry and Philosophical Grammar', in Claude J. Summers and Ted-Larry Pebworth (eds.), *Classic and Cavalier: Essay on Jonson and the Sons of Ben* (Pittsburgh: University of Pittsburgh Press), 91–104.

EMPSON, WILLIAM (1957), 'Donne the Space Man', *Kenyon Review*, 29: 337–99.

ERIKSEN, ROY (2000), *The Building in the Text: Alberti to Shakespeare and Milton* (University Park: Pennsylvania State University Press).

EVANS, ROBERT C. (1995), *Habits of Mind: Evidence and Effects of Ben Jonson's Reading* (Lewisburg, Pa.: Bucknell University Press).

FEHRENBACH, R. J., and E. S. LEEDHAM-GREEN (eds.) (1992–8), *Private Libraries in Renaissance England: A Collection and Catalogue of Tudor and Early Stuart Book-Lists*, 5 vols. (Binghamton, NY: Medieval and Renaissance Texts and Studies).

FEINGOLD, MORDECHAI (1984), *The Mathematician's Apprenticeship: Science, Universities and Society in England, 1560–1640* (Cambridge: Cambridge University Press).

—— (1991), 'Tradition vs. Novelty: Universities and Scientific Societies in the Early Modern Period', in Barker and Ariew (eds.), *Revolution and Continuity*, 45–59.

—— (1997a), 'The Humanities', in Tyacke (ed.), *Seventeenth-Century Oxford*, 211–357.

—— (1997b), 'The Mathematical Sciences and New Philosophies', in Tyacke (ed.), *Seventeenth-Century Oxford*, 359–448.

—— (1999), 'Gresham College and London Practitioners: The Nature of the English Mathematical Community', in Ames-Lewis (ed.), *Sir Thomas Gresham*, 174–88.

—— (2001), 'English Ramism: A Reinterpretation', in Mordechai Feingold, Joseph S. Freedman, and Wolfgang Rother (eds.), *The Influence of Petrus Ramus* (Basel: Schwabe), 127–76.

FERGUSON, MARGARET W. (1983), *Trials of Desire: Renaissance Defenses of Poetry* (New Haven: Yale University Press).

FERGUSSON, FRANCIS (1949), *The Idea of a Theater* (Princeton: Princeton University Press; repr. Garden City, NY: Anchor Books, 1953).

FIELD, J. V. (1999), 'Why Translate Serlio', in Ames-Lewis (ed.), *Sir Thomas Gresham*, 198–221.

FINDLEN, PAULA (1994), *Possessing Nature: Museums, Collecting, and Scientific Culture in Early Modern Italy* (Berkeley: University of California Press).

FINLAY, ROGER, and BEATRICE SHEARER (1986), 'Population Growth and Suburban Expansion', in Beier and Finlay (eds.), *London 1500–1700*, 37–59.

FISCHER-LICHTE, ERIKA (1992), *The Semiotics of Theater*, trans. Jeremy Gaines and Doris L. Jones (Bloomington: Indiana University Press).

FISHER, F. J. (1948), 'The Development of London as a Centre of Conspicuous Consumption in the Sixteenth and Seventeenth Centuries', *Transactions of the Royal Historical Society*, 30: 37–50.

FLAHIFF, FREDERICK (1986), 'Lear's Map', *Cahiers Élisabéthains*, 30: 17–33.

FLETCHER, DAVID H. (1995), *The Emergence of Estate Maps: Christ Church, Oxford, 1600–1840* (Oxford: Clarendon Press).

FLETCHER, J. M. (1986), 'The Faculty of Arts', in McConica (ed.), *The Collegiate University*, 157–99.

FORSTER, E. M. (1927), *Aspects of the Novel* (New York: Harcourt Brace).

FOUCAULT, MICHEL (1972), *The Archeology of Knowledge*, trans. A. M. Sheridan Smith (New York: Vintage).

—— (1979), *Discipline and Punish: The Birth of the Prison*, trans. Alan Sheridan (New York: Vintage).

—— (1980), 'Questions on Geography', in id., *Power/Knowledge*, ed. and trans. Alan Gordon (New York: Pantheon; first pub. 1976), 63–77.

—— (1984), 'Space, Knowledge, and Power', trans. Christian Hubert, in Paul Rabinow (ed.), *The Foucault Reader* (New York: Pantheon; first pub. 1982), 239–56.

—— (1998), 'Different Spaces', in id., *Aesthetics, Method, and Epistemology: The Essential Works of Foucault, 1954–1984*, ii, ed. James D. Faubion, trans. Robert Hurley *et al.* (New York: New Press), 175–85.

FOX, ROBERT (ed.) (2000), *Thomas Harriot: An Elizabethan Man of Science* (Aldershot: Ashgate).

FRENCH, PETER (1972), *John Dee: The World of an Elizabethan Magus* (London: Routledge & Kegan Paul).

FRENCH, ROGER (1994), *William Harvey's Natural Philosophy* (Cambridge: Cambridge University Press).

FUMERTON, PATRICIA (2000), 'London's Vagrant Economy: Making Space for "Low" Subjectivity', in Orlin (ed.), *Material London*, 206–25.

FUNKENSTEIN, AMOS (1986), *Theology and the Scientific Imagination from the Middle Ages to the Seventeenth Century* (Princeton: Princeton University Press).

GABBEY, ALAN (1990), 'The Case of Mechanics: One Revolution or Many?', in Lindberg and Westman (eds.), *Reappraisals*, 493–528.

—— (1993), 'Between *Ars* and *Philosophia Naturalis*: Reflections on the Historiography of Early Modern Mechanics', in J. V. Field and Frank A. J. L. James (eds.), *Renaissance and Revolution: Humanists, Scholars, Craftsmen, and Natural Philosophers in Early Modern Europe* (Cambridge: Cambridge University Press), 63–72.

GALISON, PETER (1997), *Image and Logic: A Material Culture of Microphysics* (Chicago: University of Chicago Press).

—— and ALEXI ASSMUS (1989), 'Artificial Clouds, Real Particles', in Gooding *et al.* (eds.), *The Uses of Experiment*, 225–74.

—— and CAROLINE JONES (eds.) (1998), *Picturing Science, Producing Art* (New York: Routledge).

GALLAGHER, CATHERINE (2000), 'Formalism and Time', *Modern Literary Quarterly*, 61: 229–51.

GASCOIGNE, JOHN (1990), 'A Reappraisal of the Role of the Universities in the Scientific Revolution', in Lindberg and Westman (eds.), *Reappraisals*, 207–60.

GENETTE, GÉRARD (1969), 'La Littérature et l'espace', in id., *Figures II: Essais* (Paris: Seuil), 43–7.

—— (1982), 'Frontiers of Narrative', in id., *Figures of Literary Discourse*, trans. Alan Sheridan (New York: Columbia University Press, 127–44); first pub. as 'Frontières du Récit', in id., *Figures II: Essais* (Paris: Seuil), 49–69.

GIARD, LUCE (1991), 'Remapping Knowledge, Reshaping Institutions', trans. Maurice Slawinski, in Pumfrey *et al.* (eds.), *Science, Culture, and Popular Belief in Renaissance Europe*, 19–47.

GIBBONS, BRIAN (1980), *Jacobean City Comedy* (London: Methuen; first pub. 1968).

—— (1996), 'The Question of Place', *Cahiers Élisabéthains*, 50: 33–43.

GILBERT, NEAL (1963), *Renaissance Concepts of Method* (New York: Columbia University Press).

GILLIES, BERTRAND (1966), *Engineers of the Renaissance* (Cambridge, Mass.: MIT Press; first French edn., 1964).

GILLES, JOHN (1998), 'Marlowe, the Timur Myth, and the Motives of Geography', in Gillies and Vaughan (eds.), *Playing the Globe*, 203–29.

—— (1994), *Shakespeare and the Geography of Difference* (Cambridge: Cambridge University Press).

—— (2001), 'The Scene of Cartography in *King Lear*', in Gordon and Klein (eds.), *Literature, Mapping, and the Politics of Space*, 109–37.

—— and VIRGINIA MASON VAUGHAN (eds.) (1998), *Playing the Globe: Genre and Geography in Renaissance Drama* (Madison, NJ: Fairleigh Dickinson University Press; London: Associated University Presses).

GIROUARD, MARK (1983), *Robert Smythson and the Elizabethan Country House* (New Haven: Yale University Press); first pub. as *Robert Smythson and the Architecture of the Elizabethan Era* (London: Country Life Limited, 1966).

GLIMP, DAVID, AND MICHELLE R. WARREN (eds.) (2004), *Arts of Calculation: Quantifying Thought in Early Modern Europe* (New York: Palgrave).

GOLDBERG, JONATHAN (1983), *James I and the Politics of Literature: Jonson, Shakespeare, Donne, and their Contemporaries* (Baltimore: Johns Hopkins University Press).

—— (1984), 'Perspectives: Dover Cliff and the Conditions of Representation', *Poetics Today*, 5: 537–48.

GOODING, DAVID, TREVOR PINCH, and SIMON SCHAFFER (eds.) (1989), *The Uses of Experiment: Studies in the Natural Sciences* (Cambridge: Cambridge University Press).

GORDON, ANDREW, and BERNHARD KLEIN (eds.) (2001), *Literature, Mapping, and the Politics of Space in Early Modern Britain* (Cambridge: Cambridge Cambridge University Press).

GORDON D. J. (1975), 'Poet and Architect: The Intellectual Setting of the Quarrel between Ben Jonson and Inigo Jones', in Stephen Orgel (ed.), *The Renaissance Imagination* (Berkeley: University of California Press), 77–101.

GORDON, SCOTT (1991), *The History and Philosophy of Social Science* (New York: Routledge).

GOTCH, J. ALFRED (1928), *Inigo Jones* (London: Methuen).

GOULDING, ROBERT (1999), '*Testimonia Humanitatis*: The Early Lectures of Henry Savile', in Ames-Lewis (ed.), *Thomas Gresham*, 125–45.

GRAFTON, ANTHONY (1999), *Cardano's Cosmos: The Worlds and Works of a Renaissance Astrologer* (Cambridge, Mass.: Harvard University Press).

—— and LISA JARDINE (1986), *From Humanism to the Humanities: Education and the Liberal Arts in Fifteenth- and Sixteenth-Century Europe* (Cambridge, Mass.: Harvard University Press).

—— —— (1990), ' "Studied for Action": How Gabriel Harvey Read his Livy', *Past and Present*, 129: 30–78.

GRANT, EDWARD (1976), 'Place and Space in Medieval Physical Thought', in Peter K. Machamer and Robert G. Turnbull (eds.), *Motion and Time, Space and Matter* (Columbus: Ohio State University Press), 137–67.

—— (1981), *Much Ado about Nothing: Theories of Space and Vacuum from the Middle Ages to the Scientific Revolution* (Cambridge: Cambridge University Press).

GRANVILLE-BARKER, HARLEY (1946–7), *Prefaces to Shakespeare*, 2 vols. (Princeton: Princeton University Press).

GREENBLATT, STEPHEN (1980), *Renaissance Self-Fashioning from More to Shakespeare* (Chicago: University of Chicago Press).

GREENFIELD, JON (1997*a*), 'Design as Reconstruction: Reconstruction as Design', in Mulryne and Shewring (eds.), *Shakespeare's Globe Rebuilt*, 81–96.

—— (1997*b*), 'Timber Framing, the Two Bays and After', in Mulryne and Shewring (eds.), *Shakespeare's Globe Rebuilt*, 97–120.

GREG, W. W. (1931), *Dramatic Documents from the Elizabethan Playhouses: Stage Plots, Actor's Parts, Prompt Books*, 2 vols. (Oxford: Clarendon Press), i: Commentary; and ii: Facsimiles.

—— (1955), *The Shakespeare First Folio* (Oxford: Clarendon Press).

GREGORY, DEREK (1994), *Geographical Imaginations* (Oxford: Blackwell).

GRIFFITHS, PAUL, and MARK S. R. JENNER (eds.) (2000), *Londinopolis: Essays in the Cultural and Social History of Early Modern London* (Manchester: Manchester University Press).

GROS, PIERRE (1994), '*Munus non Ingratum*: Le Traité Vitruvien et la notion de service', in *Le Projet de Vitruve: Objet, destinataires et réception du De Architectura* (Rome: École française de Rome), 75–90.

GUILLÉN, CLAUDIO (1971), *Literature as System: Essays toward the Theory of Literary History* (Princeton: Princeton University Press), 283–371.

GURR, ANDREW (1992), *The Shakespearean Stage, 1574–1642* (Cambridge: Cambridge University Press).

—— (1997), 'Shakespeare's Globe: A History of Reconstructions and Some Reasons for Trying', in Mulryne and Shewring (eds.), *Shakespeare's Globe Rebuilt*, 27–47.

—— (1999), 'Who is Lovewit? What is He?', in Richard Cave, Elizabeth Schafer, and Brian Woolland (eds.), *Ben Jonson and Theatre: Performance, Practice and Theory* (London: Routledge), 5–19.

—— (2000), 'The Authority of the Globe and the Fortune', in Orlin (ed.), *Material London*, 251–67.

HACKMANN, W. D. (1989), 'Scientific Instruments: Models of Brass and Aids to Discovery', in Gooding *et al.* (eds.), *Uses of Experiment*, 31–65.

HADDEN, RICHARD W. (1994), *On the Shoulders of Merchants* (Albany: State University of New York Press).

HALL, RUPERT (1959), 'The Scholar and the Craftsman in the Scientific Revolution', in Marshall Clagett (ed.), *Critical Problems in the History of Science* (Madison: University of Wisconsin Press), 3–23.

HALPERN, RICHARD (1991), *The Poetics of Primitive Accumulation: English Renaissance Culture and the Genealogy of Capital* (Ithaca, NY: Cornell University Press).

HARDING, VANESSA (1990), 'The Population of London, 1500–1700: A Review of the Published Evidence', *London Journal*, 15: 111–28.

HARDISON O. B., JR. (1988), 'The Two Voices of Sidney's Apology for Poetry', in Kinney (ed.), *Sidney in Retrospect*, 45–61 (first pub. 1972).

HARKNESS, DEBORAH E. (1999), *John Dee's Conversations with Angels: Cabala, Alchemy, and the End of Nature* (Cambridge: Cambridge University Press).

—— (2002), ' "Strange" Ideas and "English" Knowledge: Natural Science Exchange in Elizabethan London', in Smith and Findlen (eds.), *Merchants and Marvels*, 137–60.

HARRIS, EILEEN (1990), *British Architectural Books and Writers, 1556–1785* (Cambridge: Cambridge University Press).

HARRIS, JONATHAN GIL (2002*a*), 'Shakespeare's Hair: Staging the Object of Material Culture', *Shakespeare Quarterly*, 53: 479–91.

—— (2002*b*), 'Properties of Skill: Product Placement in Early English Artisanal Drama', in Harris and Korda (eds.), *Staged Properties*, 35–66.

—— (2004), *Sick Economies: Drama, Mercantilism, and Disease in Shakespeare's England* (Philadelphia: University of Pennsylvania Press).

—— and NATASHA KORDA (eds.) (2002), *Staged Properties in Early Modern English Drama* (Cambridge: Cambridge University Press).

HARRIS, JOHN, STEPHEN ORGEL, and ROY STRONG (1973), *The King's Arcadia: Inigo Jones and the Stuart Court* (London: Lund Humphries).

HARVEY, DAVID (1996), *Justice, Nature and the Geography of Difference* (Cambridge: Blackwell).

HATTAWAY, MICHAEL (1982), *Elizabethan Popular Theater: Plays in Performance* (London: Routledge & Kegan Paul).

HAYNES, JONATHAN (1992), *The Social Relations of Jonson's Theater* (Cambridge: Cambridge University Press).

HEATH, SIR THOMAS (1949), *Mathematics in Aristotle* (Oxford: Clarendon Press).

HEIDEGGER, MARTIN (1977), 'Modern Science, Metaphysics, and Mathematics', *Basic Writings* (New York: Harper & Row), 247–82.

HELGERSON, RICHARD (1983), *Self-Crowned Laureates: Spenser, Jonson, Milton and the Literary System* (Berkeley: University of California Press).

—— (1992), *Forms of Nationhood: The Elizabethan Writing of England* (Chicago: University of Chicago Press).

HENINGER, S. K., JR. (1974), *Touches of Sweet Harmony: Pythagorean Cosmology and Renaissance Poetics* (San Marino, Calif.: Huntington Library).

—— (1988), 'Sidney and Serranus' Plato', in Kinney (ed.), *Sidney in Retrospect*, 27–44 (first pub. 1983).

—— (1989), *Sidney and Spenser: The Poet as Maker* (University Park: Pennsylvania State University Press).

HERMAN, PETER C. (1989), ' "Do as I Say, Not as I Do": The *Apology for Poetry* and Sir Philip Sidney's Letters to Edward Denny and Robert Sidney', *Sidney Newsletter*, 10: 13–24.

HERRICK, MARVIN T. (1925), 'Sir John Cheke and Aristotle's *Poetics*', *Classical Weekly*, 18: 134–5.

—— (1926), 'The Early History of Aristotle's *Rhetoric* in England', *Philological Quarterly*, 5: 242–57.

—— (1930), *The Poetics of Aristotle in England* (New Haven: Yale University Press).

—— (1946), *The Fusion of Horatian and Aristotelian Literary Criticism, 1531–1555* (Urbana: University of Illinois Press).

—— (1950), *Comic Theory in the Sixteenth Century* (repr. Urbana: University of Illinois Press, 1964).

HILL, CHRISTOPHER (1965), *Intellectual Origins of the English Revolution* (Oxford: Clarendon Press); rev. as *Intellectual Origins of the English Revolution Revisited* (Oxford: Clarendon Press, 1997).

HILLMAN, DAVID, and CARLA MAZZIO (eds.) (1997), *The Body in Parts: Fantasies of Corporeality in Early Modern Europe* (New York: Routledge).

HINMAN, CHARLTON (1963), *The Printing and the Proofreading of the First Folio of Shakespeare*, 2 vols. (Oxford: Clarendon Press).

HOMANN, FREDERICK A. (1983), 'Christophorus Clavius and the Renaissance of Euclidean Geometry', *Archivum Historicum Societatis Iesu*, 52: 233–46.

HOSLEY, RICHARD (1979), 'The Theatre and the Tradition of Playhouse Design', in Berry (ed.), *The First Public Playhouse*, 47–79.

HOUGHTON, WALTER E., JR. (1941) 'The History of Trades: Its Relation to Seventeenth-Century Thought', *Journal of the History of Ideas*, 2: 33–60; repr. in Weiner and Noland (eds.), *Roots of Scientific Thought*, 354–81.

HOWARD, JEAN E. (1994), *The Stage and Social Struggle in Early Modern England* (New York: Routledge).

—— (2000), 'Women, Foreigners, and the Regulation of Urban Space in *Westward Ho*', in Orlin (ed.), *Material London*, 150–67.

—— (2001), 'Shakespeare and the London of City Comedy', *Shakespeare Studies*, 39: 1–21.

—— (2002), 'Competing Ideologies of Commerce in Thomas Heywood's *If You Know Not Me You Know Nobody* Part II', in Turner (ed.), *The Culture of Capital*, 163–82.

—— (2003), 'Shakespeare, Geography, and the Work of Genre on the Early Modern Stage', *Modern Language Quarterly*, 64: 299–322.

—— (2007), *Theater of a City* (forthcoming).

HOWELL, WILBUR SAMUEL (1961), *Logic and Rhetoric in England, 1500–1700* (New York: Princeton University Press; Russell & Russell).

HUNTER, GEORGE K. (1986), 'Bourgeois Comedy: Shakespeare and Dekker', in E. A. J. Honigmann (ed.), *Shakespeare and his Contemporaries* (Manchester: Manchester University Press), 1–15.

HUTSON, LORNA (1993), 'Fortunate Travelers: Reading for the Plot in Sixteenth Century England', *Representations*, 41: 83–103.

—— (1994), *The Usurer's Daughter: Male Friendship and Fictions of Women in Sixteenth-Century England* (London: Routledge).

INGRAM, WILLIAM (1988), 'The Early Career of James Burbage', in C. E. McGee (ed.), *The Elizabethan Theatre*, x (Port Credit, Ont.: P. D. Meany), 18–36.

—— (1992), *The Business of Playing: The Beginnings of the Adult Professional Theater in Elizabethan London* (Ithaca, NY: Cornell University Press).

IVENS, WILLIAM M., JR. (1946), *Art and Geometry: A Study in Space Intuitions* (New York: Dover).

JAMESON, FREDRIC (1971), *Marxism and Form: Twentieth-Century Dialectical Theories of Literature* (Princeton: Princeton University Press).

—— (1981), *The Political Unconscious: Narrative as a Socially Symbolic Act* (Ithaca, NY: Cornell University Press).

JAMMER, MAX (1954), *Concepts of Space* (Cambridge, Mass.: Harvard University Press).

JARDINE, LISA (1974*a*), *Francis Bacon: Discovery and the Arts of Discourse* (Cambridge: Cambridge University Press).

JARDINE, LISA (1974*b*), 'The Place of Dialectic Teaching in Sixteenth-Century Cambridge', *Studies in the Renaissance*, 21: 31–62.

—— (1975), 'Humanism and the Sixteenth Century Arts Course', *History of Education*, 4: 16–31.

—— (1986), 'Gabriel Harvey: Exemplary Ramist and Pragmatic Humanist', *Revue des Sciences Philosophiques et Théologiques*, 70: 36–48.

—— and WILLIAM SHERMAN (1994), 'Pragmatic Readers: Knowledge Transactions and Scholarly Services in Late Elizabethan England', in Anthony Fletcher and Peter Roberts (eds.), *Religion, Culture and Society in Early Modern Britain: Essays in Honour of Patrick Collinson* (Cambridge: Cambridge University Press), 102–24.

JARDINE NICHOLAS (1988), 'Epistemology of the Sciences', in Charles Schmitt, Quentin Skinner, Eckhard Kessler, and Jill Kraye (eds.), *The Cambridge History of Renaissance Philosophy* (Cambridge: Cambridge University Press), 685–711.

JEWKES, WILFRED T. (1958), *Act Division in Elizabethan and Jacobean Plays, 1583–1616* (Hamden, Conn.: Shoe String).

JOHNS, ADRIAN (1998), *The Nature of the Book: Print and Knowledge in the Making* (Chicago: University of Chicago Press).

JOHNSON, A. W. (1994), *Ben Jonson: Poetry and Architecture* (Oxford: Clarendon Press).

JOHNSON, FRANCIS R. (1937), *Astronomical Thought in Renaissance England: A Study of the English Scientific Writings from 1500 to 1615* (Baltimore: Johns Hopkins University Press; repr. New York: Octagon Books, 1968).

—— (1940), 'Gresham College: Precursor to the Royal Society', *Journal of the History of Ideas*, 1: 413–38.

—— (1942), 'Thomas Hood's Inaugural Address as Mathematical Lecturer of the City of London', *Journal of the History of Ideas*, 3: 94–106.

JOHNSTON, STEPHEN (1991), 'Mathematical Practitioners and Instruments in Elizabethan England', *Annals of Science*, 48: 319–44.

JONES, EMRYS (1971), *Scenic Form in Shakespeare* (Oxford: Clarendon Press).

JORGENSEN, PAUL A. (1962), *Redeeming Shakespeare's Words* (Berkeley: University of California Press).

JOSEPH, SISTER MIRIAM, CSC (1962), *Rhetoric in Shakespeare's Time: Literary Theory of Renaissance Europe* (New York: Harcourt, Brace & World).

KAHN, VICTORIA (1985), *Rhetoric, Prudence, and Skepticism in the Renaissance* (Ithaca, NY: Cornell University Press).

—— (1994), *Machiavellian Rhetoric: From the Counter-Reformation to Milton* (Princeton: Princeton University Press).

KASTAN, DAVID SCOTT (1982), *Shakespeare and the Shapes of Time* (Hanover: University Press of New England).

—— (1999), *Shakespeare after Theory* (New York: Routledge).

—— (2001), *Shakespeare and the Book* (Cambridge: Cambridge University Press).

KAUFMANN, THOMAS DACOSTA (1993), *The Mastery of Nature: Aspects of Art, Science, and Humanism in the Renaissance* (Princeton: Princeton University Press).

KAYE, JOEL (1998), *Economy and Nature in the Fourteenth Century: Money, Market Exchange, and the Emergence of Scientific Thought* (Cambridge: Cambridge University Press).

KEARNEY, HUGH (1970), *Scholars and Gentlemen: Universities and Society in Pre-Industrial Britain, 1500–1700* (Ithaca, NY: Cornell University Press).

KELLER, A. G. (1976), 'Mathematicians, Mechanics, and Experimental Machines in Northern Italy in the Sixteenth Century', in Maurice Crosland (ed.), *The Emergence of Science in Western Europe* (New York: History of Science Publications), 15–34.

KEENE, DEREK (2000), 'Material London in Time and Space', in Orlin (ed.), *Material London*, 55–74.

KER, N. R. (1986), 'The Provision of Books', in McConica (ed.), *The Collegiate University*, 441–519.

KERNAN, ALVIN (1959), *The Cankered Muse: Satire of the English Renaissance* (New Haven: Yale University Press).

KERNODLE, GEORGE (1944), *From Art to Theatre: Form and Convention in the Renaissance* (Chicago: University of Chicago Press).

KINNEY, ARTHUR (ed.) (1986), *Essential Articles for the Study of Sir Philip Sidney* (Hamden, Conn.: Archon Books).

—— (ed.) (1988), *Sidney in Retrospect: Selections from English Literary Renaissance* (Amherst: University of Massachusetts Press).

KLEIN, BERNHARD (2001), *Maps and the Writing of Space in Early Modern England and Ireland* (Houndmills: Palgrave).

KLEIN, ROBERT, in collaboration with HENRI ZERNER (1964), 'Vitruve et le théâtre de la Renaissance italienne', in eid., *La Forme et l'intelligible: Écrits sur la Renaissance et l'art moderne* (repr. Paris: Gallimard, 1970), 294–309.

KNAPP, PEGGY (2000), 'The Work of Alchemy', *Journal of Medieval and Early Modern Studies*, 30: 575–99.

KNIGHTS, L. C. (1951), *Drama and Society in the Age of Jonson* (London: Chatto & Windus).

—— (1959), *Some Shakespearean Themes* (Stanford, Calif.: Stanford University Press).

KNORR CETINA, KARIN (1999), *Epistemic Cultures: How the Sciences Make Knowledge* (Cambridge, Mass.: Harvard University Press).

KNOWLES, RICHARD A. (1963), '*As You Like It* and the Concept of Plot', Ph.D. diss. (University of Pennsylvania).

KNOWLSON, JAMES (1975), *Universal Language Schemes in England and France* (Toronto: University of Toronto Press).

KRISTELLER, PAUL OSKAR (1979), *Renaissance Thought and its Sources*, ed. Michael Mooney (New York: Columbia University Press).

—— (1990), 'The Modern System of the Arts', in id., *Renaissance Thought and the Arts: Collected Essays* (Princeton: Princeton University Press; first pub. 1952).

KUHN, THOMAS (1977), 'Mathematical versus Experimental Traditions in the Development of Physical Science', in id., *The Essential Tension: Selected Studies in Scientific Tradition and Change* (Chicago: University of Chicago Press), 31–65.

LACHTERMAN, DAVID RAPPORT (1989), *The Ethics of Geometry: A Genealogy of Modernity* (New York: Routledge).

LAIRD, W. R. (1986), 'The Scope of Renaissance Mechanics', *Osiris*, 2nd ser., 2: 43–68.

LAMB, CHARLES (1811), 'On the Tragedies of Shakespeare, Considered with Reference to their Fitness for Stage Representation,' in *The Works of Charles and Mary Lamb*, ed. E. V. Lucas, 7 vols. (London: Methuen, 1903).

LANGER, ULLRICH (1999), 'Invention', in Norton (ed.), *The Cambridge History of Literary Criticism*, 136–44.

LATOUR, BRUNO (1987), *Science in Action: How to Follow Scientists and Engineers through Society* (Cambridge, Mass.: Harvard University Press).

LATOUR, BRUNO (1990), 'Drawing Things Together', in Lynch and Woolgar (eds.), *Representation in Scientific Practice*, 19–68.

—— and WOOLGAR, STEPHEN (1986), *Laboratory Life: The Construction of Scientific Facts*, 2nd edn. (Princeton: Princeton University Press).

LECHNER, SISTER JOAN MARIE (1962), *Renaissance Concepts of the Commonplaces* (New York: Pageant Press).

LEE, H. D. P. (1935), 'Geometrical Method and Aristotle's Account of First Principles', *Classical Quarterly*, 29: 113–24.

LEEDHAM-GREEN, E. S. (1986), *Books in Cambridge Inventories: Book-Lists from Vice-Chancellor's Court Probate Inventories in the Tudor and Stuart Periods*, 2 vols. (Cambridge: Cambridge University Press).

LEFEBVRE, HENRI (1979), 'Space: Social Product and Use Value', trans. J. W. Freiberg, in J. W. Freiberg (ed.), *Critical Sociology: European Perspectives* (New York: Irvington), 285–95.

—— (1991), *The Production of Space*, trans. Donald Nicholson-Smith (Cambridge: Blackwell; first pub. 1974).

—— (1992), *Critique of Everyday Life*, trans. John Moore, with preface Michel Trebitsch (New York: Verso).

LEGGATT, ALEXANDER (1973), *Citizen Comedy in the Age of Shakespeare* (Toronto: University of Toronto Press).

LEINWAND, THEODORE B. (1986), *The City Staged: Jacobean Comedy, 1603–1613* (Madison: University of Wisconsin Press).

LEVIN, HARRY (1959), 'The Heights and the Depths', in John Garrett (ed.), *More Talking about Shakespeare* (London: Longmans), 87–103.

—— (1986), 'Notes toward a Definition of City Comedy', in Lewalski (ed.), *Renaissance Genres*, 126–46.

LEVIN, RICHARD (1971), *The Multiple Plot in English Renaissance Drama* (Chicago: University of Chicago Press).

LEWALSKI, BARBARA KIEFER (ed.) (1986), *Renaissance Genres: Essays on Theory, History, and Interpretation* (Cambridge, Mass.: Harvard University Press).

LEWIS, C. S. (1960), *Studies in Words* (Cambridge: Cambridge University Press; repr. 1961).

LINDBERG, DAVID C. (1990), 'Conceptions of the Scientific Revolution from Bacon to Butterfield: A Preliminary Sketch', in Lindberg and Westman (eds.), *Reappraisals*, 1–26.

—— and ROBERT C. WESTMAN (eds.) (1990), *Reappraisals of the Scientific Revolution* (Cambridge: Cambridge University Press).

LOENGARD, JANET S. (1983), 'An Elizabethan Lawsuit: John Brayne, his Carpenter, and the Building of the Red Lion Theatre', *Shakespeare Quarterly*, 34: 298–310.

LOEWENSTEIN, JOSEPH (1984), *Responsive Readings: Versions of Echo in Pastoral, Epic, and the Jonsonian Masque* (New Haven: Yale University Press).

—— (1985), 'The Script in the Marketplace', *Representations*, 12: 101–14.

—— (1991), 'Printing and "the Multitudinous Presse": The Contentious Texts of Jonson's Masques', in Brady and Herendeen (eds.), *Ben Jonson's 1616 Folio*, 168–91.

—— (2002a), *Ben Jonson and Possessive Authorship* (Cambridge: Cambridge University Press).

—— (2002b), *The Author's Due: Printing and the Prehistory of Copyright* (Chicago: University of Chicago Press).

LONG, PAMELA O. (1985), 'The Contribution of Architectural Writers to a "Scientific" Outlook in the Fifteenth and Sixteenth Centuries', *Journal of Medieval and Renaissance Studies*, 15/2: 265–98.

—— (1997), 'Power, Patronage, and the Authorship of *Ars*: From Mechanical Know-how to Mechanical Knowledge in the Last Scribal Age', *Isis*, 88: 1–41.

—— (2001), *Openness, Secrecy, Authorship: Technical Arts and the Culture of Knowledge from Antiquity to the Renaissance* (Baltimore: Johns Hopkins University Press).

LUBORSKY, RUTH SAMSON, and ELIZABETH MORELY INGRAM (eds.) (1998), *A Guide to English Illustrated Books 1536–1603* (Tempe, Ariz: MRTS).

LUPTON, JULIA REINHARD (1987), 'Truant Dispositions: Hamlet and Machiavelli', *Journal of Medieval and Renaissance Studies*, 17: 59–82.

—— (1993), 'Mapping Mutability; or, Spenser's Irish Plot', in Brendan Bradshaw, Andrew Hadfield, and Willy Maley (eds.), *Representing Ireland: Literature and the Origins of Conflict, 1534–1660* (Cambridge: Cambridge University Press), 93–115.

LYNCH, MICHAEL (1990), 'The Externalized Retina: Selection and Mathematization in the Visual Documentation of Objects in the Life Sciences', in Lynch and Woolgar (eds.), *Representation in Scientific Practice*, 153–86.

—— and STEPHEN WOOLGAR (eds.) (1990), *Representation in Scientific Practice* (Cambridge, Mass.: MIT Press).

McCONICA, JAMES (1979), 'Humanism and Aristotle in Tudor Oxford', *English Historical Review*, 94: 291–317.

—— (ed.) (1986), *The Collegiate University*, vol. iii in *The History of the University of Oxford*, gen. ed. T. H. Aston (Oxford: Clarendon Press).

MACK, PETER (1996), 'Humanist Rhetoric and Dialectic', in Jill Kraye (ed.), *The Cambridge Companion to Renaissance Humanism* (Cambridge: Cambridge University Press), 82–99.

McKENZIE, D. F. (1977), 'Typography and Meaning: The Case of William Congreve', in Giles Barber and Bernhard Fabian (eds.), in *Buch und Buchhandel in Europa im achtzehnten Jahrhundert* (Hamburg: Dr Ernst Hauswedell), 81–123.

—— (1986), *Bibliography and the Sociology of Texts*, the Panizzi Lectures, 1985 (London: British Library).

McKLUSKIE, KATHLEEN E. (1994), *Dekker and Heywood: Professional Dramatists* (New York: St Martin's Press).

McNEILL, FIONA (1997), 'Gynocentric London Spaces: (Re)Locating Masterless Women in Early Stuart Drama', *Renaissance Drama*, NS 28: 195–244.

McPHERSON, DAVID (1974), 'Ben Jonson's Library and Marginalia: An Annotated Catalogue', *Studies in Philology*, 71/5: 1–106.

McRAE, ANDREW (1996), *God Speed the Plough: The Representation of Agrarian England, 1500–1660* (Cambridge: Cambridge University Press).

MANICAS, PETER T. (1987), *A History and Philosophy of the Social Sciences* (Oxford: Blackwell).

MANLEY, LAWRENCE (1995), *Literature and Culture in Early Modern London* (Cambridge: Cambridge University Press).

MARCUS, LEAH S. (1996), *Unediting the Renaissance: Shakespeare, Marlowe, Milton* (New York: Routledge).

MARIN, LOUIS (1984), *Utopics: Spatial Play*, trans. Robert A. Vollrath (Atlantic Highlands, NJ: Humanities Press).

MARIN, LOUIS (1988), *Portrait of the King*, trans. Martha M. Houle, Foreword Tom Conley (Minneapolis: University of Minnesota Press).

—— (2001), *On Representation*, trans. Catherine Porter (Stanford, Calif.: Stanford University Press).

MARTIN, CATHERINE GIMELLI (1996), ' "Boundless the Deep": Milton, Pascal, and the Theology of Relative Space', *ELH* 63: 45–78.

—— (2001), ' "What if the Sun be Centre to the World?' Milton's Epistemology, Cosmology, and Paradise of Fools Reconsidered', *Modern Philology*, 99: 231–65.

MARKLEY, ROBERT (1993), *Fallen Languages: Crises of Representation in Newtonian England, 1660–1740* (Ithaca, NY: Cornell University Press).

MASTEN, JEFFREY (1996), *Textual Intercourse: Collaboration, Authorship, and Sexualities in Renaissance Drama* (Cambridge: Cambridge University Press).

—— (1997), 'Playwrighting: Authorship and Collaboration', in Cox and Kastan (eds.), *A New History of Early English Drama*, 357–82.

MAZZIO, CARLA (2004), 'The Three Dimensional Self: Geometry, Melancholy, Drama', in Glimp and Warren (eds.), *Arts of Calculation*, 39–65.

MAUS, KATHERINE EISAMAN (1984), *Ben Jonson and the Roman Frame of Mind* (Princeton: Princeton University Press).

MENDYK, STAN A. E. (1988), *Speculum Britanniae: Regional Study, Antiquarianism, and Science in Britain to 1700* (Toronto: University of Toronto Press).

MENON, MADHAVI (2004), *Wanton Words: Rhetoric and Sexuality in English Renaissance Drama* (Toronto: University of Toronto Press).

MERRIMAN, MARCUS (1983), 'Italian Military Engineers in Britain in the 1540s', in Tyacke (ed.), *English Map-Making*, 57–67.

METER, J. H. (1984), *The Literary Theories of Daniel Heinsius: A Study of the Development and Background of his Views on Literary Theory and Criticism during the Period from 1602–1612*, trans. Ina Swart (Assen: Van Gorcum).

MEYER, EDWARD (1897), *Machiavelli and the Elizabethan Drama* (Weimar: Emil Felber).

MONTAGU, M. F. ASHLEY (ed.) ([1946*a*]); 'Suggestions for the Better Correlation of Literature and Science', in Montagu (ed.), *Studies and Essays in the History of Science*, 237–46.

—— ([1946*b*]), *Studies and Essays in the History of Science and Learning Offered in Homage to George Sarton on the Occasion of his Sixtieth Birthday, 31 August 1944* (New York: Schuman).

MORGAN, VICTOR (1979), 'The Cartographic Image of "The Country" in Early Modern England', *Transactions of the Royal Historical Society*, 5th ser., 29: 129–54.

MORGAN-RUSSELL, SIMON (1999), ' "No Good Thing Ever Comes Out of It": Male Expectation and Female Alliance in Dekker and Webster's *Westward Ho*', in Susan Frye and Karen Robertson (eds.), *Maids and Mistresses, Cousins and Queens: Women's Alliances in Early Modern England* (New York: Oxford University Press), 70–84.

MOSS, ANN (1996), *Printed Commonplace-Books and the Structuring of Renaissance Thought* (Oxford: Clarendon Press).

MUKERJI, CHANDRA (1983), *From Graven Images: Patterns of Modern Materialism* (New York: Columbia University Press).

MULLANEY, STEVEN (1988), *The Place of the Stage: License, Play and Power in Renaissance England* (Chicago: University of Chicago Press).

MULRYNE, J. R., and MARGARET SHEWRING (1997), *Shakespeare's Globe Rebuilt*, advisory ed. Andrew Gurr (Cambridge: Cambridge University Press).

MURRAY, TIMOTHY (1987), *Theatrical Legitimation: Allegories of Genius in Seventeenth-Century England and France* (New York: Oxford University Press).

MYRICK, KENNETH (1935), *Sir Philip Sidney as a Literary Craftsman* (Lincoln: Nebraska University Press).

NEWMAN, KAREN (1991), *Fashioning Femininity and English Renaissance Drama* (Chicago: University of Chicago Press).

—— (2000), 'Toward a Topographic Imaginary: Early Modern Paris', in Carla Mazzio and Douglas Trevor (eds.), *Historicism, Psychoanalysis, and Early Modern Culture*, 59–81.

—— (2002), 'Walking Capitals: Donne's First Satyre', in Turner (ed.), *The Culture of Capital*, 203–21.

NEWMAN, WILLIAM R. (1989), 'Technology and Alchemical Debate in the Late Middle Ages', *Isis*, 80: 423–45.

—— (1997), 'Art, Nature, and Experiment among Some Aristotelian Alchemists', in Edith Sylla and Michael McVaugh (eds.), *Texts and Contexts in Ancient and Medieval Science: Studies on the Occasion of John E. Murdoch's Seventieth Birthday* (Leiden: Brill), 305–17.

—— and ANTHONY GRAFTON (2001), 'Introduction: The Problematic Status of Astrology and Alchemy in Premodern Europe', in William R. Newman and Anthony Grafton (eds.), *Secrets of Nature: Astrology and Alchemy in Early Modern Europe* (Cambridge, Mass.: MIT Press).

NEWTON, NORTON (1997), 'The Palace of Rhetoric: Geometrical and Architectural Form in Ben Jonson', *Dalhousie Review*, 77: 23–44.

NICOLSON, MARJORIE (1956), *Science and Imagination* (Ithaca, NY: Cornell University Press).

—— (1960), *The Breaking of the Circle* (New York: Columbia University Press).

NORTON, GLYN P. (1999), *The Cambridge History of Literary Criticism*, iii: *The Renaissance* (Cambridge: Cambridge University Press).

O'DAY, ROSEMARY (1982), *Education and Society, 1500–1800: The Social Foundations of Education in Early Modern Britain* (London: Longmans).

OLSCHKI, LEONARDO (1919–27), *Geschichte der Neusprachlichen Wissenschaftlichen Literatur*, 3 vols. (Heidelberg: Carl Winter's Universitätsbuchhandlung; Vanduz: Kraus Reprint, 1965).

ONG, WALTER J. (1958), *Ramus, Method, and the Decay of Dialogue* (Cambridge, Mass.: Harvard University Press).

—— (1962), 'System, Space and Intellect in Renaissance Symbolism', *The Barbarian Within and Other Fugitive Essays and Studies* (New York: Macmillan), 68–87.

ORGEL, STEPHEN (1965), *The Jonsonian Masque* (Cambridge, Mass.: Harvard University Press).

—— (1975), *The Illusion of Power: Political Theater in the English Renaissance* (Berkeley: University of California Press).

—— (1984), 'Shakespeare Imagines a Theater', *Poetics Today*, 5: 549–61.

—— (ed.) (2002), *The Authentic Shakespeare* (New York: Routledge).

—— and ROY STRONG (1973), *Inigo Jones: The Theater of the Stuart Court*, 2 vols. (Berkeley: University of California Press).

ORLIN, LENA COWEN (1994), *Private Matters in Public Culture in Post-Reformation England* (Ithaca, NY: Cornell University Press).

—— (1995), ' "The Causes and Reasons of All Artificial Things" in the Elizabethan Domestic Environment', *Medieval and Renaissance Drama in England*, 7: 19–75.

—— (ed.) (2000*a*), *Material London* (Philadelphia: University of Pennsylvania Press).

—— (2000*b*), 'Boundary Disputes in Early Modern London', in Orlin (ed.), *Material London*, 345–76.

ORRELL, JOHN (1988), *The Human Stage: English Theatre Design, 1567–1640* (Cambridge: Cambridge University Press).

—— (1993), 'Building the Fortune', *Shakespeare Quarterly*, 44: 1–10.

—— (1997), 'Designing the Globe: Reading the Documents', in Mulryne and Shewring (eds.), *Shakespeare's Globe Rebuilt*, 51–65.

OSBORN, JAMES M. (1972), *Young Philip Sidney, 1572–1577* (New Haven: Yale University Press).

OSTOVICH, HELEN (1999), ' "To Behold the Scene Full": Seeing and Judging in *Every Man Out of His Humour*', in Butler (ed.), *Re-presenting Ben Jonson*, 76–92.

OVITT, GEORGE, JR. (1987), *The Restoration of Perfection: Labor and Technology in Medieval Culture*, (New Brunswick, NJ: Rutgers University Press).

PADLEY, G. A. (1985–8). *Grammatical Theory in Western Europe*, 2 vols. (Cambridge: Cambridge University Press).

PALME, PER (1959), 'Ut Architectura Poesis', in Nils Gösta Sandblad (ed.), *Idea and Form: Studies in the History of Art*, Uppsala Studies in the History of Art, NS, 1 (Stockholm: Almquist & Wiksells).

PARKER, PATRICIA (1987), *Literary Fat Ladies: Rhetoric, Gender, Property* (New York: Methuen).

—— (1996), 'Rude Mechanicals', in Margreta De Grazia, Maureen Quilligan, and Peter Stallybrass (eds.), *Subject and Object in Renaissance Culture* (Cambridge: Cambridge University Press), 43–82.

PARSONS, WILLIAM BARCLAY (1968), *Engineers and Engineering in the Renaissance* (Cambridge, Mass.: MIT Press; first pub. 1939).

PASTER, GAIL KERN (1974), 'Ben Jonson and the Uses of Architecture', *Renaissance Quarterly*, 27: 306–20.

—— (1985), *The Idea of the City in the Age of Shakespeare* (Athens: University of Georgia Press).

—— (1993), *The Body Embarrassed: Drama and the Disciplines of Shame in Early Modern England* (Ithaca, NY: Cornell University Press).

PAVEL, THOMAS G. (1985), *The Poetics of Plot: The Case of English Renaissance Drama* (Minneapolis: University of Minnesota Press).

PAVIS, PATRICE (1982*a*), *Voix et images de la scène: Essais de sémiologie théâtrale* (Lille: Presses universitaires de Lille).

—— (1982*b*), *Languages of the Stage: Essays in the Semiology of the Theatre* (New York: Performing Arts Journal Publications).

—— (1996), 'Performance Analysis: Space, Time, Action', trans. Sinéad Rushe, *Gestos*, 22: 11–32.

PAYNE, PAULA H. (1990), 'Tracing Aristotle's *Rhetoric* in Sir Philip Sidney's Poetry and Prose', *Rhetoric Society Quarterly*, 3: 241–50.

PEACOCK, JOHN (1995), *The Stage Designs of Inigo Jones: The European Context* (Cambridge: Cambridge University Press).

PEARL, VALERIE (1961), *London and the Outbreak of the Puritan Revolution: City Government and National Politics, 1625–43* (Oxford: Oxford University Press).

PEIRCE, CHARLES SANDERS (1931–58), *The Collected Papers of Charles Sanders Peirce* i–vi, ed. Charles Hartshorne and Paul Weiss; vii–viii, ed. Arthur Brooks, 8 vols. in 4 (Cambridge, Mass.: Harvard University Press).

—— (1957), *Essays in the Philosophy of Science* (New York: Liberal Arts Press).

PEREZ-RAMOS, ANTONIO (1988), *Francis Bacon's Idea of Science and the Maker's Knowledge Tradition* (Oxford: Clarendon Press).

PERKINSON, RICHARD (1936), 'Topographical Comedy in the Seventeenth Century', *ELH* 3: 270–90.

PETERS, F. E. (1967), *Greek Philosophical Terms: A Historical Lexicon* (New York: New York University Press).

PETERS, JULIE STONE (2000), *Theatre of the Book, 1480–1880: Print, Text, and Performance in Europe* (Oxford: Oxford University Press).

PICKERING, ANDY (1989), 'Living in the Material World: On Realism and Experimental Practice', in Gooding *et al.* (eds.), *The Uses of Experiment*, 275–97.

PLATT, COLIN (1994), *The Great Rebuildings of Tudor and Stuart England: Revolutions in Architectural Taste* (London: UCL Press).

POCOCK, J. G. A. (1975), *The Machiavellian Moment: Florentine Political Thought and the Atlantic Republican Tradition* (Princeton: Princeton University Press).

POOVEY, MARY (1995), *Making a Social Body: British Cultural Formation, 1830–1864* (Chicago: University of Chicago Press).

—— (1998), *A History of the Modern Fact: Problems of Knowledge in the Sciences of Wealth and Society* (Chicago: University of Chicago Press).

POWER, M. J. (1972), 'East London Housing in the Seventeenth Century', in Peter Clark and Paul Slack (eds.), *Crisis and Order in English Towns, 1500–1700* (London: Routledge & Kegan Paul), 237–62.

—— (1978), 'The East and West in Early-Modern London', in E. W. Ives, R. J. Kaecht, and J. J. Scarisbrick (eds.), *Wealth and Power in Tudor England: Essays Presented to S. T. Bindoff* (London: Athlone Press for the University of London), 167–85.

PRAZ, MARIO (1928), 'Machiavelli and the Elizabethans', *Proceedings of the British Academy*, 13: 49–97.

PUMFREY, STEPHEN, PAOLO L. ROSSI, and MAURICE SLAWINSKI (eds.) (1991), *Science, Culture, and Popular Belief in Renaissance Europe* (Manchester: Manchester University Press).

RAAB, FELIX (1964), *The English Face of Machiavelli: A Changing Interpretation, 1500–1700* (London: Routledge & Kegan Paul).

RAINEY, RONALD (1991), 'Dressing Down the Dressed-Up: Reproving Feminine Attire in Renaissance Florence', in John Monfasani and Ronald G. Musto (eds.), *Renaissance Society and Culture: Essays in Honor of Eugene F. Rice, Jr.* (New York: Italica Press), 217–37.

RANDALL, JOHN H. (1940), 'The Development of Scientific Method', *Journal of the History of Ideas*, 1: 177–206.

RAPPAPORT, STEVE (1989), *Worlds within Worlds: Structures of Life in Sixteenth-Century London* (Cambridge: Cambridge University Press).

RATH, ERICH VON (1925–38), *Gesamtkatalog der Wiegendrucke* (Leipzig: K. W. Hiersemann).

REIF, SISTER PATRICIA (1962), 'Natural Philosophy in Some Early Seventeenth-Century Textbooks', Ph.D. diss. (St Louis University).

—— (1969), 'The Textbook Tradition in Natural Philosophy', *Journal of the History of Ideas*, 30: 17–32.

REISS, TIMOTHY (1997), *Knowledge, Discovery, and Imagination in Early Modern Europe: The Rise of Aesthetic Rationalism* (Cambridge: Cambridge University Press).

—— (2000), 'From Trivium to Quadrivium: Ramus, Method, and Mathematical Technology', in Neil Rhodes and Jonathan Sawday (eds.), *The Renaissance Computer: Knowledge Technology in the First Age of Print* (London: Routledge), 45–58.

—— (2004), 'Calculating Humans: Mathematics, War, and the Colonial Calculus', in Glimp and Warren (eds.), *Arts of Calculation*, 137–63.

REYHER, PAUL (1909), *Les Masques anglais: Études sur les ballets et la vie de cour en Angleterre (1512–1640)* (Paris; reissued, New York: Benjamin Blom, 1964).

REYNOLDS, BRYAN (2002), *Becoming Criminal: Transversal Performance and Cultural Dissidence in Early Modern England* (Baltimore: Johns Hopkins University Press).

—— and JOSEPH FITZPATRICK (1999), 'The Transversality of Michel de Certeau: Foucault's Panoptic Discourse and the Cartographic Impulse', *Diacritics*, 29/3: 63–80.

RIGGS, DAVID (1989), *Ben Jonson: A Life* (Cambridge, Mass.: Harvard University Press).

ROBINSON, FORREST (1972), *The Shape of Things Known* (Cambridge, Mass.: Harvard University Press).

ROGERS, JOHN (1996), *The Matter of Revolution: Science, Poetry, and Politics in the Age of Milton* (Ithaca, NY: Cornell University Press).

ROONEY, ELLEN (2000), 'Form and Contentment', *Modern Literary Quarterly*, 61: 17–40.

ROSE, MARK (1972), *Shakespearean Design* (Cambridge, Mass.: Harvard University Press).

ROSENBERG, ELEANOR (1955), *Leicester, Patron of Letters* (New York: Columbia University Press).

ROSS, CHERYL LYNN (1988), 'The Plague of *The Alchemist*', *Renaissance Quarterly*, 41: 439–58.

ROSS, W. D. (1953), *Aristotle* (London: Methuen).

ROSSI, PAOLO ([1968]), *Francis Bacon: From Magic to Science*, trans. by Sacha Rabinovitch (Chicago: University of Chicago Press).

—— (1970), *Philosophy, Technology and the Arts in the Early Modern Era*, trans. Salvator Attanasio, ed. Benjamin Nelson (New York: Harper & Row).

SACKS, DAVID HARRIS (2000), 'London's Dominion: The Metropolis, the Market Economy, and the Stage', in Orlin (ed.), *Material London*, 20–54.

—— (2002), 'The Metropolis and the Revolution: Commercial, Urban, and Political Culture in Early Modern London', in Turner (ed.), *The Culture of Capital*, 139–162.

SAIBER, ARIELLE (2005), *Giordano Bruno and the Geometry of Language* (Aldershot: Ashgate).

SALINGER, LEO (1986), *Dramatic Form in Shakespeare and the Jacobeans* (Cambridge: Cambridge University Press).

SALZMAN, L. F. (1952), *Building in England down to 1540: A Documentary History* (Oxford: Clarendon Press).

SAWDAY, JONATHAN (1996), *The Body Emblazoned: Dissection and the Human Body in Renaissance Culture* (New York: Routledge).

SCHAFFER, SIMON (1989), 'Glass Works: Newton's Prisms and the Uses of Experiment', in Gooding *et al.* (eds.), *The Uses of Experiment*, 67–104.

SCHMITT, CHARLES (1975), 'Philosophy and Science in Sixteenth-Century Universities: Some Preliminary Comments', in John Emery Murdoch and Edith Dudley Sylla (eds.), *The Cultural Context of Medieval Learning* (Dordrecht: Reidel), 485–537.

—— (1983*a*), *Aristotle and the Renaissance* (Cambridge, Mass.: Harvard University Press).

—— (1983*b*), *John Case and Aristotelianism in Renaissance England* (Kingston, Ont.: McGill-Queen's University Press).

—— (1984), *The Aristotelian Tradition and Renaissance Universities* (London: Variorum Reprints).

SCHOFIELD, JOHN (ed.) (1987), *The London Surveys of Ralph Treswell* (London: London Topographical Society).

—— (1994), *Medieval London Houses* (New Haven: Yale University Press).

—— (2000), 'The Topography and Buildings of London, *ca.*1600', in Orlin (ed.), *Material London*, 296–321.

SCODEL, JOSHUA (1999), 'Seventeenth-Century English Literary Criticism: Classical Values, English Texts and Contexts', in Norton (ed.), *The Cambridge History of Literary Criticism*, 543–54.

SCOTT, MARGARET (1984), 'Machiavelli and the Machiavel', *Renaissance Drama*, NS 15: 147–74.

SEATON, ETHEL (1924), 'Marlowe's Map', *Essays and Studies by Members of the English Association*, 10: 13–35.

—— (1929), 'Fresh Sources for Marlowe', *Review of English Studies*, 5: 385–401.

SELLIN, PAUL R. (1968), *Daniel Heinsius and Stuart England* (Oxford: Oxford University Press).

SERRES, MICHEL (1982), *Hermes: Literature, Science, Philosophy*, ed. Josué V. Harari and David F. Bell (Baltimore: Johns Hopkins University Press).

SHAKESPEARE, WILLIAM (*c.*1605), *The Tragedy of King Lear*, ed. Jay L. Halio (Cambridge: Cambridge University Press, 1992).

—— (1725), *The Works of Shakespeare*, ed. Alexander Pope, 6 vols.

SHAPIN, STEVEN (1994), *A Social History of Truth: Civility and Science in Seventeenth-Century England* (Chicago: University of Chicago Press).

—— and SIMON SCHAFFER (1985), *Leviathan and the Air-Pump: Hobbes, Boyle, and the Experimental Life* (Princeton: Princeton University Press).

SHAPIRO, BARBARA (1983), *Probability and Certainty in Seventeenth-Century England* (Princeton: Princeton University Press).

—— (2000), *A Culture of Fact: England, 1550–1720* (Ithaca, NY: Cornell University Press).

SHAW, DIANE (1996), 'The Construction of the Private in Medieval London', *Journal of Medieval and Early Modern Studies*, 26: 447–66.

SHERMAN, WILLIAM (1995), *John Dee: The Politics of Reading and Writing in the English Renaissance* (Amherst: University of Massachusetts Press).

SHIRLEY, JOHN W. (ed.) (1974) *Thomas Harriot, Renaissance Scientist* (Oxford: Clarendon Press).

—— (1983), *Thomas Harriot: A Biography* (Oxford: Clarendon Press).

SIEMON, JAMES R. (1994), 'Landlord not King: Agrarian Change and Interarticulation', in Richard Burt and John Archer (eds.), *Enclosure Acts: Sexuality, Property, and Culture in Early Modern England* (Ithaca, NY: Cornell University Press), 17–33.

SILVER, LARRY, and PAMELA H. SMITH (2002), 'Splendor in the Grass: The Powers of Nature and Art in the Age of Dürer', in Smith and Findlen (eds.), *Merchants and Marvels*, 29–62.

SIMON, JOAN (1966), *Education and Society in Tudor England* (Cambridge: Cambridge University Press).

SLAUGHTER, MARY M. (1982), *Universal Languages and Scientific Taxonomy in the Seventeenth Century* (Cambridge: Cambridge University Press).

SLAWINSKI, MAURICE (1991), 'Rhetoric and Science/Rhetoric of Science/Rhetoric as Science', in Pumfrey *et al.* (eds.), *Science, Culture, and Popular Belief in Renaissance Europe*, 71–99.

SMALLWOOD, R. L. (1981), ' "Here, in the Friars": Immediacy and Theatricality in *The Alchemist*', *Review of English Studies*, NS, 32: 142–60.

SMITH, BRUCE R. (1988), *Ancient Scripts and Modern Experience on the English Stage, 1500–1700* (Princeton: Princeton University Press).

—— (1999), *The Acoustic World of Early Modern England: Attending to the O-Factor* (Chicago: University of Chicago Press).

SMITH, CHRISTINE (1992), *Architecture in the Culture of Early Humanism* (Oxford: Oxford University Press).

SMITH, IRWIN (1963), *Shakespeare's Globe Playhouse* (London: Peter Owen).

—— (1964), *Shakespeare's Blackfriars Playhouse: Its History and its Design* (New York: New York University Press).

SMITH, DAVID L., RICHARD STRIER, and DAVID BEVINGTON (eds.) (1995), *The Theatrical City: Culture, Theatre, and Politics in London, 1576–1649* (Cambridge: Cambridge University Press).

SMITH, PAMELA (1994), *The Business of Alchemy: Science and Culture in the Holy Roman Empire* (Princeton: Princeton University Press).

—— and PAULA FINDLEN (eds.) (2002*a*), *Merchants and Marvels: Commerce, Science, and Art in Early Modern Europe* (New York: Routledge).

—— (2002*b*), 'Commerce and the Representation of Nature in Art and Science', in eaed. (eds.), *Merchants and Marvels*, 1–25.

SNOW, C. P. (1964), *The Two Cultures: And a Second Look* (Cambridge: Cambridge University Press).

SNUGGS, HENRY L. (1960), *Shakespeare and Five Acts: Studies in a Dramatic Convention* (New York: Vantage).

SOLOMON, JULIE ROBIN (1998), *Objectivity in the Making: Francis Bacon and the Politics of Inquiry* (Baltimore: Johns Hopkins University Press).

SPILLER, ELIZABETH (2004), *Science, Reading, and Renaissance Literature: The Art of Making Knowledge* (Cambridge: Cambridge University Press).

SPINGARN, JOEL (1924), *A History of Literary Criticism in the Renaissance* (Westport, Conn.: Greenwood Press; repr. 1976).

STERN, VIRGINIA (1979), *Gabriel Harvey: His Life, Marginalia, and Library* (Oxford: Clarendon Press).

STEWART, ALAN (2000), *Philip Sidney: A Double Life* (London: Chatto & Windus).

STILLMAN, ROBERT E. (1995), *The New Philosophy and Universal Languages in Seventeenth-Century England: Bacon, Hobbes, and Wilkins* (Lewisburg, Pa.: Bucknell University Press).

STONE, LAWRENCE (1980), 'The Residential Development of the West End of London in the Seventeenth Century', in Barbara C. Malament (ed.), *After the Reformation: Essays in Honor of J. H. Hexter* (Philadelphia: University of Pennsylvania Press), 167–212.

STONE, P. W. K. (1980), *The Textual History of King Lear* (London: Scolar).

STRONG, EDWARD W. (1932), *Procedures and Metaphysics: A Study in the Philosophy of Mathematical–Physical Science in the Sixteenth and Seventeenth Centuries* (Berkeley: University of California Press; repr. Hildesheim: Georg Olms Verlagsbuchhandlung, 1966).

STRUEVER, NANCY S. (1992), *Theory as Practice: Ethical Inquiry in the Renaissance* (Chicago: University of Chicago Press).

STYAN, J. L. (1967), *Shakespeare's Stagecraft* (Cambridge: Cambridge University Press).

SULLIVAN, GARRETT A., JR. (1994), ' "Arden Lay Murdered in that Plot of Ground": Surveying, Land, and *Arden of Faversham*', *ELH* 61: 231–52.

—— (1997), 'Space, Measurement, and Stalking Tamburlaine', *Renaissance Drama*, NS, 28: 3–27.

—— (1998), *The Drama of Landscape: Land, Property, and Social Relations on the Early Modern Stage* (Stanford, Calif.: Stanford University Press).

SUMMERS, DAVID (1987), *The Judgment of Sense: Renaissance Naturalism and the Rise of Aesthetics* (Cambridge: Cambridge University Press).

SUMMERSON, JOHN (1966), *Inigo Jones* (Baltimore: Penguin Books).

—— (1991), *Architecture in Britain, 1530 to 1830* (New York: Penguin Books; first pub. 1953).

SVENDSEN, KESTER (1956), *Milton and Science* (Cambridge, Mass.: Harvard University Press).

SWAN, CLAUDIA (2002), 'From Blowfish to Flower Still Life Paintings: Classification and its Images, *circa* 1600', in Smith and Findlen (eds.), *Merchants and Marvels*, 109–36.

TAVERNOR, ROBERT (1991), *Palladio and Palladianism* (London: Thames & Hudson).

TAYLER, EDWARD W. (1990), '*King Lear* and Negation', *ELR* 20: 17–39.

TAYLOR, E. G. R. (1930), *Tudor Geography, 1485–1583* (London: Methuen).

—— (1934), *Late Tudor and Early Stuart Geography, 1583–1650* (London: Methuen; repr. New York: Octagon Books, 1968).

—— (1947), 'The Surveyor', *Economic History Review*, 17: 121–33.

—— (1954), *Mathematical Practitioners of Tudor and Stuart England* (Cambridge: Cambridge University Press; repr. Redondo Beach, Calif.: The Gemmary, 1989).

TAYLOR, GARY (1993*a*), 'The Structure of Performance: Act-Intervals in the London Theatres, 1576–1642', in Gary Taylor and John Jowett, *Shakespeare Reshaped 1606–1623* (Oxford: Oxford University Press, 1993), 3–50.

—— (1993*b*), 'Post-Script', in Gary Taylor and John Jowett, *Shakespeare Reshaped 1606–1623* (Oxford: Oxford University Press), 237–43.

—— and MICHAEL WARREN (eds.) (1983), *The Division of the Kingdoms: Shakespeare's Two Versions of* King Lear (Oxford: Clarendon Press).

THIRSK, JOAN (1978), *Economic Policy and Projects: The Development of a Consumer Society in Early Modern England* (Oxford: Clarendon Press).

—— (2000), 'England's Provinces: Did they Serve or Drive Material London?', in Orlin (ed.), *Material London*, 97–108.

THOMAS, KEITH (1987), 'Numeracy in Early Modern England', *Transactions of the Royal Historical Society*, 5th ser., 37: 103–32.

TRAUB, VALERIE (2000), 'Mapping the Global Body', in Peter Erickson and Clark Hulse (eds.), *Early Modern Visual Culture: Representation, Race, and Empire in Renaissance England* (Philadelphia: University of Pennsylvania Press), 44–97.

TRIMPI, WESLEY (1962), *Ben Jonson's Poems: A Study of the Plain Style* (Stanford, Calif.: Stanford University Press).

—— (1983), *Muses of One Mind: The Literary Analysis of Experience and its Continuity* (Princeton: Princeton University Press).

—— (1999), 'Sir Philip Sidney's *An Apology for Poetry*,' in Norton (ed.), *The Cambridge History of Literary Criticism*, 187–98.

TUAN, YI-FU (1977), *Space and Place: The Perspective of Experience* (Minneapolis: University of Minnesota Press).

TURNER, G. L'E. (1983), 'Mathematical Instrument-Making in London in the Sixteenth Century', in Tyacke (ed.), *English Map-Making*, 93–106.

—— (1991), 'Introduction: Some Notes on the Development of Surveying and the Instruments Used', *Annals of Science*, 48: 313–17.

TURNER, HENRY S. (1997), '*King Lear* Without: The Heath', *Renaissance Drama*, NS 28: 161–93.

—— (2001), 'Nashe's Red Herring: Epistemologies of the Commodity in *Lenten Stuffe* (1599)', *ELH* 68: 529–61.

—— (ed.) (2002*a*), *The Culture of Capital: Property, Cities, and Knowledge in Early Modern England* (New York: Routledge).

—— (2002*b*), 'Plotting Early Modernity', in Turner (ed.), *The Culture of Capital*, 85–127.

—— (2007), 'Literature and Mapping in England, 1520–1688', in *The History of Cartography*, iii: *Cartography in the European Renaissance*, ed. David Woodward (Chicago: University of Chicago Press).

TUVE, ROSAMOND (1947), *Elizabethan and Metaphysical Imagery: Renaissance Poetic and Twentieth-Century Critics* (Chicago: University of Chicago Press).

—— (1968), 'Imagery and Logic: Ramus and Metaphysical Poetics', in Paul Oskar Kristeller and Philip Wiener (eds.), *Renaissance Essays from the Journal of the History of Ideas* (New York: Harper & Row), 267–302.

TYACKE, NICHOLAS (ed.) (1997), *The Seventeenth Century*, iv of *The History of the University of Oxford* (Oxford: Clarendon Press).

TYACKE, SARAH (ed.) (1983), *English Map-Making, 1500–1650: Historical Essays* (London: British Library).

ULREICH, JOHN C. (1986), ' "The Poet's Only Deliver": Sidney's Conception of Mimesis', in Kinney (ed.), *Essential Articles for the Study of Sir Philip Sidney*, 135–54.

VAN DEN BERG, KENT T. (1985), *Playhouse and Cosmos: Shakespearean Theater as Metaphor* (Newark: University of Delaware Press; London: Associated University Presses).

VAN DEN BERG, SARA (1991), 'Ben Jonson and the Ideology of Authorship', in Brady and Herendeen (eds.), *Ben Jonson's 1616 Folio*, 111–37.

VAN DORSTEN, J. A. (1962), *Poets, Patrons, and Professors: Sir Philip Sidney, Daniel Rogers, and the Leiden Humanists* (Leiden: Leiden University Press for the Sir Thomas Browne Institute).

VÉRIN, HÉLÈNE (1993), *La Gloire des ingénieurs: L'Intelligence technique du XVIe au XVIIIe siècle* (Paris: Albin Michel).

VICKERS, BRIAN (1968), *Francis Bacon and Renaissance Prose* (Cambridge: Cambridge University Press).

WALLACE, CHARLES WILLIAM (1913), *The First London Theatre: Materials for a History* (London: Benjamin Blom; reissued 1969).

WALLACE, MALCOLM WILLIAM (1915), *The Life of Sir Philip Sidney* (Cambridge: Cambridge University Press; repr. New York: Octagon Books, 1967).

WARD, JOSEPH P. (1997), *Metropolitan Communities: Trade Guilds, Identity, and Change in Early Modern London* (Stanford, Calif.: Stanford University Press).

WATSON, ROBERT N. (1976), 'Machiavel and Machiavelli', *Sewanee Review*, 84: 630–48.

—— (1986), '*The Alchemist* and Jonson's Conversion of Comedy', in Lewalski (ed.), *Renaissance Genres*, 332–65.

WEBER, MAX (1978), *Economy and Society: An Outline of Interpretive Sociology*, ed. Guenther Roth and Claus Wittich, 2 vols. (Berkeley: University of California Press).

WEIMANN, ROBERT (1978), *Shakespeare and the Popular Tradition of the Theater: Studies in the Social Dimension of Dramatic Form and Function*, ed. Robert Schwarz (Baltimore: Johns Hopkins University Press; first pub. 1967).

—— (2000), *Author's Pen and Actor's Voice* (Cambridge: Cambridge University Press).

WEINBERG, BERNARD (1950), *Critical Prefaces of the French Renaissance* (Evanston, Ill.: Northwestern University Press).

—— (1963), *A History of Literary Criticism in the Italian Renaissance*, 2 vols. (Chicago: University of Chicago Press).

WEINER, ANDREW (1978), *Sir Philip Sidney and the Poetics of Protestanism: A Study of Contexts* (Minneapolis: University of Minnesota Press).

—— (1980), 'Expelling the Beast: Bruno's Adventures in England', *Modern Philology*, 78: 1–13.

WEINER, PHILIP P., and AARON NOLAND (eds.) (1957), *The Roots of Scientific Thought: A Cultural Perspective* (New York: Basic Books).

WEISHEIPL, J. A. (1965), 'Classification of the Sciences in Medieval Thought', *Medieval Studies*, 27: 54–90.

—— (1978), 'The Nature, Scope, and Classification of the Sciences', in Lindberg (ed.), *Science in the Middle Ages*, 461–81.

WELLS, SUSAN (1981), 'Jacobean City Comedy and the Ideology of the City', *ELH* 48: 37–60.

WELSFORD, ENID (1962), *The Court Masque: A Study in the Relationship between Poetry and the Revels* (New York: Russell & Russell).

WEST, RUSSELL (2001), *Spatial Representations and the Jacobean Stage: From Shakespeare to Webster* (New York: Palgrave).

WEST, WILLIAM (2002), *Theatres and Encyclopedias in Early Modern Europe* (Cambridge: Cambridge University Press).

WESTMAN, ROBERT S. (1980), 'The Astronomer's Role in the Sixteenth Century: A Preliminary Study', *History of Science*, 18: 105–47.

WHITNEY, ELSPETH (1990), *Paradise Restored: The Mechanical Arts from Antiquity through the Thirteenth Century*, Transactions of the American Philosophical Society, 80: 1–169.

WICKHAM, GLYNNE (1959–81), *Early English Stages, 1300–1660*, 3 vols. in 4 (New York: Columbia University Press).

WIEBENSON, DORA (1988), 'Guillaume Philander's Annotations to Vitruvius', in Jean Guillaume (ed.), *Les Traités d'architecture de la Renaissance* (Paris: Picard), 67–72.

WIGHTMAN, W. P. D. (1962), *Science and the Renaissance: An Introduction to the Study of the Emergence of the Sciences in the Sixteenth Century*, Aberdeen University Studies, 143, 2 vols. (Edinburgh: Oliver & Boyd).

WILBURN, DAVID (1980), 'Shakespeare's Nothing', in Murray M. Schwartz and Coppélia Kahn (eds.), *Representing Shakespeare: New Psychoanalytic Essays* (Baltimore: Johns Hopkins University Press), 244–63.

WILLIAMS, RAYMOND (1983), *Keywords,* rev. edn. (Oxford: Oxford University Press).

WITTGENSTEIN, LUDWIG (1958), *Philosophical Investigations*, trans. G. E. M. Anscombe (New York: Macmillan; 3rd edn., 1968).

WITTKOWER, RUDOLF (1971), *Architectural Principles in the Age of Humanism*, 3rd edn. (New York: W. W. Norton).

—— (1974*a*), 'English Literature on Architecture', in id., *Palladio and Palladianism* (New York: Georges Braziller), 95–112.

—— (1974*b*), 'Inigo Jones, Architect and Man of Letters', in id., *Palladio and Palladianism*, 51–64.

—— (1978), 'Brunelleschi and "Proportion in Perspective" ', in id., *Idea and Image: Studies in the Italian Renaissance* (London: Thames & Hudson), 125–35.

WOLFE, JESSICA (2004), *Humanism, Machinery, and Renaissance Literature* (Cambridge: Cambridge University Press).

WOLFSON, SUSAN J. (1997), *Formal Charges: The Shaping of Poetry in British Romanticism* (Stanford, Calif.: Stanford University Press).

—— (2000), 'Reading for Form', *Modern Literary Quarterly*, 61: 1–16.

WOOD, NEAL (1990), 'Cicero and the Political Thought of the Early English Renaissance', *Modern Language Quarterly*, 51: 185–207.

WORDEN, BLAIR (1996), *The Sound of Virtue: Philip Sidney's* Arcadia *and Elizabethan Politics* (New Haven: Yale University Press).

WORTHEN, W. B. (1997), *Shakespeare and the Authority of Performance* (Cambridge: Cambridge University Press).

—— (1998), 'Drama, Performativity, and Performance', *PMLA* 113: 1093–107.

WOUDHUYSEN, HENRY R. (1996), *Sir Philip Sidney and the Circulation of Manuscripts 1558–1640* (Oxford: Clarendon Press).

YACHNIN, PAUL (1997), *Stage-Wrights: Shakespeare, Jonson, Middleton, and the Making of Theatrical Value* (Philadelphia: University of Pennsylvania Press).

—— (2002), 'Wonder-Effects: Othello's Handkerchief', in Harris and Korda (eds.), *Staged Properties*, 316–34.

YATES, FRANCIS (1964), *Giordano Bruno and the Hermetic Tradition* (Chicago: University of Chicago Press).

—— (1966), *The Art of Memory* (Chicago: University of Chicago Press).

—— (1969), *Theatre of the World* (Chicago: University of Chicago Press).

ZETTERBERG, J. PETER (1980), 'The Mistaking of "the Mathematicks" for Magic in Tudor and Stuart England', *Sixteenth Century Journal*, 11: 83–97.

ZILSEL, EDGAR (1941), 'The Origins of William Gilbert's Scientific Method', in Weiner and Noland (eds.), *Roots of Scientific Thought*, 219–50; first pub. in *Journal of the History of Ideas*, 2: 1–32.

—— (1942*a*), 'The Genesis of the Concept of Physical Law', in Weiner and Noland (eds.), *Roots of Scientific Thought*, 251–75; first pub. in *Philosophical Review*, 51: 245–79.

—— (1942*b*), 'The Sociological Roots of Science', *American Sociological Review*, 47: 544–62.

Index